HIDDEN
SCOURGE

HIDDEN SCOURGE

Exposing the Truth
about Fossil Fuel Industry Spills

KEVIN P. TIMONEY

McGill-Queen's University Press

Montreal & Kingston • London • Chicago

ISBN 978-0-2280-0893-4 (cloth)
ISBN 978-0-2280-0894-1 (paper)
ISBN 978-0-2280-1026-5 (ePDF)

Legal deposit fourth quarter 2021
Bibliothèque nationale du Québec

Printed in Canada on acid-free paper that is 100% ancient forest free
(100% post-consumer recycled), processed chlorine free

This book has been published with the help of a grant from the Canadian
Federation for the Humanities and Social Sciences, through the Awards to
Scholarly Publications Program, using funds provided by the Social Sciences
and Humanities Research Council of Canada. McGill-Queen's University Press
also gratefully acknowledges the financial support of the McLean Foundation
for this book.

We acknowledge the support of the Canada Council for the Arts.

Nous remercions le Conseil des arts du Canada de son soutien.

Library and Archives Canada Cataloguing in Publication

Title: Hidden scourge : exposing the truth about fossil fuel industry spills /
    Kevin P. Timoney.
Names: Timoney, Kevin, author.
Description: Includes bibliographical references and index.
Identifiers: Canadiana (print) 20210231742 | Canadiana (ebook) 20210231858 |
    ISBN 9780228008934 (cloth) | ISBN 9780228008941 (paper) | ISBN
    9780228010265 (ePDF)
Subjects: LCSH: Oil spills—Canada, Western. | LCSH: Oil spills—West (U.S.) |
    LCSH: Petroleum industry and trade—Environmental aspects—Canada,
    Western. | LCSH: Petroleum industry and trade—Environmental aspects—
    West (U.S.) | LCSH: Canada, Western—Environmental conditions. | LCSH:
    West (U.S.)—Environmental conditions.
Classification: LCC TD427.P4 T56 2021 | DDC 628.1/6833—dc23

This book was design and typeset by studio oneonone in Minion 11/14

For Abby, Anne, and Lindy, whose compasses always point true.

We are all capable of believing things which we know to be untrue,
and then, when we are finally proved wrong, impudently twisting the facts
so as to show that we were right. Intellectually, it is possible to carry on this
process for an indefinite time: the only check on it is that sooner or later
a false belief bumps up against solid reality, usually on a battlefield.

George Orwell, "In Front of Your Nose," *Tribune*, 22 March 1946

Contents

CONTENTS

viii

Prologue
Learn from the Past or Repeat It

A ten-minute drive from where I grew up in Ocean County, New Jersey, the Ciba chemical company opened a dye manufacturing plant in 1952 in Toms River. For more than forty years, the plant known as Toms River Chemical (TRC) manufactured dyes and disposed of toxic by-products such as trichloroethylene, epichlorohydrin, benzidine, and anthraquinone (Fagin 2013). The oversight was so poor and the dumping of waste so profitable that the company, in violation of its discharge permit, even quietly expanded into the chemical waste disposal business. In 1966, after contaminating the town's water supply and air and not informing the public, the company added a pipeline to the ocean that for years disgorged chemical waste less than a kilometre offshore of Ortley Beach. When the pipeline burst in 1984 and released contaminants at a street intersection in Toms River, the company, then known as Ciba-Geigy, assured local people that the pipeline carried harmless salty water that discharged into the salty ocean. Actually, the pipeline carried dangerous chemical wastes, but the pipeline leak was a minor danger. In truth, a chemical scourge had been spreading for years, mostly invisible and therefore easy to hide.

We all knew people who worked at the chemical plant. As kids we overheard adults recounting incidents about chemicals being dumped in the sand near the plant or discharged into the Toms River. Our parents warned us not to swim in the Toms River, but the warnings were not needed. We were "Pineys" after all, rural people who lived in the New Jersey Pine Barrens. We knew what a healthy Pine Barrens stream looked like, such as Cedar Creek where I grew up. The water was tea-coloured but pure, it tasted good, and was full of pickerel, painted and snapping turtles, and elvers that had swum from the Sargasso Sea. The Toms River was different; there was something unsettling about the dark water. We didn't know about carcinogens and environmental toxins, but we did know that we never saw animals living in the river and that frightened us.

It turned out that the rumours were true and our fears were justified. For forty years, local people were ingesting contaminated drinking water and breathing contaminated air. On some days, the air at TRC contained so much solvent that it dissolved the stockings of secretaries who worked at the plant (Fagin 2013). Toms River Chemical and local authorities knew that contamination was occurring as early as the mid-1950s. The lengths that the company and its partners went to conceal the pollution are shocking. By 1980, each year the company was burying 9,800 drums of chemical wastes and 6,804 m³ of chemical sludge on their property. They dumped millions of cubic metres of liquid waste into unlined pits. Seepage from their toxic waste ponds was estimated at 757 m³ per day, which entered the Toms River or groundwater. Because burning of toxic wastes produced dense clouds of coloured or black smoke, the company switched to burning wastes at night. Contamination of drinking water with dyes was concealed by the local water company's adding eight times the safe dose of chlorine to remove the colour. And of course from the outset, the company misled the public about its environmental impacts, stating in 1953, "Actually, the water discharged into the Toms River will be a great deal more palatable for fish and humans than the river itself" (Fagin 2013). Similar offensive doggerel was spouted by the company for decades. We Pineys, who drank from the pure water creeks that drained the Pine Barrens, knew better.

TRC was not alone in its chemical dumping. The notorious Reich Farm in Pleasant Plains, later designated a US Environmental Protection Agency (EPA) contaminated Superfund site (see glossary), lies 3 km northeast of the TRC plant. EPA Superfund sites pose a threat to human or environmental health. In 1971, the Reich Farm received an estimated 5,000 drums of toxic waste dumped illegally by Nick Fernicola, a contract hauler for Union Carbide. In 1973, I volunteered at an organic farm across the road from the Reich Farm; we were unaware of the toxins nearby. Fernicola dumped another 1,500 drums from Union Carbide at the Dover Landfill after bribing the landfill operators.

The leaking drums contained SAN trimer, styrene, toluene, trichloroethylene, and other wastes that spread underground and contaminated the groundwater and drinking water of thousands of people. The Manchester Township Landfill just outside Toms River was used by a drug company to dispose of its chemical wastes; the site was known locally as the Penicillin Dump. Groundwater pollution from various sources has contaminated the water of at least eleven neighbourhoods in Toms River. Today, almost everyone in the area drinks treated water whose quality is managed by a water company overseen by government and monitored by well-informed, tireless citizens backed by strong right to know legislation.

Slowly and painfully, from the late 1960s through the 1980s, the truth emerged that the groundwater and drinking water in the Toms River area had been contaminated with an array of persistent toxins, some of which were carcinogens. Much of the credit for piercing the veil of secrecy goes to a single journalist, Don Bennett, who worked for the local newspaper, the *Ocean County Observer*. It took him years to put the pieces together in large part because TRC acted like a "closed empire out there in the woods," out of sight of prying eyes. Neither the company nor branches of government would answer questions about health and safety but were always happy to talk about the company's contribution to the economy.

As concerns rose with each new revelation, studies in the 1980s and 1990s identified Toms River as a residential cancer cluster for childhood brain cancers, central nervous system cancers, and leukemia (Fagin 2013). The long fight to uncover the truth and find some form of justice was led not by government or regulators but by citizens, mostly by the parents of stricken children. One of the citizens, a high school science teacher who later became a prosecutor then a judge, recalled, "From Day One we were concerned about cancer in the community, but we didn't have the resources to look into it. We were taking on the whole social structure of the company and the politicians and agencies" (Fagin 2013). Citizens and journalists found themselves on the wrong side of a firewall.

Eventually, scientific, public health, and legal help arrived for the citizens of Toms River, some truth emerged, and there was some closure. But in large part, there was too much delay and too narrow a focus on pediatric cancer. For a host of reasons, efforts were focused on the epidemiology and toxicology of three types of childhood cancer using a study design with limited statistical power. Many childhood cancers were excluded due to the study design; there were no studies of cancers in the adult population; and there were no studies of noncancer health effects such as skin and eye irritation, allergies, seizures, respiratory illnesses, organ damage, immune and endocrine system disruption, or the psychological and emotional impacts. Because there were insufficient environmental monitoring data and essentially no data for the 1950s and 1960s, the study teams were hampered in their ability to reconstruct contaminant exposures. In short, help had arrived on the crime scene too late. Given the scarcity of the environmental chemistry data, the small human sample size, the multiple causes of cancer, the multiple chemical exposures, and the delay between exposure and carcinogenesis, the prospect of identifying a smoking gun that would hold up in court was never good. An out of court settlement to some of the families of children stricken by cancer brought closure to some, bitter disappointment for others, and still unanswered questions that persist today in 2021.

The only studies conducted of the health effects on the chemical plant workers used a flawed study design, were limited to cancer, were commissioned by and under the control of the company, and were found to have missed known cancers and failed to account for the documented "healthy worker" effect (people who are well enough to be hired tend to be healthier than the general population). Despite these shortcomings, a 1990s company study found elevated death rates from lung cancers among vat dye and maintenance workers, elevated death rates from stomach and bladder cancers among azo dye workers, and elevated death rates from central nervous system tumours among vat, azo, and plastics workers (Fagin 2013). The company's consultants explained away most of the cancers as possibly attributable to chance, smoking, or to unidentified exposures. Former company employees viewed the cancer study as the final insult.

Much to the relief of nearly everyone, TRC stopped production in 1996. The company had not simply lost its social licence, it had disposed of it in a toxic waste dump. In 1997 the company was broken up into a chemical dye division bought by BASF and a pharmaceutical division bought by Novartis. BASF moved its dye production factories to Louisiana and China while Novartis now manufactures drugs used in cancer treatment. Excavation of the older dumps at the TRC Superfund site began in 2003 with the removal of 47,000 crumbling chemical drums. Cleanup ended in 2010, cost $92 million, and removed 262,232 m³ of contaminated material. There remain 38,000 disintegrating drums of contaminants still buried in the TRC site known as Cell One, which BASF refuses to remove. Millions of cubic metres of contaminated groundwater remain under the site and under peoples' homes.

How could the toxic dumping and emissions have continued for decades? The pollution was covert, responsible authorities, including Toms River's water company and regulators, were complicit or incompetent, and politicians looked the other way. The company cultivated a social network of politicians, government staff, and friendly media willing to tell the company's story uncritically. The environmental damage continued because the company controlled information and it excelled at keeping secrets.

Although the covert disposal of toxic wastes is best known at Toms River, dumping was widespread in rural Ocean County where, as of 2015, sixteen EPA Superfund sites had been identified. There are more contaminated sites in my home county than are found in thirty-six American states. How could this happen in a largely rural area without industry? It happened in large part *because* it was rural; there were no inconvenient witnesses. From the 1940s to the early 1980s, chemical manufacturers in nearby cities hired companies to dispose of their industrial wastes, no questions asked. Often the chemical wastes would be dumped in unlined rural landfills, after which the chemicals promptly soaked into the sand.

Some waste hauling companies preferred to dump for free, without permission or notification. They would dispose of the wastes along roads, at rural farms, and in gravel and sand pits hidden in the Pine Barrens. "Midnight dumpers" would drive their eighteen-wheelers to favoured spots and dump their load of chemical drums or simply open the spigot on tank trucks and let the tank drain as they drove. The more advanced operations with links to organized crime would post lookouts with walkie-talkies during dumping sessions (Fagin 2013). Dumping of toxic wastes continued at the Jackson Landfill until at least 1978. As a result, the Jackson Landfill was declared yet another EPA Superfund site. The Cohansey Aquifer, which underlies the area, remains contaminated in some areas with lead, chlorobenzene, methylene chloride, and a host of other volatile organic compounds and heavy metals (EPA 1994).

From 1975 to 2010, my sister lived in rural Ocean County. In the 1980s with rumours of groundwater contamination, my sister had her well water tested. It contained lead, benzene, and other volatile organic compounds from nearby covert dumping of industrial wastes. We first learned of the dumping through a neighbour, an independent truck driver who admitted he had been hired to dispose of the wastes. His accounts of dumping toxic wastes were corroborated years later by the US EPA and the New Jersey Department of Environmental Protection. By then, of course, it was too late. In 2014, my sister died of cancer. We will never be certain if her death was directly related to the contaminants she had drunk for thirty-five years.

After my sister died, I researched toxic waste sites on the US EPA and New Jersey Department of Environmental Protection websites. It turns out, unknown to all of us, my sister and her three children lived within five kilometres of six EPA Superfund sites, all illegal industrial waste sites that had contaminated the soil and groundwater. The most infamous of these chemical dumps is the harmless-sounding Goose Farm, where from the mid-1940s to the mid-1970s, 4-chlor-m-cresol, benzene, ethylbenzene, octane, pentachlorophenol, polychlorinated biphenyls, toluene, and methylene chloride were dumped into a pit about 91 m long by 30 m wide by 4.6 m deep. At the Wilson Farm near my sister's home, dumping by Thiokol Corporation in the 1960s and 1970s contaminated the groundwater with lead, mercury, arsenic, other heavy metals, cyanide, methylene chloride, phthalates, and trichloroethane (EPA 2018). Toxic waste dumping in Ocean County may have hurt thousands of people and caused widespread covert damage. We can't be certain. Some questions don't have answers because the relevant data were never gathered – a point we will return to in our study of Alberta spills.

Assigning blame for what happened in Toms River and Ocean County is less important than learning from what happened. The first lesson comes from Kim Pascarella, one of the Toms River citizens who has worked for decades to protect the legacy of the lost children by continuing to seek the scientific truth (Fagin 2013). He observed, "We've learned that you can't assume somebody else is going to take care of things for you … Arrogance by these companies and by the government is what got us into all this in the first place. We know that now." We cannot depend on governments, regulators, or corporations to protect us.

The second lesson is to be vigilant to the danger signs. Industrial spills hidden from view, poor regulatory oversight, failure to gather credible data, missing information, misinformation, the prospect of large profits, and a social organization composed of industry, regulators, and politicians – these are all danger signs. Whenever these factors come together, trouble is not far away. The story has been repeated too many times. The landfill called Love Canal in Niagara Falls, New York, where the Hooker Chemical Company disposed of more than 200 chemical compounds, is perhaps the most notorious. The company later sold the land to the municipality, which, despite warnings of serious contamination, proceeded to build schools and housing on the site. The subsequent health effects were horrific and included chromosomal damage to one-third of the population and a host of cancers and birth defects. The positive legacy of Love Canal is that it led to passage of the Superfund Act and a means to deal with contaminated sites. As in the Toms River story, it was reporters, not government agencies, that exposed the dangers of Love Canal. *Hidden Scourge* also owes its origin to the work of an investigative journalist who provided me with the Alberta Energy Regulator's spill data.

Relative to the tragedy that unfolded near my childhood home in Ocean County, New Jersey, in Alberta the chemicals and the modes of discharge are different, but the pattern feels eerily similar – decades of covert contamination and complicity. The public, the first affected, finds itself on the wrong side of an information firewall, largely unaware of the risks. Consider Lynnview Ridge in Calgary. Imperial Oil operated an oil refinery in Calgary from 1924 to 1975, after which it sold the land to developers who built the Lynnview Ridge subdivision. No one told the residents that their neighbourhood was built on the lead- and hydrocarbon-contaminated land of the old refinery (CBC 2009). After contamination was discovered in 2001, it proved less expensive for Imperial Oil to purchase 140 homes and several apartment blocks than it was to pay for decontamination. But some residents refused to sell their homes below market value and fought for cleanup in the courts. Eventually, the Alberta government ordered Imperial to remediate the land around the remaining homes. Contaminated soil around the homes was removed to a depth of 1.5 to 4.5 m. Is the tragedy of Toms River and Ocean County repeating itself wherever hydrocarbons are exploited? This book tells the story.

Preface

This study began with a serendipitous observation. Several years ago, when I first examined the Alberta Energy Regulator's spill data, I noticed a curious property. If one cubic metre was spilled of, say, crude oil, one cubic metre was recovered; if five cubic metres were spilled, five cubic metres were recovered, and so on. Certainly, that can happen by chance. But tens of thousands of spills reporting an exact duplication of volumes spilled and volumes recovered cannot happen in the real world. I graphed spill volume against recovery volume. It was a straight-line 1:1 relationship. In short, the spill recoveries were too good to be true. At that point, I smelled smoke and went looking for the fire.

If the reported spill recoveries were not scientifically credible, serious questions arose. Did it mean that undetermined volumes of spilled materials remain on the landscape? Were industry-reported spill and recovery volumes accurate? After cleanup operations, was there evidence of residual contamination and biological effects? Were any of the regulator's environmental data on spills supported by science? Was the regulator protecting the environment?

Those questions prompted discussions with Keepers of the Water Council, a nonprofit citizens' water advocacy and conservation group. Keepers, along with the Dene Tha, a First Nation directly affected by fossil fuel industry spills, asked me to examine spills data in concert with a field study. I completed the initial phase of the study, focused in northwestern Alberta, in late 2016.

On the strength of the disparity between the regulator's data and the scientific data, I expanded the study to include all of Alberta, then later broadened the scope to North America wherever I could find relevant scientific data. I did so because I realized that I had stumbled onto the proverbial onion – peel away one layer and you'll find another. I found troubling layers all the way down: misleading data, errors, and missing information.

As when Alice fell down the rabbit hole, once I began to look into the regulator's data, I could not reconcile what I saw with reality as I knew it. Each realization led me deeper into a rabbit warren whose twists and turns revealed an alternate universe that led me to question not only spill data but also government and industry data about the effects of well pads, pipelines, seismic lines, emissions, and impact assessments. Nor could I reconcile reality with the regulator's own statements that it was effective, efficient, and credible and that it was protecting the public and the environment and enforcing the rules. All evidence contradicted the regulator's statements. This I found offensive.

The challenge for me as a scientist was to harness the realization that an injustice was being perpetrated and then objectively expose the facts. Each conclusion I reached, I weighed against relevant evidence to ensure logical consistency. Once accepted as a fact, the task was to make sense of it. Why, for example, would numeric values for crude oil volumes released and recovered in spills be both too good to be true and subjectively chosen rather than measured – in a word, fraudulent?

Each answer led to another question, so what began as an examination of regulatory data led to questions about the fate of our ecosystems, our government, and of our democracy itself. The process came to illustrate one of the first lessons of ecology: everything is connected.

Hidden Scourge reveals the netherworld of a regulator's environmental incident data in the light of science. It evaluates the adequacy and truthfulness of the regulator's data and compares those data with scientific data, field observations, industrial and government reports, news stories, interviews, correspondence, peer-reviewed studies, and documents obtained under freedom of information. In a few instances, I have withheld the name of a source to protect the person from retribution. The book presents findings from one of the few examinations of environmental impacts not conducted by or under the auspices of the fossil fuel industry. It separates fiction from fact by differentiating erroneous accounts of phenomena from demonstrable facts supported by evidence.

The book answers fundamental questions: How often do spills occur? What substances are spilled? Does the regulator provide scientifically credible and timely data on spills and their environmental impacts? Is there evidence of contamination after cleanup? Are the data complete? Do spills result in significant and persistent impacts? Is the regulator protecting the public interest and the environment? What are the ecological, social, and financial liabilities?

Answering those questions required a deep dive into a hidden world. I didn't intend to follow such a long and tortuous path, but once on that path, I had to follow it to the end. My efforts to unearth hidden but critical information and bring it to the attention of the public have consumed my life for the last five years. For the last four years I've worked with zero funding. I've been inspired by the volunteers of the world who act because they know their actions have meaning. I've persisted because it felt worth the effort. I've laboured to translate smoke into substance and technical concepts into plain language. I've enjoyed the daily challenge of fitting together the pieces of a puzzle. I've been helped along the way by concerned citizens and fellow scientists. Surprisingly, I've been energized by firewalls, obfuscation, and questions met with silence because whenever people work hard to hide something, whatever they're hiding has to be important. And finally, I've been lifted up by the simple joy of learning. I hope you'll find the book worth the effort.

I've written this book for scientifically literate general readers. The book is not a scientific treatise nor is it a nature guide. It's a demanding read that traverses the fields of ecology, chemistry, soils, biology, environmental science, statistics, history, policy, governance, and information management. By the book's end, I hope that you will agree that the light of science can act as a powerful disinfectant of contagious disinformation.

To understand the impacts of fossil fuel industry spills requires the language of science and the presentation of evidence. It is not enough to say that something is numerous or large or significant. When we ask how many, how big, or how significant, we must present evidence that both defines and quantifies. I arrive at general conclusions after examination of specific details, peering deep into the weeds among thousands of data points. The picture is drawn leaf by leaf, point by point. When the picture is complete and held at arm's length, the hidden is revealed.

Part 1 of the book introduces the background necessary to understand spills, provides an overview of relevant Alberta history, and describes the data to be examined. Part 2 surveys the scientific literature on the effects of spills and other industry disturbances. Parts 3 and 4 analyze and interpret the evidence. Part 5 explains how misinformation and pervasive ecological damage became the rule rather than the exception, then examines the global threat of carbon addiction, and proposes a way out of the mess.

I have tried to present the material in a lively manner, but I've avoided hyperbole, oversimplification, playing loose with the facts, or dumbing down to score rhetorical points. The world of spills is a big and messy one. Sometimes we have to traverse a morass to reach firm ground. In some chapters, the material is unavoidably technical. If you find a chapter tough slogging, please jump ahead to the chapter summary, which should provide you with the take-home messages. To make the text concise, I provide the details in a public online appendix whose sections are numbered web 2.1 and so on (available at https://escholarship.mcgill.ca/concern/books/hx11xk518). These are the all-important "trees" that comprise the forest. A glossary defines and discusses technical terms used in the book and web materials. For species, I have used common names instead of scientific names whenever generally accepted common names exist (ACIMS 2013). Otherwise, I cite both a common and a scientific name.

A NOTE ABOUT "SIGNIFICANCE"

There are two kinds of significance: objective (scientific) and subjective (personal). The former depends upon data, the latter depends upon our personal values. Because there is no absolute certainty that something is true or false, when scientists make statements they do so with the knowledge that they may be incorrect. The likelihood of being incorrect is the p-value and whenever p-values are small, the evidence is strong, and we can be confident that the conclusion is sound.

Scientifically, when something is significant, we mean that a set of observations differs from a comparison set of observations. If we say that plant communities at spill sites differ in their species composition from that of natural plant communities at $p = 0.001$, that statement will be true, on average, 999 times out of 1,000 and false once in 1,000 times. Specifically, the p-value is the probability of type I error, that is, concluding there is a difference when in fact there is no difference. P-values are used to specify the degree of confidence in a conclusion.

Also, something can be significant because it's important. For example, increased dominance by exotic species at spill sites is significant because exotic species harm native biodiversity. The personal, or subjective, significance of that statement depends on our values. If we value biodiversity, it's significant that spills harm it; if we don't value biodiversity, losing it isn't significant. Values matter: they're the lens through which we view objective facts.

WEIGH THE EVIDENCE THEN REACH
YOUR OWN CONCLUSIONS

The evidence presented in this book leads to important conclusions. How can you evaluate whether these findings are true?

To assist in your evaluation, I provide data and their sources, methods, analytical results, and documentation sufficient for you to reach your own conclusions. Based on the documentation, you could repeat this study from scratch. In other words, the study is reproducible. If in doubt about a statement, consider asking a set of questions. How reliable is the source of the claim? Was it a politician, an industry representative, a scientist? Who funded the work? Are there vested interests underlying the claim? What is the evidence and what is the quality of the evidence? Has anyone disproved the claim? Can the claim be tested? If not, the claim is a belief or opinion.

I'm not asking you, the reader, to accept my conclusions on faith. Faith is easy; it requires only a shut down of critical thinking, and there's already far too much of that in our world. Instead, I ask for something more precious – your sustained attention to the evidence, some of which may prove unfamiliar or technical. Then I ask that you reach your own conclusions.

Everyone is capable of believing things known to be untrue, and conversely of disbelieving things that are patently true. In one sense, it doesn't matter whether we believe in facts. Objective facts exist independently of subjective beliefs. It's an objective fact that using more fossil fuels means emitting more greenhouse gases and driving more dangerous climate change. Many conservatives may not be concerned about the impacts of climate change. They have a right to their opinion about the subjective importance of those impacts upon their lives, but their opinions don't change the objective facts of climate change. But in another sense, it matters profoundly whether we believe in facts. If facts don't underpin our beliefs, we wander without a compass, disconnected from reality. To believe in facts, we first need access to truthful information. Our lives, ecosystems, and civilization itself depend on free access to the truth. Therein lies the danger, as you'll see.

I feel no joy in reaching these conclusions, but there is some consolation in learning the truth. When undermined by misinformation, democratic processes falter, government ceases to serve the electorate, and people lose faith in their leaders and their government. Words matter, truth matters. Energy misinformation, sanctioned by government and regulators, is a symptom of a democracy under siege. To fight this systemic infection, we have to seek and speak the truth and require our leaders to follow our example. Democracies, like gardens, require active care and sweat to maintain.

The science is clear: the fossil fuel industry causes ecological damage wherever it is practiced. But reports emanating from the regulator and the fossil fuel industry paint a halcyon picture of prosperity and "world-class" environmental management. The cognitive dissonance between reality and the officially sanctioned alternative facts is deafening. Because the results of this study bear directly upon the responsibilities of the regulator and the government of Alberta, I invited both agencies to review a draft of this manuscript. Both declined.

The regulator, government, and its partners have created an alternative world in which facts that don't facilitate exploitation are ignored or considered invalid. It's a world in which disastrous well blowouts are portrayed as making Alberta famous and praised for providing free publicity. It's a world where scientists are fired for their integrity; where failing to provide timely and credible information demonstrates "stellar competence"; where the regulator demonstrates empathy by labelling people who voice concerns as ecoterrorists. It's a world in which spills don't damage ecosystems and no animals are harmed; where spill data are based on human decisions rather than measurements; where spills are perfectly recovered, and the land is reclaimed to a healthy, productive state. We're asked to believe in this utopian world as matters of faith, but it's a world of make-believe as the evidence will show.

In the 1970s, former Alberta premier Peter Lougheed encouraged Albertans to think like owners when it came to viewing how petroleum resources were developed. For a host of reasons, that never came to pass. Instead, we watch like sheep as our earthly home is degraded by companies that don't own the land, yet behave like land barons, putting up no trespassing signs while they strip it of its treasures. Peter Lougheed was right. We own the land and we need to act like owners. And at a more profound level, the land owns us. Our fate and the fate of the land are entwined.

A profound social and environmental injustice is being committed. The industry and its captured regulatory and government partners are responsible. We can continue to tolerate the injustice and be silent partners to this obscene negation of life, or we can strive for a more just world. Time will tell whether the orange glow on the horizon is encroaching light pollution, an approaching wildfire, or a new dawn.

PART ONE

HIDING IN PLAIN SIGHT

CHAPTER 1

Covert Spills

Chronic ills – a corrupt political class, a sclerotic bureaucracy, a heartless
economy, a divided and distracted public – had gone untreated for years.
We had learned to live, uncomfortably, with the symptoms.

George Packer, "Underlying Conditions"

INTRODUCTION

Fossil fuels have changed the world in myriad ways that have been both beneficial and detrimental. Over the past century, the increased use of fossil fuels
has transformed economies and civilization itself. The economic benefits of
fossil fuels have been and continue to be significant and indisputable. Fossil
fuels provide millions of people with employment and provide exports for
energy-rich economies. They move our vehicles, heat our homes, and power
industry and modern agriculture. Fossil fuels make modern civilization possible. Notwithstanding the benefits of fossil fuels, ongoing climate change
driven by human activities poses a threat to life on Earth and to global civilization. Burgeoning human populations, over-exploitation of resources, and
carbon-based economies are undermining the capacity of ecosystems to deliver ecological goods and services and are creating conditions where billions
of people live with inescapable pollution.

Unprecedented human-caused changes to the planet have led to rising concerns about ecological tipping points and the threats posed to global security.
In this introductory chapter, we examine the warning signs that all is not well
in our fossil-fuelled world. We then focus on the Alberta context and its history, the rising tide of confrontations, and the conjoined problem of spills and
missing or unreliable information.

WARNING SIGNS

For most of human history, energy sources were bound within a specific place and time. Wood, wind, water, and human and animal labour were local and could not be transported. Hydrocarbons changed everything. Coal replaced wood and turned water into steam that powered machines and trains that crisscrossed continents. Oil and gas, along with their pipelines and storage capacity, transformed societies and severed the relationship between space and time. When the awesome power of hydrocarbons was unleashed, we could burn up the past whenever and wherever we chose. No one dreamed it would endanger our future (Taylor 2019).

Since about 1950, the beginning of the Great Acceleration, human activities have increased to become a force that has altered planetary functions and is actively undermining the ability of Earth to support life (Steffen et al. 2011). The human population has tripled since 1950. Global economic activity, as measured by gross domestic product (GDP), has grown tenfold and average per capita GDP has tripled. In concert with this rapid global growth in economies, resource use, habitat loss, communications, technology, and human population, global energy consumption has risen fivefold; fertilizer use has risen eightfold; the number of large dams has risen sixfold; use of fresh water has risen fourfold; the number of motor vehicles has grown sevenfold; and international tourism has grown twentyfold. Since 1950, about one-half of stratospheric ozone has been depleted; surface temperatures have risen over land and sea, especially so in boreal and arctic regions; marine fish capture has risen fourfold; nitrogen inputs to coastal zones have increased fivefold; and the abundance of thousands of native terrestrial species has declined. The Great Acceleration is the most important and abrupt change in the Earth's history since the evolution of the human species (Costanza et al. 2007).

Greenhouse gas emissions have risen to levels that are unimaginably large. In 2018 alone, 55.3 billion tonnes of greenhouse gases were emitted, the equivalent of 7.3 tonnes for every person on Earth. Over recent decades, about 77 per cent of the emissions have come from the use of fossil fuels; about 23 per cent have come from land conversion and agriculture. Between 2009 and 2018, global emissions of greenhouse gases increased an average 1.5 per cent each year; in 2018 they rose by 1.7 per cent (UN 2019). In May 2018, the carbon dioxide concentration of our atmosphere reached 415 parts per million, the highest level observed in at least 800,000 years (UNDP 2019).

One of the drivers of the world's ecological problems is how we develop and use fossil fuels. Fossil fuel use contributes to pervasive ecological problems and is the primary driver of human-caused climate change, which, over the past century, has had a measurable impact on ecosystems. Temperatures have risen worldwide, precipitation patterns have changed, global sea level has risen, and flooding and coastal inundation have increased in frequency and severity. Ocean acidification and warming are driving major changes in our oceans including significant declines in coral reefs. Climate change has profoundly affected ecosystems by changing species distributions, population sizes, and the timing of reproduction and migration events, as well as causing an increase in the frequency of pest and disease outbreaks.

In the blink of an eye in geological time, humans have risen to global dominance. Wherever we turn we see the hand of *Homo sapiens* belying its scientific name. We are tearing apart the fabric of life, altering the course of evolution, and degrading our life support systems. We are at a crossroads; what road will we choose? Worryingly, we see the rise of demagogues and their followers rejecting science in favour of "alternative facts." We know that the road we are on, global dependency on fossil fuels, is driving dangerous global changes.

The hydrocarbon road leads to more pipelines, spills, emissions, and ecological damage, and ever deeper ruts in a road that locks us into carbon dependency on a planet with dangerous atmospheric, economic, and ecological feedbacks. Although people who oppose or support pipelines rarely agree, they do agree on the fundamental reason for building pipelines: pipelines facilitate the carbon economy. But the carbon economy threatens life on the planet. Where those who oppose or support pipelines differ is in the subjective importance they place on that objective fact.

We all know that energy delivery systems supply more than heat, light, and power, but one of the indirect effects of pipelines is seldom discussed. Pipelines disconnect the impacts from the benefits of hydrocarbon production. Producing areas, typically sparsely populated, suffer the brunt of the ecological damage while distant, typically urban areas, receive the benefits and hold the political power. Pipelines reinforce and maintain the asymmetry of impacts and power. By shipping energy products long distances, the consumer doesn't have to cope with the negative local consequences of energy production (Jones 2014). The damage inflicted by the Trans Mountain and other major pipelines, if confined to the pipeline right-of-ways, would be relatively minor, but that's not how pipelines work. The majority of the damage is the result of their carrying product to global markets. In so doing, they drive environmental destruction across the vast hydrocarbon-bearing landscape that feeds the pipelines, and most importantly, by facilitating the marketing and burning of fossil fuels, they are the detonator for the climate-destroying bomb of greenhouse gas emissions. The ability to separate politically powerful areas of consumption from impoverished areas of production permits the creation of environmental sacrifice zones, a process already documented in northeastern Alberta (Timoney 2015) and painfully evident in Nigeria, Louisiana, and the Middle East. Pipelines provide economic, political, and social power to some at the expense of others (Jones 2014). As such, they are a tool of injustice. But it doesn't have to be that way. Effective policies and enforced regulations can lessen the impacts and share the benefits more equitably.

6

As a species we are struggling upstream towards ecologically sustainable economies against a current of disinformation and competing political, social, and economic interests. In Alberta, under an NDP government, we began a halting journey towards sustainability with increases in renewable energy and energy efficiency and changes in policy. Carbon pricing is beginning to level the playing field by making carbon-intensive activities pay the true, heretofore hidden and deferred price of emitting carbon and consuming and polluting water and land, but the 2019 election of a conservative government in Alberta undermined the modest reforms.

Built-in inertia in economies that presently run on carbon mean that fossil fuels will remain a major geopolitical force for years to come. We cannot simply turn off a valve and wish away the crisis brought about by basing civilization on burning carbon. Will advanced civilization survive the rising tide of change and instability? Given the magnitude of the planetary emergency, there is an urgent need for societies to understand how the world is changing, why it is changing, and what can be done to improve the chances that human societies can flourish on a healthy planet. As a result, the carbon economy has come under increasing scrutiny as a growing body of evidence has documented the costs of fossil fuel's dominance in the global economy. Opposition to the fossil fuel industry has created a rising tide of confrontations focused on the routing of pipelines, contamination of air, land, and water, and the urgent requirement to transform to a climate-friendly economy in hope of averting global disaster.

Growing concerns over spills fuel much of the opposition. The covert nature of spills and lack of information, however, make it difficult to appreciate the threats they pose. Although spills occur daily, most of us have never observed one in person. Lack of personal experience arises because most spills occur in areas distant from human population centres and because authorities prevent public access to spills. Most spills are never seen by the public, and most spill effects are never documented. Like the dumping of toxins into the groundwater of Toms River, fossil fuel industry spills and their effects are covert.

THE ALBERTA CONTEXT

Alberta's economy is dominated by the fossil fuel industry. Fossil fuel revenue accounts for almost one-third of the provincial budget and slightly more than one-half the value of the province's exports (Alberta Energy 2017). Alberta's hydrocarbon resources include conventional oil and natural gas, bitumen and heavy oil, and coal, and unconventional sources such as shale gas, coal bed methane, and "tight" oil and gas (requiring hydraulic fracturing). The fossil fuel industry operates in all regions of the province as it exploits hydrocarbon reserves presently estimated at 286 million m³ of conventional oil, 26 billion m³ of bitumen and unconventional hydrocarbons, 821 billion m³ of natural gas, and 37 billion tonnes of coal (Alberta Energy 2017). The development and management of these hydrocarbon resources is overseen by a regulator charged with protecting the public interest and the environment. Here we briefly survey the history of hydrocarbon production in Alberta to set the stage for our study of spills.

The ecological and social footprint of the fossil fuel industry in Alberta has been growing for more than a century. The first Alberta oil well began production in 1902. Alberta became a province in 1905 and gained control of its natural resources in 1930 under the Natural Resources Transfer Agreement. The first long-distance natural gas pipeline began operation in 1912. The first big strike came in 1914 when the Dingman No. 1 well came into production at what would become the boomtown of Turner Valley and the centre of the Canadian hydrocarbon industry until discoveries near Leduc in 1947. And so began the great race between the turtle, the advancement of ecological understanding, and the hare, hydrocarbon exploitation.

Because the natural gas produced from the Turner Valley wells lacked a market at the time, it was seen as an impurity to be separated from the valuable "natural gasoline" and kerosene. To dispose of the natural gas in Turner Valley, Calgary Petroleum Products began wholesale flaring that continued nonstop for years; about 14–17 million m³ of natural gas were flared every day. As a result, the night sky glowed across a broad swath of southwestern Alberta (figure 1.1). Government disputes with Calgary Petroleum Products over its flaring ended in 1920 when its operation burned to the ground and the company was taken over by Imperial Oil. But the flaring continued.

Imperial soon expanded operations with a new plant and new wells. In October 1923, when a drilling team ignored an order to stop drilling, its Royalite No. 4 sour gas well blew out and released 566,000 m³ of gas per day. The gas caught fire five days later and raged for weeks. At night, the glow from the blaze reportedly could be seen 150 kilometres away. Once the fire was extinguished and the well brought under control, Imperial responded by expanding its capabilities to process gas. But years of profligate waste due to uncontrolled flaring had not only raised the ire of federal regulators, it had lowered the reservoir pressure in the Turner Valley field and made it more difficult for oil to flow to the surface. During his 1929 tour of the Turner Valley oilfield, Winston Churchill was astonished by the unbridled burning. He was moved to comment on the "pillars of flame" that gave the "landscape a truly satanic appearance". Churchill's son Randolph lamented that the oilmen were "pigging up a beautiful valley to make their fortunes" (Tolppanen 2014).

In order to bring some semblance of order to hydrocarbon exploitation, the Alberta government created the Turner Valley Gas Conservation Board in 1932, but it was ineffective because its directives were ignored by the oil companies. In 1938, the province of Alberta tried again to assert some control with formation of the Petroleum and Natural Gas Conservation Board and passage of the Oil and Natural Gas Conservation Act. The act was aimed at preventing uneconomic or wasteful methods in order to maximize recovery of hydrocarbons (Penfold 2016).

Alberta's history of fossil fuel industry incidents stretches back to the early twentieth century. For most of the first half of the twentieth century, hydrocarbon exploitation was akin to a Wild West gold rush. Early practices that released large volumes of contaminants included (a) well production testing, during which flow rates were determined while the hydrocarbons that gushed to the surface were burned (figure 1.2a); (b) "bringing-in" wells by burning all substances involved with bringing the well into production in order to prevent contamination of the hydrocarbon product (figure 1.2b); (c) explosions and fires (figure 1.2c); (d) continuous year-round flaring (figure 1.3a); (e) improper well abandonment (figure 1.3b); (f) burning or bulldozing of industrial waste

Figure 1.1 Turner Valley gas flaring in the 1930s. The flares were so bright and hot that people reportedly could read outdoors at night and homeless people during the Depression huddled by the flares to stay warm in winter.

on site; (g) storage of crude oil in earthen pits (see figure 8.2); and absence of scrubbers and other pollution control devices. As late as 1951, inspectors "tracked down sloppy conduct by scanning the horizon for greasy palls of soot. 'That's how you knew where oilfields were – by the plumes of black smoke … There was a period when board staff were asked to watch where these plumes were and get out to where they originated, find out what had happened'" (Jaremko 2013).

The environmental effects of most of these incidents have been poorly documented or not documented at all. Alberta had no energy regulator until 1938 and did not routinely record industrial incidents and spills until the mid-1970s. Environmental concerns were essentially nonexistent and pollution controls rudimentary until the 1970s. As we will observe, in spite of the profound influences of the fossil fuel industry, environmental oversight and monitoring of the industry in Alberta have not produced scientifically credible data for most of the last one hundred years. Even today in 2021, we still do not have credible publicly available data on fossil fuel industry emissions to air, land, and water – more on this later.

Considering that there are about 590,000 fossil fuel industry wells, 591,000 km of pipelines, well over two million kilometres of seismic lines, and hundreds of batteries, facilities, and processing plants distributed across Alberta, the lack of credible environmental data is astonishing. This development has taken place under the auspices of a regulator that states that it makes "sure energy development doesn't damage any aspect of our province's environment" (AER 2016a). Over the past century, the fossil fuel industry has transformed the economic, political, and natural landscape of Alberta. At the same time, the industry has conducted a successful program of capture of democratic institutions (Taft 2017; Urquhart 2018), in large part by spreading false information and undermining legislation, policy, and enforcement. In so doing, it has undermined its social licence and torn the social fabric.

Twenty-two years ago, the Pembina Institute conducted a study that examined the roots of citizen concerns about the fossil fuel industry (Marr-Laing and Severson-Baker 1999). They found that public concerns in Alberta and northeastern British Columbia had been caused by the government's unwillingness to provide effective environmental regulation and enforcement. Government indifference to the environmental and human health impacts of the industry were causing widespread anger, frustration, and fear. They showed that scientific evidence invalidated the claims of industry that no harmful effects arose from industry pollution. Slashing of resources intended for the energy regulator and agencies involved in environmental protection, along with deregulation, had undermined the capacity of government to provide meaningful auditing and inspection and had created a situation of voluntary compliance. The study concluded that unless measures were taken to address environmental and human health concerns, the public would act to slow or stop the issuance of public licences to the industry. It predicted that "The short-term economic benefits of saving a few million dollars in enforcement and regulatory infrastructure will be offset by hundreds of millions of dollars of annual losses from higher regulatory and public intervention costs and delayed project timelines." In short, the social licence of the industry would be lost. Since that time, public trust in both the industry and the government has continued to erode.

Figure 1.2 *Opposite* Early practices that released large volumes of contaminants. (a) Well production testing in the Turner Valley oil field in the 1930s. (b) "Bringing in" a well to remove drilling and well-stimulation wastes before bringing the well into production. Such wastes contaminated the product; it was more economical to contaminate the environment. (c) Aftermath of explosion and fire at the Royalite No. 23 well, 1931. The explosion occurred when nitroglycerine was put down the well (Tippett et al. 2014).

Figure 1.3 Early practices that released large volumes of contaminants continued. (a) Flaring of gases at a flare pit in the Turner Valley oil field. (b) Improperly abandoned wells present significant environmental uncertainty. This is especially true for older wells, such as this one, reportedly the Imperial Ribstone No. 2 well.

RISING CONFRONTATIONS, RISING STAKES

As the stakes have risen and the pace of planetary change has accelerated, disagreements over fossil fuel development have morphed into confrontations that grow larger and more intense with each passing year. In Canada, a recent energy confrontation escalated into a dispute in which former Alberta premier Notley along with Canadian prime minister Trudeau assumed the mantle of fossil fuel industry executives to force completion of the Kinder Morgan Trans Mountain Pipeline. In response, in early 2018, the British Columbia government called for further review of the pipeline's risks and the Union of BC Indian Chiefs vowed to oppose the pipeline. The Alberta government retaliated by imposing a boycott of British Columbia wine, suspending talks on buying BC electricity, and waging a media war against opponents of the pipeline.

In mid-April 2018, the Alberta government raised the stakes with Bill 12, which gave it the power to increase energy prices in British Columbia by restricting shipments of hydrocarbons (Edwardson 2018). Industry supported the legislation. The Canadian Association of Petroleum Producers (CAPP) was "on board" with Bill 12. The Explorers and Producers Association of Canada opined that "this impasse with British Columbia has to be brought to an end as quickly as possible … we would support the government at least acquiring the legal tools to defend Alberta's interests." The Canadian Association of Oilwell Drilling Contractors praised Bill 12 as "very prudent" and showing "bold leadership." The Alberta government defended the bill as necessary to push through construction of the Trans Mountain Pipeline. Bill 12 went into law in May 2018. The British Columbia government called the bill provocative and unconstitutional.

Prime Minister Trudeau promised he would use federal legislative muscle to ensure that the pipeline was built on time. In return, British Columbia undertook a court challenge over Ottawa's claim of sole jurisdiction over the environment. Incidentally, the economic study of the Trans Mountain project conducted by the Conference Board of Canada (Burt and Crawford 2014), which concluded that the project was economically beneficial, was funded by Trans Mountain Pipeline. In May 2018, following secret talks between the federal and Alberta governments and Kinder Morgan, the Canadian government purchased the Kinder Morgan pipeline for $4.5 billion and transferred ownership to the Trans Mountain Corp., a crown corporation (Campion-Smith and Maccharles 2018). NDP leader Jagmeet Singh responded that "climate change leaders don't spend $4.5 billion dollars on pipelines" (Canadian Press 2018).

In August 2018, a federal court of appeal quashed the approval for the Trans Mountain project citing inadequate consultation with First Nations and a flawed environmental impact study by the National Energy Board (Tasker and Harris 2018). The Alberta government retaliated by withdrawing from the federal climate action plan while the federal government reaffirmed its commitment to proceed with the project. In early 2020, the same federal court of appeal ruled that the government had consulted sufficiently with First Nations and that the project could proceed. Soon after that it was announced that the project cost had ballooned to $12.6 billion, all financed by the Canadian taxpayer. The federal government plans to sell the pipeline to the private sector and would not speculate as to whether it will sell the assets at a loss (Keller 2020). The future of Trans Mountain and other pipeline projects is uncertain. In July 2020, Zurich, the primary insurer for the Trans Mountain expansion, announced it would not renew its coverage due to expire in August 2020 (Cunningham 2020).

The tortuous history of the Keystone xl pipeline began in 2008 when Trans-Canada and ConocoPhillips proposed the line. Fast forward to January 2017 when former president Trump overturned the decision of former president Obama and reapproved the Keystone xl pipeline. In March 2020, Jason Kenney's Alberta government invested $1.5 billion of our taxes in the pipeline. But in July 2020, the United States Supreme Court upheld a Montana court ruling that the project cannot use the so-called Nationwide Permit 12 that allowed pipelines to cross rivers with minimal review. That decision came on the same day as a court-ordered shutdown of the Dakota Access pipeline and one day after Dominion Energy and Duke Energy cancelled the Atlantic Coast natural gas pipeline project (Paraskova 2020).

On 20 January 2021, on his first day in office, President Joe Biden cancelled the Keystone xl approval. The power of the fossil fuel metaorganization in Canada was on full display within twenty-four hours when Alberta and Saskatchewan premiers Kenney and Moe reportedly told Prime Minister Trudeau that they "want to go to war" with the United States over the Keystone cancellation while Ontario premier Ford told Trudeau to stand up to the bullying of Biden. Recommending waging war on the United States at this fragile juncture in North American history when democratic institutions are threatened by right-wing extremists is irresponsible. The outcome of these pipeline battles will affect all of us and circumscribe our options for addressing the climate crisis.

As a counterbalance to its support for pipelines, in June 2019 the Canadian federal government approved Bill C-69, the Impact Assessment Act and the Canadian Energy Regulator Act. The act's intent is for decisions to be made in a predictable and timely manner, to achieve reconciliation with Indigenous peoples, and to use transparent processes built on early engagement, inclusive participation, and the best available information. Among the act's purposes are averting adverse effects; ensuring that projects are considered in a precautionary but timely manner; and ensuring respect for the rights of Indigenous peoples. The act sets out financial liabilities for companies responsible for pipeline releases under the polluter pays principle. These changes, which apply only to federal jurisdiction, are reasonable and should help to protect both the public interest and the social licence of the hydrocarbon industry. They will not, however, mitigate most of the impacts of hydrocarbon exploitation because those occur under provincial jurisdiction. Despite the limited scope of Bill C-69, industry lobby groups waged a disinformation campaign to undermine support for the act and the federal liberal government. The surest sign that the act is in the public interest is that CAPP and other industry lobby groups and right-wing media never addressed the substance of the act. Instead they engaged in fear mongering and fanning the flames of separatism. I'll not provide those groups with a forum for their inflammatory rhetoric. Instead, I ask you to read Bill C-69 and reach your own opinion.

How did we get here? Why are citizens forced to assume public liabilities so that private corporations may profit? How can regulatory agencies approve projects that cause permanent climate and ecological impacts when the science is clear they are inimical to the public interest? How did government by and for the people come to be replaced by governments held in the thrall of corporations? The fossil fuel industry realized that the best return on investments come not from better machinery, they come from regulatory capture and information control. The industry has taken a "whole government" approach by investing and participating in political parties, government ministries, civil servants, universities, think tanks, regulators, lobby groups, monitoring agencies, and the media (Taft 2018). The industry sits at the table with politicians, senior civil servants, regulators, and monitoring agencies to provide oversight on legislation, enforcement, environmental protection, and land claims. The tendrils of the industry have spread like a vast fungal mycelium, exerting influence over all decision making. Industry has a right to provide its opinion, but it does not have the right to provide government oversight. Although New Democrats, Liberals, or Conservatives may be in office, it's the fossil fuel industry that's in power (Taft 2018), and rampant ecological degradation is its outcome. In short, governments infected by regulatory capture do not base their decisions on the public interest.

Worldwide, over the period 2006–20, democracy and pluralism have been under assault, including recent rapid erosion of democratic institutions in the United States and India, the world's two largest democracies (Freedom House 2020). In 2019, sixty-four countries experienced deterioration in political rights and civil liberties while only thirty-seven countries experienced improvements. People are angry, misinformed, and frightened, and they are embracing fundamentalism and conservative populist movements funded by the same vested interests that created the chaos. Starving people of education and information engenders bigotry, intolerance, fear, and distrust of education. They become more conservative and easier to manipulate. As policy, it's brilliant: it's cheap, effective, and self-reinforcing. In many countries, taxes and royalties have been eviscerated, unions and job security have been crushed, welfare has been gutted, voting rights curtailed, regulations repealed, and education and health care defunded or undermined. We are becoming squatters in the ecological and economic wreckage wrought by decline in our democracies and the increased concentration of economic power (Taylor 2019).

16

SUMMARY

Planet Earth is undergoing unprecedented changes. Climate change is one of the chief threats to the future of advanced civilization and global ecosystems, the main driver of which is the rising level of carbon dioxide in our atmosphere from the burning of fossil fuels. Significant changes to the composition and behaviour of the Earth's atmosphere are driving global changes that are unprecedented in human history. But hydrocarbon exploitation damages more than our atmosphere. Our landscapes are irrevocably changed as native ecosystems are replaced and soils and water are damaged.

Environmental damage, planned and unplanned, occurs on a daily basis. Often the effects are hidden and the data, if any exist, are unavailable to the public. In the aftermath of a spill, instead of reliable data and credible scientific assessments, we're presented with vague and reassuring press releases. Misinformation and lack of information are undermining the public's faith in government and the social licence of the fossil fuel industry.

The history of hydrocarbon exploitation presents an opportunity to examine whether industry activities have resulted in significant environmental impacts and whether information pertaining to impacts is accurate, credible, complete, available to the public in a timely manner, and supportive of a social licence. What is the truth about fossil fuel industry impacts? Fortunately data exist that allow us to determine that truth. In the next chapter, I introduce you to the data and how I analyzed them.

CHAPTER 2

The Data and How They Were Analyzed

In God we trust; all others must bring data.

Anonymous

INTRODUCTION

Why do we all know about the 1989 *Exxon Valdez* oil spill off the coast of Alaska but few of us have heard of Alberta's 1948 Atlantic No. 3 blowout that released six times the crude oil released by the *Exxon Valdez*? There are three reasons and all derive from how information is gathered and distributed. An obvious reason is the passage of time – modern news coverage travels farther and faster than it did seventy years ago. Secondly, marine spills receive more attention than do inland spills. Thirdly, and most importantly, we're taught a version of history that's acceptable to those in power.

Although there are many studies on crude oil spills in marine environments, there are relatively few studies and little available data on spills in inland environments (Fisher and Sublette 2005). To illustrate, conduct a Google Scholar search using the term "oil spill." You'll observe that about 95 per cent of the studies pertain to marine spills. The lack of available data on inland spills is remarkable given that they occur daily across much of North America and affect us all in some way. In many cases, neither the volumes spilled nor the composition of the spills is reported (Cozzarelli et al. 2017). The situation improved recently with release of some data summaries on inland spills in the United States (Allison and Mandler 2018a), but release of spill-specific data remains a rarity. Scarce available information on inland spills is a global phenomenon.

No global or national scientifically credible datasets exist on inland spills and their impacts. What exists instead is a seat of the pants patchwork of data of varying quality reported by industry to various agencies. For example, in Texas, spills are reported to the Texas Railroad Commission, in Saskatchewan to the Ministry of Energy and Resources, in North Dakota to the Ministry of Health, and in Montana to the Montana Board of Oil and Gas and/or the Montana Department of Environmental Quality. In Alberta, "upstream production" spills are reported to the Alberta Energy Regulator while other spills are reported to other agencies or not at all. Globally, there are more holes in the patchwork of information than there are patches.

Hydrocarbon misinformation is everywhere. We're told that spills from the Keystone XL Pipeline will pollute the Ogallala Aquifer while the other side tells us that spills can be prevented and are easily remediated. In Alberta, there's a standard media release that assures the public that the spill is under control, no wildlife has been harmed, and steps are being taken to prevent this in the future. The press release of former Alberta premier Alison Redford in reference to a 2012 Plains Midstream pipeline oil spill into the Red Deer River (missing from the AER's spill database) demonstrates typical government "spin." She stated that "this does not happen very often, and when it does we're able to get a handle on it quickly" (Vanderklippe and Walton 2012). She assured the public that government would take whatever steps are required to prevent this in the future (Canadian Press 2012). The same assurance-without-substance boiler-plate was again used after a 2015 Nexen spill when Premier Rachel Notley informed the public that an investigation would "ensure that it doesn't happen again" (*Financial Post* 2015). Industry uses similar spin, as in, "Canadian Natural is also taking proactive measures to prevent this type of incident in the future" (CNRL 2013). Such assurances are, of course, unscientific nonsense.

Why is there so little credible information on inland spills? Most information about spills is gathered by industry and its contractors, the quality and reliability of which vary widely. The public does not have access to this information because industry is not obligated to release it. In some cases, government agencies gather data, some of which may be available to the public. As regulations require, some industrial data are submitted to government. Some of these data are retrievable; some data are irretrievable or have been destroyed or lost; much of the data is scientifically suspect. Secondly, spill sites can be difficult to find because accurate location data may not be available, because many sites are remote, and because public access to spills is restricted. Although inland spills are common, publicly available scientific research and environmental information on spills are scarce. The vast majority of spills remain hidden from view.

Where do we turn to get accurate information? We have to build our understanding of spills from the ground up by analyzing the available evidence. In this chapter, we review the data and how they were analyzed. I examined three lines of evidence: field data, regulatory data and documents, and the scientific literature.

FIELD DATA

I used field data from four sources and four regions: northwestern Alberta, north-central and northeastern Alberta, the Rumsey Block in southern Alberta, and the Canol Road in the Northwest Territories (figure 2.1). In total, the field data represent 454 plots. We conducted fieldwork in northwestern Alberta in 2016 at sites representing crude oil spills, saline spills, and control sites in northwestern Alberta on the traditional lands of the Dene Tha First Nation (figure 2.1a, figure 2.2; for details and methods, see web 2.1–2.8). For north-central and northeastern Alberta, I compared natural control and industry reclaimed sites distributed across northeastern and north-central Alberta (figure 2.1b, web 2.9; data provided courtesy of Dr Brett Purdy). For the Canol Road, Northwest Territories, I compared alpine tundra natural controls with seventy-year-old crude oil spill plots (figure 2.1c, web 2.10; data provided courtesy of Dr Pete Kershaw). For the Rumsey Block in south-central Alberta, I compared natural grassland controls with remediated well site and pipeline plots (figure 2.1d, web 2.11; data provided courtesy of Mae Elsinger).

I analyzed the data on species, soil, and vegetation attributes by a variety of methods. Although some methods, such as ordination and classification, may seem abstruse, they aren't difficult to understand. In essence, all the methods have the same goal – to detect patterns and relationships in an objective and reproducible manner. For details and an example, see web 2.7. From 2018 to 2020, I made further field observations of spills and other disturbances in order to address questions raised in the analyses and to expand the comparisons between the regulator's data and scientific data.

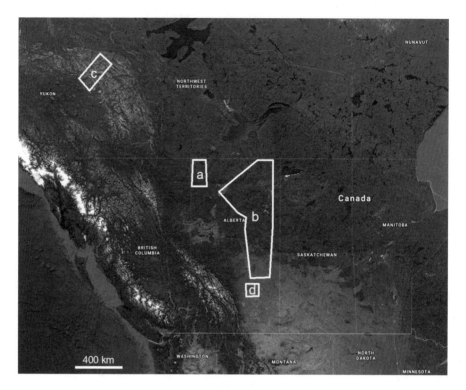

Figure 2.1 Locations of the four main field study regions: (a) northwestern Alberta, (b) north-central and northeastern Alberta, (c) Canol Road, Northwest Territories, and (d) Rumsey Block, Alberta.

Figure 2.2 *Opposite* The study sites in northwestern Alberta.

REGULATORY DATA AND DOCUMENTS, SPILLS INCLUDED AND EXCLUDED

Broadly speaking, spills occur during four different phases of hydrocarbon exploitation: during "upstream" production, during processing and refining, during distribution of products, and during consumption by users. Upstream production spills are the focus of this book. In Alberta, the regulator's Field Inspection System (FIS) database reports unintentional releases of substances from the conventional upstream oil and gas industry in Alberta since 1975. "Upstream" spills occur during production of hydrocarbons. By definition, spills that occur during refining, distribution, storage, or consumption are ex-

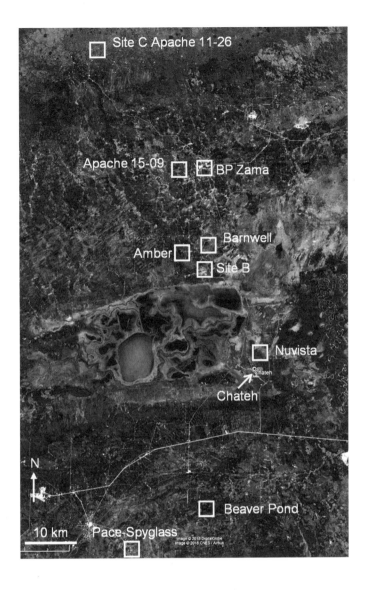

cluded. The regulator has no available information on releases that occurred before 1975. Many releases are missing both prior to and after 1975 – more on this topic later. The AER's database contains no data on releases from refineries and the distribution system downstream of refineries, from interprovincial pipelines and fuel storage facilities, from trucks and railway cars, for underground releases that go undetected, nor for intentional disposal of hydrocarbons such as plowing in of drilling waste and burial of contaminated soil, nor from the millions of point source releases by users (table 2.1). There are few data for releases resulting from production of unconventional hydrocarbons such as bitumen (see chapter 8, "Other Missing Spills"). Because most spills

Table 2.1 Inland spills resulting from hydrocarbon production and use

Spill type	Comments
Conventional Upstream, Post-1974	Comprises the vast majority of tracked spills in Alberta; the focus of this book
Missing Conventional Upstream, Post-1974	Unreported spills
Conventional Upstream, Pre-1975	No records, small number known, mostly anecdotal evidence; likely many thousands in Alberta
Unconventional Upstream Refineries, Processing Plants, Tank Farms, and Bulk Storage	Spills from production of bitumen and related
Production Distribution Pipelines, Intraprovincial	"Downstream" of refineries, etc.
Production Distribution Pipelines, Interprovincial	Tracked by National Energy Board (now the National Energy Regulator)
Trucks, Railway Cars	
Users	Millions of fuel spills by end users (airports, RCMP stations, marinas, farms, gas stations, public, outboard motors, etc.), typically gasoline, diesel, jet fuel
Miscellaneous	Poorly or unmonitored releases related to flaring, leaking abandoned wells, plowing in of drill waste, production testing, dumping, flare ponds, underground releases, seepage from tailings ponds, fracking

Note: See also chapter 8.

22

and releases are either poorly monitored or unmonitored, the available spill record is exceedingly incomplete.

Currently in Alberta, when an upstream spill occurs, industry is required to report the incident to the regulator – if it's a reportable incident (see glossary). The regulator records the information in a release report that is transcribed into the FIS database. FIS is the main tool the regulator uses to record location, ownership, technical, engineering, and environmental information about spills. Until mid-2019, a freedom of information request (shorthand, a FOIP, for Freedom of Information and Protection of Privacy Act) was required to get FIS information. For each spill, FIS provides what the AER asserts to be the volume spilled and volume recovered for various substances, the spill date, the date that cleanup was complete, the company responsible, the cause of the spill, the location, habitat effects, and other data (web 2.8).

I analyzed three vintages of the FIS data; the most recent spans the period 1 January 1975 to 30 June 2019 and includes 74,975 spills. The task of analyzing the regulator's data presented challenges and opportunities. Normally, data analysis involves a progression from proofing to hypothesis testing and statistical analyses and finally interpretation and discussion. In the case of the regulator's data, analyses required extensive data checks and validity tests of the data themselves (independent of hypothesis tests) that led down a rabbit hole we'll explore in later chapters (see also web 2.12).

23

OTHER REGULATORY INFORMATION

I submitted a freedom of information request for all relevant environmental information on the spills in northwestern Alberta (figure 2.2 and web 2.1) and requested the same information directly from industry. For the majority of the spills, little or no useful environmental information was provided by the AER. The information consisted largely of engineering reports (such as pipeline failure technical information), response and communications plans, photographs of equipment, duplicate FIS records, and engineering field notes and data – in short, not environmental information. See chapter 15, web 2.1 and 11.2 for background.

I analyzed four other industry-reported datasets on spills resulting from hydrocarbon production in order to broaden the context: upstream spills from Saskatchewan (19,511 spills, 1990 to 2018), North Dakota (8,690 spills, 2006 to 2014), and Montana (1,851 crude oil and produced water spills, 1997 to 2020; see web 6.18), and product spills from Canada National Energy Board interprovincial pipelines (1,336 spills, 2008–19). Together, the five datasets contain information on 106,363 spills (figure 2.3 and web 2.13). I gathered the five datasets into a single Excel file for your use (see web 2.12). Despite this robust number of spills, these comprise only a fraction of the total number and volume of spills because most spills go unmonitored or unreported. Therefore, the situation described from the available data represents the minimum effect of spills.

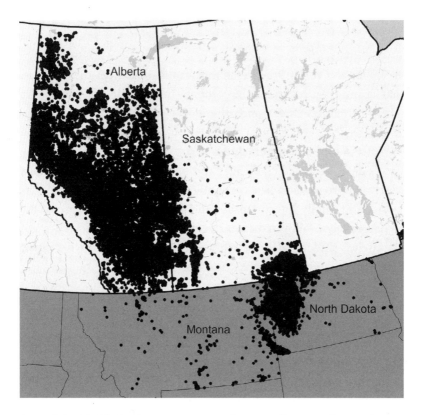

Figure 2.3 Fossil fuel industry upstream production spills reported to regulators in Alberta, Saskatchewan, Montana, and North Dakota. See also web 2.13.

THE SCIENTIFIC AND OTHER LITERATURE

I used academic papers, reports, and their data to establish the scientific knowns and unknowns and to provide context for the regulatory and industry-reported information. Media reports provided important background and were often the only source of information available.

SUMMARY

Despite the ubiquity and daily occurrence of inland spills, data and scientific information are scarce and often difficult to find. I analyzed three main lines of evidence to evaluate spills from conventional oil and gas production: field data, regulatory data, and the scientific literature. I used standard methods to allow for direct comparisons among datasets and have placed the detailed analyses in various web files.

CHAPTER 3

An Overview of Spills

When true simplicity is gained,
To bow and to bend we shant be ashamed.
To turn, to turn, it will be our delight,
Till by turning, turning, we come 'round right.

Shaker hymn, "Simple Gifts"

INTRODUCTION

To better understand spills and their ecological effects, we begin with an overview of the number, kinds, sources, and locations of spills. Let's begin with the basics.

What is a spill? A spill is an unplanned release of a substance into the environment. In this broad sense, a spill may be in liquid, solid, or gas phase, or a mixture of phases. Spills may be onto land, into water, into air, or spread underground. "Release" is a more general term used for spill and may be a more accurate term because spills imply both a liquid and a falling downward. A "blowout" is a catastrophic high pressure release from a well and may include gas, liquids, and solids.

Crude oil is a mixture of volatile and nonvolatile hydrocarbons in combination with varying amounts of natural gas, carbon dioxide, saline water, and sulphur compounds. "Saline produced water," known as brine in the United States, is a by-product of oil and gas production. It varies in composition in concert with the geological source but is usually strongly saline. Both crude oil and saline spills contain varying amounts of volatile organic compounds (VOCs), polycyclic aromatic hydrocarbons (PAHs), heavy metals, naturally occurring radioactive material, and oilfield chemicals such as alkylphenols and phthalates that are known endocrine disruptors. Spills of crude oil and saline water are better understood as spills of complex chemical emulsions.

Spill Bookkeeping

Nothing is simple with the regulator's data. In order for a spill to be recorded by the regulator, it's supposed to fit the criteria of a "reportable release" (see glossary), but often reported releases don't fit the criteria.

Multiple releases require some bookkeeping terms. Let's say a spill includes crude oil, fresh water, waste, and saline produced water. For the purpose of our bookkeeping, such a spill would be a primary crude oil spill, a secondary fresh water spill, a tertiary waste spill, and a quaternary saline spill.

"Waste" spills are typically not spills – they are a general category for miscellaneous materials recovered. But – there's always a "but" in AER data – hundreds of "waste" spills are actual spills with non-zero volumes released. For some waste spills, volume recovered is left blank or reported as zero, such as a release of 38,500 m³ of waste and zero recovered.

"Fresh water" spills can be complex mixtures that contain saline produced water, waste, raw production gas, or crude oil. In other words, they are not fresh water in the sense of potable water. For more on AER's use of the term "fresh water," see the glossary.

Natural gas releases are reported in thousands of cubic metres. Liquid volumes are reported in cubic metres. One cubic metre equals 264 US gallons, 1,000 litres, or 6.29 petroleum barrels. A cubic metre of water weighs 1,000 kilograms, 2,200 lbs. A spill of a cubic metre of crude oil or saline water can do a lot of damage. An Olympic swimming pool contains 2,499 m³.

Underground releases from pipelines, and particularly from well bores, are an insidious form of release that can remain undetected. They require careful monitoring and sophisticated groundwater plume mapping, are widespread, and can result in permanent groundwater contamination. Given that we see only surface incidents, and that hydrocarbons are conveyed within a vast underground network of well bores and pipelines, it's possible that we're failing to detect most underground releases. Underground releases are not discussed further in this book because there are insufficient data. Similarly, we know that releases of gases and liquids commonly occur at abandoned wells, but monitoring is too rudimentary to assess the extent of the problem. Serious knowledge gaps highlight the degree to which regulators ignore the risks associated with the development and transport of hydrocarbons. These failures to protect the public interest are worsened by the absence of PhD-level environmental chemists, ecologists, and public health scientists in most regulatory bodies.

SUBSTANCES SPILLED

Crude oil and saline produced water releases are the two most common fossil fuel industry spills and present the greatest ecological concerns. Together they account for the majority of spills in Alberta, but this division is a simplification. Often crude oil spills contain large volumes of saline produced water and vice versa. After all, the term "produced water" means just that, it's water that is produced along with the crude oil or natural gas that is being removed from its geological formation. You can think of crude oil and saline produced water spills as a sliding scale that ranges from 100 per cent oil and 0 per cent produced water to 0 per cent oil and 100 per cent produced water. Although not reported as such, a large proportion of these spills are a mixture of both – they're emulsions.

Of the 74,975 Alberta spills reported by the regulator (current to July 2019), 61 per cent released crude oil and/or saline water. Spills of solely crude oil, mixtures of crude oil and saline water, and solely saline water accounted for 25 per cent, 15 per cent, and 20 per cent of the total spills. Other commonly released substances include raw production gas, "fresh water," marketable production gas, "unknown," condensate, "waste," crude bitumen, and process water,

Why Are Spills Common and Why Are They So Often Reported to Be Harmless?

Hydrocarbons are easy to transport but difficult to contain (Penfold 2016). They flow smoothly through well bores and pipelines and into tanks but escape containment just as easily to spread through air, soil, and water. Spills have been common for decades, but why are they so common?

Simple questions can have complex answers. First we need to understand the difference between the reported spill rate and the actual spill rate. Let's say companies in provinces "A" and "B" experience the same actual rate of spills. Companies in province "A" are conscientiously reporting spills and companies in province "B" are lax in their reporting. Unless we know the actual spill rates,

27

we may conclude that companies in province "B" are doing a better job than those in province "A." We would be mistaken because companies in province "A" are providing truthful information and those in province "B" are not. Spills may appear to be common or rare simply because there is good or poor reporting. With poor regulations and enforcement, the greater the likelihood that spills are not being reported, and the greater the likelihood that we will think the spill rate is low. If companies know there is only a small likelihood of enforcement or if the fines imposed are small relative to profits, spills will be common.

Reporting thresholds also influence spill rates. If province "A" has a spill volume reporting threshold of 0.1 m³ and province "B" has a reporting threshold of 2 m³, spills will appear to be more common in province "A." It's therefore difficult to compare spill rates across jurisdictions or even over time if reporting thresholds change. Whether companies are truthfully reporting spills or reporting thresholds change, the reported number of spills is always lower than the actual number of spills – how much lower we'll examine in a later chapter.

Independent of the effect of truthful reporting and thresholds, what can make spills common? Spills are common wherever there is poor oversight during operations, where infrastructure is old or poorly maintained, and where corrosion is widespread. Spills are common wherever the costs of preventing spills exceed the costs incurred by spills. The latter cost is not simply the cost of responding to a spill. Failure to respond to a spill draws down the value of a company's social licence … if that failure is communicated to the public. If not, there is no economic incentive to prevent spills. And finally, spills are common where the level of exploitation is high; this is simple math … the greater the number of chances for spills, the greater the number of spills.

Economic incentive influences how the impacts of spills are documented. Consultants tasked with documenting impacts are hired by the company responsible for the spill. Finding impacts costs the energy company money and renders it unlikely that the consultant will be hired again. If the regulator is willing to accept superficial impact reports, then why go looking for problems? If this sounds extreme, it is. Later in the book we'll examine how the impacts of spills are routinely underestimated. The truth is that, for every spill in which credible scientific data have been gathered, harm has been detected.

What Do Spills Look Like?

When most of us picture an oil spill, we see an oil slick at sea, blackened shore-lines, and dying oil-soaked birds. Inland crude oil and saline water spills are different, in part because inland spills do not form extensive slicks as they do over open ocean (plate 3.1). Fresh crude oil spills onto dry land or snow resemble black stains; on lakes or rivers, they appear as slicks or iridescent sheens. Often they are concealed by vegetation or spread across wetlands and resemble dark water. Fresh saline spills look harmless, but their damage is insidious. At first, they look like water-soaked ground or a flooded wetland … they can be essentially invisible. But come back in two months and you'll find dead or dying vegetation. Because of lack of timely information and denial of access, in the vast majority of incidents the public is left to identify spill sites not by the spilled liquids, which are no longer visible, but by the effects of the spills. Once crude oil and saline spills have had time to exert their effects, spill sites can be identified by patches of barren soil, altered soil structure and chemistry, and by altered species assemblages. We can think of these alterations as a spill "signature." Old spills are often covered in grasses, mostly exotic grasses. Saline spills can also be identified by plant species that grow in salty conditions, plants known as halophytes, and often by a whitish salt crust at the soil surface.

In the aftermath of a spill, industry may attempt to recover the retrievable portion (known as "free fluid") with vacuum pumps and skimmers. It may excavate to remove contaminated soil and gather contaminated vegetation. Whatever spilled material remains soaks into the ground, is concealed under vegetation or organic matter, disperses into a water body, or flows down river. We'll explore how spills affect the biota in some detail. Suffice for now to understand that most spill sites will support some kind of plant growth. One of the great misconceptions about vegetation response to disturbance is that, because plants have reestablished, all is well. Except in the case of highly saline spills, vegetation will establish after a spill without human assistance. But green vegetation is not necessarily healthy nor is the soil underneath it. Indeed for many species, such as foxtail barley and smooth brome, it's the spill or other disturbance that creates the opportunity for the invasive or weedy species to replace the damaged native vegetation. In contrast, establishing a healthy plant–soil–animal community after disturbance is not easy. In every fossil fuel industry site that I have examined over many years, the vegetation has been demonstrably different from that surrounding the site.

What Makes Spills Harmful?

Spills are harmful because they alter the chemical, physical, or biological conditions beyond the ranges of tolerance of the biota. Spills can induce acute and chronic stress, changes in growth, density, survival, and reproduction, increases in birth defects and disease, and changes in biotic composition. The stresses can arise from direct toxicity or indirectly through soil damage. A saline spill can destroy soil structure after which movements of water and gases through the soil are restricted. Oil contamination can render soils water repellent and thereby reduce water availability to plants and reduce salt leaching. Spill impacts can result from the remediation operations through soil compaction and removal, vegetation removal, flushing of sediments, excavations, the addition of chemicals, and the introduction of species. Spill effects persist because the damage to the biota and soils coupled with the residual contaminants left behind together establish a new domain (see chapter 10).

Why are saline spills harmful? Consider what happens if the saltshaker lid falls off when you're salting your soup. You can't remove the salt because it has dissolved. You can discard the soup, but we can't discard ecosystems. If salts are not diluted, leached, flushed from the system, rendered unavailable, or otherwise removed, salts can persist indefinitely and exert long-term effects. A brine-saturated soil can require a hundredfold dilution with fresh water to lower the salt content sufficiently for unhindered plant growth (Munn and Stewart 1989).

One of the best measures of salinity is electrical conductivity, the ability of soil or water to conduct an electrical current. Salt ions such as sodium and chloride are particularly good at conducting electricity. Saline spills have high conductivity; the current is carried by the ions. It's important to understand how toxic salt can be. As an example, consider the soil on the roadside adjacent to our home. Before road maintenance was privatized, the soil grew the typical disturbance tolerant plants such as brome grass. Recently the soil was damaged by applications of brine mixes to melt winter snow and ice on the road. Now only salt-tolerant weeds grow along the roadside. The soil conductivity along the roadside in spring 2019 (2,200 μS/cm) was fifty times higher than that of the nearby undisturbed forest soil. Only about ¼ teaspoon of table salt dissolved in a litre of distilled water is needed to equal the conductivity of the soil damaged by the road brine mix, sufficient to harm most native plants.

SPILLS IN OVERVIEW

Spills Are Messy

Spills are messy in the normal sense of the word, but they are also messy in the uncertainties that they pose. The messiness derives from several facts. First and foremost, spills contain complex substances. Of the 74,975 spills reported by AER, 53,743 of those spills reported only a single substance, but most often, a single substance such as crude oil is a complex mixture. The same complexity applies to spills of saline produced water, raw production gas, raw bitumen, and other categories. Importantly, the volumes reported in combined spills of crude oil and saline water in Alberta are subjective values rather than actual measurements (web 6.18.7), which deepens their uncertainty.

The chemical composition of spills is rarely determined, so we rarely know the contaminant exposure faced by the ecosystem. Produced water can contain petroleum condensates, paraffin, corrosion inhibitors, scale inhibitors, acids, surfactants, and other additives used to enhance production (Colgan et al. 2002). Although some of these additives such as paraffin are relatively safe, others such as phthalates are not.

There are often multiple releases in a single spill. In 28,694 spills, the regulator listed two to four spilled substance categories. Therefore, the total number of releases exceeds the number of spills: there were 103,669 total reported substance releases. But even this bookkeeping oversimplifies the messiness of spills. The regulator's substance categories overlap and some are ill defined. For example, condensate, crude oil, and raw production gas are separate categories but crude oil and production gas contain condensates.

In 2,046 spills, the released substance was not identified and is therefore unknown. Adding to the uncertainty, we'll observe that the regulator's spill and recovery, location, habitat and wildlife effects, area affected, and sensitive areas data are not credible (chapters 6 and 7). There are furthermore thousands of spills missing from the regulator's records (chapter 8).

Sources of Spills

Spills come from a variety of sources including pipelines, crude oil group batteries and other production facilities, waste pits and storage tanks, from drilling and production at wells, from processing and refining, from transport via

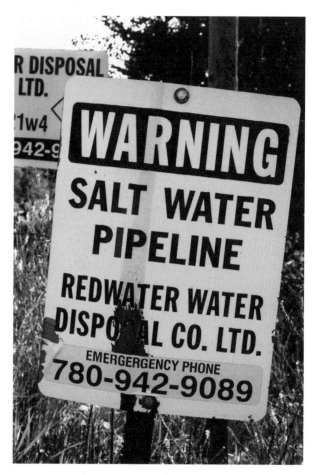

Figure 3.1 After saline water is produced during extraction of hydrocarbons, it must be disposed of at water injection wells where it is injected underground. Saline spills often occur during transport along water and multiphase pipelines and at oil wells and crude oil group batteries. By volume, water pipelines are the largest source of saline water releases in Alberta. 5 August 2018.

32

railroad cars and transport trucks, and during the sale, storage, or use of fuels. Spills that occur from the refinery stage downstream to the consumer are not part of the regulator's database.

Multiphase pipelines, crude oil group batteries, and oil wells are the three most common sources of crude oil spills within the upstream hydrocarbon production system. By volume of crude oil released, crude oil group batteries, crude oil pipelines, and multiphase pipelines are the three largest sources (web 3.2). Multiphase pipelines, water pipelines, and crude oil group batteries are the three most common sources for saline spills. By far the largest volume of saline water released comes from water pipelines (figure 3.1) followed by oil wells and multiphase pipelines (web 3.2).

In Alberta, the six types of pipelines are together responsible for 35 per cent of crude oil spills and 38 per cent of the volume of crude oil spilled, and for 52 per cent of saline spills and 55 per cent of the saline water volume spilled. In Saskatchewan, pipelines account for 31 per cent of crude oil spills and 23 per cent of the crude oil volume spilled, and 43 per cent of saline spills and 57 per cent of the saline volume spilled.

Because pipelines, wells, and crude oil group batteries are important sources of spills, let's review the major kinds. By substances carried, six kinds of pipelines are used in Alberta. (1) Water pipelines carry nonpotable water, typically saline produced water and associated substances. (2) Multiphase pipelines carry emulsions of crude oil, gases, saline production water, condensates, "fresh water," and other materials. The emulsions are also known as "oil effluent." (3) Crude oil pipelines convey crude oil. (4) Natural gas pipelines convey mixtures of methane, other light hydrocarbons, and condensates. (5) Sour gas pipelines convey natural gas containing $\geq$ 4 ppm hydrogen sulphide. (6) "Other" pipelines convey unspecified substances.

Smaller diameter gathering pipelines, up to about 20 cm diameter, carry materials from wells and batteries to facilities. Pressurized larger diameter transmission pipelines, up to 1.5 m diameter, convey products over long distances. Pipelines that move materials solely within a province are under provincial jurisdiction. Pipelines that carry hydrocarbons across provincial boundaries are interprovincial pipelines and are under the jurisdiction of the National Energy Board (NEB, renamed the Canada Energy Regulator in 2019). Pipelines of various sizes convey finished products to end users.

There are two main types of wells. Production wells convey hydrocarbons and other substances from the geological formation up to the surface. Injection wells, also called waste disposal wells, convey waste fluids such as saline produced water from the surface down to a disposal zone underground. The volume of waste liquid injected underground by the fossil fuel industry in Canada is not known. In the United States, about 2 billion gallons (7.6 million m³) of saline produced water were being injected underground *per day* in 2013 (Testa and Jacobs 2014). Ideally, underground waste disposal is accomplished in ways that protect surface water and groundwater from contamination. Groundwater contamination from wastewater injection and abandoned wells has been reported, however, as has insufficient monitoring of underground contamination.

33

Where Do Spills Occur?

Crude oil and saline water spills are widely distributed across Alberta with the exception of the Rocky Mountains and portions of northeastern Alberta, across western and southeastern Saskatchewan, and in western North Dakota (figure 2.3), but they're not uniformly distributed. In Alberta, clusters of spills exist near Chateh, Grande Prairie, Whitecourt–Slave Lake, and eastern Alberta from Cold Lake to south of Lloydminster; in the region west of Edmonton and Red Deer, east of Calgary, and west and northwest of Medicine Hat. Within the Dene Tha traditional territory in northwestern Alberta (web 3.3), crude oil and saline water spills are clustered to the north and south of the Hay–Zama Lakes. Thousands more spills have occurred than are reported and mapped (see chapter 8).

Although mapping reveals geographic clustering of spills, clustering is greater than depicted because many locations receive multiple spills. For example, in Alberta as of 2017, 4,120 locations had received multiple crude oil spills and the top one hundred locations had suffered an average of thirteen spills. For saline spills, 2,600 locations had received multiple spills and the top one hundred locations had suffered an average of sixteen spills. Similar spill clustering takes place in Saskatchewan and North Dakota. Crude oil group batteries suffer severe impacts from their multiple spills.

Crude Oil and Saline Spills: What Companies Spill the Most?

In theory, this question should be easy to answer. In reality, few questions that rely on regulatory data are straightforward. Why? In short, we don't know the actual number and volume of spills nor in many cases what was spilled or the company responsible. What we know is the reported number and volumes of spills, and those numbers are a fraction of the true spill rates as you'll see.

With these caveats in mind, for crude oil and saline spills in Alberta, the companies responsible for the most spills and the largest spill volumes include Imperial, BP, Husky, CNRL, Encana, Obsidian, Chevron, and Repsol (web 3.4). That a moderate-sized producer such as Obsidian experiences spill rates on par with the multinationals merits closer investigation. On average, BP is responsible for the largest crude oil spills; Chevron, Imperial, and BP are responsible for the largest saline spills. The absence of major producers such as

Never Confuse Reported Values with Actual Values

With industry-reported regulatory data we can never be certain of truth-fulness. Even a simple question such as what companies spill the most crude oil and saline water can be difficult to answer. As you'll see in later chapters, there are thousands of missing spills and reported spill rates and volumes are unreliable. Then there are thousands of companies. In Alberta, Saskatchewan, and North Dakota, 2,118, 694, and 350 different company names, respectively, are responsible for reported spills. Some companies are listed under multiple names and spellings, and numbered corporations can change their "names." There are hundreds of spills by unknown companies and thousands of spills of unknown substances. We might assume that companies with the most spills are the biggest polluters but the truth may be that those companies are diligent in their reporting while companies with few spills may be negligent in their repor-ting. And finally, to place spill rates in context, we need to relate spills to production. For example, if companies A and B are both responsible for say, 1,000 m^3 in spill volumes each year, while company A produces 100,000 barrels of crude oil and company B produces one million barrels of crude oil, company A is doing a poorer job of spill prevention. Because annual company production data are unknown, we can't relate spill rates to production rates.

35

Syncrude and Suncor from this list is due to bookkeeping (spills in northeast-ern Alberta are tracked by Alberta Environment, and those companies spill bitumen, dilbit, tailings, and wastewater, etc., not crude oil or saline water *per se*). In Saskatchewan, the largest spillers of crude oil and saline water include Husky, CNRL, Crescent Point, Wascana, Obsidian, Enbridge, Baytex, and Nexen (web 3.5). On average, Enbridge is responsible for the largest crude oil spills; Cona Resources, NAL, and CNR Petro Resources are responsible for the largest saline spills. North Dakota's largest spillers of crude oil and saline water include Continental Resources, Hess, Whiting Oil and Gas, Tesoro, BNSF, En-bridge, SM Energy, and Arrow (web 3.6). On average, Continental Resources and Whiting Oil and Gas are responsible for the largest crude oil spills; Hess and SM Energy are responsible for the largest saline spills. In Alberta, fifteen companies are responsible for 48 per cent of crude oil spills and 43 per cent of the total oil volume, and 54 per cent of saline spills and 63 per cent of the total saline volume. In Saskatchewan, fifteen companies are responsible for 57 per cent of crude oil spills and 59 per cent of the total oil volume, and 61 per cent of saline spills and 63 per cent of the total saline volume. In North Dakota, fifteen companies are responsible for 63 per cent of crude oil spills and 65 per cent of the total oil volume, and 63 per cent of saline spills and 69 per cent of the total saline volume.

SUMMARY

Spills are unplanned releases of substances into the environment. Although it's common to refer to spills by simple names such as crude oil, in reality, most spills are composed of complex mixtures. Crude oil and saline water spills are the most common spills that occur during upstream production. They occur daily and are widely distributed wherever hydrocarbons are produced. Thousands of companies are responsible for spills, but relatively few companies are responsible for most spills. There are many thousands of unreported spills.

Crude oil group batteries, crude oil pipelines, and multiphase pipelines are responsible for the largest volumes of crude oil spills. Water pipelines account for the largest volume of saline spills followed by crude oil group batteries and oil wells.

Most spills are hidden from public view. Crude oil spills onto dry land or snow resemble black stains; on lakes or rivers, they appear as slicks or iridescent sheens. In contrast to oil spills, recent saline spills look like harmless patches of wet ground. Both oil and saline spills can be concealed by vegetation or spread across wetlands and resemble dark water, or in some cases remain underground. The effects of saline spills are insidious and persistent. With this background on the basics of spills, we can now examine what science tells us about their effects.

PART TWO

THE INCIDENT AND THE AFTERMATH

CHAPTER 4

The Effects of Spills

There are no unsacred places; there are only sacred places and desecrated places.

Wendell Berry, "How to Be a Poet"

INTRODUCTION

In the last chapter I presented an overview of spills by defining and describing the kinds of spills, what inland spills look like, and where, when, and how often they occur. In this chapter I take you on a brief tour of the scientific literature on inland spills with a focus on Canadian and northern case studies. First, we examine the general effects of crude oil, saline water, and complex spills then focus on important studies that lay the scientific groundwork to help us understand the effects of spills and place the views and data of the regulator and industry in context. Building a strong foundation is seldom easy but is always a good idea. I've provided details and reviews of additional spill studies in the web resources. If you find the material overly technical you may want to skip to the chapter summary.

CRUDE OIL SPILLS

Crude oil contains thousands of compounds and the effects of its spills are correspondingly complex. When spilled, crude oil releases a mixture of volatile (that evaporate) and nonvolatile hydrocarbons along with condensates, carbon dioxide, saline water, sulphur, nitrogen, metals, and minerals. Hydrocarbons in crude oils are composed of gas-phase and liquid-phase straight carbon chains, aromatic rings, resins, and solids known as asphaltenes. Crude oils differ in their toxicity, mobility, and persistence in relation to their chemical composition, to the biological species exposed, to the soil properties, and the ease with which the oil can move through the environment.

Less soluble hydrocarbons, such as most PAHs, tend to be immobile, do not evaporate, do not easily biodegrade, and can bioaccumulate, impose chronic toxicity, and persist as tar balls and asphalt pavements. Medium solubility hydrocarbons, such as naphthalene, can dissolve partially in water and migrate short distances; they tend to evaporate over time but can leave residues. High solubility hydrocarbons such as benzene, toluene, and xylene can migrate and have high acute toxicity but tend to evaporate quickly if exposed to air (see Lee et al. [2015] and Testa and Jacobs [2014] for more on the composition of crude oil).

The effects of spills vary by the composition of the spill and length of exposure, by the delay between spill and response, by the type and intensity of cleanup operations, and by the ecosystems and species that are exposed. The season in which the spill occurs, soil and site characteristics, exposure to waves, flowing or nonflowing water, the size and connectivity of lakes and wetlands, permafrost, water currents, and ice can all influence the effects of a spill and the success of a cleanup. A midwinter spill on frozen ground at a bird breeding colony would have less direct impact on birds than the same spill when the colony is occupied, but the same midwinter spill could result in a greater impacted area because the oil spreads out over frozen ground.

Short-term effects of oil spills on marsh plants range from reduction in gas exchange and carbon fixation to mortality (Pezeshki et al. 2000). Physical impacts to plants come mostly from coating of foliage and the soil surface. Wetlands are sensitive to oil spills in large part because they collect water, sediments, and spills from within their watershed. The impact of oil on vegetation is generally most significant on organic soils, which makes peatlands sensitive to spills (more on sensitive areas in chapter 7). Penetration of oil into the soil can result in persistent effects such as water repellency that can limit plant growth for decades (we'll observe this in our examination of the Atlantic No. 3 blowout).

Wildlife that escapes direct mortality can succumb to starvation, injury, or the toxic effects of oil ingested while preening (Ramirez 2010). Animals can suffer delayed effects after contact with oil or other chemicals. Sublethal doses of oil can impair reproduction in birds. Cold stress can be lethal if oil

Figure 4.1 Following a pipeline spill near Swift Current, Saskatchewan, that released 69 m³ of crude oil and 1,300 m³ of produced water in September 2008, workers use an *in situ* burn in an attempt to remove crude oil from a contaminated wetland.

damages the insulation provided by feathers or fur. Ingestion or absorption of small amounts of oil can render animals more susceptible to disease or predation. Oil sheens in waste pits or contaminated ponds pose a threat to nesting aquatic birds because small amounts of oil applied to eggs are extremely toxic to embryos.

Spill effects can be mitigated or worsened by cleanup operations. Although biodegradation eventually removes most hydrocarbons after terrestrial oil spills, it can take decades and may never be complete. Conventional cleanup methods in wetlands contaminated by spills involve excavation, trenching, use of sorbent pads, bellholes, and low-pressure flushing. These methods are expensive, can have limited effectiveness, and can cause long-term harm (Moore et al. 1997). *In situ* burning is sometimes used to remove spilled hydrocarbons (figure 4.1) and can be a significant source of air pollution and damage to vegetation, soils, and wildlife. However, burning is probably less damaging overall than conventional cleanup methods and is least harmful during periods when plants are dormant. As we'll observe, remediation operations can damage ecosystems more than the spills themselves. In large part, the irreparable damage comes from the profound soil disturbance that creates problematic chemistry, degraded soil structure, and persistent nonnative species on a substrate devoid of the natural soil biological communities that provide ecological resilience.

Hydrocarbons undergo chemical and physical changes at rates that are influenced by temperature and the soil biota (Boufadel et al. 2015; Lee et al. 2015). Leaving crude oil in place to be degraded by resident microbes (a process known as natural attenuation), sometimes assisted by addition of nutrients and bacterial inoculation, can be more effective and less damaging than intrusive methods. However, natural attenuation has its limitations. Oil residues in soil tend to clump, become hydrophobic, and exclude soluble nutrients and oxygen and can create a barren soil (see plate 3.1d). Once hydrophobicity develops, oil-degrading microbes may be unable to colonize and degrade the residues (Vavrek et al. 2004). In water, hydrocarbon degradation is influenced by the dissolved oxygen concentration; the relative amounts of carbon, nitrogen, and phosphorus; salinity and pH; and time elapsed since the spill. Multidecadal persistence of spilled hydrocarbons is common, as you'll soon read.

Guidelines for "acceptable" levels of exposure to petroleum hydrocarbons in soil have been developed (CCME 2008a), which is fine, as long as we understand their limitations (web 4.1, 4.2). The guidelines are based on a handful of species, most of which are agricultural, they don't consider organic soils, and they rely upon short-term growth responses that may be irrelevant to the chronic exposure typical of natural ecosystems. Importantly, there are no guidelines for chronic hydrocarbon exposure of native species in natural ecosystems. Hydrocarbon exposures that don't affect reproduction or that are safe for chronic exposure can be more than ten times lower than acute mortality thresholds (CCME 2008b). Therefore, even if a spill site lies within "acceptable" acute guidelines, the biota may suffer impacts because damage accumulates during chronic exposure – yet we have no chronic guidelines.

Despite decades of research, significant unknowns persist about the effects of crude oil spills such as their impacts in arctic waters, shores, rivers, and wetlands; about effects on species at the population, community, and ecosystem levels; and about spill behaviour across a spectrum of crude oil types and environments (Lee et al. 2015). Improvements in spill response, prevention, decision support systems, and risk assessment haven't kept pace with advances in the technology of hydrocarbon exploitation.

42

SALINE SPILLS

Unlike hydrocarbons, salts can't be biodegraded or burned off. By analogy, we might think of hydrocarbon spills as infections that the body's natural defenses can detoxify to some extent. In contrast, saline spills are like lead poisoning in that the body has no effective way to remove the toxins; the salts are stored and do long-term damage. Saline spills cause environmental impacts that equal or exceed those of crude oil spills, but our senses can deceive us. We see no black and viscous residue, we aren't sickened by fumes, and we see no dying animals coated in oil, yet toxins have nonetheless been delivered. Saline spills typically contain more than just salts; they also contain varying amounts of hydrocarbons, heavy metals, oilfield production chemicals, and radionuclides such as radium. But it's the salt, mostly plain table salt, that makes saline spills so toxic.

Typical saline spills contain about 90 per cent or more of sodium chloride. Salt is commonplace and seemingly innocuous; we consume it every day. A dependable person is "the salt of the earth" and an undependable person is "not worth his salt." Yet if we consume too much salt, we develop hypertension and heart disease. Saline spills cause ecological hypertension. A typical salinity of a saline spill is about four times that of seawater (Keiffer and Unger 2002), but salinities can range from a minimum of 1,000 mg/L to as high as 400,000 mg/L, a salinity more than eleven times that of seawater (Colgan et al. 2002; Vavrek et al. 2004). Imagine pouring seawater on your garden. Your plants would die and you would have to abandon your garden because the salts don't degrade. Salts are the unwanted gift that keeps on giving.

As soil sodium levels increase, clay minerals disperse. This results in soil swelling, loss of soil pores, collapse of soil structure, reduced water and air movements, and inhibition of water and nutrient uptake by plants (Vavrek et al. 2004). Excess salt interferes with all water-based metabolic processes, and since all life runs on water, it's understandable that salts can create havoc. Saline spills damage the soil microbial community, the beating heart of the soil.

Removal of salts is essential to minimize the collateral damage stemming from the hydrocarbons, metals, and radionuclides in saline spills (Vavrek et al. 2004). The effects of a saline spill depend on the spill volume and chemical composition and on biological and physical factors such as the plant and

43

animal species present, the climate, soil properties, and how water moves through the ecosystem (Vavrek et al. 2004). Because of their limited capacity to leach salts, ecosystems with a high water table, such as wetlands, are sensitive to saline spills. Similarly, soils high in clay and pH tend to be sensitive to saline spills.

Chemical soil amendments have a high failure rate and can even add soil salts wherever soil drainage is impeded. Establishing healthy vegetation after spills is exceedingly difficult. One reclamation biologist described his experience with soil reclamation in Manitoba: "The worst problem was salinity, and little could be done to remedy it other than pouring on a lot of nitrate fertilizers to displace sodium from the soil colloids. But that lasted only as long as the groundwater table didn't rise to the surface during wet periods and bring with it the salts that had been leached to deeper levels" (D. Downing, pers. comm., 18 January 2017). The persistence of salts in areas subjected to spills is worsened in arid regions where rainfall is insufficient to facilitate leaching.

In the United States, petroleum exploration and production have damaged soils, surface water, groundwater, and ecosystems in all thirty-six oil-producing states (Kharaka and Dorsey 2005). The damage has resulted primarily from releases of large volumes of saline water, hydrocarbons, and improperly abandoned wells. Land clearing, roads, tank batteries, brine pits, pipelines, and other land uses have exacerbated the damage. In many regions, nine barrels of saline water are produced for every barrel of oil (Keiffer and Unger 2002). In North Dakota it's even worse: eighteen barrels of saline water are produced for every barrel of oil (Meehan et al. 2017). Over the last decade, rising rates of oil exploitation in North Dakota have outstripped the state's emergency response capacities resulting in failure to protect the safety and security of North Dakotans and the state's ecosystems (Cwiak et al. 2015).

Saline water releases from oil and gas exploitation pose a host of risks to the environment, many of which remain poorly understood or unknown due to the complex mixtures of chemicals involved (Cozzarelli et al. 2017). Produced water from conventional natural gas wells in the United States is typically ten times more toxic than produced water from oil wells (Ramirez 2010). Surface water and groundwater in the Williston Basin in the Prairie Pothole Region of the western United States were contaminated with produced saline water at thirty-four of the forty-eight industry sites investigated; seven more sites were potentially contaminated (Gleason and Tangen 2014). Hydrocarbon production was confirmed as the source of the contamination, specifically from oil and gas wells, tank batteries, reserve pits, pipelines, and illegal dumping. Water contamination at a minimum of 71 per cent of industrial sites is alarming.

In terrestrial ecosystems, excess sodium and chloride result in breakdown of soil structure and inhibition of water and nutrient absorption due to osmotic imbalances that cause drought-like symptoms and long-term reductions in growth (Environment Canada 2001). Direct toxicity causes leaf burn and tissue death and damage to the soil biota. Contamination of soil, surface water, and groundwater from brine spills in North Dakota has been detected years to decades after the spills (plate 4.1; Lauer et al. 2016; Cozzarelli et al. 2017; Meehan et al. 2017).

Excess sodium is a more persistent problem than is high salinity because exchangeable sodium usually persists after soluble salts are removed (Alberta Environment 2001). Guidelines for exposure to salts rely upon short-term exposures that are amenable to laboratory study. As noted for hydrocarbons, short-term exposures may not be relevant to chronic exposures. We can get away with oversalting our food occasionally (acute exposure) but not oversalting every day (chronic exposure). In ecosystems, harmful chronic sodium chloride concentrations are four to twenty-two times lower than harmful acute exposures (Environment Canada 2001).

It doesn't take a lot of salt to cause major changes in ecosystem composition. In Canadian freshwater ecosystems, species richness decreases as salinity increases with most of the decrease occurring at salinities ranging from 1,000 to 3,000 mg/L (Environment Canada 2001). A salinity of 3,000 mg/L is less than one-tenth the salinity of seawater.

As with the petroleum guidelines, the use of existing "acceptable" levels of salinity and conductivity may not be protective of natural ecosystems. Levels of salinity, sodicity, pH, and conductivity considered "acceptable" are largely based upon responses of species commonly used in reclamation (e.g., Howat 2000). The focus on reclamation species means that there is little information available for the majority of native species. Levels of salinity that permit reclamation species to survive are irrelevant to most native species. It would be more protective to determine if there are chemical, physical, or biological differences between spill sites and control sites. If there are significant differences, then there has been an effect, by definition. Whether that effect is acceptable is a societal decision. Currently, there is insufficient information on the ecological effects of saline spills in aquatic environments (Gleason and Tangen

2014). Environment Canada (2001) provided a review of effects on birds and mammals after exposure to excess salts. Strangely, in its recent synthesis of human-caused bird mortality, Environment Canada (Calvert et al. 2013) did not assess the effects of salt exposures to birds.

Remediating damaged soil in place, such as by adding calcium to replace sodium, establishing plants that remove contaminants, and adding mycorrhizal fungi has been touted as a possible alternative to excavation and soil replacement (Vavrek et al. 2004). Reestablishment of native communities and their ecological functions may be the best measure of remediation success. Knowledge gaps include the lack of risk assessment for the complex mixtures of chemicals in saline spills, the lack of best management practices for soil amendments, and the unknown tolerance limits for most native species. A large-scale, multisite, long-term experiment is needed to evaluate restoration status across a range of environments.

COMPLEX SPILLS AND COMPLEX HISTORIES

Anticipating and managing the impacts of spills can be challenging because spills are often complex mixtures. Without accurate data on a site's history it's impossible to understand why the soil and the biota are impaired. Observations at fossil fuel industry sites in Alberta demonstrate that establishing cause–effect relationships can be impossible due to inadequate records and complex disturbance histories. I illustrate with two examples from near my home.

Recently I inspected a well site in northern Strathcona County, Alberta, and found damaged soil and impaired vegetation indicative of a saline spill but found no record of a spill (figure 4.2a). Nearby, I inspected a crude oil group battery and found saline, barren, and damaged soil and vegetation, but the only record of a spill was that of water-based drilling mud, which the regulator certified as being cleaned up (figure 4.2b). What chemicals and what events were responsible for the damage? We don't know. What are we to conclude? Firstly, that the number of salinized sites exceeds the regulator's number of saline spill sites. Secondly, that incomplete records and complex disturbance histories make it difficult for environmental managers and municipal planners to protect both ecosystems and the public from unforeseen contaminant exposures.

Figure 4.2 Damaged soil and impaired vegetation, but what were the causes? (a) The soil surrounding this well is barren (conductivity 1,020–1,350 μS/cm). Outside the barren zone, the plant community is a mixture of halophytes, exotics, and pollution-tolerant species such as Nuttall's salt-meadow grass, foxtail barley, quack grass, common dandelion, slough grass, wild oats, and common plantain (conductivity 600–980 μS/cm; conductivity in the nearby grain field is 270 μS/cm). There is no record of a spill at this well. (b) At this crude oil group battery, saline barren soil surrounds the storage tank and the wells (conductivity 15,590 μS/cm). The only living plant in this zone is Nuttall's salt-meadow grass. Beyond the barren zone, the plant community is an impaired saline community of Nuttall's salt-meadow grass, foxtail barley, common dandelion, summer-cypress, and smooth perennial sow-thistle (conductivity 2,100 μS/cm). There is no record of a saline spill here. Both images 5 August 2018.

What does the science tell us about complex contaminant exposures? Although a saline spill might contain no more than 3 per cent hydrocarbons, this amount of oil can hinder ecosystem response. Oil contamination can render soils hydrophobic and thereby reduce water availability to plants and reduce salt leaching. Hydrocarbons and metals in soils can persist longer than salts if the salts can migrate out of the soil profile. Heavy metals present in complex spills include barium, cadmium, chromium, copper, lead, mercury, nickel, strontium, and zinc. Accumulation of these metals in plants and animals can result in significant ecological effects and movement through the food chain. Little is known of the toxicity of most oilfield chemicals. The impacts of a combined oil and brine spill may be so significant that natural recovery is impossible.

48   Chemicals in complex mixtures can act jointly to influence overall toxicity (European Commission 2011), but risk assessments on the combined effects of chemicals are not commonly conducted nor are they required. There are major knowledge gaps relating to where, how often, and to what extent humans and the environment are exposed to complex chemical mixtures. An understanding of the responses of all species in an ecosystem to chemical mixtures will be difficult if not impossible to attain. And that assumes that we know what was spilled. How are we to manage a contaminated site, or warn the public, if we don't know what happened? Complex chemical mixtures at spill sites tend to pose a greater risk than do simple spills because the plants, animals, and microorganisms must metabolize and detoxify a range of substances, some of which interact to increase toxicity. It's analogous to the synergistic effects of alcohol and sleeping pills. Given the frequency of multisubstance spills, complex contaminant burdens present significant environmental stressors.

The next sections narrow the focus to site-specific studies on the effects of spills into water and onto land that are relevant to spills in northwestern Canada. If you don't need the details, you may want to skip to the chapter summary.

SPILLS INTO WATER

Aquatic environments are sensitive to spills. Despite statements that spills rarely enter fresh water, spills into water are relatively common but are rarely documented with scientific rigour. Instead, the regulator issues its standard press release that assures us that "no impacts to wildlife were reported" as it did following a 15 August 2019 spill of 40 m³ of crude oil/saline water emulsion from a Bonterra Energy pipeline into Washout Creek, a tributary of the North Saskatchewan River (CBC 2019). Failure to find impacts should never be construed as absence of impacts. The studies below document a range of impacts from inland spills in western Canada and the United States. They also demonstrate a failure by industry and the Alberta Energy Regulator to document the effects of spills, a topic to which we'll return in later chapters.

On 1 June 1975, Federated Pipe Lines Ltd reported a pipeline spill of 445 m³ of crude oil onto a hillside and then into the Moosehorn River about 57 km south of Great Slave Lake (Bishop 1976) (details in web 4.3). The spill harmed the macroinvertebrates in the Moosehorn and Swan Rivers and effects were noted as far as 16 km downstream four to ten days after the spill. Erosion caused by improper road and site clearing practices associated with oil exploration and development also damaged the invertebrates during flash flooding with sediment-laden water. Paradoxically, the flash flooding may have facilitated flushing of the oil from the river bottom.

On 22 June 1992, about 1,208 m³ of naphtha/diesel product spilled from a Suncor pipeline, flowed overland off the pipeline right-of-way and into the House River (HBT Agra Ltd 1992). As with the previous spill, the regulator's records are dubious (web 4.4). The spill killed fishes and caused declines in species richness and abundance of fishes and invertebrates. Larval mayflies, caddisflies, and true flies (Diptera) were absent at two of the three study sites; stoneflies, dragonflies, and damselflies were the only groups found at all three sites; snails were found only at the control site. Because the study was completed soon after the spill, it did not examine long-term effects but recommended that a monitoring program be established. I found no record of follow-up monitoring.

Rupture of a Canadian Natural Resources Ltd pipeline released an unknown volume of light crude oil into the southwest fork of the Waskahigan River near Valleyview, Alberta, in May 2005 (AAR 2006). High concentrations of hydrocarbons were found in riverbank sediments in fall 2005 within 200 m of the pipeline break. Hydrocarbons (including PAHs) were transported downstream and caused endocrine-disruption in sculpins, longnose suckers, and lake chub indicative of reduced reproductive capacity. Use of a containment boom may have caused hydrocarbons to accumulate in the shoreline sediments. Again we see evidence of poor record keeping by the regulator – there is no record of this spill despite the existence of the postspill report (AAR 2006). I found

49

no explanation why this large, recent, and documented spill is absent from AER records.

Around 5 a.m. on 3 August 2005, forty-three Canadian National Railway cars derailed near the summer village of Whitewood Sands on the north shore of Wabamun Lake 65 km west of Edmonton, Alberta. Eleven cars containing viscous Bunker C fuel oil and one car containing pole treating oil ruptured and spilled. Oil dispersed over much of the eastern half of the lake and by 10 August had fouled emergent vegetation along portions of about 20 km of shoreline (Pimblett and Mitton 2015).

At the vast majority of spills, public observation and access can be prevented. The Wabamun spill was different, however, because it occurred near a major city at a popular lake with public and media access and railway spills are not under the jurisdiction of a provincial energy regulator. For perhaps both of those reasons, scientifically credible documentation of the impacts took place.

Damage to the lake was exacerbated by the disorganized and ineffective response and by aggressive attempts to recover oil from vegetation and sediments. Use of sorbent booms was ineffective and there was an inadequate supply of containment booms. One scientist recalled, "Wabamun was complete chaos. CNR had the wrong type of boom on hand, and by the time they got the right ones, the whole lake was covered" (name withheld, pers. comm., March 2019). Within days of the spill, a storm from the north detached the poorly secured containment booms from the vicinity of the spill. The booms and their load of oil were then blown across Wabamun Lake (plate 4.2a) after which oil spread along the south and east shores (plate 4.2b; H. Wollis, pers. comm., July 2019). Boats were used in attempts to corral the escaped oil with containment booms (Pimblett and Mitton 2015).

Failure to secure the containment booms allowed oil to disperse across the lake and directly into flocks of birds, which resulted in extensive mortality (H. Wollis, pers. comm., July 2019). Four days after the spill, oil was still flowing into Wabamun Lake at the derailment site with no containment booms in place (plate 4.2c), yet the railway had been cleared and trains were running. The Wabamun response placed a higher priority on economic production than on ecological protection.

Neither CN nor any branches of government or regulators were prepared for the spill with the appropriate spill response protocols or equipment. The result was a panicked, *ad hoc* response in which pressure to recover the oil from the lake led agencies such as Alberta Environment to allow otherwise illegal activities such as flushing and vacuuming of lake bottom. A wildlife biologist who responded to the spill recalled that one of the pollution specialists at Alberta Environment told him that "had a milk truck spilled its load on the highway there would have been a better response." Wollis observed that

> CN did not declare what had been spilled. The tanker of pole treating compound was nasty stuff and some of our people working near it reported strange symptoms so we pulled them off. There was no protective clothing available nor procedures to follow. Similarly, residents were given no cautionary direction ... The clean up efforts were haphazard and the consultant displayed little evidence that it knew what it should do to remove the oil while protecting reed bed vegetation and sediments ... I was appalled by the lack of expertise of the cleaning consultant and the lack of common sense of its field managers. (H. Wollis, pers. comm., August 2019)

As in the case of the Pine River oil spill (next example), the cure may have proved worse than the disease.

Oil recovery involved extensive removal of vegetation and harmful flushing and vacuuming of sediments (Thormann and Bayley 2008; Boufadel et al. 2015). The spill and its cleanup damaged bulrush marshes, killed fishes, benthic invertebrate communities, birds, and other wildlife, reduced or degraded fish habitat, western grebe nesting habitat, and migratory bird habitat, left persistent residual oil and tar balls in shoreline and marsh areas, and contaminated fish spawning areas at concentrations sufficient to impair embryo survival (Birtwell 2008; Thormann and Bayley 2008; Boufadel et al. 2015) (web 4.5). Dead fish continued to be observed into October 2005. More than 300 dead western grebes, mostly adults, were found after struggling to shore, which represented a fraction of the total grebes killed. Large numbers of young birds are believed to have died in the open lake and sank out of sight.

More than a year and a half after the spill and a major cleanup effort, oil persisted in the lake as large (>5 cm), high-viscosity and high-density mats and patties, often tangled into vegetation, and as small (<5 cm) spherical balls of soft, fluid oil surrounded by a tough layer of weathered oil (Hollebone et al. 2011). Significant amounts of PAHs were found in the oil. Oil persisted in the grebes' nesting habitat at least through 2009 (Wollis and Stratmoen 2010).

As of 2019, fourteen years after the spill, consumption of any fish species from the lake is prohibited (2019/2020 fishing regulations). The prohibition stems from concerns about the health of Wabamun Lake's fish populations resulting from the oil spill and from mercury contamination caused by the former Wabamun coal-fired power plant.

The Pine River oil spill is one of Canada's better-studied oil spills. On 1 August 2000, a pipeline break released 952 m³ of light sour crude oil into the Pine River in British Columbia, a tributary of the Peace River (Lee et al. 2015). Spill effects extended downstream 80 km and resulted in the death of about 15,000 to 27,900 fishes from six species (web 4.6). The number of dead fish found during survey totalled only about 6 to 11 per cent of the estimated total mortality, a powerful demonstration of the fact that animals found dead represent a fraction of actual mortality.

Petroleum hydrocarbons accumulated in depositional reaches and PAHS and cadmium reached concentrations sufficiently high to present health risks to fish and other aquatic life. Algal biomass increased above normal levels at one location, an effect also observed at the Pace-Spyglass spill (chapter 11). Bottom-dwelling invertebrates declined for several months, which meant that food supplies for fishes decreased during the critical period prior to overwintering. The spill response caused extensive and permanent damage, more damage than would have resulted if nothing had been done to remediate the spill – a classic illustration of the cure being worse than the disease (web 4.6). I summarize spills into inland waters in the United States in web 4.7.

SPILLS ONTO LAND

In inland environments, spills onto land are more common than are spills into water. Here we survey results from several relevant studies, all of which observed persistent physical and biological effects. As we'll learn, residual contamination after cleanup is the rule, not the exception. The problem, of course, is that follow-up studies are rarely conducted. When they are conducted, they are typically done by consultants hired by the fossil fuel companies.

One of the first scientifically credible studies to document long-term contamination with petroleum hydrocarbons was conducted near Lesser Slave Lake, Alberta (Wang et al. 1998). The study found hydrocarbon contamination in the soil twenty-five years after cleanup at three spills (Nipisi, Rainbow, and

Old Peace River) that took place in 1970–72. Although the Nipisi spill was one of the largest inland spills in Canadian history in which an estimated 9,551 m³ of oil were released onto 10 ha (also see Jaremko 2013), none of these major spills are present in the regulator's database. Soil sampled from the upper four cm was highly contaminated with petroleum hydrocarbons (20,000–256,000 mg/kg). Soil sampled at 10 to 40 cm depth was also highly contaminated (total petroleum hydrocarbons 10,000–165,000 mg/kg).

An experimental crude oil spill caused changes in the thawed active layer in soil underlying a black spruce forest in the Northwest Territories (Seburn and Kershaw 1997). After three years, active layers in the oiled forest, right-of-way (ROW), and trench were significantly deeper than their controls. After eight years, the depth of the active layer had doubled in the oiled ROW and had more than tripled in the oiled trench (Seburn et al. 1996). The persistent increase in the permafrost thaw depth was related to the high oil concentration, especially in areas where oil had pooled on the ground, which has major implications for spills on soils underlain by permafrost.

Three oil spills near Edmonton caused persistent damage to soils and vegetation (Roy and McGill 1998), the most significant of which were barren, water repellent soils with degraded structure and residual tar balls; the soils were unable to grow plants for decades (web 4.8). Severe water repellency and breakdown of soil structure took decades to develop and the areal extent of the barren soils increased over time. The oil spills caused persistent and severe damage to formerly healthy and productive terrestrial ecosystems, a conclusion supported by my observations at the Atlantic No. 3 blowout in summer 2018, seventy years after the event (see chapter 3, plate 3.1). Studies of other oil spills have confirmed that soil damage and water repellency can persist for decades (Gordon et al. 2018). In contrast to the foregoing scientifically credible monitoring of spill effects, typical postspill monitoring in Alberta, if it is conducted at all, would not pass scientific peer review (web 4.8.3).

Six studies from Canada's north documented significant spill effects on vegetation. The first is the longest-term study of a crude oil spill in Canada. Pete Kershaw and his colleagues have documented the multidecadal effects of spills of Norman Wells crude oil on alpine vegetation along the Canol Road, Northwest Territories (Kershaw et al. 2013) (web 4.9). Vegetation and soils remain strongly affected seventy years after the spills (figures 4.3 and 4.4). The researchers estimated that 160 to 300 years might be required for full vegetation recovery. I analyze original data from the Canol study in chapter 10.

Figure 4.3 Oil spill–affected vegetation and soil in erect deciduous shrub tundra thirty-five, fifty-five, and seventy years after crude oil spills. After seventy years, the soil here remains essentially bare due to residual oil effects.

Figure 4.4 *Opposite* Multidecadal effects of a crude oil spill are evident in (a) increased bare ground and (b) reduced total plant cover and (c, d) reduced species richness in decumbent shrub tundra and erect deciduous shrub tundra in spill plots relative to control plots at thirty-five, fifty-five, and seventy years after the spills.

When sweet crude oil was applied experimentally to subarctic spruce and low arctic tundra near Inuvik, Tununuk Point, and Tuktoyaktuk, Northwest Territories, all plant species declined in cover and all actively growing plant tissue was destroyed (Wein and Bliss 1973). Moss and lichen species were the most sensitive and all but one species (juniper hair-cap moss) suffered complete mortality. Effects increased in proportion to oil application rates and varied by species, vegetation type, and season of application (winter spills caused more damage than anticipated). After two years, effects were still becoming evident as black spruce root systems were damaged by the oil, spruce needles were browning, and some trees had dropped most of their needles.

Experimental spills of unweathered crude oil caused the death of any green plant tissue in direct contact with oil in two subarctic forests near Norman Wells, Northwest Territories (Hutchinson and Freedman 1978). All lichens and mosses quickly died while responses of vascular plants varied. Some species

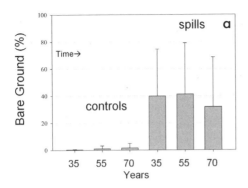

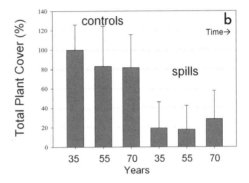

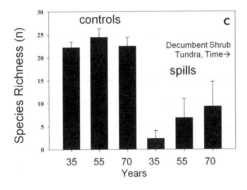

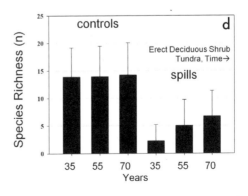

succumbed during the first year while deaths of black spruce took up to four years. Total vascular plant cover decreased. Although regrowth of some species was rapid, in other species, no regeneration was noted after five years. Where oil percolated into the soil, it later migrated laterally, especially in response to heavy rainfall. The effects of subsurface oil contamination were delayed; little effect was observed after two years, but vegetation damage spread in extent after five years. Crude oil in the forest soil remained toxic throughout the study.

It can be difficult to determine cause and effect in complex disturbances as shown in a study (Seburn et al. 1996) of the response of subarctic plant species to a crude oil spill over a three-year period near Tulita (Fort Norman), Northwest Territories. Norman Wells crude oil was experimentally applied via an open-ended pipe buried one metre below the surface within a simulated pipeline trench. Because of saturated soil conditions, most of the oil flowed to the surface and spread over the pipeline ROW. Interpretation of the spill responses was confounded by the prespill excavation of the trench, the clearing of the ROW two to three years prior to the spill, the prespill planting of agronomic exotic grasses, and the postspill redistribution of the oil. All species were still responding to the combined machinery-related soil and vegetation disturbance and the oil spill over the three-year period. In the heavily oiled ROW, with the exception of cotton grass (*Eriophorum*), the cover of all native plant species had declined. In contrast, the cover of agronomic grasses planted two to three years before the spill increased over time. Native lichens, grasses, forbs, and shrubs were the most negatively affected by the disturbances while exotic grasses and some sedges and mosses appeared to tolerate the disturbances. For oil spill studies from Alaska, see web 4.10.

Hydrocarbon-contaminated soils in southern Saskatchewan exhibit a disturbance signature of reduced vegetation and litter cover and plant species diversity, reduced soil nitrogen and phosphorus, and elevated pH, hydrocarbon concentrations, and soil carbon to nitrogen ratios (Robson et al. 2004). High cover of foxtail barley, crested wheat grass, salt grass, and forbs such as summer-cypress typified contaminated soils. Summer-cypress comprised 13 per cent of the total vegetation cover, more than the total cover of all forb species combined on uncontaminated soils. Shrub cover on uncontaminated soils was about twenty-seven times higher than on contaminated soils.

Industry reported impacts or injury to surface water, crops or livestock, soil, fish, or wildlife in 34 per cent of 16,906 oil and saline releases in Oklahoma that occurred from 1993 to 2003 (Fisher and Sublette 2005). The median volumes of spills that caused environmental injury were 1.6 m³ for crude oil and 9.5 m³ for saline water. We will apply these results in chapter 13 when we observe that the damage rate for Oklahoma spills is on the order of forty times greater than the damage rates reported in Alberta. We will also observe that industry-reported rates of damage are far lower than those reported in scientific studies (for a related study, see web 4.11).

Spills into water often accumulate on shores such as when crude oil released into the Gulf of Mexico during the BP Deepwater Horizon blowout accumulated in coastal marshes. For vascular plants, resilience to spills is assisted by endophytic fungi and bacteria that grow within their plant hosts. Researchers examined whether oil contamination affected the important symbiotic relationships between fungi, bacteria, and smooth cord grass (*Spartina alterniflora*), the dominant marsh grass in the region (Kandalepas et al. 2015). Cord grass plants from oiled areas lost all or most of their leaf fungal endophytes, and root endophytes shifted to species that metabolize hydrocarbons. Loss of the critical endophyte-vascular plant relationships was an enduring outcome of the spill, which may undermine the ecological health of the marshes. Similar studies have not been conducted in Canada.

SUMMARY

All spills of crude oil and saline water are harmful. The spills may harm soils or water, flowering plants, mosses, lichens, bacteria, or fungi, invertebrates or vertebrates, ecological services, or all of the above. The harm varies in relation to the substances spilled, their volume and areal extent, the receiving ecosystem, the season and climate, the cleanup, and the persistence of the effects.

After a spill, the biota must respond to the altered conditions or perish. From temperate regions northward across boreal, subarctic, and arctic regions, and from lowlands to alpine environments, the effects of crude oil and saline spills are recognizable as a disturbance signature of shifted species assemblages, increased mortality, physiological stress, and impaired reproduction; declines in biodiversity, productivity, and symbiotic relationships; loss of native species and native vegetation communities; decreased plant stature and density; and increased bare ground and abundance of weedy exotics, halophytes, grasses, and composites (see web 10.12.1 and chapter 10). Spills typically result in an increased proportion of pollution-tolerant and disturbance-tolerant species and a corresponding reduction in woody plants, mosses, lichens, and native species in general.

The short-term nature of most studies on the effects of spills is a major deficiency. This isn't a fault of those conducting the studies. Indeed, most studies point to a need for further monitoring. But as we'll observe in later chapters, the effects of spills and other industry disturbances can persist for decades. A second deficiency of spill effect studies is that most focus on one to a few indicators such as invertebrates, vegetation, or fishes. Yet we all know that ecosystems are intricately linked in a web of relationships, many of which are critical to ecological resilience during times of stress. An effect on one ecosystem component affects all components. The problem is that we're often unaware of those effects. Much of the change is invisible without the requisite knowledge and diagnostic tools.

Failure to document the effects of spills and failure to keep accurate records result in absence of data, not absence of effects. It will prove important to remember that spills are harmful is the rule not the exception when we examine the views of the regulator and industry as they pertain to spill impacts.

CHAPTER 5

The Effects of Other Fossil Fuel Industry Activites

I am not resigned to the shutting away of loving hearts in the hard ground.
Edna St Vincent Millay, "Dirge without Music"

INTRODUCTION

Hydrocarbon exploitation by its very nature disrupts ecosystems. All phases of the exploitation disrupt nature, from the initial exploration in which seismic lines slice up landscapes to the ensuing roads, pipelines, wells, and facilities that further fragment ecosystems and damage soil, air, water, vegetation, and wildlife. From the initial extraction and processing of the hydrocarbons to their refining and transport to markets and their eventual emissions and disposal of waste products, impacts to the environment are inescapable. The damage can be lessened by the use of best practices and effective regulations and enforcement, but it can't be eliminated. Some damage wrought by hydrocarbon exploitation is patent, such as habitat loss. Other damage is more subtle, such as loss of sensitive species. Much of the damage is hidden in the form of shifts in species abundance, loss of ecological relationships, and invisible contamination.

Hydrocarbon exploitation and use is the primary driver of human-caused climate change. It degrades ecosystem services, such as provision of clean water, fisheries, and support of biodiversity, and imposes increased social, human health, and economic burdens and uncertainties. For humans, hydrocarbon exploitation and use result in increased exposure to contaminated air, land, and water. Health effects include increased psychosocial and respiratory stress and heart disease, preterm births, reduced birth weights and neural tube defects, cardiovascular diseases, reduced cognitive function, and premature death (Di et al. 2017; Cushing et al. 2020). These adverse effects are disproportionately felt by poor people, women, the elderly, and people of colour. Better datasets and improved analytical techniques suggest that, contrary to long-held beliefs, there is no safe level for air pollutants such as fine particulate matter (Di et al. 2017).

Relative to undisturbed ecosystems, landscapes disturbed by the fossil fuel industry are more fragmented, have higher rates of rare species endangerment, lower diversity of native plant species and plant communities, are often dominated by exotic and weedy species; have a greater prevalence of contaminated and/or degraded soils and decreased water quality and quantity; have impaired nutrient cycling and productivity; and provide lower quality habitat for native animals (Flather et al. 1998; Cody et al. 2000; Brooks et al. 2004; CFIA 2008; Elsinger 2009; Naugle 2011; Rooney and Bayley 2011a, b; Kershaw et al. 2013; Gleason and Tangen 2014; Timoney 2015). As well, bitumen mining causes permanent loss of peatlands and their stored organic carbon (Rooney et al. 2012).

THE USUAL SUSPECTS

Because of their large areal footprint, the ecological effects of the hydrocarbon industry's normal operations exceed the effects of spills. It's therefore important that we consider them to place spills within the broader context of cumulative effects (chapter 14). Spills don't occur in a vacuum: industry sites are exposed to a variety of disturbances. When we attempt to understand how an ecosystem came to be impaired we may find ourselves peering through a lens clouded by cumulative effects. As a starting point, first we need to establish the predisturbance condition. Then we need to document any disturbances and their effects. We can detect a disturbance signature at all industrial sites but, due to multiple disturbances, we may be at a loss to identify what particular disturbance caused a particular effect (see web 5.1 for a case study). Here I summarize the effects of the development and operation of pipelines, wells, seismic lines, and hydraulic fracturing.

IMPACTS OF PIPELINES, WELL SITES, AND OTHER LAND USES

The impacts of pipelines, well sites, and improper waste disposal and storage have been well documented in the United States and Canada (for a review, see web 5.2). Persistent impairment of soil, groundwater, vegetation, and wildlife result from hydrocarbon exploitation (figure 5.1, plate 5.1). At the landscape scale, habitat loss and fragmentation and damage to surface and groundwater flows are typical. The soils at these industrial sites, even after "certified" reclamation (according to regulators), exhibit increased salinity, pH, conductivity, hydrocarbons (including PAHS, BTEX, fuel), metals, increased bare ground and soil compaction, impaired flows of water and air through the soil, and reduced soil fertility, organic matter, nutrients, and symbiotic bacteria and fungi. These changes result in decreased growth, stature, and biomass, increased dominance by exotic and weedy species, and declines in native species and plant community diversity and increased mortality and risks to wildlife. Poor record keeping and monitoring mean that the ecological damage is more extensive than available records indicate.

61

IMPACTS OF SEISMIC LINES

Seismic lines cause numerous impacts that are influenced by climate, soils, permafrost, predisturbance vegetation, distance to nearest roads, and other factors (table 5.1). Many of the changes are driven by changes in soil temperature, moisture, and light conditions. Conventional seismic lines (6–10 m wide) cause shifted species assemblages, deforestation, and dissect and fragment the landscape (Dabros et al. 2018). Fragmentation, in turn, harms biodiversity and ecosystem processes and is a major factor in the decline of woodland caribou. Some of the most seriously degraded landscapes are found in the Dene Tha territory of northwestern Alberta where the cumulative effects of seismic lines, pipelines, wells, facilities, spills, logging, and increasing wildfires have transformed the landscape beyond recognition and contributed to the decline of woodland caribou. Documenting the effects of seismic lines can be difficult due to poor record keeping (see chapter 16, "A Seismic Event").

The effects of conventional seismic lines are consistent over broad regions from the arctic south to temperate regions (for a review, see web 5.3). Differences in plant community composition between seismic lines and controls persist for decades and in many areas have resulted in permanent changes to vegetation including deforestation and dominance by assemblages of disturbance-adapted exotic and weedy species. Damage is most severe in wetlands such as fens and is worsened wherever seismic lines are subjected to all-terrain vehicle use.

Although modern, high-density seismic lines have been touted by industry as "low impact," recent studies demonstrate significant impacts. In some areas these linear disturbances can reach densities of 90 km/km^2 in which interior habitat, that is, unaffected habitat, is obliterated. "Low impact" seismic lines affect the physical environment and plant assemblages and reduce species richness well beyond the seismic lines proper (web 5.3.1).

HYDRAULIC FRACTURING (FRACKING)

In recent years, fracking has been added to the panoply of ways in which the fossil fuel industry affects Earth's ecosystems. Fracking involves the pressurized injection of acids, biocides, corrosion and scale inhibitors, surfactants, and other chemicals along with sand. Its purpose is to fracture the bedrock so that trapped hydrocarbons can be pumped to the surface. Fracking chemicals, which include carcinogens, mutagens, reproductive and developmental toxins, and endocrine disruptors enter the environment through spills and leaks, volatilization, and disposal of wastewater (Cushing et al. 2020). Fracking has resulted in the contamination of drinking water wells with volatile organic compounds such as gasoline- and diesel-range organics as well as the carcinogenic bis(2-ethylhexyl) phthalate commonly used in fracking (Drollette et al. 2015).

Figure 5.1 *Opposite and following page* Abandoned industry sites near Chipewyan Lake. (a) Location map; (b) Reclamation certified well site nineteen years after abandonment dominated by exotic smooth brome and alsike clover; (c) Nova gas pipeline ROW dominated by exotic red fescue, alsike clover, alfalfa, timothy, and smooth brome; (d) Sites examined near Harbor-Liege airstrip as seen in a 2014 Landsat 8 image: (1) gas well abandoned in 1983; (2) semibarren clay deposit (probably drilling mud) with a depauperate flora; (3) water injection well abandoned in 1991; (4) an abandoned compressor station; a tank leak here or at the water injection well was responsible for an unrecovered spill of 64 m^3 of saline produced water; (5) abandoned Harbor-Liege airstrip; (e) Close-up of semibarren clay twenty-six years after abandonment, September 2009.

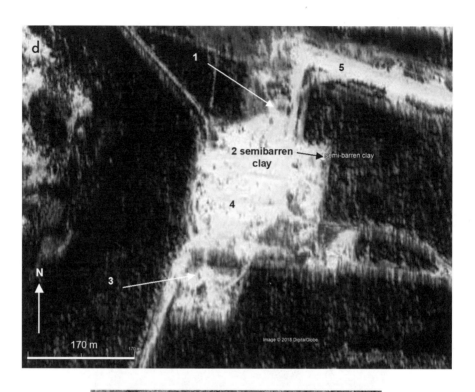

Table 5.1 Effects of seismic lines

Physical and soil effects
ponding, rutting, erosion, and compaction
degradation of permafrost and development of taliks (permanently unfrozen ground between the active layer and underlying permafrost)
changes in evapotranspiration, albedo, and thermal regime
soil subsidence
loss of stored soil carbon
disrupted lateral flow of water

Vegetation effects
increased exotic species
persistent changes in vegetation species composition
increased grasses, sedges, forbs, deciduous shrubs, and edge species
decreased evergreen shrubs, bryophytes, lichens, and forest interior species
declines in forest cover and primary productivity

Wildlife effects
changes in bird and mammal abundance
increased wolf predation on woodland caribou
increased motorized recreation, hunting, trapping, poaching, and human–wildlife conflicts

Socioeconomic effects
damage to First Nations territories
increased risk of human-caused wildfires
loss of productive forests
increased financial liability to society due to unfunded reclamation

Note: See also web 5.3.

Fluids produced by fracking include natural gas, crude oil, condensates, saline water, and whatever fracking compounds are returned to the surface. The problem, of course, is what to do with the waste fluids. Well injection of the wastes, which even in normal situations can cause underground contamination, is especially problematic in fracking operations. Safe disposal of wastewater assumes geological integrity – the ability of the geological formations to contain the wastewater without leaking. After fracking, the ability of the bedrock to provide containment has been compromised, which allows toxic wastewater injected underground to migrate.

A team of scientists reviewed wastewater handling, treatment, and disposal of hydraulic fracturing operations and reached some unsettling conclusions (Goss et al. 2015). How fracking compounds undergo chemical changes and how they move through the environment remain unknown. Despite concerted efforts, the reviewers could not determine the sources of the water used, the proportion of wastewater that is reused, recycled, treated at municipal sewage treatment or industrial treatment plants, surface discharged, or injected below-ground nor could they determine the chemical composition of the wastewater. Lack of critical information prevented the evaluation of wastewater management. The adequacy of wastewater disposal regulations for protecting the environment over the long term remains unknown for the United States, British Columbia, and Alberta.

The available databases don't serve the needs of people external to the regulator and industry. In other words, regulators and industry are not gathering the relevant environmental data critical to society. The reviewers identified significant knowledge gaps in regulatory outcomes, compliance, and best management practices. They observed that First Nations have not imposed regulations for wastewater handling, treatment, and disposal on their lands. First Nations may not presently have the capacity to dispose of fracking fluids safely. Social acceptance of hydraulic fracturing varies widely and current risk management may be unable to deal with hydraulic fracturing. Regulatory and industrial practices, which may have gone unchallenged in the past, may no longer be acceptable to the public. The reviewers were unable to identify what approaches might be successful for gaining and retaining a social licence.

Areas where fracking wastewater has been injected underground already cover a broad region in Alberta and British Columbia (figure 5.2). As a result, a large-scale uncontrolled ecosystem experiment is being conducted. Because the rate of exploitation is outstripping the rate of growth in scientific knowledge, the effects of fracking are likely to pose unpleasant surprises. Our culture has a penchant for imposing environmental uncertainties on future generations. The recent spate of earthquakes caused by fracking may be just the initial shock waves.

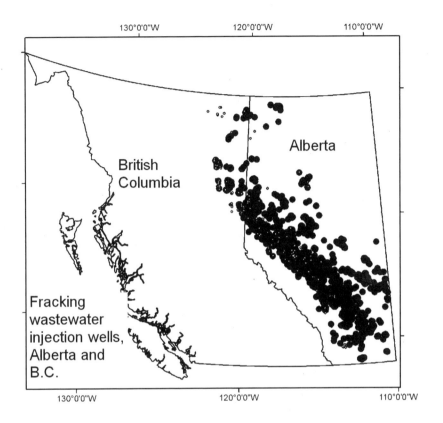

Figure 5.2 Locations where fracking wastewater has been injected underground in Alberta and British Columbia.

SUMMARY

Similar ecological effects are observed at spills, pipelines, well pads, seismic lines, and other industry-affected sites. Impaired soils and vegetation arise from a host of activities including construction and maintenance, use of heavy machinery, filling and excavation, waste disposal, topsoil stripping and storage, chemical applications, and introduction of exotic or inappropriate species. The soils and vegetation of remediated sites remain impaired relative to those of undisturbed sites. Increased soil salinity, hydrocarbons, and metals; decreased plant cover, biomass, and organic matter; decreased diversity of native species and communities, and increased bare ground, exotic species, and exotic-dominated communities are typical forms of impairment. At sites with complex disturbance histories, there may be several causes of impairment. Seismic lines reduce biodiversity, cause shifted species assemblages, increased occurrence of exotic species, and deforestation, and dissect and fragment the landscape.

The social and environmental risks posed by fracking remain poorly understood. The higher cost of recycling or reusing fracking wastewater means that the most common method of disposal is via injection wells, typically in the same region as the fracked well. We don't know the cumulative effects of fracking because the relevant data are not being gathered but it's reasonable to infer that widespread groundwater contamination may be occurring.

It's difficult if not impossible to restore ecosystems to healthy conditions once they have been damaged by industrial activities. Persistent ecosystem damage presents a major concern for future generations. With a scientific foundation now in place, in the next three chapters we examine the regulator's evidence.

PART THREE

REGULATORY EVIDENCE

CHAPTER 6

Inaccurate Locations, Suspect Spill Data, and the Falcon Effect

Turning and turning in the widening gyre
The falcon cannot hear the falconer;
Things fall apart; the centre cannot hold;
Mere anarchy is loosed upon the world,
The blood-dimmed tide is loosed, and everywhere
The ceremony of innocence is drowned;
The best lack all conviction, while the worst
Are full of passionate intensity.

William Butler Yeats, "The Second Coming"

INTRODUCTION

Regulatory capture occurs when a regulator ceases to serve the public interest and instead serves the interests of the industry it regulates. Social scientists and legal scholars have documented the political, economic, and social effects of regulatory capture (MacLean 2016). In the next several chapters, we examine the scientific effects of regulatory capture.

When striving to understand how and why an ecosystem has changed we first need answers to three questions: What happened? When did it happen? Where did it happen? It would be reasonable to expect that a regulator's incident data would allow us to answer those questions. But from the outset of the study, deficiencies were evident. The regulator's data reported inaccurate spill locations, inconsistent or vague spill descriptions, and suspect and/or subjective data. Missing information and missing spills added to the uncertainty. Data deficiencies and uncertainties can make it impossible to evaluate the effects of spills. That uncertainty presents a danger to society.

In this chapter we begin our journey down the rabbit hole of regulatory data by examining two major deficiencies – inaccurate locations and unreliable spill data – that undermine our ability to understand and monitor the effects of spills. This chapter is long and some of the material is technical. I have placed much of the documentation in web materials.

INACCURATE LOCATIONS

Suppose you need to know if there is a spill near your home. You consult the regulator's data and go to a spill location near your home. Surprise, it's not there. What do you do? You can't ask the regulator because the regulator will only repeat the same erroneous location. If you are lucky, you may be able to determine the location by studying imagery on Google Earth. Or, maybe you can find someone who can guide you to the spill. Or you find that a spill occurred at a facility, such as a well, that retains its identification sign. The spill location and the sign location match (e.g., 5-31-56-20W4) – great, but then you read "No Trespassing – Authorized Personnel Only." It shouldn't be that difficult to find or visit a spill, but it is.

One of the first lessons I learned during the fieldwork is that the AER provides inaccurate locations for spills. How inaccurate? It varies, but the inaccuracies are sufficient to make it difficult if not impossible to find spills. Descriptions of inaccurate spill locations can be boring, the same way a forensic accountant describing bookkeeping irregularities can be boring until the jury realizes it's heard evidence that will put a fraudster in prison. So please bear with me while I describe some inaccurate spill locations and why that's important. Five examples illustrate the problem (see also web 5.1).

(1) Every spill studied during the fieldwork would have been difficult to locate without being guided to the site by local knowledge holders. For example, the regulator's location for the Barnwell saline spill is displaced to the west by about 500 m from the actual spill (figure 6.1). It's not clear how such large errors can be committed, go uncorrected, and be provided to the public.

(2) When initially reported by the regulator, the location for the Apache 15-09 spill was wrong by 40 km (see web 6.1 for details).

(3) The Total Joslyn blowout location is off by 505 m of the actual incident location (see chapter 13).

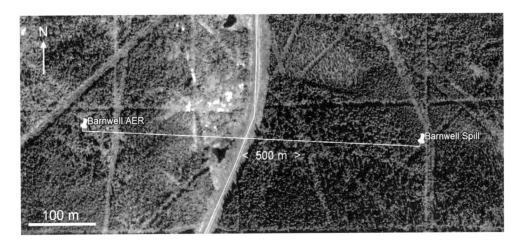

Figure 6.1 Example of an inaccurate spill location. The Barnwell pipeline spill location provided by the regulator ("Barnwell AER") is misplaced 500 m to the west of the actual location ("Barnwell Spill"). 24 August 2003, twelve years prior to the spill.

(4) A satellite image of a 2002 crude oil spill in southern Alberta revealed that the AER location was misplaced by 147 m. The AER's information about this spill was inaccurate or missing (figure 6.2).

(5) The AER location for a 2015 Nexen spill is misplaced 2.7 km from the actual spill location. It gets worse. In the Environmental Protection Order to Nexen (AER 2015a), the regulator provided the location as "800 metres south of 7-31-085-5W5W ('the Spill Site')." Firstly, the meridian "W5W" is not valid. Secondly, the position provided by the regulator places the spill 237 km west of the actual spill location. In that legal document, it would be reasonable to suppose that staff had checked the document for accuracy. That supposition would be incorrect. If we give the regulator the benefit of the doubt and assume it meant the 4th, not the 5th meridian, the location is still misplaced, in this case 10.5 km to the ENE of the actual spill. Such consistency of misinformation is hard to fathom. Although coincidental, there is some consolation in the fact that when I attempted to use the regulator's online location conversion tool to convert the Nexen spill location from township and range to latitude/longitude, I received the message "Corrupted Content Error. The site at http://www1.aer.ca/GISConversionTools/conversion_tools.html has experienced a network protocol violation that cannot be repaired." Indeed. If I slipped with

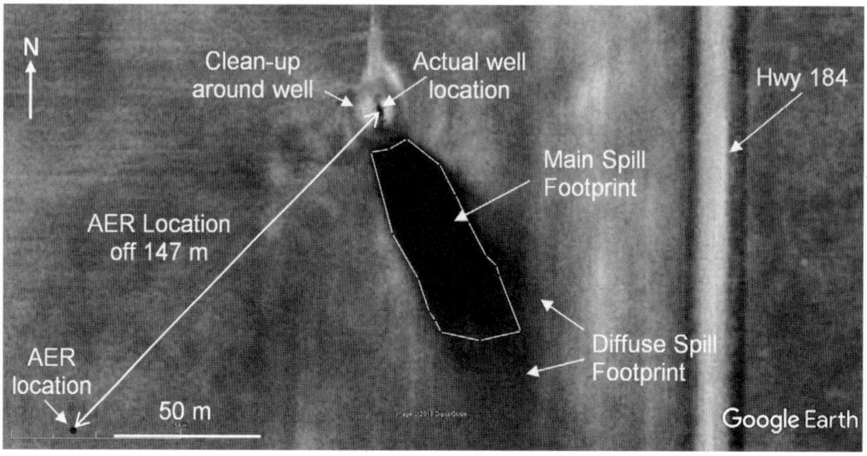

Figure 6.2 A crude oil spill captured on a satellite image illustrates inaccurate and missing data. According to the AER, this spill at an oil well in SW Alberta released 0.6 m³ of crude oil on 21 September 2002; there was zero recovery. A cleanup date of 1 October 2002 indicates that the incident was closed on that date. The record contains no data on wildlife/habitat effects or areal footprint of the spill but notes that the release extended offsite. This Landsat image was obtained six days after the spill and four days before the cleanup date. Some cleanup may have been conducted on the lease near the well as indicated by the sharp boundary of the spill footprint south of the well. The main spill footprint of 1,563 m² is approximate and does not include the diffuse edge. It's impossible for a release of 0.6 m³ crude oil to spread over 1,563 m² and blacken the ground sufficiently to be detected on old, low resolution satellite imagery.

a knife and had to depend upon the regulator to provide my location to an ambulance, I'd bleed out before the ambulance found me.

What makes AER locations inaccurate? The regulator uses the township and range system (known as "legals") to refer to industry sites. A facility might be identified as 5-31-56-20W4, meaning subdivision 5, Section 31, Township 56, Range 20, west of the 4th meridian. To convert to latitude/longitude, the regulator assumes that the spill is positioned in the centre of a subdivision, a location accurate to 16 ha (forty acres). Applying geometry, even if the regulator supplies the correct legal (which it may not, see figure 6.1), the actual spill location may differ from its AER location by up to 283 m, a significant error when attempting to find spills. Fifty-five of the reported spills were located only to quarter section, not to legal subdivision, a position accurate to 64 ha (160 acres).

The regulator introduces additional errors when it reports the location of the facility responsible for the spill rather than for the spill itself. Sometimes the location is entirely unrelated to the spill because someone made an error (examples 2 and 4 above). In the case of pipeline spills, an inaccurate location presents a serious difficulty because a spill can occur at any position along a pipeline's length. Finally, even if a spill location is accurate and the spill can be located on a satellite image, access can be prevented by private roads, locked gates, and no trespassing signs. In fact, the public is prohibited access to virtually all industry sites, spills or no spills (figure 6.3). We're not allowed access to spill sites even though most spills occur on public land.

In sum, it's best to view legals as names rather than as locations. Legals are shorthand identifiers useful to industry and the regulator, but they aren't a substitute for accurate locations. The magnitude of the inaccuracies is sufficient to hinder or prevent the public or city planners from locating spills.

Figure 6.3 Preventing access to spill sites hinders the growth of scientific knowledge and undermines the public interest. (a) A locked gate and (b) a no trespassing notice blocks public access to eight industrial sites and eleven spills. One site reports five spills, one of which is the 1982 Bruderheim oil spill site (studied by Roy and McGill 1998) that has developed a water repellent soil. 5 August 2018.

Legals provide another example of industry-reported data, accepted by the regulator without verification, that fall short of a minimum scientific standard. The result is that critical information about spills and their effects is unavailable to the public. That AER spill locations are not reliable presaged a consistent pattern in the FIS data, that of unreliable and missing data.

UNDERESTIMATION OF SPILL VOLUMES

Underestimation of spill volumes is a prevalent form of misinformation and is not confined to crude oil and saline water spills. The Amoco sour gas well blowout near Lodgepole, Alberta provides an example. The regulator reported a release of 18,000 m³ of condensate and ten million m³ of raw production gas, but independent environmental studies (Monenco Consultants 1983; Baker 1990) estimated significantly higher volumes, up to triple the amount of condensate and between 8–10 times as much raw gas. The official estimate of gas released is an order of magnitude lower than what was independently assessed – there is no excuse for this degree of misinformation.

The Lodgepole blowout vented condensate and sour gas with an incredibly toxic hydrogen sulphide content of 20–33 per cent to the atmosphere for sixty-eight days from October to December 1982. The blowout released 485 tonnes of sulphur each day, damaged the local water supply, resulted in loss of 260 hectares of natural habitat, and rained condensate onto 445 hectares. A scientist who later studied the effects on the surrounding forests recalled to me, "There was dark, gooey condensate over everything. It was an unpleasant field experience – messy and smelly" (B. Weerstra, pers. comm., April 2019). Health effects from the blowout were observed as far away as Edmonton. On the morning of the blowout, 230 km south of Lodgepole, Weerstra "woke up to the strong smell of sulfur, which was quite alarming … people were going to the Canmore Hospital complaining of headaches." I lived west of Edmonton at that time, about 110 km ENE of the blowout, and remember smelling hydrogen sulphide for much of the autumn. The Lodgepole blowout was a major incident that everyone living in Alberta at that time remembers. In spite of this, the regulator continues to provide misinformation about the incident.

Later in the book we'll explore cases of underestimating and underreporting spill volumes. For now, I'll relate one recent example. In January 2016, AER misrepresented the volume of the Apache 15-09 saline spill (one of the fieldwork sites) as a release of 9,500 m³. However, the regulator knew as early as October 2013 that the volume of the spill was 15,363 m³ (AER 2015b).

Another way in which the regulator misrepresents spill volumes is simply not to report them. Uncontrolled releases of bitumen at four well sites at Canadian Natural Resources Limited's Primrose Lake operations in 2013 and 2014 provide an example (Timoney and Lee 2014). The bitumen releases took place as a result of overpressuring the bedrock during high-pressure cyclic steaming operations. No one knows the volume of bitumen released because most of the bitumen remained underground after escaping the hydrocarbon reservoir. The volume of bitumen recovered, however, estimated at 1,940 m³, made the Primrose incident the fourth largest bitumen release in Alberta history. An additional 70,000 tonnes of contaminated soil were removed. The regulator's data fields are blank for substances released or recovered in this incident. Similarly, a spill of crude oil at a Suncor pipeline on 1 November 2007 resulted in a public notification due to potential hazard (notification is given in only 0.8 per cent of spills). The oil escaped into a river, habitat was affected, and the spill area exceeded 1,000 m². Yet the regulator's data reported zero crude oil was released, the volume recovered was left blank, and no other compounds were reported spilled.

77

Elsewhere in context I provide other examples of hydrocarbon and saline water releases for which the regulator reports no release or recovery volumes or fails to report the incident entirely. The significance of this underreporting is obvious: the regulator's data underestimate both the number of spills and the total volumes released to the environment.

CRUDE OIL SPILLS: HOW MANY, HOW LARGE, AND WHAT ARE THE REPORTED VOLUMES SPILLED AND RECOVERED?

Over the period 1975 through 2018, the regulator reported 30,168 crude oil spills that released a cumulative volume of 1.8 million barrels (more than 114 Olympic-sized swimming pools) at a rate of 1.9 spills/day. Crude oil spills in Alberta remain a daily occurrence (web 6.2 and 6.20). These totals are gross underestimates of the actual releases as we'll soon see. The total spill volume, by necessity, can't account for undocumented incidents. Furthermore, the volumes reported spilled and recovered are unverified.

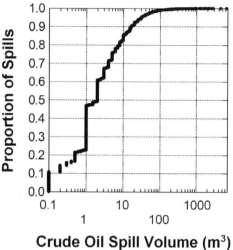

Figure 6.4 Proportion of reported crude oil spills in Alberta in relation to spill volume.

How large are crude oil spills in Alberta? *Reported* spill volumes range from 0.1 to 6,500 m³ with a median spill volume of 2 m³. You can see that the distribution of crude oil spill volumes is not a smooth one (figure 6.4) as would be expected with measured data from what is known as a continuous distribution. Why is this important? Suppose that you asked someone to measure the heights of all the school children in your province so that you could study how better nutrition has contributed to taller children relative to fifty years ago. You receive the data and plot the children's heights and you see that a disproportionate number of children are reported as exactly four feet, five feet, and six feet tall. It would be clear that the data were "cooked." The same is true with the spill volumes: some volumes, such as 0.1 m³, 1, and 2 m³, are far more numerous than expected if the volumes had been determined by measurement (figure 6.4). The reason is that the majority of spill volumes are chosen by human judgment rather than by measurement. Consider the implications of guessing rather than determining spill volumes by measurement (more on this topic later).

Thousands of spills report perfect oil recovery (figure 6.5, web 6.4). Overall, the median recovery for crude oil primary spills was 100 per cent. Industry's volumes spilled and recovered are accepted by the regulator with little or no verification, a hallmark of a captured regulator (web 6.2 and 6.3).

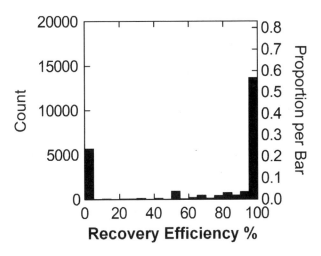

Figure 6.5 Frequency of crude oil spills in Alberta in relation to recovery efficiency.

IS CRUDE OIL SPILL RECOVERY INFLUENCED BY THE ENVIRONMENT?

AER classifies spills into three uninformative "environments": "Air/Land," "Flowing Water," and "Muskeg/Stagnant Water." Hampered as we are by the regulator's classification, we can ask whether crude oil recovery is influenced by the environment. Reported crude oil recovery efficiencies were higher in Muskeg/Stagnant Water than in the Air/Land and Flowing Water types and higher in the Air/Land type than in Flowing Water. Reported crude oil recovery was high, with a median recovery of 100 per cent in both Muskeg/Stagnant Water and Air/Land, and a Flowing Water median recovery of 66.7 per cent. The extremely high efficiencies of crude oil recovery are not possible (for details, see web 6.2, 6.5).

IS CRUDE OIL SPILL RECOVERY RELATED TO SPILL VOLUME?

Small spills are easier to recover than large spills and therefore spill recovery efficiency should decrease as spill volume increases. Strangely, the correlation between spill volume and recovery efficiency ranges from weakly negative to weakly positive (web 6.6). I therefore asked a simpler question: do spills with zero cleanup differ in volume from those reporting perfect recovery? In Flowing Water, smaller spills more often reported perfect recovery (web 6.7). Conversely, in the Air/Land and Muskeg/Stagnant Water categories, larger spills more often reported perfect recovery. The relationship between spill recovery efficiency and spill volume, if one exists, is inconsistent. Inexplicably, crude oil recovery efficiencies in Alberta appear to be unrelated to spill volume. This raises another red flag.

UNEMPIRICAL SPILL AND RECOVERY VOLUMES: THE FALCON EFFECT

Although there was no consistent relationship between spill volume and recovery of crude oil, the scatter plots were not random. There were families of smooth curves, which was significant by itself, but the data contained a deeper level of structure (figure 6.6 and web 6.8). The overall visual effect of the data pattern is that of a pointillism-rendered falcon with its wings tucked back, stooping onto its prey. For brevity, I called the data pattern the "falcon effect." It could also be called the "faked data" effect. How does it arise?

Many variables can influence spill recovery efficiency in the real world, such as environment type, response delay, season, company culture, and pressure to report favourable results. I realized that understanding why crude oil recovery efficiency exhibited such an unexpected pattern in relation to spill volume could be important to the environmental health of the tens of thousands of spill sites. I therefore devoted a significant amount of effort into determining the cause of the falcon effect.

Eventually, the reason for the families of curves became evident. The falcon effect is generated when guessing rather than measurement is used to determine spill and recovery volumes (web 6.8–6.10). The guessing is constrained by the number of possible whole number answers. For crude oil spills of 2 m^3, for example, only three whole number recovery volumes represent 94 per cent of the answers: 2 (41 per cent of values), 0 (37 per cent), and 1 (16 per cent). Once this guessing is repeated over thousands of spills and a range of spill volumes, the falcon appears.

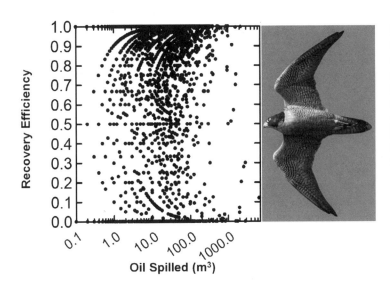

Figure 6.6 The falcon effect evident in the relationship between crude oil recovery efficiency and spill volume. Thousands of points overlap, particularly at recovery efficiencies of 0.0, 0.5, and 1.0.

An Engineer Explains the Guessing Underlying the Falcon Effect

I asked an industrial engineer (Alan Dunn, P.Eng., pers. comm., 26 September 2016) to interpret the relationship between recovery efficiency and the volume of crude oil spilled. He explained:

The data likely are "cooked," though perhaps not in a malicious way. Energy companies do not track product, for the most part, except when there is custody transfer. If one put one hundred barrels in one end of a line and only got ninety out the other end, it would be simple to say that ten got away somehow. The reality is that there may be hundreds of suppliers all the way from ten barrel pump jacks to 1,500 barrel monsters pumping into the pipeline at different times and at different rates. Flow rates vary, capacitance is provided in the network to balance it all out. So the only way to determine how much was spilled is to go out in the field and measure it. This is not easy. Hours, days, or weeks might pass before anyone realizes there is a leak, finds it, isolates it (if possible) and begins survey and repairs.

[During spill recovery] the spilled commodity is normally "mined" along with a large amount of soil or water or whatever. Unless every dump truck load or vacuum truck load was analyzed in excruciating detail, then one must depend on estimates and sampling.

So we don't know how much we had and we don't know how much we lost. Now come up with a number for the regulator and the press.

I experienced a frisson of excitement with this realization, one akin to my first reading of Darwin's Origin of Species many years ago. As natural selection driven by random mutations could give rise to wondrous forms such as peregrine falcons, so too could guessing constrained to a limited set of acceptable values give rise to a falcon. The implication of choosing rather than measuring spill and recovery volumes is significant. Numeric spill and recovery volumes are presented by the regulator without an admission that the data are guesses. That fact raises an important question: how much oil remains in the environment after cleanup operations? When the regulator reports perfect oil recovery, is there residual contamination? The answer, as will be shown, is yes.

82   SALINE SPILLS: HOW MANY, HOW LARGE, AND WHAT ARE THE REPORTED VOLUMES SPILLED AND RECOVERED?

Over the 1975–2018 period, the regulator reported 26,669 saline water spills (1.7 spills/day) with a cumulative volume spilled of 6.2 million barrels (394 Olympic-sized swimming pools). The total reported volume of saline water released was 3.4 times greater than the total reported crude oil spilled volume. As with crude oil spills, saline spills in Alberta are a daily occurrence. The total reported volume of saline water released to the environment represents a small fraction of the actual total saline water volume released (web 6.11–6.12).

How large are saline spills in Alberta? Reported spill volumes range from 0.1 to 48,079 m³ with a median spill volume of 4 m³. Some saline volumes (such as 0.1, 1, 2 m³) are far more numerous than would be expected if the values were measured (figure 6.7). The reason for the deviation from random expectations is that the majority of saline spill volumes are determined by human judgment rather than by measurement. As with crude oil spills, the implications of unmeasured saline spill volumes are significant.

Overall the median saline water recovery was 84 per cent. The thousands of spills reporting perfect saline water recovery raise questions of data validity (figure 6.8). As with crude oil spills, saline volumes spilled and recovered are reported to the regulator with little or no independent verification (web 6.11).

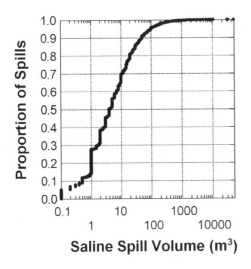

Figure 6.7 Proportion of reported saline spills in Alberta in relation to spill volume.

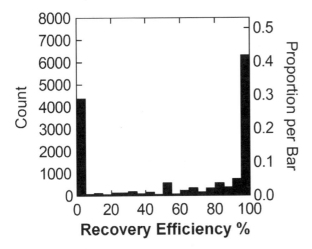

Figure 6.8 Frequency of saline spills in Alberta in relation to recovery efficiency.

IS SALINE SPILL RECOVERY INFLUENCED BY THE ENVIRONMENT?

Reported saline water recovery efficiencies were higher in Muskeg/Stagnant Water than in the Air/Land and Flowing Water types and higher in the Air/Land type than in Flowing Water. In Muskeg/Stagnant Water median recovery was 100 per cent, in Air/Land, median recovery efficiency was 86.2 per cent, and in Flowing Water, median recovery was 40.0 per cent (web 6.13).

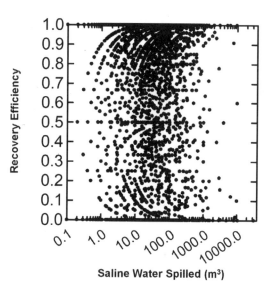

Figure 6.9 The relationship between saline water recovery efficiency and spill volume. The falcon effect is evident.

IS SALINE WATER RECOVERY RELATED TO SPILL VOLUME?

Contrary to expectations, reported saline water recovery efficiencies in Alberta are weakly related or unrelated to spill volume (web 6.11, 6.14). Although there were no evident relationships between spill volume and recovery of saline water, scatter plots revealed that the data points were not random. The falcon effect due to guessing spill and recovery volumes remains evident (figure 6.9, web 6.15).

Do saline spills with zero cleanup differ in spill volume from those with perfect recovery? In both Flowing Water and Muskeg/Stagnant Water, spill volume did not influence spill recovery (web 6.16). In the Air/Land category, larger spills more often reported perfect recovery. The relationship between saline spill volume and recovery is inconsistent and illogical. Given that the data are not based on real-world measurements raises more red flags. It's analogous to going to the doctor to discuss the results of your medical tests only to find that no tests were taken, someone just made up the results.

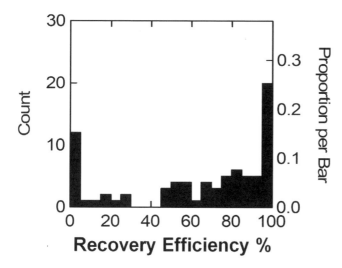

Figure 6.10 Frequency of crude oil spills in North Dakota for the 2010–11 season in relation to reported recovery efficiency.

COMMENTS ON CRUDE OIL AND
SALINE WATER RECOVERY

Cleanup after some recent major oil spills helps to place the Alberta spill recoveries in context (Boufadel et al. 2015; Lee et al. 2015): *Terra Nova*, Newfoundland, 2004: 5 per cent recovered; *Exxon Valdez*, Alaska, 1989: ~10 per cent recovered; BP Deepwater Horizon, Gulf of Mexico, 2010: 16 per cent recovered; Pine River, British Columbia, 2000: 82–92 per cent recovered; Enbridge, Kalamazoo River, Michigan, 2010: 134 per cent recovered; and Lac Mégantic, Quebec, 2013: recovery volume about 493 times the volume of the spill. Significantly, even in spills where reported recovery volume exceeded the spill volume, there were large environmental impacts and persistent contamination, as documented in the Enbridge and Lac Mégantic spills. Indeed after the Lac Mégantic cleanup, oil remained in sediments and along the banks of a 30 km stretch of the Chaudière River; most contaminated areas might never again be inhabitable (Boufadel et al. 2015).

In the real world, oil and saline water recovery is difficult. Overall, the median crude oil recovery in Alberta was 100 per cent. In comparison, the median oil recovery in North Dakota oil spills was 65.3 per cent (North Dakota 2011) (compare figures 6.5 and 6.10). Only 3.4 per cent of oil spills in North Dakota reported perfect recovery in comparison to 53.8 per cent of oil spills in Alberta. Perfect crude oil recovery is reported in Alberta sixteen times more often than in North Dakota. See web 6.18.8 for spill recovery in Montana.

Given the real-world delay between spills and cleanup, especially in remote areas, it strains credulity that 60 per cent of saline spills in wetlands report perfect recovery. It is particularly difficult to understand how crude oil spilled into flowing water can be perfectly recovered in 31 per cent of spills (web 6.17). Similarly, how can saline water, spilled into flowing water, be perfectly recovered in 15 per cent of spills? In order to do so, an entire watercourse would have to be diverted the instant a spill began. A retired Alberta government fisheries biologist confirmed this: "With many spills and pipeline breaks in flowing water, the material had flowed downstream before any action was taken by industry ... Often the clean-up was destructive and cosmetic" (Carl Hunt, pers. comm., March 2019).

The higher than expected proportion of spills with 0 per cent and 100 per cent recovery suggests that factors other than technology, engineering, environmental context, and effort influence the reported recovery volumes. A company may "fill in the blanks" on volumes recovered by duplicating the estimated volume spilled (web 6.18), by stating that no volume was recovered, or by estimating a common fraction, often one-half. There is no publicly available evidence on Alberta spills that can shed light on such internal bookkeeping practices. Questions posed to the regulator on this and related topics are examined later in the book. In essence, the regulator trusts the industry to report truthful spill volumes and recovery volumes and then records these data without verification. Overweening trust between a regulator and the industry it regulates indicates regulatory capture.

Oil spill volumes in the United States appear to follow a smoother frequency distribution, indicative of more measurement and less guessing than in the Alberta data (figure 6.11), but the United States data may be influenced by marine spills which are easier to measure than are inland spills. If instead we compare Alberta spill volumes with those from Saskatchewan and North Dakota, we find that reported spill volumes in all three jurisdictions are influenced by human subjectivity (web 6.18.5). In short, wherever data exist on inland spills, reported spill volumes are not credible.

Accounting for differences in spill volumes and rates across jurisdictions can be difficult without knowledge of how the data are gathered. In Alberta, the median spill volumes for crude oil and saline spills were 2 m³ and 4 m³, respectively. Comparison of spill volumes in Alberta with those reported from

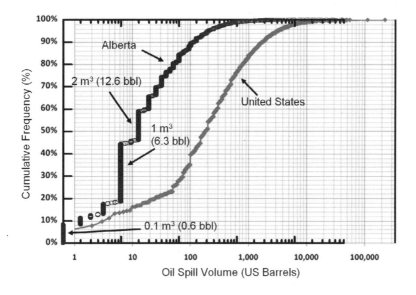

Figure 6.11 Frequency of crude oil spills in relation to spill volumes from United States coastal and inland pipelines and Alberta. In the Alberta spill volumes, note the stepped pattern indicating higher than expected frequencies of favoured spill volumes.

four American states illustrates the importance of reporting criteria. Median crude oil and brine spill volumes at oil well releases were 0.45 m³ in Pennsylvania, 0.8 m³ in North Dakota, 3.0 m³ in Colorado, and 4.9 m³ in New Mexico (Allison and Mandler 2018a). There is no reason to think that spill volumes in, for example, Pennsylvania are eleven times smaller than those in New Mexico. Spill volumes are influenced by differences in reporting thresholds. In other words, reporting thresholds influence the reported spill rates. The most efficient way to decrease the spill rate, and thereby appear to be protecting the environment, is to raise the reporting threshold. We'll observe this technique in chapter 15 when we compare the regulator's FIS data with its online spill reporting.

Alberta crude oil and saline water recovery efficiency are strongly discontinuous, with higher than expected frequencies of no recovery and perfect recovery (figure 6.12 and web 6.20). In Alberta and elsewhere, industry is reporting unrealistically high recovery rates and unempirical data (web 6.18). Discrepancies between the 2013 and 2017 versions of the regulator's data and internal reports further undermine confidence in the regulator's publicly available spill and recovery data (web 6.19).

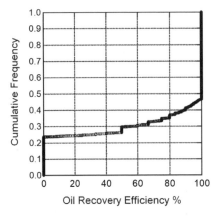 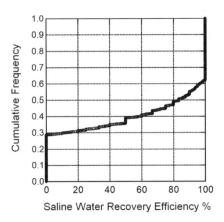

Figure 6.12 Frequency distributions of Alberta spill recovery efficiencies for primary oil spills and primary saline spills.

ANNUAL FREQUENCY AND VOLUME OF REPORTED CRUDE OIL AND SALINE SPILLS, 1975–2018

The annual number of reported crude oil spills in Alberta has varied from 353 to 1,652 spills/year while the spill volume has varied from 1,776 to 15,622 m³/year (figures 6.13a and b). For saline releases, the spill rate has varied from 196 to 949 spills/year while the spill volume has varied from 6,099 to 74,181 m³/year (figures 6.13c and d; web 6.20). Whether variations in the number and volume of reported spills represent actual variations in spill rates or changes in reporting practices, or both, is difficult to ascertain (web 6.20). Because there is often no clear distinction between crude oil and saline spills, combining the two spill types can provide the big picture view of changes over time (figures 6.13e and f). Here we see that the number of reported spills increased from the mid-1970s to the late 1990s and has since declined. The trend in total release volumes is unclear. Just as the number of vehicle accidents tracks the number of vehicles on the highways, trends in spill rates should track the production of crude oil. For example, the number of vehicle accidents over a given time period is a function of the probability of an accident per kilometre of travel. The greater the total distance travelled by all vehicles, the greater the number of accidents. By the same token, the number of spills in a given time period should be a function of the total production of hydrocarbons per unit time. What do we find?

The production of conventional crude oil in Alberta declined from about 186,000 m³/day in 1975 to about 71,000 m³/day in 2018 (figure 6.13e), and as expected, the trend in crude oil spill volume (figure 6.13b) correlates with crude oil production (web 6.20), but then the wheels fall off the bus. There is no significant correlation between annual crude oil production and either the annual number of crude oil spills or the volume of saline spills. Strangely, annual crude oil production is negatively correlated with the number of saline spills. For the reported data to be accurate would require an increasing rate of saline spills while crude oil production is declining and presumably spill prevention technology is improving. How could this occur? After all, crude oil and saline produced water are, by definition, produced during crude oil production and spills should occur in proportion to production. The simplest explanation for the lack of correspondence between crude oil production and spill rates is underreporting of spills.

When it comes to determining spill rates, bookkeeping practices are another source of uncertainty. Because there are no rules for how industry classifies spills, we might observe an apparent decrease in spill rates simply by industry reporting the spills as a different substance – such as reporting crude oil spills as "total hydrocarbon" spills. Indeed, the reported annual number of spills of all substance categories over the past forty-five years has not declined; it more than doubled from 1975 to 1998; from 1998 to 2018, the annual spill rate continued to rise (figure 6.14).

How do Alberta spill rates and volumes compare to those of other jurisdictions? Bearing in mind that the patchwork of spill data is composed of more holes than patches, annual numbers of crude oil and saline spills are about 60–70 per cent higher in Alberta than in Saskatchewan and up to 80 per cent higher than in North Dakota. Annual spill volumes are about 60–130 per cent higher in Alberta than in Saskatchewan and 50–400 per cent higher than in North Dakota (web 6.18). Alberta's spill rates dwarf those of Montana: crude oil and saline spills are sixteen and eighteen times more frequent, respectively, in Alberta and total crude oil and saline spill volumes are eight and eleven times higher, respectively, in Alberta than in Montana (web 6.18.8).

SUMMARY

This chapter required some tough slogging. Let's consider what we have learned. Over the period 1975 through 2018, there have been 1.9 crude oil spills/day in Alberta with a total reported volume spilled of 290,578 m³ and a median recovery efficiency of 100 per cent. Over the same period, there have been 1.7 saline spills/day with a total reported volume spilled of 979,849 m³ and a median recovery of 86 per cent. The annual number and total volume of crude oil and saline spills in Alberta greatly exceed those observed in Saskatchewan, North Dakota, and Montana. The number and volume of reported spills underestimate the true values, a fact of considerable importance that we will examine in later chapters.

The preponderance of perfect spill recoveries raises a red flag about the truthfulness of the regulator's data. It's as if the regulator is shouting "nothing to see here folks," but all that shouting only serves to raise questions. It's not known how much contaminant remains after cleanup. Comparison with data from other jurisdictions further calls into question the validity of the regulator's data. The data tell us more about the culture of the regulator and its partners than they do about spills and the environment. The regulator's data are too good to be true. Unverified industry-reported data are inherently uncertain. The only certainty is that reported incident rates underestimate the true incident rates.

The annual number and volume of crude oil and saline spills in Alberta may have declined in recent years. We can't be certain due to the unreliability of the industry-reported data. In fact, the annual reported number of spills of

Figure 6.13 *Opposite* Crude oil and saline spills in relation to conventional crude oil production. Annual number and volume of (a, b) crude oil spills, (c, d) saline water spills, and (e, f) combined crude oil and saline spills in Alberta, 1975–2018. For crude oil, the long-term mean spill rate is 686 +/- 226 s.d. spills per year and 6,604 +/- 3,562 m³ per year s.d. For saline water, the long-term mean spill rate is 606 +/- 225 s.d. spills per year and 22,269 +/- 13,166 m³ per year s.d. For combined crude oil and saline spills, the mean annual total spills are 1,292 +/- 403 s.d., and mean annual total volume 28,873 m³ +/- 13,567 s.d. Long-term daily combined mean release rates are 3.5 spills/day and 79.0 m³/day. The bold black lines in panels e and f are the long-term mean spill rates. The apparent decline in crude oil and saline spills over the past twenty years may be an artifact of bookkeeping because the total number of spills from all categories shows no trend over that period.

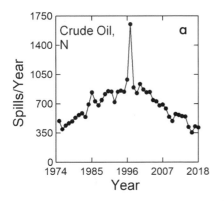

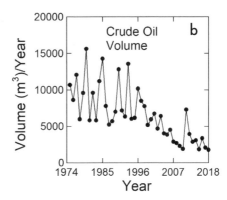

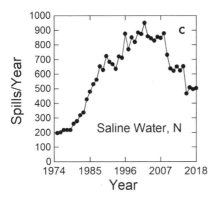

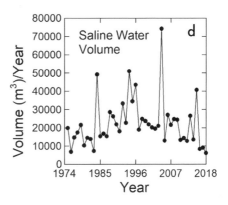

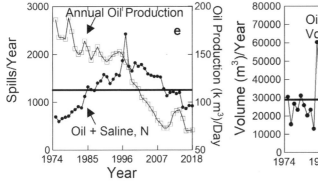

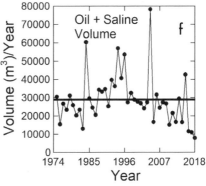

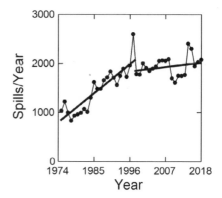

Figure 6.14 Total primary spills per year of all substances in Alberta. The long-term average is 1,681 +/- 421 spills per year. The bold lines are linear regressions.

all substances is apparently increasing. The total number of spills reported and the total volumes spilled underestimate the true spill rates. Inaccurate spill locations and poor data quality control create further uncertainty and difficulty in assessing the effects of spills. The lack of correlations between annual crude oil production and both the annual number of crude oil spills and the annual volume of saline spills suggest underreporting of spills. The illogical negative correlation between annual crude oil production and the annual number of saline spills further undermines confidence in the regulator's data.

In the absence of rules and objective methods for determining spill and recovery volumes, most reported volumes are little more than subjective estimates. The falcon or faked data effect, observed in spill recovery data, results from guessing preferred fractions of the spill volume as the value for the recovery volume. The three most common recovery guesstimates are, in decreasing order, perfect recovery, zero recovery, and one-half recovery.

In the next chapter, we continue our assessment of the validity of the regulator's spill data.

CHAPTER 7

Spill Forensics

Contrariwise, continued Tweedledee, if it was so, it might be;
and if it were so, it would be; but as it isn't, it ain't. That's logic.

Lewis Carroll, *Alice in Wonderland*

INTRODUCTION

We grow a lot of our own food. In summer 2018, we had a big carrot and beet crop, hundreds of pounds of each. Unfortunately, after we put up our carrots in sand that was too moist, we lost the entire carrot crop to rot. The beets were still fine, so, following the unofficial motto of the US Marine Corps, we adapted, improvised, and overcame to make up for the carrot deficit. We learned new ways of using beets such as in bread, chocolate cake, burgers, and dips. The "adapt, improvise, overcome" approach has much to recommend it when information from a regulator proves to be corrupted with rot. In that case, it's fruitful to compare the regulator's data with scientifically credible information. In so doing, we learn not about the natural environment but rather about the regulatory environment.

Accurate environmental data are essential to risk management. The previous chapter demonstrated that the regulator's spill and release data exhibit properties that would be unexpected in scientific data. In this chapter we continue to evaluate the credibility of the regulator's data with a forensic audit and then examine how often spills are reported in sensitive areas, how often unknown substances are spilled, how often unnamed corporate entities are responsible for spills, how much time elapses between a spill and its cleanup, the frequency of spills for each day of the week, the causes of spills, and spill footprints.

Now immersed within the regulator's spill data, we find ourselves deep down a rabbit hole. To make sense of the regulator's data, we will seek science-based measured values and data based on consistent logic but will instead find ourselves in Wonderland trying to get straight answers out of Tweedledum and Tweedledee. We'll observe that the regulator's environmental data tell us less about the natural environment than about the effects of regulatory capture.

This chapter presents a forensic audit. What do I mean by that? There are three senses of "forensic" that apply here. First, the chapter uses specialized methods of evidence detection. Second, the chapter involves the application of scientific methods to legal problems, in this case whether the legal authority, the regulator, is protecting the public interest. Third, we consider facts that are suitable for public discussion and debate.

A FORENSIC AUDIT OF AER SPILL, RECOVERY, AND EFFICIENCY DATA

Sometimes "pure" scientific research can have unforeseen and immense practical applications. Sequencing the human genome led to advances in medicine, agriculture, anthropology, evolution, and the treatment of cancers. It also led to a major advance in forensic detection of criminals who left samples of their DNA at crime scenes. Similarly, the discovery of patterns in how often digits occurred in data, now known as Benford's Law, while seemingly purely academic, led to advances in detection of fraud and falsified data. First, a little history.

Benford's Law, also known as Newcomb-Benford's Law and the first-digit law, was described in a paper titled "The Law of Anomalous Numbers" (Benford 1938). Although the physicist Frank Benford is credited with the law, this strange property of predictable frequencies in digits was first noted by the Nova Scotia–born astronomer Simon Newcomb. Newcomb's (1881) discovery began with a serendipitous observation. He noticed that the first pages in books of logarithms, those that began with the digit 1, were the first to wear out. He observed that the leading (or first significant) digit in logarithms is more often 1, followed by 2, and so on. Fittingly, Benford's Law, discovered while thumbing through pages of logarithms, is itself based on a logarithm.

Benford determined that the frequency of the first significant digits 1–9, D, followed a frequency distribution equal to $\log_{10}(1 + 1/D)$. The law also describes the expected frequencies for second, third, and fourth digits. Datasets that conform to Benford's Law are composed of numbers that are randomly assigned rather than chosen by humans. Benford frequencies persist even when values are transformed into different units such as quarts, barrels, or cubic metres or multiplied or divided by constants.

Benford's fulsome description of the law involved study of twenty-nine different kinds of data, such as town population sizes, physical constants, molecular weights, numbers in an issue of *Reader's Digest*, street addresses, river discharge rates, and death rates. Other datasets that conform to Benford's Law include stock prices, house prices, accounts receivable and accounts payable, electoral and socioeconomic data, those with a wide numerical range, values that are derived from mathematical combinations (e.g., quantity x price, such as electricity bills), data without a predefined maximum, and measured releases to air of environmental toxins such as lead and ethylbenzene (de Marchi and Hamilton 2006; Diekmann 2007; Bredl et al. 2012). Significantly, datasets composed of numbers influenced by human decisions, where values are chosen based on psychological thresholds rather than derived from measurement, are not expected to conform to Benford's Law.

The usefulness of Benford's Law, when combined with statistical tests of departure from expectation, lies in its ability to detect fraudulent, falsified, approximated, or human-influenced data. Benford's Law has been used to detect tax, accounting, and electoral fraud, untruthful census data, and inaccurate environmental data. A Benford analysis demonstrated that industry-reported values for air releases of lead and nitric acid in the United States were inaccurate (de Marchi and Hamilton 2006). When people were asked to fabricate statistical estimates with several significant digits, the faked numbers did not follow Benford's Law (Diekmann 2007). Even with conscious effort, humans find it difficult to simulate data derived from measurements, a useful fact when examining datasets for misconduct (Mosimann et al. 2008).

As another test of the validity of the regulator's spill and release data, in this section I present a forensic audit based on Benford's Law. Here we examine the frequency of first significant digits in crude oil and saline spill data, and

95

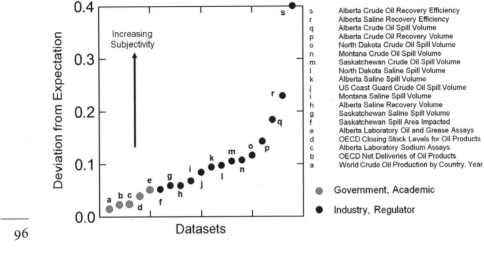

Figure 7.1 Data pertaining to the fossil fuel industry and the environment differ in their degree of subjectivity as measured by deviation from an expected Benford distribution. Data and details in web 7.1–5, 7.14–17.

compare these findings with United States Coast Guard spill data, laboratory oil and grease assays and dissolved sodium assays, and economic data (for details, see web 7.1–7.5).

The frequency of first significant digits in the regulator's crude oil spill volume, recovery volume, and percent recovery data departed strongly from expected Benford's Law frequencies (figure 7.1). US Coast Guard crude oil spill data also did not conform to a Benford distribution, which makes sense given that the Coast Guard also relies upon industry-reported data (see chapter 15). The saline spill and recovery results corroborate the oil spill and recovery results. The frequency of first significant digits in saline spill volume, recovery volume, and saline per cent recovery data departed strongly from Benford's Law frequencies. In contrast, laboratory assays of oil and grease and dissolved sodium in water samples from the Athabasca and Peace Rivers conformed to a Benford distribution. The lab assays demonstrate that when hydrocarbons and salts are measured rather than guessed, the data conform to a Benford distribution.

IMPORTANCE OF THE BENFORD RESULTS

Industry-reported data pertaining to spills represent decisions, rather than measurements, with varying degrees of subjectivity. The Alberta situation is not unique. Crude oil and saline spill volumes reported by industry in Saskatchewan, North Dakota, and Montana similarly don't conform to a Benford distribution. In contrast, laboratory and academic datasets and those pertaining to hydrocarbon economics rely upon measurement much more than do industry data pertaining to the environmental impacts of hydrocarbon production.

What might influence the choice of values to assign to spill and recovery volume decisions? Uncertainty, the lack of quantitative tools such as gauges, and time constraints may play a role. Pressure to report a favourable result creates a tendency to underestimate spill volume, overestimate recovery success, and minimize impacts. In the absence of measurements, why not understate the spill volume, state that the spill has been perfectly recovered, and state that there are no impacts? Why be the bearer of bad news, especially if no one is checking?

The crude oil and saline spill results raise important questions. How much crude oil and saline water is actually being spilled? How much is being recovered? And how much residual contamination remains in the environment? The significance of spill data being derived from subjective decisions can't be overstated.

CRUDE OIL AND SALINE SPILLS
IN SENSITIVE AREAS

Sensitive areas are an important component of informed ecosystem management. Before we consider the regulator's data, let's first define sensitive areas. A sensitive area is one whose form, function, and composition are easily affected by disturbance. By form, we mean the structure of an ecosystem – what it looks like – is it a multilayered old-growth forest, an even-aged pine plantation, or an agricultural field? By function we mean the processes that operate in the ecosystem – how much water moves through the system, how much organic matter is fixed each year, how it responds to fire or flooding. By composition we mean all the life forms that make that ecosystem their home.

Ecologists, biologists, geologists, land managers, and planners have identified a variety of sensitive environments that can be used to inform management. These include seepage areas, peatlands, wetlands, riparian zones, watersheds for domestic water supplies, critical breeding, spawning, and overwintering habitat, migratory staging areas, biodiversity hotspots, hibernacula, and critical habitat for threatened and endangered species and communities. The protection of sensitive areas should be a high priority for any land manager charged with protecting the public interest. In order to do that, an agency must have both a scientifically defensible sensitive areas system and management criteria for those sensitive areas. Sensitive ecosystem types and landscape attributes that confer ecological sensitivity are routinely incorporated into geographic information systems. British Columbia uses a sensitive ecosystems inventory to identify at-risk and fragile ecosystems in order to support land-use decisions that will protect ecological integrity (Sensitive Ecosystems Inventories 2017). In Alberta, some years ago, the concept was used to guide land management. Operators of upstream oil and gas facilities in environmentally sensitive areas were encouraged to conserve and reclaim land and mitigate environmental effects (Alberta Environment 2003).

As originally intended, the AER's sensitive area designations were reportedly based on the Alberta Sustainable Resource Development sensitive areas. But were they in practice? The regulator classified 0.21 per cent of crude oil spills and 0.27 per cent of saline spills as occurring in sensitive areas (web 7.6). For spills into flowing water, all of which would be considered ecologically sensitive, the regulator classified 0.96 per cent of crude oil spills and 0.67 per cent of saline spills as sensitive. These low levels of ecological sensitivity underestimate the true extent of sensitive areas, but by how much? To get that answer required a science-based map of ecological sensitivity.

I contacted Alberta Environment and Parks (AEP) and requested that it provide an estimate of the total areal extent of sensitive areas in the province (for details, see web 7.6). AEP could not provide that value for the simple reason that it doesn't have all of the relevant data nor does any agency. It could, however, provide the areal extent of sensitive wildlife occurrences and their critical habitat and the extent of Alberta wetlands. Although these layers comprise a subset of sensitive areas in Alberta, the data provide a defensible science-based *minimum* estimate of ecological sensitivity.

If we exclude national parks, where hydrocarbon exploitation does not occur, about 22.7 per cent of the province supports sensitive wildlife and 28.1

per cent supports wetlands. Some wildlife and wetland areas overlap so we can't use the simple sum to arrive at total sensitive area. When we correct for overlap, 46.2 per cent of Alberta outside of the national parks supports either sensitive wildlife or wetlands. On average, the occurrence of spills in sensitive areas should be proportional to the areal extent of sensitive areas and the industrial footprint. The AER underrepresents the occurrence of sensitive areas by a factor of about 171 times for saline spills and 220 times for crude oil spills. Its underrepresentation of ecological sensitivity would be even greater if other sensitive ecological information were included. The AER's sensitive area data grossly misrepresent the ecological reality.

HOW THE AER'S SENSITIVE AREAS DATA MORPHED INTO MEANINGLESSNESS

99

Within the AER, there was intense debate in 2017 as to how to use and apply the sensitive areas designation (name withheld, pers. comm., April 2017). Part of that debate followed a report on the occurrence of spills in sensitive areas in Alberta. The purpose of the report (*Environmental Performance Report, Pipeline Releases 2015 and Sensitive Environments*) was to demonstrate how sensitive area information can be useful in the management of spills. The report documented high rates of damage to sensitive environments resulting from pipeline spills and concluded that sensitive areas should be identified by policy and legislation. AEP endorsed that view. In response, AER suppressed the report, terminated the employment of the chief scientist author of the report, and eliminated the concept of sensitive areas from its spill information system (see below). The AER's suppression of the report illustrates the inability of the regulator to tolerate "bad news"(see chapter 16).

Because the AER's sensitive areas did not conform to mapped sensitive areas and did not appear to be ecologically based, I asked the regulator for clarification (web 7.7). The correspondence demonstrates loss of corporate memory over time, lack of ecological grounding, and that staff inconsistently applied decision rules. A senior source within AER (name withheld, pers. comm., May 2017) explained that the regulator lacks environmental and data/information management accountability. For the AER, charged with protecting the environment, it's remarkable that sensitive areas and other environmental data have not been used to inform spill response and management.

Other governments, forestry companies, and national parks use sensitive layers because they result in better management. Does the AER use ecological information within a GIS? A source explained: "The AER does have access to many ecological GIS layers ... We don't generally use them in our day to day field operational business" (W. Gilbart, AER, pers. comm., 11 January 2017). Why this is so is not clear but it belies a lack of both ecological knowledge and a commitment to wise management.

Rather than make its sensitive area designation scientifically defensible and useful, the regulator instead chose to classify all spills in sensitive areas from 2009 to the present as nonsensitive areas. In the regulator's spin words, it "enhanced" its database "to prevent inspectors from ever checking off this data item as 'Yes.' It will now always ever show as 'No'" (web 7.7). The illogic of this change is patent. If the only valid answer to a question is no, then there's no question. But it's worse than that. Given that all ecosystems are sensitive to fossil fuel industry disturbances, requiring that all areas subjected to spills be classified as nonsensitive is tantamount to disinformation and unscientific nonsense. We can dismiss the regulator's sensitive area designations as fiction.

SENSITIVE AREAS AND LAND OWNERSHIP

Because sensitive areas were intended to indicate ecological sensitivity, that freehold private lands were designated sensitive three times more frequently than were public lands demonstrates a nonecological subjectivity (web 7.6). It's also strange that all spills on First Nations reserve lands or within Metis settlements were classified as nonsensitive areas given the strong connections and feelings that Indigenous people have about their lands. Finally, land ownership was unknown in 6,473 crude oil spills and 3,859 saline spills (current to 2017); this is a major data gap. Why would the regulator be unable to determine land ownership at spill sites? Failure to determine land ownership suggests that the regulator is unconcerned that landowners are not being informed of spills. That lack of concern affects all of us because the public owns most of the land in the province.

SPILLS: UNKNOWN SUBSTANCES AND UNKNOWN CORPORATE ENTITIES

As of June 2019, the substances released in 2,046 spills were unknown. Let's think about that. How could neither the regulator nor the company know what was spilled? Most unknown substance releases took place at pipelines (74 per cent). Are we to believe that no one knows what is spilling from these pipelines? There were no data on wildlife/habitat effects in 70 per cent of unknown substance spills; 30 per cent observed "no affect"; 0.3 per cent stated that animals were affected; and 0.3 per cent stated that animals were injured or killed. When habitat/wildlife effects were assessed, the AER reported no effects in 99.4 per cent of the spills. There were no cleanup dates for 56 per cent of spills of unknown substances. All unknown substance spills postdate 16 January 1994; why this is so is not clear (AER provided no explanation).

Numbered corporations (registered as a number rather than a name) were responsible for 913 reported spills of all substances in Alberta compared to only fifty-six spills by numbered corporations in Saskatchewan. In Alberta, the median spill recovery was 0 per cent for numbered corporations compared to a median recovery of 50 per cent for spills of all substances by named corporations. What were the effects of these spills? Were their impacts ever studied? Numbered corporations shield owners from unwanted publicity. Although a registry search can be made ($25/company), it does not disclose owners, it lists only directors and shareholders. In the event of a spill, a numbered corporation can declare bankruptcy then reincorporate with a new number and continue operations. A numbered corporation can't develop a bad environmental reputation, which perhaps explains why in at least one-half of all their spills, no recovery was attempted. Why spend money when there is no penalty for doing nothing?

HOW MUCH TIME ELAPSES BETWEEN SPILL AND CLEANUP?

How many days elapse between the occurrence of a crude oil or saline spill and completion of cleanup? Here we can compare data from Alberta and Montana with NEB interprovincial pipeline data. In Alberta, cleanup was complete on the day of the spill in 27 per cent of spills and in Montana in 6 per cent of spills (web 7.12). In 50 per cent of spills, cleanup was complete within two days in Alberta and within six days in Montana. If we repeat this exercise for spills of all substances in Alberta, we observe a similar result: in 31 per cent of spills, the regulator stated that cleanup was complete on the day of the spill and in 51 per cent of spills, cleanup was complete within two days.

Given what is known of the delay between the initiation of a spill, its detection, and the ensuing response to get a crew on site, often to a remote location, stop the release, contain the spill, and clean up the spill, a delay of zero days between a spill and completion of its cleanup is simply not credible. Consider that at interprovincial pipelines, for spills of hydrocarbons, and those of crude oil in particular, 88 per cent and 89 per cent respectively, require more than one hundred days for cleanup compared to only 21 per cent and 12 per cent of spills in Alberta and Montana (web 7.12). The median time required for cleanup of interprovincial hydrocarbon and crude oil spills is 424 days and 584 days, respectively, in comparison to the Alberta and Montana median time of only two and six days needed for cleanup.

Case studies of spills discussed elsewhere in the book demonstrate that the remarkably swift cleanup of spills reported to regulators by industry is another case of data that are too good to be true. As we'll see in the case studies, issuance of a cleanup date does not mean that the site has been successfully decontaminated or remediated. The strongest inference we can draw from the data is that unbelievably fast cleanup is just that, it's not believable.

DO MORE SPILLS OCCUR ON PARTICULAR DAYS OF THE WEEK?

Given that spills during the upstream production of hydrocarbons are unplanned events, they should occur with equal frequency for all days of the week, but do they? I determined the daily frequency of spills for five jurisdictions (National Energy Board, Alberta, Saskatchewan, North Dakota, Montana) and found large differences in the observed and expected frequencies of spills (web 7.12.1–2). Alberta and Montana spills departed most strongly from the expectation of temporal randomness while North Dakota and National Energy Board spills showed smaller departures. Less frequent spill reporting on the weekend appears to be an industry-wide phenomenon. If reduced vigilance on the weekend results in some spills not being reported, they would tend to be smaller spills. I tested this hypothesis for spills of crude oil and saline produced water in Alberta. For both types of spills, reported spill volumes were indeed higher on Saturdays and Sundays (web 7.12.3). Spills are reported more frequently on weekdays because companies are catching up on spills not reported on the weekend. Reduced vigilance on the weekend results in a shift towards larger spill volumes.

WHAT CAUSES CRUDE OIL AND SALINE WATER SPILLS?

Anyone concerned about fossil fuel industry spills is likely, at some point, to ask, "why do spills occur?" The regulator keeps track of spills by using eight cause categories, twenty-two cause types, and 101 failure types (web 7.8–7.11). The regulator's spill cause data are a mess. For example, the failure type "internal corrosion" is grouped under fourteen different cause types including those unrelated to internal corrosion such as "accidental," "construction," "contravention," "external corrosion," "non-procedural," and "vandalism." The regulator's spill categories arose over time as *ad hoc* guesses with no clear logic, rules, or data verification. Furthermore, all spills between 1975 and early 2002 lack data for both cause category and cause type. Given the state of the data, can we make some sense of the AER's spill causes? I apologize for the confused results – it's difficult to make sense from nonsense; I can only report what the regulator has recorded.

103

From 2002 to the present, by cause category, equipment failure accounted for 65 per cent of crude oil spills and 74 per cent of saline spills while operator error accounted for 22 per cent of crude oil and 15 per cent of saline spills (web 7.8). These results contrast strongly with a US study of spills at hydraulically fractured wells, which found that operator error was the most common cause of spills (Allison and Mandler 2018a).

The top five spill cause types were common to both crude oil and saline spills: internal corrosion, malfunction, mechanical/structural, accidental, and oversight. The three most frequent failure types were shared by crude oil and saline water spills: internal corrosion, equipment failure, and operator error. Other important failure types for crude oil spills included external corrosion, line failure, stuffing box failure, tank overflow, and valve failure and for saline spills included external corrosion, construction damage, line failure, tank overflow, and valve failure. By volume of crude oil spilled, the top three failure types were equipment failure, operator error, and internal corrosion. By volume of saline water spilled, the top three failure types were internal corrosion, construction damage, and operator error.

OBSERVATIONS ON THE CAUSES OF SPILLS

The regulator's spill causes have been cobbled together over time without logic or standard definitions and without consistent application. Although it is widely known that aging energy infrastructure increases the risk of spills (Sublette et al. 2006), infrastructure age is not part of the AER's FIS database. Many of the spills attributed to internal corrosion and equipment failure are ultimately attributable to the corrosiveness of saline produced water and failure to maintain infrastructure. For something as critical as assigning causes for spills, the regulator's data are remarkably illogical, inconsistent, and incomplete.

Here are five examples that illustrate corrupt data: (a) "Contravention" is not a spill cause. A spill may contravene a law, but a contravention can't cause a spill. (b) The failure type "cumulative release" can't cause a spill. The AER is nonsensically saying that a release is the cause of a release. (c) Of the 101 failure types, one is "equipment failure," but seventy-four other failure types are also kinds of equipment failure. (d) Failure types such as corrosion may be ultimately accounted for by insufficient maintenance, carelessness, or some other form of operator error. (e) The regulator lists "adverse effect" as a spill failure type but defines it as "impairment of or damage to the environment, human health, or safety or property." An adverse effect is by definition an effect not a cause (see web 7.11). But the adverse effect data are illogical at a more fundamental level. In none of the spills for which the AER states there was an adverse effect did the AER state there was an effect on habitat or wildlife.

Recall that Benford analysis detected guessing, rather than measurement, as the source for spill and recovery volumes. In that case, there were only nine discrete possibilities, the numbers 1 through 9, whose statistical distribution could be determined and compared to the Benford distribution. In the case of the causes of spills, we have a different situation: 101 possible failure types, many of which are vague or overlap with other categories and some of which are illogical. Guessing from a poorly defined set of *ad hoc* categories produces random noise. What should be a straightforward summary of the causes of spills becomes an exercise in grasping smoke.

The most important result of the analysis is a sobering one. Despite the importance of understanding why spills occur, the regulator demonstrates its inability to gather meaningful, logical, and consistent data. Study of the regulator's spill causes tells us little about spills. Instead it tells us about a dysfunctional regulatory culture.

SPILL FOOTPRINTS

We conclude this chapter by asking how large an area is impacted by a given spill. Most datasets studied by scientists convey both relevant information, that is, a signal, and irrelevant or random variations, that is, noise. In radio communications, data with a high signal to noise ratio convey clear meaningful sounds such as music with a minimum of garble and static. In science, data with a high signal to noise ratio convey meaningful information and a minimum of inexplicable variation. As we have seen in the case of regulatory data pertaining to spills, there is often a low signal to noise ratio. In many of those cases, the industry-reported data turn the science on its head such that the noise is the important message. The relationship between the volume of spills and the areal footprint of those spills provides another case in point. We examine the data by asking a simple question: if liquid of known volume is released, what is its footprint?

Unfortunately, the Alberta footprint data are not credible (see web 7.13). We can however use the Saskatchewan footprint data. The first clue that the Saskatchewan data contain surprises comes when we plot spill volumes against spill footprints (web 7.13). The diagrams produce a cloud of points clustered in the corner of the plots (like a dust bunny in the corner of a room) known by the felicitous metaphor the "dust bunny distribution" (McCune and Root 2015), a common result when there is a weak relationship between two variables. To build on the metaphor, we can take an MRI of the dust bunny by using a log–log plot. When we do that, we can see that spill footprints increase with increasing spill volumes (figure 7.2 and web 7.13), which is expected, however it's the variation in the relationship that's most significant. A host of factors can influence how widely a spill spreads, such as liquid volume and viscosity, temperature, slope, topography, snow, saturation of the substrate, and soil organic content. But in the Saskatchewan data, for a given spill volume, footprints ranged over an astonishing ten-thousandfold and for a given footprint, spill volumes also ranged over ten-thousandfold. Variation in natural conditions can't explain how a spill of 1 m³ of crude oil could produce footprints ranging from 1 m² to 10,000 m² – it's not possible under real world conditions. Impossibly small spill footprints were also common: of 6,005 saline-crude oil releases of ≥ 10 m³, 404 spills report footprints of 0 m². It's difficult to believe that a spill of at least 10,000 litres would not leave a footprint.

Overall, there were 857 crude oil and/or saline spills with reported footprints of 0 m². Moreover, there's no meaningful relationship between spill volume and the proportion of a spill footprint that flows off industry leases, further evidence that the industry-reported data are not credible (web 7.13). Finally, Saskatchewan saline and crude oil spill volumes and area impacted all fail Benford analysis tests, which reinforces the view that subjective choices rather than measurements produce the values (web 7.14).

If we set aside the extreme variability for a moment, we observe that as spill volumes increase over the range from < 1 m³ to 1,000 m³, concentrations within the spill footprints increase ten- to fiftyfold. A pattern emerges: spill concentrations, expressed as litres per m², increase significantly with increasing spill volumes (web 7.13.3). So, although we can't use the Saskatchewan data to understand the impact of individual spills, a signal emerges from the noise. The larger the spill volume, the larger are both the extent *and* the intensity of the impact. This makes sense in that as a spill disperses horizontally, it also disperses vertically as it seeps into the ground. The larger the spill, the longer it takes for the spill to disperse, which leaves more time for the spill to permeate the substrate rather than spread horizontally.

Figure 7.2 *Opposite* The message in the cloud of data points. Saline water (a), crude oil (b), and combined saline water and crude oil spill volumes (c) in relation to spill footprints for Saskatchewan spills. The reference lines are LOWESS regressions. Thousands of points overlap. The x- and y-axes are log-scaled.

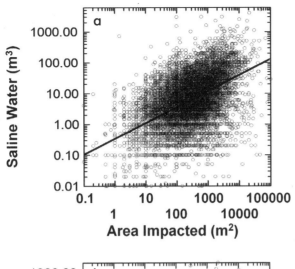

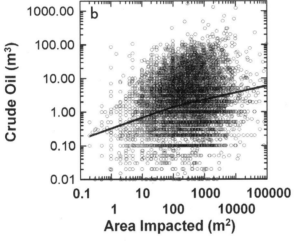

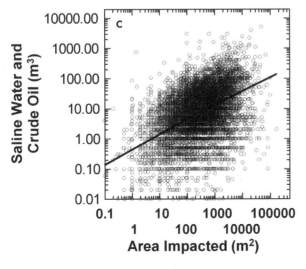

SUMMARY

Industry-reported crude oil and saline spill volume, recovery volume, and recovery efficiency data result from subjective decisions rather than actual measurements. As a result, we don't know how much is being spilled or recovered or remaining in the environment after cleanup.

Relative to a scientifically defensible occurrence map of sensitive areas, the AER grossly misrepresents the occurrence of spills in sensitive areas. The tendency to designate privately owned lands as sensitive more often than public land suggests that nonecological considerations influence decisions about sensitivity. All spills on First Nations reserve lands and within Metis settlements were classified as nonsensitive areas. Land ownership was unknown at more than 10,000 crude oil and saline spills.

As Henry David Thoreau observed, it is better to avoid the beginnings of evil. To do so, we need to prevent spills. Without a clear understanding of the causes of spills, there is little hope of preventing them. Sadly, the AER's spill cause data prove to be subjective choices from an illogical *ad hoc* list, an untenable situation tolerated by a captured regulator. After 75,000 spills, the Alberta regulator's spill cause data provide shockingly little insight into avoiding the beginnings of evil.

Spills of unknown substances and spills by unnamed corporate entities present uncertainty and environmental risk to the public. More often than not, unnamed corporate entities report no recovery of spilled materials. The strongest inference we can draw from the data on the delay between spill and cleanup is that the unrealistically rapid cleanup is too good to be true.

Fewer spills are reported on Saturdays and Sundays and weekend spill volumes tend to be larger than those on weekdays. The data suggest deficiencies in monitoring and reporting.

For a spill of a given volume, the areal impact of spills ranges over tenthousandfold; similarly, for a spill of a given footprint, industry estimates of the spill volumes also range over ten-thousandfold. This extreme variability is not possible in nature. The data don't tell us how individual spills behave in the environment. But when we look at the big picture a pattern emerges: big spills cause both more extensive damage *and* more intensive damage than small spills.

Fossil fuel industry incidents are daily occurrences and have been for decades. Spills, in particular, are more common than the industry and its supporters would have us believe. Despite good intentions, spills occur and their effects linger and spill response can be slow and inadequate. Industry and the regulator continue to experience difficulty in identifying the causes of spills, preventing spills, responding to spills, and communicating truthfully about spills. The public deserves better management, monitoring, and record keeping. Which brings us to the next topic, spills for which there are no records – missing spills.

CHAPTER 8

Exploring the Unknown: Missing Spills

well, I just think it would be good if one of us
maybe stood up and said a few words,
or, so as not to involve the police,
at least quietly wrote something down.

Billy Collins, "Passengers"

INTRODUCTION

Decades ago near my childhood home in New Jersey, a tragic history of industrial pollution and regulatory complicity unfolded. There were many danger signs that seem obvious in retrospect: industrial spills hidden from view, poor oversight, failure to gather credible data, and failure to provide the public with complete and accurate information. A social organization composed of industry, regulators, and politicians united by financial interests excluded the public from participation in protecting their health and the environment. We can choose to learn from that past or repeat the same tragic mistakes.

It's reasonable to expect that a regulator would maintain a complete database of spills. After all, spills present environmental and social risks, and who else can we expect to monitor spills if not the regulator? But such is not the case. No spills that occurred prior to 1975 are included in the regulator's database and many spills that occurred since 1975 are also missing. Many thousands of spills are not monitored by any agency. Missing spills and other covert releases impose unquantifiable threats to ecosystems and to society.

In this chapter we get a glimpse into the unknowns posed by missing spills and abandoned wells. I document some of the missing spills, estimate the number of pre-1975 missing spills, discuss the two largest releases in Canadian history (both missing from the regulator's database), then examine the danger of undocumented releases from abandoned wells.

MISSING SPILLS

Of the nine spills I studied in the fieldwork in northwestern Alberta, four are missing from the regulator's records (Amber, Beaver Pond, BP Zama, and Site B spill sites; see web 2.1–2.7 and 8.1). North of Site B we know that a large spill of crude oil took place in the early 1970s that flowed into a creek known by Dene Tha as "Old Man Creek" (figure 1.2q in web 2.5). The Dene Tha were hired to soak up the crude oil with straw bales; some crude oil was transferred to barrels. Despite the fact that this large oil spill flowed into a creek and required the emergency hiring of local people, there is no record of it in the AER database. Its occurrence would have remained a missing spill without the long memory of local knowledge holders.

Records for thousands of pre-1975 spills are missing from the regulator's data (figure 8.1). The reason for the absence of pre-1975 spills is simple: the regulator did not keep a retrievable record of spills until the mid-1970s. In the official history of the regulator, Jaremko (2013) writes, "In 1970, the ERCB responded swiftly to a rash of oil spills. The blunders included the biggest pipeline leak in Alberta history, which dumped about 50,000 barrels of oil … onto a muskeg bog in the Nipisi area near Lesser Slave Lake. At the time of the disaster, the ERCB only had two employees responsible for pollution control. The bureau created for the role was in its infancy, and formal procedures for reporting and investigating spills were just getting underway." The volume of the Nipisi spill was estimated by Wang et al. (1998) to be 9,539 m³ (60,000 barrels or 3.8 Olympic-sized swimming pools). Another major pre-1975 spill, also unrecorded, is a 6 June 1970 release of an estimated 3,000 m³ of oil (1.2 Olympic-sized swimming pools) from a Suncor pipeline into the Athabasca River and the Peace–Athabasca Delta (Hogge et al. 1970).

Not only are there are no electronic records of pre-1975 spills, there may be no pre-1975 records whatsoever. No one seems to know. There may be miscellaneous accounts of individual spills, but there is certainly no database. To the Old Man Creek, Nipisi, and Athabasca River spills noted above, we can add four pipeline spills of crude oil, an Amoco spill of unspecified volume into Freeman Lake in August 1970, an Amoco spill of 158 m³ into the Freeman River

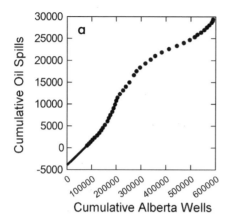
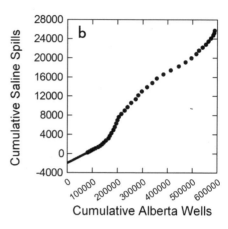

Figure 8.1 Cumulative number of (a) crude oil spills and (b) saline spills in Alberta in relation to cumulative number of licensed wells for the period 1975–2016. The solid line
extrapolates the number of missing spills back to the time of zero wells.

in the Swan Hills in September 1970 (Canadian Press 1970); an Imperial Oil
spill of 4,452 m³ 30 km west of Edmonton in January 1971 (Canadian Press
1972); and a Gulf Alberta spill of 1,113 m³ upstream of Driedmeat Lake near
Camrose in 1973 (*Calgary Herald* 1973; Kheraj 2011). Given that the hydrocarbon industry has been active in Alberta since the early twentieth century, the
lack of pre-1975 records presents a major unknown.

Missing spills are not restricted to pre-1975 incidents. A major spill into the
Athabasca River from a Suncor flare pond took place in February 1982. An Alberta Fish and Wildlife officer noted a cloudy area and then an oily sheen on
the open water and observed "there is no evidence that in the initial period
these increasing rates of emissions into the Athabasca River gave any concern
to the employees of Suncor." The spill, missing from the regulator's records,
caused shutdown of commercial fishing on Lake Athabasca and reportedly
caused illnesses among people in Ft Mackay (Struzik 1982a,b; Alberta Provincial Court 1983).

Even recent well-publicized spills, such as the Plains Midstream crude oil
spill into the Red Deer River in August 2012, are missing. This pipeline release
of 463 m³ of crude oil affected people and businesses along 40 km of river
downstream of the spill and also affected businesses upstream (ERCB 2014).
The regulator stated that the spill impacted wildlife, water, soils, and vegetation
but provided no description of those impacts.

Perhaps the most egregious recent missing spill is "a geyser of fluids and poisonous hydrogen sulphide" that erupted from a CNRL well near Karr Creek, Alberta on 2 May 2016. According to the helicopter pilot and whistleblower, Matthew Linnitt, the release took place when workers failed to properly close a valve (McSheffrey 2019). Linnitt, working alone on site, attempted to access the site's emergency breathing equipment but found that the workers who had improperly sealed the valve had removed the emergency breathing gear. Lacking cellphone service, Linnitt ran from the fumes and waited at a distance until his air monitor told him the sour gas levels had decreased to safe levels. He then had to decide to "report what happened and risk being fired for revealing that CNRL had violated safety protocols, or he could lie to save his job." He falsified the incident report. Then in 2019, Linnitt was no longer able to live with the lie and confessed publicly. He had falsified the Karr Creek incident report "after his initial report, which outlined the missing air packs, triggered a 'call from my foreman informing me that if I did not rewrite the report I would be fired.'" In the immediate wake of the incident, Linnitt had alerted CNRL of the false incident report, but CNRL concluded instead that Linnitt had falsely claimed that his report was false! Later that month, his services were terminated by both CNRL and the helicopter company. CNRL failed to act to address the foreman's threat that led to a false incident report in which people could have been killed by poisonous gas. To make matters worse, if that's possible, although required by regulations, CNRL did not report the release to the AER. Linnitt even contacted the AER directly to report the incident and "made contact with a woman who promised to return his call after determining how to proceed with his complaint. He never heard back from her, and the AER said it has no complaint record for the Karr Creek location on Linnitt's incident report" (McSheffrey 2019). This dangerous release, brought to the attention of the AER by the eyewitness, remains missing from the FIS database; no action was taken by AER against CNRL for failing to report.

It's fair to ask why there are any spills missing from the regulator's database. The regulator can't honestly provide a database of spills to the public without admitting that there are spills missing, which it refuses to do. Unavailability or absence of documentation on contaminated sites can impose environmental, social, and economic liabilities. Lack of timely access to accurate scientific information hampers a government's ability to ensure rational planning, development, and effective management of contaminated sites.

Missing Spills Are Not Unique to Alberta

In 2014, routine pipeline maintenance revealed an unreported underground oil spill on the Trans Mountain pipeline under the Coldwater
Reserve near Merritt, British Columbia (CBC 2018a). The oil spill, of unknown volume, took place in 1968 during pipeline rerouting. The spill
went unreported and undetected for forty-six years during which time
the Antoine family grew crops, raised cattle, and drew water from a well
for their home and farm. Testing at the spill site detected crude oil and
gasoline contamination both in the soil and in the groundwater. One
report noted that all of the contamination may not have been identified.
Another report stated that at least 1,530 m^3 of soil should be removed.
As of 2018, fifty years after the spill and four years after the spill was discovered, the family still waited for remediation and for fair compensation
from Kinder Morgan. The chief of the Coldwater Band, Lee Spahan,
believes that Kinder Morgan has been "trying to keep it quiet" since discovery of the spill four years ago. Looking back over the past four years,
Ms Antoine is not certain she could have done things differently. She
observed, "There's such an imbalance in the power of knowledge … It's
frightening because it feels like I am going to be forced to accept that
nothing gets done."

114

ESTIMATING THE NUMBER OF PRE-1975 SPILLS

Is there any way to estimate the number of pre-1975 spills? By the end of 1974,
there were 76,512 energy wells licensed in Alberta. We can use the relationship
between the cumulative number of wells and the cumulative number of crude
oil and saline spills in Alberta to backcast in time (figure 8.1). A similar relationship between North Dakota oil production volume and the number of
brine spills has been demonstrated (Lauer et al. 2016). Extrapolating back to
zero wells based on the relationships between cumulative number of wells and
cumulative crude oil and saline spills suggests at least 4,000 crude oil spills
and 1,800 saline spills missing from the regulator's database occurred before
1975. By a similar process, we can extrapolate missing spill volumes of 90,000

m³ of crude oil and 100,000 to 150,000 m³ of saline water. These estimates grossly underestimate the true number and volume of missing releases.

Estimating pre-1975 missing spills and missing spill volumes assumes that the relationship between the number of wells and spills has been constant over time. Such an assumption is conservative. Relative to the number of wells, spills and other contaminant releases were more frequent in the early twentieth century than at present. Early practices that released large volumes of contaminants included well production testing, "bringing-in" wells by burning all contaminants on site, continuous and widespread flaring, explosions and fires, improper well abandonment, bulldozing of industrial waste on site, and storage of crude oil in earthen pits (chapter 2). In the early days, oil pipelines were sometimes simply laid unprotected on top of the ground (figure 8.2). The total number and volume of contaminant releases will never be known.

Shockingly, the largest crude oil and saline spills in Canadian history, the 1948 Atlantic No. 3 blowout near Devon, Alberta, and the eighty-seven-year-long release of salt water from "Old Salty" in northwestern Alberta, are missing from the regulator's database. The Atlantic No. 3 spill was a six-month-long "rampage" that released 1.5 million barrels (Jaremko 2013) that ranks among the world's largest inland oil spills. At the time, it was the largest inland well blowout in world history and still ranks among the world's largest releases. Currently, the two largest inland oil spills known are the 1979 Mingbulak blowout in Uzbekistan (2.1 million barrels) and the 1994 Kolva River pipeline spill in Russia (2.0 million barrels). In comparison, the *Exxon Valdez* spill released 0.26 million barrels of crude oil into Prince William Sound, Alaska, in 1989 and is considered one of the most devastating human-caused disasters. It ranks as the second-largest oil spill in United States waters behind the Deepwater Horizon spill of 2010. Yet few people are aware of Alberta's Atlantic No. 3 blowout, a crude oil release six times larger than the *Exxon Valdez* spill, seventy-seven times larger than the Enbridge Kalamazoo River spill, and 2,381 times larger than the Lac Mégantic spill. But all these spills are dwarfed in volume by the saline water released by the Alberta abandoned well known as "Old Salty." It released an estimated 679 million barrels (272,000 Olympic-sized swimming pools; see below), 136 times the volume of the BP Deepwater Horizon spill.

Figure 8.2 Oil production practices in Alberta during the 1940s as shown in *The Story of Oil*. (a) Dumping of crude oil into an underground storage pit excavated in the oil field. (b) Pumping crude oil stored in an aboveground oil pit into a transport truck. (c) An unprotected aboveground crude oil pipeline in southwestern Alberta.

OTHER MISSING SPILLS

Documenting the majority of contaminant releases is not possible for the simple reason that there is little or no available information. Sometimes contaminated sites are discovered during excavation or construction (see web 8.3). The prevalence of undocumented release sites is hinted at in an early documentary by the National Film Board, *The Story of Oil* (NFB 1946), that described production practices in Alberta oil fields during the 1940s. It noted that the absence of pipelines to move crude oil from wells resulted in the need to store crude oil in the field: "The receiving pit may be just a large hole dug in the ground. The pit stores the oil until it is pumped out again to be cleaned or to be sent to the railroad as fuel." Crude oil was stored both below ground and above ground. Where are these pits? Were they ever remediated?

117

As we'll see, undocumented releases from open-air storage of crude oil and hydrocarbon waste continues even today. Similarly, "oil or saltwater staining," which refers to spills where crude oil or some other substance has soaked into the ground, are not necessarily recorded in the spills database (see web 8.2 for unreported spills noted as stains); their total number is unknown (also see web 6.19).

The regulator's database does not include spills from interprovincial pipelines (see chapter 15). Although spill rates in interprovincial pipelines are dwarfed by those in provincial pipelines, the historian Sean Kheraj (2011) wrote that by January 1975, a rash of Interprovincial Pipeline Company oil spills in the main pipeline running east from Alberta caused Alberta Environment Minister Bill Yurko to commission a report. The *Regina Leader-Post* reported that this pipeline failed repeatedly between 1973 and 1975 resulting in a total reported spill volume of 18,939 m³ between Alberta and Minnesota.

Nor can we turn to the Canadian federal contaminated sites registry. The contaminated sites registry apparently tracks contaminants only if sites are under federal jurisdiction. Nor does the regulator's database include spills, licensed wastewater discharge, and other releases reported to Alberta Environment arising from bitumen production. In the bitumen sands region alone, we documented 1,432 reported incidents of land, surface water, or groundwater contamination for the period 1996–2012 (Timoney and Lee 2013), none of which are in the AER's records. For the reader who needs proof of this fact, I provide forty-four examples in web 8.3. Moreover, there are only five Alberta Environment records of releases in northeastern Alberta prior to 1996, simply because no records were kept (see web 8.3 for examples). Nor are tailings spills from the bitumen sands region adequately monitored by the AER. In spite of thousands of releases of toxic tailings since the mid-1960s, the earliest record of tailings releases reported by the AER dates from 2014.

Hydrocarbon spills from railroad cars and federal pipelines are tracked by the Transportation Safety Board of Canada and/or the Canada Energy Regulator (formerly the National Energy Board). Despite the fact that Canada's interprovincial pipelines have operated since the early 1950s, incident data don't exist prior to 1961, and readily available data begin only in 2008 (Kheraj 2019). Moreover, the federal data are industry-reported and are inadequate to assess both the causes and the environmental consequences of interprovincial pipeline incidents in Canada (Belvederesi et al. 2017). It's another case of the appearance of monitoring without the substance. Some railway spills, such as the derailments at Lake Wabamun, Alberta, and Lac Mégantic, Quebec, have had major environmental and social consequences. Railway car spills remain common and spill large volumes of crude oil that sometimes cause toxic infernos (plate 8.1). Shockingly, two large crude oil spills from Canadian Pacific trains, both of which were followed by major fires, recently took place within ten kilometres of each other near Guernsey, Saskatchewan, one on 9 December 2019 and one on 6 February 2020 (Shield 2019, 2020). In the December spill, some of the CP Rail crude oil containers were retrofitted TC-117 tank cars, which have added safety features absent from the DOT-111 tank cars involved in the 2013 Lac Mégantic disaster. In the February spill, TC-117J tank cars with improved thermal protection and thicker steel were involved (Smith 2020). The recent spills indicate that the safety improvements to crude oil tank cars are insufficient to prevent tank ruptures and subsequent spills and fires. Spills by transport trucks are also common and are not tracked by any single agency (plate 8.2).

To make matters worse, the vast majority of spills are not monitored adequately or not monitored at all. These include spills at refineries, gas stations, airports, RCMP stations, marinas, railyards, industrial sites, at farms, and by the public and, especially in the north, at fuel caches, airstrips, fire attack bases, fly-in fishing camps, mining camps, weather stations, and Distant Early Warning sites. Release of hydrocarbons from outboard motors, especially from 2-stroke engines, has been a major source of water pollution for decades. Hydrocarbon leaks at bulk storage facilities represent another major source of contamination. In the United States, above ground storage tanks were once bottomless, which allowed product to seep into the subsoil (Testa and Jacobs 2014; see figure 8.2). Later, storage tanks were constructed with single steel bottoms that would corrode and leak. Present leak containment systems at bulk storage sites are greatly improved. Abandoned gas stations exist in almost every community in North America and often remain unremediated as vacant lots because the cost of cleanup exceeds the value of the land and governments seldom have the power or will to enjoin responsible parties to remediate the contamination. In short, our lives are immersed in a vast network of contaminated sites, most of which are invisible. For the most part, they exist not out of malice or negligence but simply because hydrocarbons are toxic and spill readily.

The total number of spills and contaminated sites will never be known. Worryingly, wherever study is conducted, more sites are identified than would be assumed from the public record. At least 1,766 contaminated sites exist in Calgary (Anderson 2017) and at least 210 contaminated sites exist near the town of Swan Hills (Dance et al. 2015). It's challenging to document spills for which there are no public records. Eyewitnesses are needed, such as in the spills observed by the Dene Tha at Old Man Creek, Beaver Pond, and Amber. But eyewitnesses are scarce and those willing to go on record are scarcer.

THE ATLANTIC NO. 3 BLOWOUT

The Atlantic No. 3 blowout, the largest crude oil spill in Canadian history (figure 8.3a), began on 8 March 1948 near Devon, Alberta. This is its story.

An unsafe practice known as drilling "blind and dry" (continuing drilling even though drilling mud is not recirculating back to the surface to control downhole pressure) was the reported cause (MacInnes 2017). Crude oil and natural gas from the blowout flowed north from the well, not south (we'll return to that point later), and formed a lake of oil and bubbling gas covering about sixteen hectares. Soon afterward, ten to fifteen thousand barrels of oil per day were reportedly being recovered (Stewart 1988); some parties profited handsomely from the disaster. Frank McMahon, who acquired the lease under questionable circumstances, and whose company was responsible for the disaster, became a millionaire as a result of the blowout, which increased the flow of oil to the surface to many times that of a normal well (Stewart 1988).

Six months after the blowout began, on 6 September, the derrick, undermined by craters of bubbling oil and gas, collapsed. A spark ignited the lake of hydrocarbons into a growing conflagration, the likes of which Canadians had never seen (figures 8.3 b and c). A CBC reporter was dispatched in an aircraft to report on the fire visible from Edmonton. As he flew around the towering column of flames and black smoke, he observed, "It's the worst oil fire I've ever seen. This brings back memories of the bombing of Berlin" (Stewart 1988). The fire was extinguished two days later after pumping great volumes of water from the North Saskatchewan River down a relief well. The well was finally brought under control several months after the fire when "Moroney suppositories" were forced down the well bore (Stewart 1988). The spill released an estimated 1.5 million barrels of crude oil (Jaremko 2013). The infamous *Exxon Valdez* spill released one-sixth the volume released by Atlantic No. 3. The largest known accidental oil spill in history, the BP Deepwater Horizon spill, released an estimated five million barrels.

Aspects of the disaster as related by the regulator (Jaremko 2013) bear repeating:

> Only 1.6 kilometres east of the 1947 Leduc discovery, a blowout at the 1948 Atlantic No. 3 follow-up well called global attention to the large scale of Alberta's new found wealth. The spill turned a farm field into a flaming mini-lake under a mushroom cloud of black smoke. The spectacle went around the world on newspaper front pages and movie theatre newsreels
>
> …
>
> It was Alberta's most spectacular blowout – and just 40 kilometres southwest of downtown Edmonton, within easy reach of news media and motion picture crews. The six-month rampage generated a well-recorded cavalcade of follies. McMahon's Atlantic Oil Co. tried to stop runaway oil flows of 15,000 barrels per day by stuffing a comic array of materials into the hole in the theory that they would swell and congeal into a plug: 10,000 bags of cement, carloads of ping-pong balls, [1.5 tonnes of] chicken feathers, and cotton seed [hulls]. A worker blew up a gas-filled outhouse by ducking inside for a forbidden cigarette; he survived a 60-metre flight in the rocketing biffy, but earned an unprintable nickname for life. After flooding a 40-acre crop field with 1.5 million barrels of oil, the spill caught fire. An 800-foot pillar of flame sent a mushroom cloud of smoke 7,000 feet into the sky for 60 hours, making Alberta famous – and catching investors' eyes with images on newspaper front pages and in movie theatre newsreels around the world …

Figure 8.3 Atlantic No. 3 blowout, 1948. (a) Ground level view near the rig covered in craters of bubbling oil and gas. Human in white circle for scale. Craters bubbled with oil and gas for six months until the blowout caught fire in September 1948. (b, c) Aerial views of the blowout after it caught fire, six months after the blowout began. Compare with figure 8.4 and plate 8.3.

The ERCB took over control of the site, supervised industry wild-well taming and cleanup crews, and made the company responsible for the mess cover its costs out of proceeds from selling recovered oil. The site grows organic crops today.

An AER website (resource.aer.ca, MacInnes 2017) provides further telling observations:

> [The resulting inferno] soon caught the eye of news media and many others around the world. More than anyone [*sic*] else, images of the towering inferno sent a clear and convincing message to global investors: Alberta was indeed an oil province. When video reels of the fire hit theatres everywhere, from New York to Paris, that's when the international money started flooding in ... Even today, Atlantic No. 3 is credited with bringing international attention to Alberta's energy industry. It reportedly brought $40 million of free publicity into the province ... One year after the disaster, the land was levelled and seeded. Three more years passed and grain was planted just south of the well site, where it continues to grow.

Interestingly, the site in the "2005 After" photograph in the regulator's history (MacInnes 2017), meant to depict the well site fifty-seven years after the blowout, is not of the well site; it's a photo of an area about 620 m northwest of the well site.

The regulator's version of the history would have benefitted from fact checking. As to the view that the regulator made the company responsible for the blowout pay for the cleanup, we learn (Alberta Oil 2010) that on 26 January 1949, representatives from eleven producing companies in the Leduc oil field met with the regulator chairman "to decide how money collected from the sale of oil recovered from the Atlantic blowout would be divvied up, and to decide what – if any – penalty should be applied to Frank McMahon's Atlantic Oil Co." Soon afterward, on 29 March 1949, the Alberta government passed the Atlantic Claims Act which prevented anyone from taking legal action against the Atlantic Oil Company or the regulator without prior written consent from Alberta's attorney general. These are not the actions of an independent regulator protecting the public interest.

As to the regulator taking control over the blowout, we are not told that two months elapsed between the blowout and the regulator taking control when it handed the operation to V.J. Tip Moroney (Kerr 1986). From Kerr's account we learn,

> After the Board, as Trustee, had paid all its bills, it still had $1,000,000 from crude revenue which it handed over to Frank McMahon in early 1949. That's how Frank was able to start on his way to building a gas pipeline from northeast B.C. to northwest U.S.A. And the Rebus lessors? They had collected huge royalty revenues up until the Board took over. Neither they nor Frank had been in any hurry to kill the well [i.e., stop the blowout], but the bald facts are that without Moroney in charge, the entire reservoir could conceivably have been depleted with unbelievable losses.

123

The regulator's story of the employee who rocketed sixty metres into the air in a flying biffy is fiction. It doesn't require a degree in physics to realize that an explosion that hurled an employee sixty metres into the air would be fatal. An eyewitness observed that the corrugated metal walls of the outhouse were blown off, but the employee remained seated and suffered only minor burns (Stewart 1988). Playing loose with the facts characterizes much of the regulator's incident reporting. The largest crude oil disaster in Canadian history shouldn't serve as fodder for jokes.

The official history of the disaster also fails to relate the confrontation between Imperial Oil and local people (Stewart 1988). The company had decided to construct a pipeline through the local cemetery to carry the oil from the blowout. When word got out, a priest accompanied by local farmers armed with shovels, picks, axes, and pitchforks confronted Imperial Oil at the cemetery. The Imperial Oil representative recalled, "They were weapons to be used to make sure nobody came on that graveyard." The message was clear: you will not build a pipeline through the graves of our family members. Imperial relented and routed the pipeline to avoid the cemetery. This tableau, part of the history of Alberta's largest crude oil disaster, demonstrates what can happen when people act together when they possess information about a clear and present danger. The story of local people rising up to stop a pipeline is not a narrative that the regulator, the industry, and its allies in government want to communicate to the public.

Officially, the disaster is portrayed as a spectacular event that provided millions of dollars in free publicity and an advertisement to energy investors, an event in which the regulator took charge and put regulations in place to prevent future blowouts. Readers of "Alberta Energy History Prior to 1970" (Alberta Energy 2018) will find no mention of the Atlantic No. 3 blowout. Its 1948 entry notes the drilling of the Imperial Leduc No. 2 well but fails to mention the blowout at the adjacent No. 3 well. Think about that. The largest inland oil well blowout in Canadian history is left out of "Alberta Energy History" by Alberta Energy.

The happy story in which the land was reclaimed within three years and now grows organic crops is fiction. No organic crops are grown on the soils subjected to the crude oil spill. Furthermore, the land noted by the regulator as being reclaimed within three years of the blowout south of the well would be irrelevant even if it were true because the oil accumulated north, not south, of the well. And still further, fifty years after the disaster, the local landowner, J.A. Rebus, told researchers (Roy and McGill 1998) that large patches of damaged, nonwettable soil had existed for decades and that this soil had not been tilled, seeded, or fertilized for most of the past thirty years, maybe longer. The Glenbow Museum Archives stated that the surrounding farmland remained unusable fifty years after the incident (Alberta Culture and Tourism 2018). The area is now a registered Alberta historic site described as a twenty-three hectare parcel of land composed of dormant fields seeded to grass. The website description on the historic site states, "The scars of Alberta's greatest oilfield disaster are still evident in the bald patches in the seeded field" (HERMIS, n.d.).

What of the ecological effects? The soil at the Atlantic No. 3 site was studied by Roy and McGill (1998). Writing fifty years after the blowout, they observed that substantial amounts of oil had percolated into the subsoil. The soil had become severely water-repellent and its structure had broken down. The soil in 1998 still contained significant amounts of oil, 6,500 mg of residual oil per kg of soil. The areal extent of the impaired soil appeared to be expanding over time.

In July 2018, I visited the Atlantic No. 3 site to determine if the ecological effects persist. Bare soil patches and stressed vegetation attest to the long-term effects at the Atlantic No. 3 site (figure 8.4). Seventy years after the disaster, the effects of the blowout are evident. Patches of barren soil are the most obvious signs (plate 8.3a). Below the loose powdery surface layer, the soil is a compact,

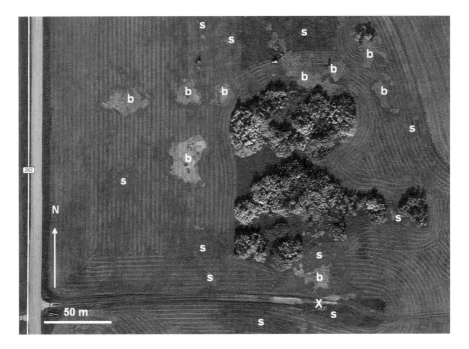

Figure 8.4 Soil and vegetation damage persists seventy years after the Atlantic No. 3 blowout evident in the bare soil patches (b) and the discoloured stressed vegetation (s) in the seeded hayfield that surrounds the aspen grove. A white X marks the approximate location of the former Atlantic No. 3 well. Study of satellite images revealed the consistent presence of soil damage over the years. 29 September 2015.

platy hardpan (plate 8.3b). Readers knowledgeable about soils might be shocked to learn this soil, once a fertile Black Chernozem, has been degraded to a Regosol. A plant community of exotic species borders the barren patches. The exotics smooth brome, common dandelion, Canada thistle, quack grass, and lamb's quarters, along with mats of the pollution-tolerant cyanobacterium *Nostoc* and colonies of purple horn-toothed moss (*Ceratodon purpureus*, a worldwide indicator of disturbance and sterile soils, plate 8.3c and d) form the impaired plant community. Aspens in the grove at the centre of the site are stressed and stunted (plate 8.3e); the understory of the grove is dominated by smooth brome.

In updating the history of Atlantic No. 3 to 2018, I contacted a member of a historical society who, I was told, knew a great deal about the blowout. The most interesting point he made was not about the blowout but about how fossil fuel industry history is portrayed. He began by asking me why I wanted to know about Atlantic No. 3, then said he would help me as long as I did not write anything negative about the industry. There, in a nutshell, is the problem. If as a prerequisite for assistance, we have to tell a favourable story, we engage in information distortion.

The scarcity of available environmental information and the public's lack of awareness of the disaster are not coincidental. If information can't be found, it's as if incidents don't happen. It would be useful to know how much crude oil was recovered and how much was left in the ground. Was contaminated soil removed? What volume of crude oil was dispersed in the air to settle over the countryside? One account stated that crude oil mist dispersed as much as five kilometres from the blowout. What volume of oil burned in the inferno? How many animals died? The one truly fortunate aspect of the disaster is that the hydrocarbon was sweet crude oil. Had it contained appreciable amounts of hydrogen sulphide or saline water, the impacts would have been worse.

Although the Atlantic No. 3 disaster is interesting, how the history has been portrayed is of equal significance. The narrative is analogous to telling the story of the *Exxon Valdez* disaster as a successful marketing campaign by Exxon. The regulator's narrative of the disaster lacks discussion, or even recognition, of the environmental impact of the disaster. Instead, Atlantic No. 3 is portrayed as an "attention grabber" that made Alberta "famous" (Jaremko 2013). The regulator's self-laudatory and self-exculpatory version of history plays loose with the facts and distracts with apocryphal stories, telling us about a flying biffy, successful reclamation, and organic crops. The history has been subjected to a dizzying amount of spin. As the agency responsible for the disaster, the energy regulator presents a distorted version of events that places its activities in a favourable light. We'll examine how the regulator and its allies systematically distort information in chapters 15 and 16.

Seventy years after the event, the soils and vegetation remain impaired; Atlantic No. 3 is a toxic waste site. In the United States, Atlantic No. 3 would be a Superfund Site. In Alberta, it's a historic site. The Atlantic No. 3 blowout raises a cautionary note to which we'll return in later chapters. Those in power control the information that writes history and shapes our opinions. To control history is to control the future. Truthful, accessible, and complete environmental information is necessary for democracy to survive.

OLD SALTY

The history of Peace River Oils #1 well (known to the industry as "Old Salty," "The Well from Hell," and "The World's Longest Blowout") illustrates several salient properties of a captured regulator: chronic pollution tolerated by government and the regulator, covert contaminant releases, undocumented impacts, major spills missing from the regulator's database, and underreporting of spill volumes.

Peace River Oils # 1 (PRO1) was drilled in 1916 in an attempt to exploit hydrocarbon reserves (figure 8.5). Unlike most other early twentieth century wells drilled in the area which were reportedly abandoned successfully in the mid-1950s, PRO1 continued uncontrolled discharge until 2003. The regulator attempted to cap the well but was unsuccessful. During one of those attempts, saline produced water was released onto adjacent cropland. The spill from that attempt was apparently recorded as FIS incident 19880874, a release of 10,000 m³ saline water (zero recovery) and one million m³ of sour raw production gas (zero recovery). Although this 1988 release was large, it represents a tiny fraction of the total contaminant release from PRO1.

Peace River Oils did not strike oil at PRO1; instead, it perforated a high-pressure saline aquifer. The expulsion of water and raw production gas was so great that a crater formed and "swallowed" the drilling rig. The crater then acted as a high discharge saline spring. The company attempted to stop the well blowout several times but gave up and left. By 1954, perhaps earlier, responsibility for capping the well had passed to the regulator. In 1955, the regulator attempted to cap the well but concluded that it lacked the technology. In 1982, when PRO1 lay at the bottom of an 8 m deep crater, a second relief well was drilled but still failed to staunch the flow. Workers observed that the pressure at the well was so great that bowling ball-sized rocks shot out of the hole like bullets (Weber 2003).

In 1988, seventy-two years after the discharge began, it was discovered that the produced water contained hydrogen sulphide. How could that happen? How could seventy-two years pass before someone in authority noticed that the discharge contained poisonous sour gas? Frustrated local people asked how a regulator responsible for preventing pollution, and that was legally responsible for the well, could allow the pollution to continue for decades. In 2001, after complaints were filed, Environment Canada became involved (a rare intervention) and ordered the regulator to cap the well.

The discharge of saline water at the wellhead was estimated at 30–50 L/sec (Alberta Environment 1989). To place the immensity of this release in context, consider that a discharge of 40 L/sec releases 1.26 million m³/year, or 30 *Exxon Valdez* disasters each year. Alberta Environment (1989) conducted the only publicly available study of the impacts. The study was undertaken in response to a request from the regulator, which was in turn a response to complaints. It summarized the situation by stating the well is located about 20 km downstream of Peace River [townsite] and discharges thirty to fifty litres per second of salt water into the Peace River. It noted that natural gas containing 1 per cent toxic hydrogen sulphide escapes in sufficient amounts to support a continuous flame at the wellhead and that the salt water flows to the river under pressure and may enter the river in other places such as in a backwater one quarter mile away from the well. Salt water may also have contaminated the Quaternary deposits, which are a major aquifer in the area. At the average sodium chloride content at the well head, PRO1 discharged 37,000 tonnes of sodium chloride each year. It was pure dumb luck that Old Salty discharged directly into the Peace River. At the average Peace River discharge there, the river diluted the effluent from PRO1 by an average of about 46,000 times. By sheer good fortune, the toxic saline discharge was diluted and carried by a riverine super-highway downstream to the Mackenzie River and then out to the Beaufort Sea.

During the 1988 and 1989 fieldwork, water, soil, and air quality data were gathered at PRO1, the domestic well on the Nixon property, and the Peace River. PRO1 discharge contained sodium, chloride, and total dissolved solid concentrations similar to those of seawater and moderate to high concentrations of barium, boron, lithium, strontium, ammonia, hydrogen sulphide, and hydrocarbons. The concentrations for dissolved chloride and sodium are the highest on record in Alberta Environment's surface water quality data for the Peace River watershed. The hydrocarbons (0.3 to 31 mg/L) included weathered crude oil, chloroform, benzene, phenol, other phenolic compounds, and PAHs. Concentrations of several constituents exceeded environmental guidelines for irrigation of agricultural land and for protection of aquatic life. Toxicity tests demonstrated that PRO1 discharge was "extremely toxic." In the Peace River, invertebrates 100 m downstream of PRO1 were less diverse and abundant than invertebrates 100 m upstream of PRO1.

Within a 60 m radius of the well, hourly average hydrogen sulphide concentrations ranged from two to twenty-two times higher than hourly air

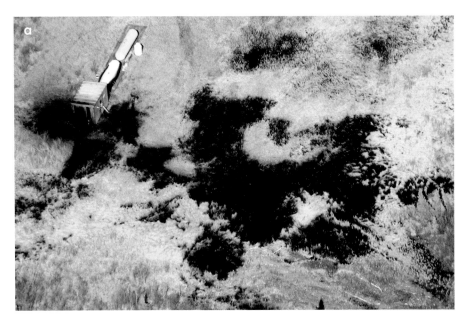

Plate 3.1 What do inland spills look like? (a) The 2012 Pace-Spyglass crude oil spill in northwestern Alberta soon after it occurred. The crude oil continued to spread through the bog-fen wetland. (b) The 2013 Apache saline spill in northwestern Alberta some weeks after it was discovered. Note the dead and dying trees. The white ellipse indicates the source of the spill. Later, the wetland was replaced by an excavated pond with persistent salinity.

Plate 3.1 *continued.* What do inland spills look like? (c) Part of the area affected by the 1948 Atlantic No. 3 blowout near Devon, Alberta, seventy years after it occurred. Barren, water-repellent soil patches have been evident for decades. 23 July 2018. (d) This spill site near Bruderheim, Alberta, received at least two spills (1993, 2006), both containing saline produced water and crude oil. The heavily impacted site, inspected in 2018 and 2019, is primarily barren soil with scattered Nuttall's salt-meadow grass and common dandelion. Some of the barren soil is hardpan that fragments into flakes when struck with a tool much like the water-repellent soil at the Atlantic No. 3 site. 5 August 2018. See also plate 8.3b.

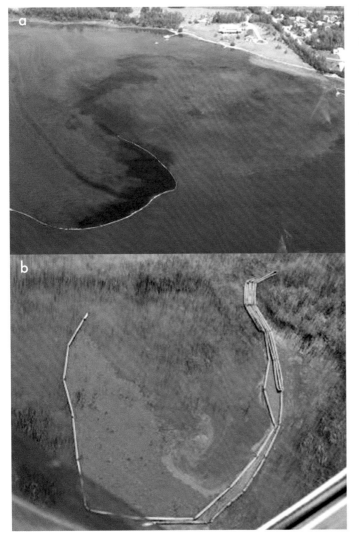

Plate 4.1 *Above* The soil and living community at this fifty-year-old saline spill in northwestern North Dakota have been permanently damaged.

Plate 4.2 *Left and following page* Wabamun Lake oil spill. (a) Three days after the spill, the poorly secured oil containment booms were unmoored during a storm. Here we see them drifting and releasing oil near Ascot Beach (6 August 2005). (b) Oil spread across the lake to foul portions of the south shore. Here we see an unmoored and folded boom lodged along the south shore (9 August). (c) Although the railway had been cleared and trains were running again, oil continued to flow into Lake Wabamun at Whitewood Sands (black arrow, 6 August).

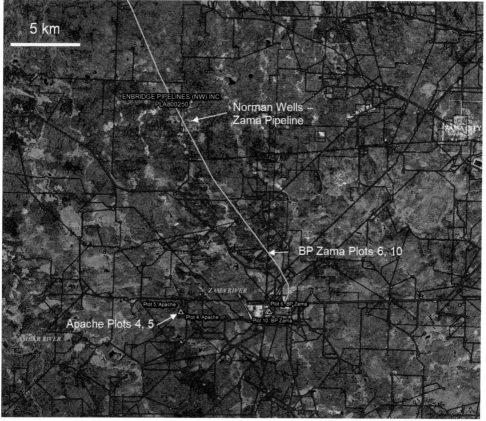

Plate 5.1 Linear disturbances near the southern terminus of the Norman Wells–Zama Pipeline (blue-green, an interprovincial pipeline built in 1985) in relation to the BP Zama and Apache spill plots (chapters 9, 10). The vegetation and soils overlying the extensive fossil fuel industry infrastructure (shown in red) differ markedly from those of native communities.

Plate 8.1 Derailments of trains transporting oil. (a) Derailment of a Canadian Pacific freight train on 9 December 2019 near Guernsey, Saskatchewan involved thirty-three oil tank cars and one hopper car, release of about 1,500 m³ of crude oil, and a major fire that burned for more than a day. Unburned oil soaked into the ground. Canadian Pacific did not believe that local waterways had been affected and stated that the area would be cleaned up and restored. (b) Ten km from that derailment and fire, on 6 February 2020, another CP crude oil train derailment involved thirty-one cars, a dozen of which caught fire, which caused a spill of 1,200 m³ of crude oil and another toxic fire that required evacuation of eighty-five people. An eyewitness stated the fire "looks like an inferno ... Like a war zone" (Shield 2020, Smith 2020).

Plate 8.2 A tanker truck crash on 16 November 2019 on the Pouce Coupe River Bridge near Dawson Creek, British Columbia spilled 40 m³ of crude oil. About 75 per cent of the oil burned in the ensuing fire while the remainder flowed onto the land and into the river (Canadian Press 2019a). The impacts of thousands of tanker truck spills have not been determined.

a

Plate 8.3 *Opposite and this page*
Ecological damage persists at the
Atlantic No. 3 site, seventy years
after the blowout. (a) One of many
barren water repellent areas. (b)
Water repellent degraded soil in a
hardened barren soil patch. When
struck with a tool, the soil shatters
into flakes and chunks. (c) Exotic
Canada thistle on the edge of a
barren soil patch. (d) A moss community of the disturbance indicator
Ceratodon purpureus. (e) Stunted
and stressed aspen trees in the
central grove. 23 July 2018.

Plate 9.1 *Top* Wood bison tracks filled with crude oil are common in the contaminated soil at the Amber site. 20 July 2016.

Plate 9.2 *Bottom* The oil waste pit at the Pace-Spyglass site more than four years after the spill and after the AER had classified the site as cleaned up. There are no wildlife deterrents at this pit. Contaminated waste pits with no wildlife deterrents pose a chronic threat to wildlife (Trail 2006; Ramirez 2010, 2013). 22 July 2016.

Plate 9.3 *Top* Four years after clean up, oil floats on the water surface (white arrows) in the disturbed marsh habitat at the Pace-Spyglass spill. The contaminated wetland poses a danger to migratory and resident wildlife. There are no wildlife deterrents. 22 July 2016.

Plate 9.4 *Bottom* In summer 2016, the excavated pond at the Apache 15-09 spill was essentially devoid of visible invertebrates, algae, waterfowl, and aquatic plants. Near the plot, only one small vascular plant (probably bur-reed), one backswimmer (Notonectidae), and a few blue damselfly adults were observed. This pond was created when the contaminated bog-fen was excavated during clean up. 21 July 2016.

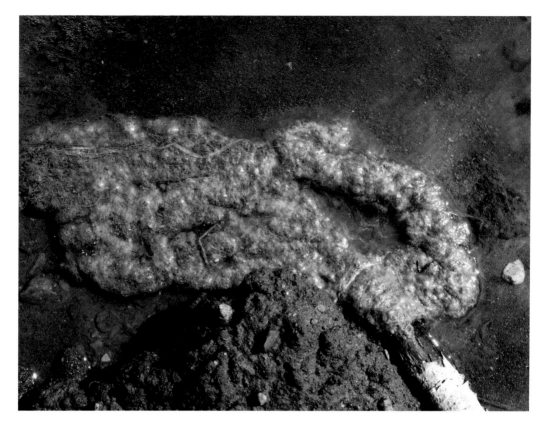

Plate 9.5 One of many blue-green algal (cyanobacterial) mats along the shore of Apache pond 15-09. Cyanobacteria were the dominant biota. See the Postscript following chapter 18 for later observations of this area.

Plate 10.1 The Amber oil spill site. Alsike clover, common horsetail, reed canary grass, smooth perennial sow-thistle, fowl bluegrass, and scentless chamomile tolerate soil highly contaminated with crude oil. 20 July 2016.

Plate 10.2 Knotweed (*Polygonum monspeliense*) growing in Plot 4 at the 15-09 Apache saline spill. This species is characteristic of hard, parched, or "waste soil." 21 July 2016.

Plate 10.3 The abundance of Nuttall's salt-meadow grass at the 11-26 Apache2 saline spill site indicates that salts remain in the soil. Other indicators of degraded or disturbed soil conditions here include alsike clover, common plantain, smooth perennial sow-thistle, and common horsetail. This site was remediated to a standard meeting or exceeding that required by the regulator. 21 July 2016.

Plate 10.4 Natural control and crude oil spill plots in 2012, seventy years after spills. (a) erect deciduous shrub tundra; (b) decumbent shrub tundra

Plate 10.4 *continued* (c) sedge meadow tundra, control; (d) sedge meadow tundra oil spill. Note the loss of woody vegetation at the spill sites. The contrast in vegetation between oil spills and adjacent controls seventy years after the spills is striking.

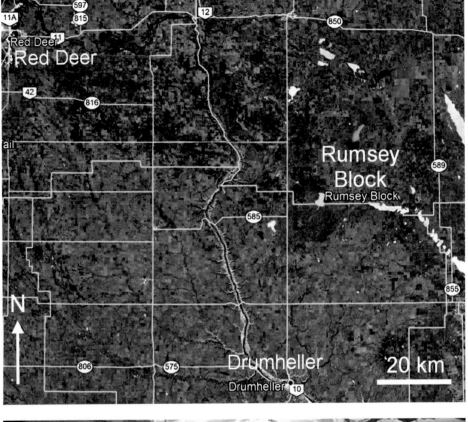

Plate 11.1 Aerial view of the Pace-Spyglass oil spill during clean up in summer 2012. The bluish-black liquid is a mixture of crude oil and water. The injection well source of the spill is indicated by the black ellipse. A water truck is circled in red for scale.

Plate 10.5 *Opposite top* The Rumsey Block, located about 48 km NNE of Drumheller in south-central Alberta, contains the world's largest intact example of native aspen parkland – plains rough fescue landscape.

Plate 10.6 *Opposite bottom* This spectacular biodiverse patterned salt marsh in the Lobstick Creek area of Wood Buffalo National Park is one of many saline communities that are absent from industrially salinized landscapes. Rare and endangered whooping cranes nest in this wetland. For a description of this and other natural saline plant communities, see Timoney (2015). 10 August 2001.

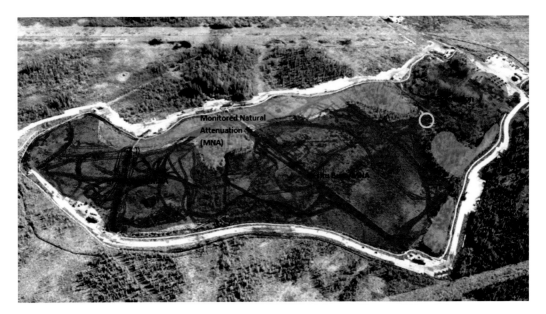

Plate 11.2 *Top* The excavation area (brown), *in situ* burn (red), and monitored natural attenuation (green) areas according to the burn plan. Plot 8 (established in 2016) is located at the turquoise circle. The excavated area is now a contaminated marsh.

Plate 11.3 *Bottom* Aerial view from 2012 showing where Plot 8 (white ellipse) was established four years after the spill. The bluish-black liquid is a mixture of crude oil and water. The circular reddish objects are inflatable tanks used to contain oil.

Plate 11.4 Oil had escaped the containment booms and persisted in water and soil four years after cleanup. This is not an iron-bacteria sheen; it's crude oil. Plot 8, 21 June 2016.

Plate 11.5 The source of the spill. (a) Ground view of the sedge fen at the spill site on the date of spill detection, 19 May 2012. (b) Aerial view of the injection well and spill, 19 May 2012. The well was located in the shack (later removed during cleanup operations).

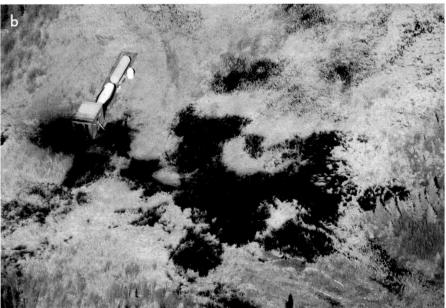

Plate 11.6 *Top* The spill on 20 May 2012. The well is circled. Dark areas within the polygon are a mixture of crude oil and water.

Plate 11.7 *Bottom* The spill on 24 May 2012. The black liquid is a mixture of crude oil and surface water.

Plate 11.9 A pied-billed grebe coated with crude oil after landing in a waste oil pit similar to the pits at the Pace-Spyglass and Amber spills.

Plate 11.8 *Opposite* Ineffective wildlife deterrents. The AER accepts wildlife deterrents known to be ineffective. (a) A plastic snow fence surrounds the well head source of the oil spill (the shack has been removed). (b) Bald eagle and owl effigies. (c) Plastic snow fence and car lot pennants over oil-contaminated water. (d) Skimming of spilled crude oil and a plastic snow fence and pennants intended to deter wildlife. See plate 11.9.

Plate 12.2 The oil waste pit at the Amber site presents a chronic hazard to wildlife. There are no wildlife deterrents nor is there wildlife monitoring. See web 8.2 for incidents and other records. 20 July 2016.

Plate 12.1 *Opposite* (a) The bog-fen at the Pace-Spyglass spill site has been replaced by a contaminated marsh of disturbance-adapted and pollution-tolerant graminoids. (b) Open water supports an unusual assemblage of algae and cyanobacteria. Scientific study of this assemblage would shed light on ecosystem response to oil pollution in a boreal peatland. 22 July 2016.

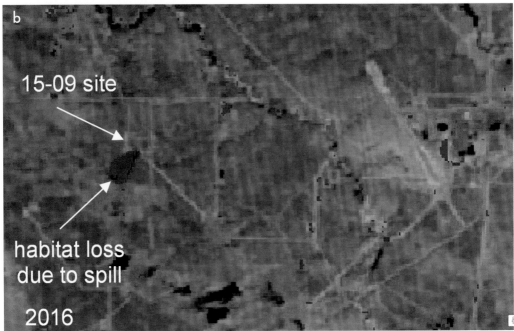

Plate 12.3 Apache 15-09 spill. (a) The heavily impacted industrial landscape near the Apache 15-09 well site prior to the spill, circa 2005. (b) Forest loss in the area receiving the saline spill (red area) was detected by the Global Forest Change program. Other red areas are also recent forest losses. Magenta and olive hued areas in this 2016 Landsat image are industrially disturbed landscape.

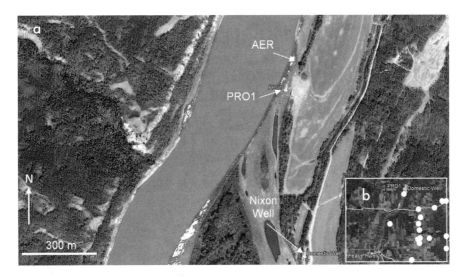

Figure 8.5 Aerial views of PRO1. (a) Location of PRO1 ("Old Salty") on the east bank of the Peace River, three years after being capped, and the Nixon domestic water well 750 m to the south. Note the AER's incorrect location for PRO1 (AER), misplaced 150 m NE of the true location. (b) PRO1 in relation to the town of Peace River (TPR) and other AER FIS spills in the area (white dots). 3 May 2006.

quality guidelines (Alberta Environment 1989). The Nixon's domestic well, 750 m south of PRO1 (figure 8.5), contained phenols, high concentrations of chloride, and heavy hydrocarbons whose fingerprint matched those from PRO1. Toxicity tests indicated that the domestic well was "extremely toxic." Croplands north and south of the well exhibited poor growth or no growth at all. Vegetation effects were associated with a soil that was high in chloride, sodium, and electrical conductivity and that smelled of sour gas. Radioactivity in the soil around the well was elevated ten times above normal due to discharge of the radioactive groundwater (Weber 2003).

The location of PRO1, at the water's edge of the Peace River, was simultaneously the worst and best possible location. It was the worst location because it meant that most of the effluent flowed immediately into the Peace River. During flood stages of the Peace River, PRO1 was submerged. It was the best location for the same reason because the Peace River has, by far, the greatest dilution power of any river in Alberta. Despite the dilution, Alberta Environment water quality measurements taken in summer during high river discharge detected the effluent plume 30 km downstream. The effluent plume would have been detectable much farther downstream during winter when

Peace River discharge fell to as low as 14 per cent of the mean discharge and 4 per cent of peak discharge, but there are no winter data.

Several lessons can be learned from "Old Salty." The history illustrates the danger posed by poor monitoring and regulatory failure. Few people were aware of the hidden contaminant releases – they were out of sight at an isolated location in the Peace River valley, similar to the dumping of industrial wastes in the rural Pine Barrens of New Jersey. Given that only one publicly available impact study was ever conducted, the full extent of the impact of eighty-seven years of uncontrolled discharge will never be known. Nor will we ever know the total volume of saline water spilled by the fossil fuel industry since its inception. What is certain is that the AER's total reported spill volume represents a small fraction of the actual volume released. At "Old Salty" release of immense volumes of contaminated water and toxic raw production gas continued for eighty-seven years with the full knowledge of government and various regulators.

The history of PRO1 lays to rest any claim that Alberta's energy regulators are effective protectors of the environment. In September 2003, PRO1 was finally capped by the Orphan Well Association at a cost of $5 million, one-half of the association's annual budget (Weber 2003; Turcza 2004), both a bargain for the public and a pittance of the annual profits for the industry.

Over its lifetime, PRO1 released an estimated 109.6 million m^3 of saline water, about 114 times larger than all recorded saline water releases in the FIS database. Moreover, this is the volume disgorged from just the well head. An unknown volume of contaminated water spread horizontally through the underlying sand and gravel. It's difficult to contemplate the immensity of this release. Consider that this volume translates to fourteen days of saline water disposal for the entire United States based on 2013 disposal rates. Or consider that the total discharge from PRO1 amounted to 38 per cent of the current volume of all conventional crude oil reserves in Alberta. Let's suppose that, if instead of being diluted and carried downstream by the Peace River, the discharge was spread evenly over the land at a rate sufficient to cause significant harm (100 L/m^2). The discharge from this single well would have poisoned about 1,080 km^2, or an area 33 km by 33 km.

The history of PRO1 is reminiscent of other major incidents in Alberta's energy history. It demonstrates stunning indifference and incompetence both in allowing the discharge to continue for eighty-seven years and in failing to monitor the environmental effects. Instead, government and industry have

spun a tale that places them in a favourable light. They refer to PRO1 affection-
ately as "Old Salty," the focus of an "epic well-control effort," and the reason
for establishment of the Orphan Well Association (Jaremko 2013). The disastrous Atlantic No. 3 blowout is remembered for its free publicity and its positive impact on energy investment. The Turner Valley industrial complex is
remembered for "its spectacular flare pit, referred to for years as Hell's Half
Acre." One Turner Valley resident recalled that, for many years, he didn't know
what it was to sleep in the dark. Turner Valley's industrial incidents are remembered for focussing worldwide attention on Alberta's resources. The Atlantic No. 3 and Turner Valley industrial complex are commemorated as
Alberta Historic Sites. History is written by the victors. In Alberta, that means
history is written by the fossil fuel industry.

131

THE DANGERS OF ABANDONED WELLS

Although "Old Salty" posed the most serious known ecological threat of any
abandoned well, it is only one of roughly 170,000 abandoned wells in Alberta.
Leakage from abandoned wells is yet another form of covert "spill" in which
hydrocarbons, produced water, and other substances escape as liquids or gases.
It has long been known that leakage from aging and abandoned wells can contaminate soils and groundwater (IAHS 1990; Taylor et al. 2000). In areas of saline wastewater injection, poorly plugged abandoned wells and corroded well
casings provide conduits for contaminants to flow into freshwater aquifers
(Gorman 2001). Groundwater pollution from abandoned wells can damage
aquifers beyond repair (Zaporozec 1981). Once groundwater is degraded, the
pollution may persist indefinitely.

Contamination from abandoned wells has been known for decades in the
United States. In 1952, an official of the Texas Railroad Commission, the state's
energy regulator, noted that hardly a day passed without receiving a complaint
about surface or groundwater pollution "which invariably can be traced to
improper plugging" of abandoned wells (Gorman 2001). In Alberta, with insufficient abandoned well monitoring and little publicly available environmental data, we can only guess which wells are leaking. At the surface, major
leaks are indicated by dead vegetation and bubbles in pools of liquid near
abandoned wells (Testa and Jacobs 2014). If you observe a spring at the former
well pad, you can be sure the abandoned well is leaking.

Sources of contamination can be difficult to identify because groundwater can flow great distances yet migrate slowly; contamination can arise years later and distant from the faulty well. In fully developed oil fields such as exist in Alberta, hundreds of abandoned wells may be a potential source of contamination of a town's water. It can be prohibitively expensive to track down the source of the contamination and then stop the leak. Proving legal and financial responsibility for the leak can be difficult, especially if the well has had multiple owners. More important than who is responsible are the facts that the well has contaminated the groundwater and that remediation is probably not feasible. Who pays for delivery of fresh, safe water to the affected people?

Leakage from abandoned wells is an international problem. Contaminants of concern released from abandoned wells include methane and other vocs, brine, crude oil, metals, drilling mud, and carbon dioxide. Carbon dioxide corrodes the cement plugs used in abandoned wells and can therefore contribute to well failure. Contaminated soil, old equipment, and industrial waste add to the hazards at abandoned well sites. Methane is a common pollutant at abandoned wells that poses risks to both human health and the climate. The climate risk posed by methane is significant because its global warming potential in the atmosphere is about twenty-eight to thirty-six times greater than that of carbon dioxide. Yet, because monitoring is inadequate, we still don't have precise numbers on either the total number of abandoned wells or their total methane emissions. In January 2021, scientists estimated that there were four million abandoned wells in the United States and 370,000 abandoned wells in Canada that release a total of 629 tonnes of methane per day (Williams et al. 2021). They concluded that annual methane emissions from abandoned wells are 20 per cent higher in the United States and 150 per cent higher in Canada than reported in national inventory reports.

Causes of groundwater contamination were investigated for 185 well incidents in Ohio; 22 per cent were caused by leakage from orphaned wells and 61 per cent were caused by well drilling and production (Allison and Mandler 2018b). Study of 138 abandoned wells in Wyoming, Colorado, Utah, and Ohio found that 40 per cent of unplugged wells leaked methane compared to less than 1 per cent of properly plugged wells. Abandoned wells accounted for 2–4 per cent of total methane emissions from oil and gas activity in those states (Allison and Mandler 2018b). In the city of Los Angeles alone, there are an estimated 900 unplugged abandoned wells. The Texas Railroad Commission plugged about 35,000 abandoned wells from 1984 to 2008 at a cost of $163 mil-

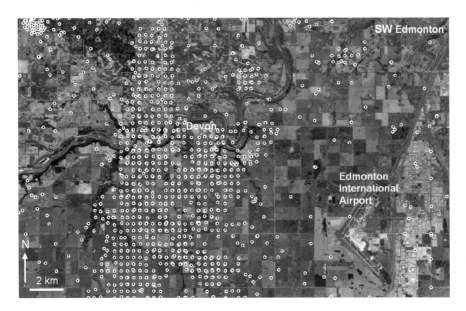

Figure 8.6 Abandoned wells southwest of Edmonton near Devon, Alberta. Abandoned wells pose an unassessed and unmonitored environmental risk. How many people living in the area are aware of their proximity to abandoned wells?

lion while 15,000 abandoned wells in Oklahoma were plugged since 1994 at a cost of $100 million. In Appalachia, the greatest pollution hazard from abandoned wells was found at sites located on or near valley sides and in areas of permeable sediments (Harrison 1983), such as at "Old Salty" in Alberta.

Well type and location, wells drilled at an angle (whipstocked), abandonment method, low hydrocarbon prices at the time of abandonment, regulatory changes, leak testing, and uncemented casings all influence the likelihood of leakage from abandoned wells (Bachu and Watson n.d.). Abandoned wells in Alberta may pose a significant threat to humans and ecosystems, but getting a credible answer from the AER is a challenge. Although abandoned wells leak a host of compounds, the AER lacks a comprehensive monitoring and risk abatement program.

Consider the simplest of questions: how many abandoned wells are there in Alberta? According to the AER, there were 85,164 abandoned wells in Alberta as of September 2016. But a report coauthored by the AER's former chief environmental scientist, Dr Monique Dubé, estimated that there are about 170,000 abandoned wells in rural areas alone, of which about 17,000 are leaking (figure 8.6). About 3,400 of these wells are leaking at levels that pose health risks to humans. These estimates don't tell us where the leaking wells are located. The earliest abandoned wells pose the most danger. Alberta Energy noted that the first energy well abandoned in Alberta in 1935 was plugged with "a few wheelbarrows of cement." There are an additional 38,000 wells abandoned prior to 1964 that the regulator classifies as exempt from cleanup requirements; an indeterminate number of these wells leak. In Alberta's cities, there are 1,500 abandoned wells, about 150 of which are leaking near houses and businesses. Of thirty-six leaking wells that were studied, nine were leaking methane at concentrations that pose a risk of neurological damage to humans; one-sixth were leaking at the life-threatening level of more than 10,000 ppm. A further 1,165 abandoned wells in towns have not been assessed for leaks.

Regarding the health dangers posed by abandoned wells, Dr Dubé asked, "Why doesn't the AER have a handle on what constitutes a real risk in terms of toxicology and environmental exposure from abandoned wells? Why has it taken so long, and why don't we acquire the expertise to rapidly assess the risks of these liabilities and move on them quickly?" The abandoned wells report, completed in November 2016, was suppressed by the regulator (Nikiforuk 2017b, c). A related 2015 report by Alberta Health, *Methane from Leaking Abandoned Wells: Health and Safety Concerns*, was also suppressed. When an investigative journalist asked government for a copy, he was told officials could not find it. The public should not have to rely upon investigative journalists to obtain copies of suppressed reports to learn about the risks of abandoned wells. That's the job of a responsible regulator.

Abandoned wells are often located near people's homes. In some cases, homes have been built on top of abandoned wells. In 2010, residents of Calmar, Alberta, sought compensation and explanations when they learned that their homes had been built on top of an abandoned gas well (CTV Edmonton 2010). Imperial Oil later purchased five of the homes so that it could drill and excavate the offending well. An industry expert, Don Hunter, explained that sometimes well records get lost. Elsewhere, residents in Leduc County were not aware of wells next to their homes and under the pavement in their neighbourhoods. One abandoned well was located in a schoolyard. An official with the town of Calmar noted that it's common practice to build roads and parks on top of abandoned wells.

Health effects are often reported by those who live near abandoned wells. Mark Dorin's family, of Didsbury, Alberta, lived cheek by jowl with a leaking gas well for more than a decade (Bakx 2019). Dorin's mother, Shirley, experienced health effects from the exposure. She stated, "My garden is very close

... to the oil well, which had been supposedly shutdown. I would notice a really severe headache when I would be out in the garden." The family hired a lawyer and complained to the province. After more than four decades of frustration and chronic health effects, the family is still waiting for the well to be properly abandoned.

SUMMARY

Tens of thousands of spills and covert releases missing from the regulator's records pose social and economic liabilities and environmental uncertainty. Shockingly, the two largest releases in Canadian history, both from Alberta, are missing from the regulator's database (the saline blowout at Peace River Oils # 1 and crude oil blowout at Atlantic No. 3). These two releases alone dwarf the entire total release volumes reported by the regulator; their impacts have not been documented adequately, and on the rare occasions when they are discussed, are done so in a light-hearted vein. Environmental information and monitoring of abandoned wells are inadequate. The human health and climate changing effects of leakage from abandoned wells have been underestimated.

Lack of timely access to accurate scientific information about spills and other contaminated sites hampers local governments' ability to ensure rational planning and development and debars the public from participation in environmental protection. Citizens and municipalities wishing to know where contaminated sites are located shouldn't have to conduct forensic research.

Viewed as a whole, the regulator's data misinform on all aspects relevant to the impacts of spills be they spill and recovery volumes, per cent recovery, spill locations, effects on habitat and wildlife, the occurrence of spills in sensitive areas, spill footprints, and the causes of spills. Then there is the information that is simply missing, characterized by thousands of spills with blank data fields, spills of unknown substances, spills by unnamed companies, and spills onto land whose owners are unknown. Then there are the thousands of missing spills and the tens of thousands of spills that lie outside the jurisdiction of the regulator.

The regulator's data have been cobbled together over the years from unverified information supplied by industry. In short, it's a mess. In a way, it's worse than having no information because the regulator's data provide the appearance of monitoring without the substance.

In the prologue I recounted the tragic history of pollution in Toms River and Ocean County, New Jersey. Chemical, waste disposal, and water companies had contaminated the drinking water and groundwater of many communities, but instead of openness and corrective actions, the people got secrecy. Citizens learned that they could not depend upon government to protect them, they had to protect themselves and that protection required their active involvement. It took tragedy for the people, the government, and the industries to learn that working together is the only viable way to protect public and environmental health. That history teaches us to be vigilant to the danger signs. Decades ago near my home in Ocean County, New Jersey, and today in Alberta the danger signs are the same: spills hidden from view, poor regulatory oversight, failure to gather credible data, and failure or refusal to provide the public with complete and accurate information. A social organization composed of industry, regulators, and politicians united by financial interests excluded the public from participation in protecting their health and their environment. We are repeating those same mistakes today across a broad swath of North America. We have created a vast minefield where millions of people must live with the spectre of contaminated sites and abandoned wells. Meanwhile, those responsible sit safely behind a firewall.

In the next part of the book, we examine the field evidence relating to spills. We begin by focussing on the effects of spills on soil and water in the territory of the Dene Tha in northwestern Alberta.

PART FOUR

SCIENTIFIC EVIDENCE

CHAPTER 9

Spill Effects on Soil and Water Chemistry on the Dene Tha Lands

One must be a sea to receive a polluted stream without becoming impure.

Friedrich Nietzsche, *Thus Spoke Zarathustra*

INTRODUCTION

In the previous three chapters we examined a variety of regulatory data. In the next six chapters we examine an array of scientific evidence. In this chapter, we begin with soil and water chemistry from sites in northwestern Alberta (figure 2.2). We then examine the effects on vegetation and flora from the four study regions (chapter 10), explore the Pace-Spyglass oil spill (chapter 11), examine wildlife exposure to contaminants (chapter 12), compare the regulator's rates of habitat and wildlife damage with scientific data (chapter 13), and conclude with an examination of the cumulative effects of the fossil fuel industry (chapter 14). We'll observe that the scientific evidence stands in stark contrast with the regulator's data.

Back in 1538, Paracelsus, the father of toxicology, observed that the concentration of a substance influenced its toxicity. That principle has been paraphrased as "the dose makes the poison." In order to assess the chemical effects of spills we therefore need to understand both the inherent qualities of the substances and their concentrations. In chapter 4, we surveyed inherent qualities – how and why spills of hydrocarbons and salts affect ecosystems. In this chapter, we quantify their postcleanup concentrations at the spill sites in northwestern Alberta on the territory of the Dene Tha First Nation. Some of the material in these chapters is technical (see glossary as needed). I've put most of the details in the web materials. If you find the text to be slow going, you might consider skipping to the chapter summaries for the main lessons learned.

SOIL HYDROCARBONS

Spills of hydrocarbons introduce complex chemical mixtures into the environment. Because hundreds of different compounds may be present, it's challenging to characterize hydrocarbon spills. One standard assay that has proven useful is to measure the total concentration of F1–F4 hydrocarbons, four large groups of hydrocarbons that differ in their number of carbon atoms. The F1 group includes hydrocarbons with six to ten carbons that are often acutely toxic and evaporate quickly such as benzene, toluene, ethylbenzene, and xylenes (known as BTEX) and most of the compounds in gasoline. F2 includes hydrocarbons with eleven to sixteen carbons, such as most of the compounds in kerosene and diesel oil; F3 includes hydrocarbons with seventeen to thirty-four carbons such as lubrication oils; and F4 includes hydrocarbons with thirty-five or more carbons such as waxes. Although this classification is a useful one, it doesn't include light gases or condensates with fewer than six carbons. Nor does it tell us much about toxicity because each of the F1–F4 groups includes compounds that range from harmless to hazardous. With this background in mind, we can survey the main results (for details, see web 9.1).

BTEX hydrocarbons were detected at all three oil spills (Beaver Pond, Pace-Spyglass, Amber: web 9.1–9.3). Given that both the Beaver Pond and Amber sites have been subjected to years of weathering, it's not surprising that volatile hydrocarbons were low there. In contrast, soil at the Pace-Spyglass spill contained benzene, ethylbenzene, m & p-xylene, and o-xylene and a high concentration (480 mg/kg) of total F1 hydrocarbons. As we'll learn later, gasoline was poured onto the Pace peatland to facilitate a prescribed burn during cleanup. This is the probable reason for the BTEX and high concentration of F1 hydrocarbons, a fact that would not be known without the diligent observations of First Nations people.

At natural control sites, total hydrocarbon concentrations ranged from 59 to 1,340 mg/kg while those at disturbed but nonoil spill sites reflected those of natural controls. Natural hydrocarbons such as waxes predominate in the soils of those sites. At the oil spill sites, total hydrocarbon concentrations ranged from low at the enigmatic Beaver Pond site, to 3,600 mg/kg at the Pace-Spyglass oil spill, to an astonishing 211,700 mg/kg at the Amber oil spill. At the Pace-Spyglass oil spill Plot 8, total hydrocarbon concentrations were two to three times higher than control values. However, soil data (AER 2017a) from elsewhere at the Pace-Spyglass site documented acutely toxic hydrocarbon levels hundreds of times greater than those observed at Plot 8 (see chapter 11 and table 11.1).

At the Amber spill, the F3 concentration was a toxic 86,000 mg/kg. The soil at the Amber spill is saturated with hydrocarbons to the extent that wood bison wandering through the area sink into contaminated mud (plate 9.1). The ability of some plant species to grow on the edge of this spill is remarkable. One study observed that the maximum concentration of soil total petroleum hydrocarbons in which plants were found alive was 7,624 mg/kg (Lee et al. 2010); at Amber, the plants were growing on soil containing twenty-eight times that level of hydrocarbons.

Oil persists in the sediments and in the water at the Pace-Spyglass spill (plates 9.2 and 9.3, and web 9.2), yet the regulator reports perfect recovery of the oil. At both the Pace-Spyglass and Amber spills, the air was redolent with hydrocarbons. There were clear differences in the chemistry of the crude oil spill sites and control sites (web 9.4 and 9.5). These sites, in spite of whatever remediation they may have received, contain sufficient hydrocarbons to be demonstrably different from natural soils and pose a persistent threat to the biota.

SOIL SALINITY

At the Barnwell saline spill, soil conductivity, pH, calcium, magnesium, and sulphate were elevated above the control. Elevated conductivity at the site indicates that the effects of the spill may persist (see web 9.6 for details on all the sites).

At the Apache saline spill, soil conductivity, calcium, magnesium, potassium, and sulphate were elevated. Conversely, soil levels of chloride and sodium were higher in the control soil. Addition of a soil amendment at the Apache spill site would help to explain the lower sodium and chloride levels and the lower chloride:sulphate ratio, and the higher calcium and sulphate levels in the spill soil than in the control soil. Unfortunately, Apache did not provide the soil information that I requested.

At the BP Zama (Apache Zama) saline spills site, all soil salinity indicators were strongly elevated. Levels of soil chloride, conductivity, sodium, potassium, and sulphate were the highest recorded at any of the sites. Calcium, pH, and magnesium were also strongly elevated. The extremely high sodium and soil conductivity at the spill site present severe limitations to plants (Alberta Environment 2001).

At the Pace-Spyglass oil spill, chloride and pH were elevated, and sulphate levels were lower relative to the bog control and the marsh-fen control. The chloride:sulphate ratio at the spill site was the highest observed at any site and indicates that the spill or cleanup efforts may have elevated the chloride level of the wetland.

The Amber site was divided into the battery site (Site A1) and the oil spill site (Site A2). The dry soil at Site A1 was extremely compacted, perhaps due to multiple passes by heavy machinery. In contrast, the soil at Site A2 was soft and saturated with crude oil. Chloride, calcium, and sodium levels were relatively elevated at the oil spill and potassium was relatively elevated at the battery site. At both sites, sulphate levels and conductivity indicated spills.

The 11-26 Apache2 saline spill was divided into a hygric soil (Site C1) and a mesic soil (Site C2). Soil chloride levels at these sites were the second highest observed at any of the sites. Soil sodium was elevated, especially at Site C2. The high soil chloride levels are troubling given that the site was cleaned to a standard meeting or exceeding that required by the Alberta Energy Regulator (Kallal 2016).

Claims of perfect recovery of saline water are untenable. There was a clear chemical signature at the spill sites (web 9.7–9.8) indicated by elevated levels of conductivity, pH, calcium, chloride, sodium, magnesium, potassium, and sulphate. The saline spill sites, in spite of whatever remediation they may have received, remain saline and demonstrably different from natural soils in their chemistry. Given that the AER database reports a total of 26,669 saline spills from 1975 through 2018, the landscape ecological impacts of saline spills have been significant. Within the territory of the Dene Tha, there had been 2,910 spills of all substance types as of 2018. The total area affected in the spills is not known because the AER's spill footprint data are not credible (chapter 7 and web 7.13). Field checking of actual spill footprints against those listed in the regulator's database demonstrate systematic underestimates.

POND CHEMISTRY

During remediation at the Apache 15-09 and 11-26 saline spills, ponded depressions were created during removal of contaminated soil. Water quality at both ponds in 2016 was poor (web 9.9–9.10) as indicated by elevated conductivity, magnesium, manganese, copper, selenium, iron, arsenic, calcium, chloride, sodium, and sulphate.

Fieldwork at the 15-09 pond revealed a paucity of aquatic animals and plants three years postexcavation, suggesting persistent impaired habitat and water quality (plate 9.4). Given the poor water quality, it's fortunate that few animals were using the ponds. Mats of cyanobacteria (blue-green algae) were the most abundant life in the pond (plate 9.5).

At the Nuvista spill, postspill excavation to remove contaminated materials created ponds during the winter of 2015–16. Although flooding during June and July 2016 of the Nuvista spill site prevented our on-ground study of the spill, water chemistry data permit an overview. Pond water samples taken in May 2016 showed elevated concentrations of arsenic, barium, chromium, copper, iron, lead, manganese, selenium, silver, uranium, vanadium, zinc, chloride, and total dissolved solids (web 9.11).

143

SUMMARY

Spills are recognizable by their chemical signature. Field data from the Pace and Amber crude oil spill sites documented elevated hydrocarbons and some elevated salinity indicators, absence of effective wildlife deterrents, and either that the sites were considered remediated or the spill was missing from the regulator's records. Soils at the saline spill sites were elevated in conductivity and salinity. Soil chemistry varied between sites and may have been influenced by postspill soil amendments, but requests to the regulator and industry for chemistry and remediation information were ignored. Poor water quality at the excavated ponds at both Apache spill sites was evident in their elevated pH, conductivity, and concentrations of many cations and anions. At the Nuvista site, nine months after the spill, and after excavations to remove contaminated materials, water at the site contained high levels of metals that exceeded protection guidelines. The contrast between the regulator's information and the scientific evidence reveals a failure by the regulator to gather and provide credible environmental data. Persistent contamination at spill sites can be expected after cleanup.

CHAPTER 10

Spill and Related Effects on the Vegetation and Flora in Four Study Regions

Desert Recipe
Choose a healthy piece of land. Peel and discard the green outer layer. Sterilize and compress the soil into a hardpan, then marinate in salt water. Apply a greenwash of liquid sugar and dye. Keeps indefinitely. Market as a healthy alternative to nature.

INTRODUCTION

In this chapter we examine the effects of spills and related disturbances on vegetation and plant species. We begin with the field data from the northwestern Alberta, then consider data from north-central and northeastern Alberta, the Canol Road in the Northwest Territories, and the Rumsey Moraine in southern Alberta.

COMMUNITIES AND SPECIES FROM NORTHWESTERN ALBERTA

Vegetation at natural and industrially disturbed sites clearly differed (web 10.1–10.8). Disturbance caused soil contamination and impairment, shifts in vegetation species composition, and decreased native plant species richness. These results contradict the regulator's records, which reported completion of cleanup operations and no effects on habitat or wildlife (web 10.1.1, 10.1.2). Plant species at disturbed sites formed assemblages typified by introduced reclamation species, and weedy, disturbance-adapted species. Disturbance is the primary gradient with natural sites exhibiting higher total plant cover and disturbed sites lower total plant cover. Soil moisture is the second most important gradient; vegetation species composition changes from dry to wet sites.

Barrens and weedy meadows at the disturbed sites replaced the spruce forests and woody and graminoid wetlands of the natural landscape controls. In some situations, the lack of forest cover is related to insufficient time for forests to develop while in other situations, it's doubtful that forests could ever develop given the soil limitations imposed by disturbance. Saline spills had the lowest total plant cover, followed by pipeline right-of-ways and battery sites, then oil spills; natural communities had the highest plant cover. Twelve species indicated natural vegetation, two species indicated wet soils, and four species indicated disturbed sites (web 10.6). The presence of black spruce, Labrador tea, and leatherleaf, and various lichen species indicate undisturbed conditions. Conversely, the presence of common dandelion, fowl bluegrass, and the weedy moss *Bryum caespiticium* indicates disturbance.

146

Plant Species Tolerant of Spills and Industrial Disturbance

The prevalence of indicator species reveals a widespread disturbance signature. By the same token, the absence of species found only in natural communities tells you that you are observing something different from natural conditions. Finding one indicator species tells you something; finding a community of these species tells you a lot more. Study of the vegetation and the soil helps reconstruct the history of a place. Once we know what is, and what was, we have a good idea of what will be.

Indicator species analysis provides a means to identify species characteristic of natural and industrial sites (plates 10.1–10.3, web 10.7). Many of the species able to grow at spill sites are widespread generalists tolerant of a broad range of ecological conditions. Soil chloride, conductivity, calcium, magnesium, potassium, and sulphate concentrations influenced vegetation composition more than did hydrocarbons (web 10.8). Five species were strong indicators of disturbance: yellow and white sweet clovers (which depress native plant species diversity), cultivars of slender wheatgrass (commonly used in reclamation), rough hair grass (weedy native species that thrives after soil disturbance), and common yarrow (tolerant of a wide range of conditions).

Plant species characteristic of industry sites in northwestern Alberta help us to interpret site history. Alsike clover is a common, pollution-tolerant exotic forb that is widely planted and persists after introduction (plate 10.1). Foxtail barley is a weedy grass tolerant of the soil salts and disturbance common along roadsides, pipelines, and at battery sites. It increases in abundance on grazed lands because it's unpalatable to bison, horses, and cattle. Smooth perennial sow-thistle is a pollution- and disturbance-tolerant, weedy exotic forb common in meadows. Common horsetail is a weedy native plant that is one of the most common plants in North America and is highly tolerant of disturbance; it's a common roadside species. Common plantain is a weedy exotic of waste ground. One of its common names is "whiteman's foot," suggestive of its tendency to follow human disturbance. Fowl bluegrass is a disturbance-tolerant native grass of wet meadows. Water sedge is a pollution- and disturbance-tolerant native marsh sedge. Fireweed is a common native weedy forb known for its ability to spread rapidly after fire. Scentless chamomile is an aggressive weedy exotic of fields, waste ground, and roadsides; its association with industrial disturbance presents a biodiversity concern. Finally, knotweed (*Polygonum monspeliense*, plate 10.2), a weedy exotic forb, is characteristic of parched, hard, and saline waste soils.

147

The Effect of Industrial Disturbance on Plant Species Richness

Industrial disturbance favoured the occurrence of exotic and weedy species (table 10.1). The proportion of weedy species was highest at spill sites, high at disturbed sites, and low at control sites. Disturbance killed all lichen species; at control sites, 24 per cent of the flora was composed of lichens. Similarly, industrial disturbance strongly depressed mosses and liverworts. Relative to controls, disturbance and spills raised the proportion of vascular plant species in the flora. Although the proportion of vascular plant species increased with disturbance, vascular plant species richness was suppressed by disturbance. There were forty-four vascular plant species at disturbed sites and forty-eight vascular plant species at spill sites relative to fifty-seven vascular plant species at control sites.

Industrial disturbance caused shifts in the proportion of species from major plant families. At natural control sites, the grass, composite, and bean families comprised an average of 5, 4, and 0 per cent of the flora whereas at industrial sites, those families comprised an average of 24, 16, and 12 per cent of the total flora. The increased proportion of grass, composite, and bean species at industrial sites is due in large part to the corresponding loss of lichens, most bryophytes, and many vascular plant species. The grass, composite, and bean families are known for their disturbance-adapted and salt-tolerant species.

Table 10.1 Plant species at industrial and control sites in northwestern Alberta tallied by native vs exotic species, nonweedy vs weedy species, and plant groups

| Site type | Species | Native vs exotic | | Weedy | | | Group | |
	n	native	exotic	yes	no	vascular	bryophyte	lichen
Disturbed	45	32	13	19	26	44	1	0
Spills	56	45	11	32	24	48	8	0
Control	123	119	4	14	109	57	37	29
	%	native	exotic	yes	no	vascular	bryophyte	lichen
Disturbed	100	71	29	42	58	98	2	0
Spills	100	80	20	57	43	86	14	0
Control	100	97	3	11	89	46	30	24

Note: See web 10.3 for the reduced species richness at industrial sites.

THE INDUSTRIAL DISTURBANCE SIGNATURE IN INDEPENDENT VEGETATION AND SOILS DATA

Data gathered by other scientists at natural control and industrially affected sites provide replicates so that we can determine if the vegetation and soil effects observed in northwestern Alberta are observed elsewhere.

Industrially Reclaimed Sites and Controls, Northeastern and North-Central Alberta

Vegetation and soils of naturally saline sites and reclaimed sites differed in species composition related to differences in soil sodium absorption ratio, electrical conductivity, and sodium, calcium, chloride, sulphate, and potassium concentrations (web 10.9–10.11). Nineteen plant species indicated natural control sites and twenty-six species indicated reclaimed sites (web 10.12). Total vascular plant species richness was much greater in naturally saline vegetation (161 species) than at industrially reclaimed sites (100 species, web 10.12.1).

Reclaimed sites were indicated by exotics and disturbance-adapted plants such as water sedge, small bottle sedge, bluejoint reedgrass, Pumpelly brome, bird's-foot trefoil, common cattail, both yellow and white sweet clover, and fireweed. In contrast, indicators at natural sites were predominantly native halophytes and widespread generalists such as western willow aster, slender wheatgrass, Nuttall's salt-meadow grass, tufted white prairie aster, and sea milkwort.

Of the twelve vegetation community types I identified, eleven were found at natural sites while only four were found at reclaimed sites (web 10.13). Reclaimed sites supported lower community diversity and a greater abundance of exotic and/or weedy plant species. Of the four community types found at reclaimed sites, three were characteristic of disturbance: water sedge – small bottle sedge marsh; a weedy meadow type dominated by brome, bird's-foot trefoil, white sweet clover, yellow sweet clover, and fireweed; and common cattail – slough grass marsh.

Although various studies have observed that industrial disturbance causes an increased proportion of species from the grass, composite, goosefoot, and other families (web 10.12), all rules have exceptions. In the case of naturally saline plant communities, industrial disturbance reverse this pattern. These communities have by their nature a high proportion of halophytes and therefore the grass, composite, and goosefoot families are well represented prior to disturbance. When these communities are disturbed and reclaimed, many native halophytes are extirpated because they're not adapted to soil disturbance (web 10.12.1). Therefore, disturbance decreases the proportion of species from those families.

Alpine Crude Oil Spills and Controls, Canol Road, Northwest Territories

Species composition in erect deciduous shrub tundra, dwarf shrub tundra, and sedge meadows differed at natural sites and spill sites seventy years after the spills (web 10.14–10.19). Thirty species or cover types indicated natural sites and eighteen indicated crude oil spills (web 10.20). I identified twenty community types (web 10.21, 10.22). Most community types were composed of plots that belonged to either the natural or oil spill groups, indicative of sharp differences in the species composition of natural and oil spill sites. The absence of exotic species in the local alpine flora combined with the lack of reclamation meant that the spill sites lacked the exotic and agronomic species typical of sites farther south.

In natural erect deciduous shrub tundra, the dominant cover types were star-tipped reindeer lichen, organic matter, and bog birch whereas at oil spills, the dominant cover types were cryptogamic crust, juniper hair-cap moss, miscellaneous bryophytes, and organic matter (plate 10.4a). In natural dwarf shrub tundra, the dominant cover types were organic matter, northern white mountain avens, and cryptogamic crust whereas in oil spills, the dominant cover types were organic matter, mineral soil, and residual tar (plate 10.4b). In natural sedge meadow tundra, the dominant cover types were organic matter, standing water, peat moss, and cryptogamic crust; the dominant cotton grass was sheathed cotton grass. In oil spill sedge meadow tundra, the dominant cover types were organic matter, residual oil, and mineral soil; the dominant cotton grass was narrowleaf cotton grass (plates 10.4c and d).

The Canol data provide strong evidence of crude oil's multidecadal effects on plant communities. Oil spills resulted in reduced plant species richness, lichen richness, and vascular plant richness, reduced shrub and total vegetation cover and reduced organic matter, and increased bare mineral soil (table 10.2). Even to a casual observer, after seventy years, the vegetation of the oil spills clearly differs from the undisturbed alpine tundra (plate 10.4).

Pipeline Right-of-Ways, Well Sites, and Controls, Rumsey Block, South-Central Alberta

The Rumsey Block (plate 10.5) study documents a persistent industrial effect on soils and vegetation in a south-central Alberta aspen parkland – plains rough fescue landscape (for details, see web 10.23 and Elsinger 2009).

Pipelines vs Controls
Four indicator species were identified for pipeline ROWs and four species were identified for adjacent controls (web 10.23). Three of the four pipeline indicator species are used in reclamation seed mixes: northern wheat grass, awned wheat grass, and western wheat grass. Plains muhly and bastard toadflax indicated ditchwitching of pipelines and field mouse-ear chickweed and intermediate oat grass indicated ploughing of pipelines. Green needle grass and western porcupine grass indicated an agronomic seed mix while low sedge and pasture sagewort indicated a Rumsey 1983 seed mix. Plains rough fescue and prairie crocus were the best indicators of undisturbed conditions.

Well Sites vs Controls
Of the twelve indicator species for well sites (web 10.24), eight were undesirable exotic species: smooth brome, Kentucky bluegrass, common dandelion, quack

Table 10.2 Species richness and cover at control and oil spill plots, seventy years after crude oil spill (Canol Road)

Attribute (averages)	Control (120 plots)	Spill (105 plots)
Species richness (n)	11.3	7.5
Lichen richness (n)	5.8	4.0
Vascular plant richness (n)	4.6	2.4
Total vegetation cover (%)	81.7	58.4
Exposed mineral soil (%)	2.9	26.0
Exposed organic matter (%)	28.6	22.0

grass, thistle (including Canada thistle), sheep fescue, yellow sweet clover, and intermediate wheat grass. Three of the indicators were native species introduced in reclamation seed mixes: slender wheat grass, western wheat grass, and green needle grass. For undisturbed prairie adjacent to well sites, there were eighteen indicators, all of which were native species (web 10.24).

Effects on Species Richness and Total Plant Cover
Reclaimed well sites had lower native species richness and cover and more exotic species and higher cover of exotics than did native prairie (web 10.25). Pipelines supported fewer native species than did native prairie.

Effects on Soil
Construction and reclamation resulted in major soil changes (web 10.26, 10.27). Soils at reclaimed well sites were more strongly impacted than were those at pipelines. Relative to controls, pipeline soil bulk density, electrical conductivity, pH, magnesium, and clay were higher and organic carbon and total nitrogen were lower. Relative to controls, well site soil bulk density, electrical conductivity, pH, magnesium, calcium, potassium, sodium, and clay were higher and sand, organic carbon, and total nitrogen were lower.

Although the soils at the well sites and pipelines were not subjected to known spills, the soils exhibited similar attributes such as increased electrical conductivity and bulk density. Why? Mixing of surface and subsurface soils, use of heavy machinery, and the manner in which surface soils are handled degrade the soils (Elsinger 2009). The loamy prairie topsoil of organically enriched and aerated soil aggregates is the product of centuries of organic matter accumulation, root growth, invertebrate tunnelling, decomposition, and mycorrhizal activities. Because topsoils are living communities, they can't be stripped, stockpiled, stored, and put back in place without damage. Stored soil loses its structure and biota. When the soil is put back in place and mixed with the subsoil (which is higher in conductivity, pH, calcium, and magnesium), and compacted by heavy machinery, the reclaimed soil resembles the degraded soil typical of spills.

THE INDUSTRIAL DISTURBANCE SIGNATURE
AND DOMAINS OF ATTRACTION

Data from the four study regions and the scientific literature reveal that industry creates a disturbance signature in the form of persistent shifts in vegetation and soils relative to natural controls. Most native species lose in their interactions with the fossil fuel industry. The "winners" are most often exotics and weedy, disturbance-adapted species (web 10.28). In table 10.3 we put a face on the disturbance signature in the form of indicator species and ecosystem attributes that can tell us about ecosystem conditions across much of western Canada and the adjacent United States. Some indicators, such as elevated electrical conductivity, can be expected wherever spills occur. Other indicators, such as an increased depth of the active layer on permafrost soils, are region or habitat specific. Similarly, species indicators can differ between ecological regions. The persistence of industrial signatures depends on the severity of the perturbation, the climate, moisture regime, the landform, the species introduced, and the nature of the prespill ecosystem. A disturbance signature can be expected to persist from years to indefinitely.

THE DISTURBANCE SIGNATURE:
CONTRA-INDICATORS

Once as a young adult with keen eyesight I took a walk during a snowstorm. That evening a local trapper who had followed my tracks asked me what I thought of the marten. I asked "what marten?" He responded "the marten in the trap that you walked within ten feet of today." So much for keen eyesight. Three decades later and some years after my eyesight started to fail, my nephew and I canoed across northern Saskatchewan and Manitoba. As we paddled

Table 10.3 The fossil fuel industry disturbance signature

Species indicators (presence indicates disturbance)
Various habitats, various regions

exotic grasses: creeping foxtail, crested wheat grass, downy chess, hard fescue (*Festuca trachyphylla*), intermediate wheat grass, Kentucky bluegrass (native and exotic), orchard grass, quack grass, red fescue, sheep fescue, smooth brome, timothy, wild oats
exotic legumes: alfalfa, alsike clover, bird's-foot trefoil, red clover, white sweet-clover, yellow sweet-clover
exotic composites: annual hawk's beard, Canada thistle, common dandelion, pineapple weed, scentless chamomile, sow-thistle species
other exotics: common plantain, knotweed (*Polygonum monspeliense*), red-root pigweed, summer-cypress
native species: aspen, biennial sagewort, common horsetail, common vetch, common yarrow, fireweed, many-flowered yarrow, narrow-leaved hawkweed, slender wheatgrass (planted)
cosmopolitan weedy mosses: *Barbula convoluta, Bryum caespiticium, Ceratodon purpureus, Funaria hygrometrica, Leptobryum pyriforme, Pohlia nutans*

Wetlands, moist habitats, and salinized soils

graminoids: alpine rush, bluejoint reedgrass, common cattail, creeping spike-rush, fowl bluegrass, foxtail barley, Nuttall's salt-meadow grass, reed canary grass, rough hair grass, salt grass (s. Saskatchewan), short-awned foxtail, slough grass, small bottle sedge, toad rush, tufted hairgrass, water sedge
non-graminoids: *Chara* (an alga), marsh cinquefoil, marsh horsetail, meadow horsetail, spearscale saltbush, spiked water-milfoil, widgeon-grass, yellow rattle

Reclamation mixtures in plains rough fescue grassland

grasses: awned wheat grass, green needle grass, intermediate oat grass, northern wheat grass, plains muhly, slender wheatgrass, western porcupine grass, western wheat grass
non-grasses: bastard toadflax, field mouse-ear chickweed, low sedge, pasture sagewort

Alpine tundra

Carex membranacea, juniper hair-cap moss, sweet-flowered androsace

Floristic indicators

increased pollution-tolerant and salt-tolerant species
increased proportion and cover of agronomic/forage, weedy, exotic, or introduced/planted species
decreased moss proportion and cover; if present, are cosmopolitan weedy species
lichens absent or few; if present, tend to be cryptogamic crusts or growth form of overlapping scales (squamulose)

increased blue-green algae (cyanobacteria) on land and in water

decreased native species proportion, cover, and diversity

shifts in the proportion of species from particular plant families (for example, increased proportion from grass, composite, bean, goosefoot, sedge, knot/dock, and rose families)

Vegetation and landscape indicators

increased weedy meadows and weedy marshes, decreased peatlands

decreased native grassland, forest, and shrub vegetation

woody plants replaced by nonwoody plants

decreased vegetation type diversity

decreased vegetation cover, biomass, height, and density

hydraulic isolation of wetlands; steeper slopes (narrower littoral zone); reduced wetland areal extent

increased landscape fragmentation

decreased resilience to stress

Physical indicators

increased bare ground; decreased organic matter and plant litter

increased depth of active layer on permafrost soils

damage to river channels, riparian habitat, and wetlands; increased erosion and deposition; disruption of horizontal flows of water

mature, predisturbance soils replaced by young soils without horizons (Regosols)

development of water repellency and long-term growth impairment

loss of soil structure (granular aggregates break down to single-grain); loss of porosity, voids, and permeability

increased clay, bulk density, penetration resistance (hardness), and soil compaction

increased concentrations of petroleum hydrocarbons, PAHs, sodium, chloride, calcium, magnesium, potassium, electrical conductivity, sodium absorption ratio, pH, sulphate, heavy metals, and radioactivity; visible residual tar, oil, or salt crust

decreased capacity to exchange gases and water

decreased primary productivity, nutrient cycling, cation exchange capacity, fertility, nitrogen, phosphorus, organic carbon

in water, increased electrical conductivity, salinity, total dissolved solids, chloride, sulphate, sodium, iron, alkalinity, ammonium, naphthenic acids, barium, boron, bromide, lead, lithium, radium, selenium, strontium, vanadium, and endocrine disruptors; residual tar balls; decreased pH in case of acidic fracking water

Species contraindicators (presence indicates nondisturbance)
Various habitats, various regions

almost all woody plants, mosses, and lichens; most native plants (examples: white spruce, black spruce, Labrador tea, leatherleaf)

Marshes and meadows [a]

---

awned sedge, common great bulrush, <u>common tall sunflower</u>, <u>cordgrass</u>, <u>few-flowered aster</u>, <u>Macoun's wild rye</u>, <u>narrow reed grass</u>, <u>northern reed grass</u>, <u>oak-leaved goosefoot</u>, <u>prairie bulrush</u>, <u>saline plantain</u>, <u>salt-marsh sand spurry</u>, <u>samphire</u>, <u>sea milkwort</u>, <u>seaside plantain</u>, <u>slender arrow-grass</u>, spangletop, <u>tufted white prairie aster</u>, western willow aster, <u>western sea-blite</u>

Plains rough fescue grassland

---

plains rough fescue, prairie crocus

Alpine tundra

---

bog bilberry, bog birch, Lapland rose-bay, moss campion, northern white mountain avens; lichens: crinkled snow lichen (*Cetraria nivalis*), curled snow lichen (*C. cucculata*), green witch's hair lichen (*Alectoria ochroleuca*), Iceland lichen (*Cetraria ericetorum*), reindeer lichen (*Cladonia arbuscula*), star-tipped reindeer lichen (*Cladonia stellaris*)

[a] halophytes restricted to natural saline communities are underlined
Note: For other indicators, see chapters 4 and 5 and web 9.1 to 10.28.

towards an esker back-lit by the low sun, I noticed a distant silhouette that didn't fit against the expected background in the understory of the spruce forest. We stopped paddling and I pointed out the shape to my nephew. I whispered, "Joe, there's a lynx sitting in the spruces ahead. I'll point the bow towards it. It's looking straight at us. Can you see it?" We quietly resumed paddling. When we got to within 200 metres or so, the lynx stood up and slowly ambled off, at which point my nephew finally saw the lynx. Recognizing a lynx or a disturbance signature requires first looking in the right direction, then learning to recognize patterns, and later, the deviations from those patterns.

Because the impacts of the fossil fuel industry result in the permanent loss of natural vegetation and most native species, undisturbed landscape serves as a contra-indicator of industrial impacts. Although this may seem obvious, there are two keys in learning the signature of contra-indicators. The first is learning to recognize ecosystems the way we know friends, that is, each person, each habitat, and each species has a name linked with a history and a repository of knowledge. The second is learning to recognize where an ecosystem lies on the gradient from undisturbed native to completely non-native.

There are no shortcuts to learning the contra-indicators, but there are some general principles. The first principle is that industrial disturbances eliminate most forest and native shrub communities. At the plant-group level, industrial disturbances eliminate most trees, woody plants, lichens, and mosses. At the community and species-levels, industrial disturbances eliminate most native communities and native species. If you find yourself in a woody community, or one dominated by native species, the community contra-indicates industrial disturbance. Conversely, if you find yourself in an herbaceous community dominated by exotic species and species tolerant of disturbance, you're seeing a disturbance signature.

Once you've put a name on the community, the next task is to identify as many of its species as you can because each species conveys information. If you find a salt meadow community dominated by cord grass, sand spurry, and western sea-blite, you know that you're in a native saline community, a contra-indicator of disturbance. If instead you find a salt meadow community dominated by foxtail barley and reed canary grass (*Hordeum, Phalaris*), you're in a disturbed saline community. Given sufficient information about the soils and the vegetation, you can determine where the site lies on the disturbance gradient from unaffected ecosystem to permanently damaged ecosystem (see web 9 and 10 for examples).

NATURAL VS HUMAN-CAUSED SALINE COMMUNITIES

One of the curious aspects of saline spills is that the plant communities that form in their aftermath bear little resemblance to natural saline plant communities. In central and western Canada, naturally saline sites support a great diversity of community types, species, and rare or unique habitats (plate 10.6; table 10.3 underlined species) (among many: NWWG 1988; Fairbarns 1990; Purdy et al. 2005; Timoney 2001, 2015). In contrast, saline spill sites support only a handful of plant communities and species. The greater biodiversity at naturally saline sites is due in part to their greater diversity of soil and water chemistry. Other factors also limit biodiversity after saline spills including soil degradation (such as loss of soil biota and collapse of soil structure), introduction of exotics, and lack of nearby seed sources. Whatever the reasons, depauperate human-caused salinized communities have as much in common with biodiverse naturally saline communities as, to paraphrase Mark Twain, lightning has in common with lightning bugs.

RECLAMATION IS A BAIT-AND-SWITCH

The differences between natural vegetation and industry-affected vegetation are stark and persistent (see also chapters 4 and 5). It's a wonder that the regulator and industry can speak of "certified" and "successful reclamation" with a straight face. Reclamation is one of those concepts that sounds good on paper, but reclamation as practiced in Alberta presents a low bar (see glossary terms: reclamation and certified reclaimed). Almost any site can qualify for certified reclaimed status, even sites with permanently damaged soils dominated by exotics (web 5). Certified reclaimed is not the equivalent of ecologically healthy. Consider a healthy soil supporting a forest full of native songbirds. Now damage the soil and remove the forest and the native songbirds and replace them with brome grass and starlings – that's the essence of reclamation.

157

Industry's promise of reclamation is a bait-and-switch, a falsehood that relies upon disinformation. Reclamation is not, as implied, the return of a healthy vegetation-soil community. It's the establishment of impaired vegetation on damaged soils. Granted, plants can be made to grow on industrial sites and if that's all that's required for reclamation, let's admit it and stop the false statements about restoring nature. If instead, we require that healthy natural vegetation and a healthy soil are present when industrial sites are returned to the people, then the industry does not practice successful reclamation. Having to state such an obvious fact is akin to having to state that the emperor has no clothes. But such is the effectiveness of disinformation – the truth may come as a rude awakening.

PERSISTENT DOMAIN SHIFTS

The evidence points to a sobering fact. The industrial signature represents a domain shift. What do I mean by that? In nature, all ecosystems function within a domain whose boundaries are defined by ranges of variability that don't exceed the resilience of the ecosystem. Under normal conditions, sites vary over time, but the variation remains bounded within the domain. If we conceptualize a domain as a bowl and the condition of a site as a marble rolling around within the bowl, the position of the marble is defined by the state of the ecosystem (figure 10.1a). If the ecosystem is pushed too hard, the marble spills over the rim of the bowl and undergoes a domain shift. Regime shifts, thresholds, alternative stable states, and tipping points are synonyms for domain shifts.

For example, a white spruce forest may be logged, its topsoil removed, and the underlying mineral soil compacted during hydrocarbon exploitation. The site may be later reclaimed, but the native white spruce forest with a healthy living soil, lichens and caribou, warblers, and other songbirds is gone forever. A weedy meadow with few birds has taken its place (figure 10.1b). In the bland parlance of landscape ecology we say the land cover type has undergone "conversion."

When industry disturbs an ecosystem, the physical, chemical, and biological changes are too severe for the ecosystem to return to its predisturbance condition. In some cases, the postdisturbance dominance by exotics such as smooth brome and reed canary grass results from intentional introduction even though the detrimental effects of these and other exotics on native biodiversity are well known (GISD 2018). Whether that new domain is acceptable to society isn't an ecological question, it's a social and psychological one. After all, does it matter what species populate the landscape or that the soil and water contain contaminants? What does it matter if biodiversity has been lost? To some, it matters profoundly, to others, it matters not at all.

The importance of biodiversity is well documented (IPBES 2019). But beyond providing us with ecological goods and services such as clean air, clean water, fisheries, and recreation, what does biodiversity do for us? Biodiversity is important because the network of relationships amongst nature's species supports life itself. When biodiversity declines, the web of symbiotic relationships falls apart and habitat value, productivity, and the ability to tolerate and respond to stress all decline. In human terms, biodiversity is our extended family. Now suppose that each year, someone replaces a portion of your family and friends with strangers. Over time, your extended family, even your parents and siblings, is replaced with strangers. There's no common ground, no shared stories and songs, no mutual resilience, just strangers in an increasingly strange land. And when the times turn tough, as they always will, the relationships of mutual support are gone. There's no one to share your burdens, provide counsel, or comfort you. That's biodiversity loss. Biodiversity imparts resilience to stresses such as drought, floods, erosion, disease, and insect attacks. As our Earth's ecosystems come under increasing stress, we are going to need all the biodiversity we can get.

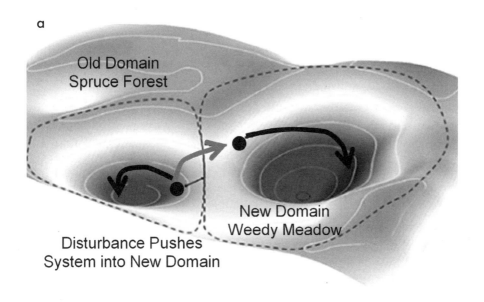

a

Old Domain
Spruce Forest

Disturbance Pushes
System into New Domain

New Domain
Weedy Meadow

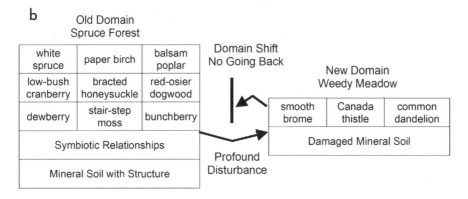

b   Old Domain
     Spruce Forest

white spruce	paper birch	balsam poplar
low-bush cranberry	bracted honeysuckle	red-osier dogwood
dewberry	stair-step moss	bunchberry
Symbiotic Relationships		
Mineral Soil with Structure		

Domain Shift
No Going Back

Profound
Disturbance

New Domain
Weedy Meadow

smooth brome	Canada thistle	common dandelion
Damaged Mineral Soil		

Figure 10.1 Domain shifts. (a) The domain of attraction as visualized with the bowl and marble analogy. If the system is perturbed beyond the threshold of stability, it enters a new domain with a new range of variability and a new stable point or attractor. (b) Changes in tree, shrub, and forest floor species, soils, and vegetation during a domain shift from a predisturbance native boreal mixed-wood white spruce forest to a postdisturbance species-poor weedy meadow. Domain shifts are the rule at industrial disturbances such as spills, reclaimed well sites, roads, seismic lines, and pipelines.

SUMMARY

Industrial disturbance causes impaired soils with shifted species assemblages and reduced diversity of native species and communities, in particular for lichens, mosses, and native woody plants. Indicators of disturbance and contra-indicators can be equally important: the absence of expected common species, and of nonweedy native species in general, can provide silent testimony. What isn't said is often the message; what is missing is often as important as what is present. The results are consistent across datasets and with the scientific literature. Industry activities result in persistent loss of biodiversity. Such sites have undergone domain or regime shifts and will not return to their predisturbance condition.

Disturbance signatures vary by climate, ecological region, and site history. The persistence of disturbance signatures has important implications for naturally stressed ecosystems such as arctic and alpine environments and shorelines as these sensitive areas come under increasing pressure of hydrocarbon exploitation. At the risk of being the pest who keeps insisting that the emperor has no clothes, the fossil fuel industry causes permanent ecosystem damage. To believe otherwise requires detachment from reality.

CHAPTER 11

Behind the Firewall:
The Pace-Spyglass Oil Spill

Slowly the poison the whole blood stream fills.
… The waste remains, the waste remains and kills.

William Empson, "Missing Dates"

INTRODUCTION

Postspill reports can constitute important sources of information but because they're commissioned by industry, access to those reports is restricted. Although I tried, I was unable to obtain reports for most of the incidents studied in the fieldwork. The Pace-Spyglass spill was one exception. Those documents, made available by the Dene Tha First Nation, and augmented by fieldwork and documents released under FOIP, provide a unique opportunity to see behind the regulatory firewall. In this chapter we examine a case history of an oil spill and the industrial and regulatory responses. For details, please see web 11.1. To aid in your understanding of the Pace oil spill, plates 11.1–11.8 provide ground and aerial views.

BACKGROUND ON THE SPILL

Pace Oil & Gas Ltd was responsible for a spill discovered on 19 May 2012 attributed to equipment failure/internal corrosion of an aboveground pipe at an injection well (plate 11.1). The ultimate source of the crude oil was a production well. Inexplicably, crude oil from the production well was reportedly pumped to the injection well (Pace 2012a). The AER record stated that all of the crude oil in the 800 m³ spill was recovered; there was release offsite into "muskeg/stagnant water," the wetland was not sensitive, and there was "no affect" [*sic*] on wildlife or the public.

Review of the Pace report to the regulator provides context and raises questions. The report did not explain how 800 m³ of crude oil were spilled at an *injection* well. Injection wells are used to dispose of wastes such as saline produced water. Why was crude oil being pumped to an injection well used for disposal? Pace stated that the spill was discovered by Pace personnel, but the AER report (2014b) stated that the spill was discovered by Plains Midstream. Pace stated that surface water, groundwater, and soil BTEX, F1-F4 hydrocarbons, PAHs, metals, and salinity parameters were repeatedly sampled at a network of locations, but no results were provided. The report stated that a contractor provided wildlife deterrents that included "air horns and quads along the perimeter of the spill site ... a perimeter fence around the site with safety and silt fencing, placement of effigies, flagging, strategic light placements, audio deterrents and human presence 24 hours." That may have occurred, but by 2016 the only deterrents in place were an orange plastic snow fence and strings of car lot pennants, neither of which have wildlife deterrent value. The report stated that "wildlife observations are reported daily ... Additional measures for wildlife protection include the use of trail cameras ... recording of wildlife sightings," but the Pace report provided no wildlife data.

Pace received approval to burn off residual oil in the peatland. The burn map (plate 11.2) indicated that the spill footprint was to be subjected to an *in situ* burn. AER (2014b) stated, "ESRD approved a controlled remedial burn of the site to remove light hydrocarbons from the spill footprint. The site was ignited at 17:50 on June 9, 2012, and a second burn was done on June 15, 2012." According to Dene Tha members Norm and Joe Chonkolay, gasoline was added to the wetland to facilitate ignition. Pouring gasoline into the peatland may explain the fact that four years later the Pace soil contained the highest levels of BTEX and F1 hydrocarbons observed at the field sites.

The regulator concluded that the spill had been cleaned up four years prior to our fieldwork, but the purported perfect recovery of oil is contradicted by soil data and on-site observations. Four years after the spill cleanup, excavation, and remedial burn, the soil at Plot 8 contained an unacceptably high 3,600 mg/kg of total hydrocarbons (web 9.1 and plate 11.3). Residual oil was visible as a surface sheen on the water (plate 11.4). Probing of soil underwater revealed oil trapped below the surface. Even higher levels of hydrocarbon contamination were observed elsewhere in the wetland (table 11.1).

Plates 11.5 to 11.8 help us understand the magnitude of the spill and the wild-life danger that it poses. Note the ineffective wildlife "deterrents" in place for over four years and counting. Initially deterrents reportedly consisted of owl and bald eagle effigies, air horns, a plastic snow fence, and car lot pennants. At some point early in the postspill period, the only deterrents left in place were the snow fence and the car lot pennants. None of these deterrents has any value. Protective nets over the contaminated water and waste pit, which would have had some deterrent value, were not used. Removal of the contami-nated waste pit, which did not occur until *six years* after the spill (in 2018, see Postscript) would have been the most effective wildlife protection.

It's been known for years that the deterrents employed by the company, and approved by the regulator, have no value. When I showed the deterrents to a former Canadian Wildlife Service biologist, he nearly wept. The US Fish and Wildlife Service (USFWS 2011) has warned regulators that use of pennants (flagging) as a wildlife deterrent at oil pits is ineffective. Apparently, the AER didn't get the memo; wildlife mortality is the predictable result (plate 11.9). In the United States, fossil fuel companies that expose migratory birds and other wildlife to imminent endangerment are subject to administrative orders and penalties of $7,500 per day in violation of those orders. Potential harm to wild-life is all that is required to trigger enforcement actions under the Migratory Birds Treaty Act. In Canada, we have similar protections under the Migratory Birds Convention Act. For unknown reasons, despite documented endanger-ment of migratory birds and protected species, no enforcement actions were taken in response to the Pace-Spyglass spill. The AER's acceptance of ineffective wildlife deterrents demonstrates negligence. But under the captured regulatory regime, the AER is immune to judicial remedy. It can act negligently and there is nothing the public can do other than challenge its immunity.

THE REGULATOR'S REPORT AND INSPECTIONS

The regulator's report and inspections (AER 2014b, 2017a) demonstrate limited competence in the assessment of ecological impacts. Here I offer some obser-vations (for details, see web 11.1). Because Pace did not own spill recovery equipment, it was forced to rent equipment, which resulted in a twelve-day lag between detection of the spill and a full crew being on site. But no one knows when the spill began. The detection date may have been two weeks after

163

the release began; a month may have elapsed between the spill and the full-scale response. Soon after the spill, AER allowed Pace to restart operations at the injection well. Restarting operations at the well prior to completion of a study of causality posed unquantified risks.

Estimates of the spill volume increased from five to one hundred and then to 800 m³, 160 times larger than the first estimate. The regulator stated that based on an aerial view of the spill and an updated spill volume of 100 m³ (later raised to 800 m³) it sent an inspector, an investigator, and an incident response coordinator and reclassified the spill from an alert to a level-1 emergency. Because most spills do not exceed 100 m³, this revelation confirms that field inspection is an unusual occurrence. The company estimated the spill volume based on rate of evaporation, spill depth and extent, recovery volume, and oil remaining. This was a level-1 emergency that received more scrutiny than the vast majority of spills, yet the spill volume was a rough estimate and the perfect spill recovery reported was clearly false.

Industry and the regulator stated the spill occurred at an "unoccupied beaver dam" but presented no evidence that the habitat was unoccupied by beaver. Dene Tha First Nation people, however, observed oil-contaminated beavers. Although the regulator and industry repeatedly stated that soil, water, wildlife, and vegetation monitoring were taking place, my requests for the data were ignored. The regulator described the wetland as "varied vegetation cover, including black spruce, sage leaf willow, and graminoids (e.g., low rushes, sedges, reed grasses)." What was called "sage leaf" and "sage leaf willow" are vernacular names not used in Alberta for hoary willow (*Salix candida*), names indicating unfamiliarity with Alberta's flora. Although it's possible that hoary willow was present, I didn't observe it, and it's certainly not a dominant species. Nor are there rushes and reed grasses present. The vegetation near the spill site is a bog-fen peatland. The regulator concluded that the spill response met with its expectations, but four years later, the site remained contaminated, its vegetation was damaged, and the site posed a threat to wildlife (see chapter 12).

The regulator misunderstands how vegetation responds to oil spills. It stated in September 2012 that "the site was showing positive signs of vegetative regrowth and results from initial environmental monitoring were showing that site remediation efforts were working." Plant growth after an oil spill can be rapid if a spill does not contain appreciable salts. Hydrocarbons can cause an increase in microbial activity and a flush of plant growth. For many plant species, rapid growth is a stress response, not a sign of health. In order to understand the vegetation response, credible knowledge of the species present before and after the spill is necessary, which the regulator did not possess. Death of the native species and rapid growth by invading disturbance-adapted plants such as common cattail is not evidence of effective remediation. Contaminated vegetation can draw animals into an area where they are then exposed to toxins. Finally, there can be a lag between a spill and ecosystem response that unfolds over years. Concluding that remediation is successful four months after a spill is unscientific nonsense.

The regulator is not a competent evaluator of vegetation, wildlife, or ecosystems; its errors in basic ecology would be laughable if they didn't have tragic consequences. Inexplicably, the Royal Society of Canada in its report on crude oil spills in Canada (Lee et al. 2015) essentially quoted the regulator's evaluation of the spill: "no wildlife or aquatic life mortalities noted; remediation efforts reported as being effective with vegetative regrowth noted." See chapter 15 for a discussion of the Royal Society report.

Internal inspections (AER 2017a) illustrate the barely intelligible and unreliable information that characterize AER's incident reporting. One report stated "a release of oil emulsion from a surface pipeline for an injection well. release amount reported was 5m. On May 21, 2012 a site visit was conducted, area was observed results indicated a much larger spill occurred. estimated volumes was in access of 100m3 was released." Although the regulator noted a satisfactory inspection with no need for reinspection, the spill cleanup was just beginning. A second AER report (26–27 August 2015) stated, "No non-compliances were identified ... Observations found: Contaminated soil (hydrocarbon soaked) within the immediate surface area of the well. The area within the lease boundary is still matted with swamp mats and could potentially be masking Hydro carbon liquids below the mats. No enforcement was issued for this inspection. the contaminates identified within the well area were direct impacts due to a large Hydro-carbon release that occurred in 2012." More than three years after the spill, a field inspection observed "hydrocarbon soaked" soil. Despite persistent contamination, the inspection was deemed "satisfactory," reinspection was not required, and no enforcement actions were taken.

The regulator found that Pace had failed to review its emergency response plan and failed to provide training of emergency response personnel. The company was not aware of the composition of the spill until after field testing.

165

How can a company respond to a spill in a timely and effective manner if it's not aware of the spill composition? Had the regulator exercised due diligence, it would have known prior to the spill that Pace's emergency response capabilities were insufficient. Also, because old pipes are common in much of Alberta, corrosion presents an ongoing hazard, especially where equipment contacts salty water. The chloride content at the Pace well was similar to that of seawater. The pipe failure point was above ground at the wellhead and easily observed; failure of a thirty-five-year-old saline water disposal pipe could have been predicted and prevented.

TOXIC LEVELS OF HYDROCARBONS IN THE SOIL

Alarmingly high levels of hydrocarbons remained in the wetland three years after the spill (table 11.1), sufficiently high to pose a clear health danger. Some compounds exceeded environmental guidelines by a factor of more than 200. These levels of toxicity are in some samples hundreds to thousands of times greater than the concentrations we observed at the Plot 8 sample of July 2016. In some samples, the contaminant levels are nothing short of astonishing. For example, the soil surface at site 15-10 was composed of 63 per cent hydrocarbons three years after the spill and its remediation. The absence of effective wildlife deterrents at the site is inexcusable as is the regulator deeming that the spill had been cleaned up.

CONCLUDING QUESTIONS AND COMMENTS

In spite of a cleanup involving skimming, ditching, pumping, excavation, application of chemicals, and two remedial burns, significant levels of hydrocarbons remained in the wetland four years after the spill. In an effort to understand how the regulator could justify certifying the Pace-Spyglass spill site as remediated, I wrote to the AER (web 11.2). I asked the regulator to explain how such a situation could be deemed acceptable. I received a letter from AER's chief environmental scientist at that time (Dr Monique Dubé) stating, "We are working with staff in the organization to review your queries and examine the data and will get back to you shortly with a formal response from the AER."

Table 11.1 Dangerous soil hydrocarbon levels at the Pace-Spyglass site

Sample	Depth (m)	BTEX (mg/kg)					Petroleum hydrocarbons (mg/kg)		
		Benzene	Toluene	Ethyl-benzene	Xylenes	F1	F2	F3	F4
BG15-01	0–0.3							295	80
BG15-01	0.4–0.6						12	170	49
BG15-02	0–0.3						18	181?	51
BG15-02	0.5–0.7							52	
Pond edge	N/A			0.20	1.34	414	6,030	16,500	6,010
15-01	0–0.2				0.75	292	61,600	149,000	48,700
15-02	0–0.2						11,900	97,600	41,800
15-03	0–0.3					301	7,950	15,800	5,320
15-04	0–0.3					22	26,000	186,000	74,100
15-05	0–0.3	0.092	0.30	0.42	2.52	58	97,700	372,000	156,000
15-06	0–0.3						7,790	146,000	72,800
15-07	0–0.3						16,100	335,000	170,000
15-08	0–0.4				0.95?		4,690	32,700	16,000
15-09	0–0.3					835	25,900	42,900	16,200
15-10	0.0?						54,300	399,000	178,000
15-11	0–0.3			0.07	1.41	175	33,500	158,000	67,100
15-12	0–0.3			0.04		345	54,100	160,000	68,400
15-13	0.0?	0.029	2.89				240	1,880	1,080
15-14	0–0.1	5.15		5.69	127	4,120	2,040	6,440	3,060?
15-14	0.1–0.2	98.8	167	28.1	2,910	13,700	59,200	75,300	28,900
15-14	0.2–0.5	49.4?	67.4?	217	1,370	13,800	29,600	39,500	13,100
15-14	0.7–0.85	3.07	20.9	9.22	60.8	758	1,080	2,060	1,070
15-15	0–0.2	0.068	0.24	0.94	18.5	1,850	99,800	214,000	82,200
15-16	0–0.2	0.166		0.36	2.58	468	11,000	30,900	11,600
15-17	0–0.4			0.42	8.29	171	73,300	143,000	53,800
15-18	0–0.2		9.36		0.22		20,900	170,000	75,800
15-19	0–0.2	0.045		0.15	0.89	295	369	569?	328?

Note: Underlined values denote chemical concentrations that exceed acute exposure guidelines.
Although I requested it, the regulator did not supply the report (AER 2017a) in a text readable format. I have typed this table from a difficult-to-read scan and inserted "?" where values were illegible.
Data gathered on 23 September 2015. To eliminate cluter, I have blanked the nondetects. Acute exposure guidelines (and detection levels) in mg/kg: benzene 0.046 (<0.005), toluene 0.52 (<0.05), ethyl-benzene 0.11 (<0.01), xylenes 15 (<0.05), petroleum hydrocarbons, F1 210 (<10), F2 150 (<10), F3 1300 (<10), F4 5600 (<10).

Three weeks later, Dr Dubé's employment was terminated. The removal of Dr Dubé, a respected scientist who was striving to improve the regulator's environmental performance, demonstrates the regulator's lack of commitment to improve its scientific credibility. After the removal of Dr Dubé, responsibility for answering my questions shifted to AER Public Affairs. I provide the full response in web 11.2. In answer to my question as to how a highly contaminated area could be deemed cleaned up, the AER told me, "The identified off-site impacts indicated by Parkland Geo in September, 2015, were excavated during February 2016 while frozen ground conditions permitted access to these impacted areas. Open bodies of water were created resulting from the fall 2015/winter 2016 remediation. In the event that any hydrocarbons accumulate in these water bodies preventable measures were implemented to insure containment and to deter any wildlife and/or migratory birds, following spring break up, ongoing site monitoring was conducted which included additional sampling and site assessment. Site maintenance included vegetation control and temporary containment management."

I find myself struggling to breathe in the dense cloud of smoke. The AER's barely intelligible missive describes activities that took place prior to this study's 2016 fieldwork during which we observed that remediation had not contained the contaminants nor protected wildlife or migratory birds from daily exposure. Contraventions of the Migratory Birds Convention Act and the Pest Control Products Act occurred without investigation or enforcement. "Vegetation control" damaged the wetland (see chapter 12).

SUMMARY

Study of the Pace-Spyglass crude oil spill does nothing to assuage fears that spills are poorly managed and result in long-term damage that isn't communicated to the public. The regulator's handling of the spill demonstrates a lack of ecological knowledge and due diligence, a failure of enforcement, and an inability to understand and control the environmental impacts of spills. The regulator's designating this spill as having no environmental effect is stunning.

As I stood at the site four years after the spill and saw and smelled the crude oil in a wetland without wildlife deterrents, the sick feeling in my stomach stemmed from more than hydrocarbon fumes. The wetland remains contaminated and its vegetation impaired and continues to present a chronic risk to wildlife. As to how the regulator could designate the spill site as remediated, it's significant that the regulator does not track environmental changes at spill sites over time in relation to benchmarks or targets. Nor does the regulator require standard monitoring and sampling designs. Its documentation of spills is not credible, evaluation of spill effects is haphazard and amateur, and decisions as to when a site has been remediated are subjective and arbitrary.

169

CHAPTER 12

Exposure to Contaminants at the Spill Sites

Live or die, but don't poison everything.

Anne Sexton, "Live or Die"

INTRODUCTION

The Pace-Spyglass spill illustrated a failure to protect the environment, but the history of that spill isn't unusual. What makes the Pace-Spyglass spill different is the wealth of "behind the firewall" evidence that was available. Although the evidence from the Pace-Spyglass spill demonstrated clear residual effects, upon close inspection, evidence from every spill examined demonstrates residual effects. Because no agency monitors contaminant exposures at spill sites, and spills occur wherever hydrocarbons are exploited, residual ecosystem effects pose a widespread and unassessed risk. But the problem of chronic exposure runs far deeper than spills. In the western United States, daily exposure to hazardous materials at infrastructure such as dehydrator tanks, reserve pits, skim pits, and wastewater disposal sites kills more birds than do spills (Ramirez 2013).

In this chapter we examine evidence of contaminant exposures at five of the field study sites. Documenting these exposures was difficult and required help from the Dene Tha, digging up unpublished information, and submission of information requests. I found but a fraction of the information that apparently exists. But like seeing the tip of a rat's tail disappear into a hole in the wall, sometimes a fraction tells the essentials of a story, such as the creature attached to it and the state of the home.

PACE-SPYGLASS CONTAMINANT EXPOSURES
TO WILDLIFE

Contaminants remained in the wetland at the Pace-Spyglass spill four years after the spill and likely still persist there. In summer 2016, a sagging plastic snow fence surrounded the site that deterred the movements of exactly zero animals. There were no active bird deterrents. The hawk and owl effigies, audio deterrents, and lights present in 2012 had long since been removed, and regardless, none of these methods have been shown to be effective wildlife deterrents. Animals at the Pace-Spyglass site are exposed to contaminants every day, year-round.

During their monitoring, Dene Tha members Norm and Joe Chonkolay noted oiled beaver, woodland caribou (a federal SARA-protected species), moose, black bear, wolverine (an Alberta "may be at risk" species), Canada lynx (an Alberta "sensitive species"), red fox, and pine marten in the area of the spill (figure 12.1). That wildlife have experienced years of exposure to contaminants at the spill, long after the regulator deemed the spill cleanup complete, is cause for concern. That fact becomes harder to bear when we observe that human visitors at the spill can wear breathing protection while, of course, wildlife cannot (figure 12.2).

The Chonkolays documented an oiled solitary sandpiper (figure 12.3) that was in distress and could not fly. After a phone conversation, a representative of the energy company checked with "environment" (government or the regulator?), after which he told the Chonkolays that they could "go ahead and get rid of the bird," effectively counselling to commit a crime under the Migratory Birds Convention Act. Fortunately, the bird's rescuers did not agree with that recommendation. Instead, they "cleaned the bird up good and released it. The bird flew around and we made sure that it was ok"; they documented the incident (figure 12.4).

During the sampling in June and July 2016, we observed killdeer feeding at the water's edge of the oil-contaminated shore near Plot 8 (figure 12.5), a yellowthroat warbler, several blue-winged teal, and a great blue heron on site and heard sandhill cranes calling nearby.

Figure 12.1 *This page and opposite*
Wildlife contaminant exposures caught
on camera at the Pace-Spyglass spill.
(a) black bear, 14 June 2015; (b) woodland caribou cow and calf, 7 July 2015;
(c) woodland caribou cow, 11 July
2015; (d) Canada lynx, 30 June 2015;
(e) Canada lynx, 21 July 2015. The
wooden platforms visible under the caribou are "swamp mats" laid down at the
spill site to facilitate the movements of
heavy machinery.

OTHER CHEMICAL EXPOSURES AT THE
PACE-SPYGLASS SPILL

Without the persistence and dedication of Dene Tha members (figure 12.6), much of the environmental history and impacts of the Pace-Spyglass spill would not have come to light. Joe Chonkolay documented the postspill response of industry and the regulator (pers. comm., 11 Sept. 2016). Micro-blaze was the first chemical applied after the spill (July 2012). "The second was X-Cide 102W Industrial Liquid Bactericide, sprayed on June 14th and 15th of 2013. Both were sprayed by the company Infinity Vegetation Recovery of Rainbow Lake, AB. I contacted the AER rep, Catherine Evans, and she said [that she]

Figure 12.2 *Top* Protection against breathing toxic fumes was provided to staff responding to the Pace-Spyglass oil spill. It's appropriate to protect the health and safety of humans, but it's also appropriate to protect the health and safety of wildlife. Wildlife exposed to chronic contaminants cannot don breathing protection or have their food and water delivered from safe areas.

Figure 12.3 *Bottom* The oiled solitary sandpiper rescued at the wellhead. 30 May 2014.

On Friday May 30th 2014, Norman and I (Joe chonkolay) came to spillsite at location 14-21-108-07, we came in and found a sandpiper bird covered in oil, we caught the bird and I (Joe) call Chris the consultant and Stuart in Calgary, we told him that we found the bird and Stuart told us to hold on to the bird, He (Stuart) called again and said the he will make some calls to Edmonton. I told him that we will take the bird to Rainbow office and said OK, but he called again and said the we have to keep the bird on site as there will be some one to come pick the bird up we waited till about 2:30 pm when Stuart called and said the he talked with the environment and he gave us the go ahead to get rid of the bird in an most humanly possible. I talked it over with Norman and he didn't agree with it. we cleaned the bird up good and released it. The bird flew around and we made sure that it was ok.

Figure 12.4 *Top* Notes documenting discovery of the oiled solitary sandpiper at the Pace-Spyglass spill. 30 May 2014.

Figure 12.5 *Bottom* Killdeer feeding in the oil-contaminated wetland at Plot 8, 22 July 2016. The yellow bladder in the foreground is an oil-containment boom; oil slicks were observed outside the containment. Lymnaeid snails and adult blue damselflies were also present. Killdeer have suffered significant population declines in the boreal taiga plains region of Alberta since the 1970s.

Figure 12.6 Dene Tha members Joe and Norm Chonkolay are the registered trappers for the area that includes the Pace-Spyglass oil spill. Here they are describing the environmental history of the incident. 22 July 2016.

didn't approve the latter chemical ... Spyglass ... wanted this chemical sprayed. It was trucked in by Baker Hughes."

It's understandable that Micro-blaze was applied. It assists in breakdown of hydrocarbons in soil and water and is composed of several strains of microbes along with surfactants and nutrients. In contrast, the motivation for applying X-Cide 102W to the wetland is not known. X-Cide 102W is a broad-spectrum bactericide used to kill bacteria in industrial nonpotable waters, flooding and water injection operations, in drilling muds, workover fluids, packer fluids, water disposal systems, tank bottoms, and in petroleum-based waters (Ash and Ash 2004). The bactericide is not authorized for use in wetlands and is toxic to fishes and birds. Label directions state that the user should not allow the compound to enter lakes, streams, ponds, and public water supplies. It was an offense under the Pest Control Products Act to apply it to the Pace-Spyglass wetland. Although the unlawful use of X-Cide was brought to the attention of AER by the Dene Tha, no enforcement actions were taken.

The use of X-Cide at the Pace-Spyglass spill may have contributed to the extremely low levels of sulphate observed in the soil and to the unusual cyanobacterial and algal community at the site. Is the strange aquatic community (plate 12.1) related to the oil contamination, the excavation and mechanical disturbances, the application of Micro-blaze, the application of X-Cide 102W, or a combination of all these factors? Elsewhere, an experimental spill of Norman Wells crude oil into a lake in the Mackenzie River valley was also followed by a cyanobacterial bloom (Hellebust et al. 1975).

WILDLIFE CONTAMINANT EXPOSURE AND MORTALITY

Like the Pace-Spyglass site, the Amber site illustrates how wildlife is subjected to chronic contaminant exposures. Known to local people as the "Boneyard," this site contains an oil spill, a leaking pit of abandoned crude oil, abandoned shacks and tanks, and industrial waste and debris (figures 12.7–12.8 and web 8.2). There are no wildlife protections. It is unclear how long contaminant exposure has existed at Amber because the AER records for this site are a mess (web 2.4). The most recent inspection in 2010 found the environment "satisfactory." We are left with two alternative explanations for the exposure to the crude oil. Either a 50 m³ crude oil spill in 1998 was never cleaned up, or the spill was never recorded and may come from chronic leakage of the crude oil sump pit or from an underground pipeline. In the absence of reliable records we can only guess. The only certainty is that the crude oil waste pit presents a constant danger to wildlife. The toll this exposure has taken on the area's wildlife is not known but given the high concentrations of contaminants, the open oil sump pit, the lack of animal deterrents, and the abundant bison tracks and scats at the site, it's clear that the AER is failing to protect the environment. Concerned First Nations people are the only reason we know about this site.

Ungulates mistake exposed salts as mineral licks and seek open habitat where wolves can be detected at a distance. This behaviour brings bison, moose, and other ungulates into daily contact with the salinized, open habitat of the industrial landscape. In so doing, they can be exposed to contaminants in soil, water, and vegetation (figure 12.9 and plate 12.2). Again, we do not have the details about this exposure because no agency is monitoring, but we can at least see the tip of the rat's tail. Consider that, for humans, a safe chronic

Loading / Unloading
Procedure
1. Position Wheel Chocks
2. Connect Ground Cable
3. Don Breathing Apparatus
4. Couple Hose Load / Unload
5. Uncouple Hose
6. Remove Breathing
   Apparatus
. Remove Cable and Chocks

Do Not Enter Dyke
Without Breathing Apparatus

Figure 12.7. The Boneyard at the Amber site. (a) Miscellaneous contaminants exist with the crude oil. The contaminated soil would be considered "oil or salt water staining" and not necessarily reported as a spill. (b) Air at the site reeks of hydrocarbons on a warm day. Although the sign warns to "don breathing apparatus" and "do not enter dyke without breathing apparatus," animals can't read signs or don protective apparatus. (c) Bison patties attest to regular contaminant exposure at this site strewn with industrial waste. 20 July 2016.

Figure 12.8 The Bone-yard, continued. (a) Foam insulation and other waste in various states of disintegration indicate that this site has been contaminated for years. (b) Electrical components have also been abandoned. This toxic site was considered "cleaned up" by the regulator. 20 July 2016.

consumption of C20-C35 petroleum hydrocarbons (roughly equivalent to the F3 fraction) is 0.03 mg/kg/day (Ohio EPA 2010). Assuming a similar response for bison (which is not known), a safe ingestion by a 300 kg bison would be 9 mg/day. Ingestion of 10 g of contaminated soil at the Amber site, such as might be consumed if the animal licked an oil-coated hoof, would result in ingestion of ninety-six times the safe daily dosage.

Figure 12.9 Wood bison near the Amber oil spill site. Wood bison, an endangered species, can't avoid daily contact with industrial sites in northwestern Alberta. 20 July 2016.

Ungulates are of course not the only animals exposed to crude oil in Alberta. The number of bird deaths resulting from exposure to oil and other waste pits in Alberta, such as the leaking oil pit at the Amber site (plate 12.2), is unknown. Such deaths do occur. For example, in August 2015, Syncrude reported thirty dead great blue herons (later increased to thirty-one) at an abandoned sump pond north of Fort McMurray, a location known as 691 Pumphouse Sump (Shannon 2015). Two years after the grisly discovery, Syncrude was charged for failing to ensure that wildlife did not come into contact with a hazardous substance (AER 2017b). In 2019, Syncrude was fined $2.75 million, of which $1.8 million was for charges under the federal Migratory Birds Convention Act.

Syncrude did not discover the dead birds on its lease; it was a contractor who stumbled upon them while looking for a shortcut. Later investigation found a heron rookery with twenty-six nests located only 300 m from the toxic pond (Canadian Press 2019b). How this 1 km long by 400 m wide pond could for years have no wildlife deterrents, why there was no wildlife monitoring, and how neither government nor industry were aware of a heron rookery within 300 m of a waste pond defies understanding. To my knowledge, the death of thirty-one great blue herons is the largest reported mass mortality of herons at one location in Canada, perhaps in North America. The great blue heron is a sensitive species in Alberta; its entire provincial population is dependent upon fewer than one hundred nesting colonies (Alberta Government 2017a). It's unknown whether all the herons died in a single mortality event or whether the birds accumulated over time. The level of negligence underpinning these deaths is horrifying.

Bird mortality at oil waste pits in the United States has been studied by the US Fish and Wildlife Service (Trail 2006), which helps to place the oil pits at Pace and Amber in context. Between 1992 and 2005, 172 bird species from forty-four families were recovered from oil sump pits. Ninety-two per cent of the birds were protected species. About 500,000 to one million birds die annually in the United States as a result of exposure to oil pits. Exposure to oil pits is not the only contaminant pathway. Contaminated vegetation consumed by wildlife is a common pathway as is ingestion of contaminated grit, and exposure to high levels of salinity, metals, radioactivity, and PAHs in soils and water, and bitumen wastewater and tailings ponds (Millennium 2007; Timoney 2013).

181

Study of mortalities at oil and gas facilities in the western United States over the period 2007–10 observed that chronic exposure to dehydrator tanks, reserve pits, skim pits, and crude oil wastewater (see glossary) was responsible for 51, 24, 5, and 4 per cent of bird deaths; in comparison, oil spills were responsible for 1 per cent of bird deaths (Ramirez 2013). The high proportion of bird mortalities at dehydrator tanks could be due to their small size and therefore ease of detecting dead birds. Reserve pits in contrast are far larger, making detection of dead birds more difficult. Because wildlife mortality at Canada's oil and gas sites is not monitored, we don't know if similar death rates apply here. One thing is certain: chronic exposures do more harm than acute exposures.

The veil of secrecy maintained by the AER about industry-caused wildlife mortalities extends to the unconventional hydrocarbon production in the bitumen sands region. At least forty-three species of birds have died as a result of tailings pond exposure in northeastern Alberta; estimated mortality there has ranged from 458 to 5,029 birds per year (Timoney and Ronconi 2010). In 2015, the AER commissioned Dr Colleen Cassady St Clair to study Alberta's bird protection. The report (St Clair 2016) stated that it's impossible to prevent birds from landing on tailings ponds; that new landing deterrent systems, implemented without adequate evidence or evaluation, may be less effective and more detrimental than the deterrents they have replaced; that press releases have been "grossly misleading, if not willfully deceitful in relation to the available evidence about both landings and mortalities"; that there is a "persistent lack of realism, openness and honesty in public claims about monitoring results ... [and] in the number of birds that are portrayed to land or die on the industry's" tailings ponds. In an experience that echoed my AER experiences, the scientist noted that "Five months and multiple escalating requests were required to obtain these [bird monitoring] data" which refutes "claims by both federal and provincial governments about the openness and transparency of monitoring the environmental impacts of the industry ... there's no transparency." St Clair's report found a lack of oversight regarding the monitoring of landings and deaths and the scientific validity of the monitoring data. Will we ever know the true death toll? Not if the AER has its way. The AER suppressed the report. *The Narwhal* later requested the report through FOIP, but the AER refused to release it. The AER's decision was overruled after appeal to the privacy commissioner and the report was released in January 2021. Habitual misinformation and information suppression are traits of a captured regulator.

EXPOSURE TO HIGH SALINITY AT THE
APACHE SALINE SPILLS

Exposure to saline spill water at the Apache spill sites caused widespread mortality of plants and animals and impaired saline plant communities, elevated soil conductivity, and poor water quality. At the Apache2 (11-26) spill, court documents support this view (web 12.1). The agreed statement of facts between the Crown and Apache (Kallal 2016) observed that "32 tonnes of affected soil were removed from the 11-26 Site and the area around the Site was turned into a pond for migratory waterfowl and to provide drinking water for wildlife." This is a good example of how events and information are spun to appear positive. Recall from chapter 9 that soil conductivity, sodium, and chloride remained highly elevated after cleanup despite the fact that the site was cleaned to a standard meeting or exceeding that required by the regulator (Kallal 2016). The vegetation and soil remain impaired. The pond created for migratory waterfowl and drinking water for wildlife may instead pose a threat to waterfowl, wildlife, and aquatic life, in effect luring animals into a contaminated area.

Although the FIS data state that the Apache 15-09 spill had "no affect" on wildlife or habitat, the truth is that Apache was found guilty of damage to 42 ha of public land. The saline spill, with a concentration about four times that of seawater, released about 1,214 tonnes of chloride onto 42 ha. It's not surprising that the spill was toxic. As early as June 2013 an aerial photograph showed yellowed and discoloured vegetation. James Ahnassay, then chief of the Dene Tha First Nation, observed that "every plant and tree died" in the area of the spill (Vanderklippe 2013). Internal documents demonstrated poor monitoring and assessment, insufficient oversight by the company and the regulator, no monitoring of impacted wetland vegetation, extensive contamination, hundreds of animal deaths, and failure of AER to record animal deaths (AER 2017c; web 6.1.1). Although Apache reported the deaths of 382 wood frogs and four birds, the AER database contains no record of these deaths. Documents obtained through FOIP reveal that the spill began on 5 May 2013, thirty-one days before the Dene Tha were notified. Apache first reported that the saline spill totalled 30 m³, 500 times lower than the later determined volume of 15,363 m³.

The 15-09 spill footprint was subdivided into four divisions by Apache. Division 1 was the upland surrounding the well. This area was impaired by industrial activities before the spill and is a weedy meadow; 383,011 tonnes of salt-contaminated soil were removed from Division 1 and disposed of at the Tervita Landfill. Division 2 (figure 12.10) is a bog-fen that received the brunt of the toxic discharge. Division 3 was reportedly a "large beaver pond," and Division 4 was a "pond/wetland complex." In Division 1, the mean conductivity exceeded a startling 100,000 µS/cm, sufficiently toxic to kill most organisms. In Division 2, conductivity and chloride concentrations remained highly elevated above natural conditions, ranging from two to thirty times the freshwater protection guideline. Some areas with an elevated chemical spill signature were located more than 2 km from the well, demonstrating that the affected area exceeded the 42 ha in the court document.

Animals exposed to the spill contaminants included American robins, various warbler, sparrow, blackbird, wren, thrush, and sandpiper species, greater scaup, blue-winged teal, mallard, bufflehead, greater yellowlegs, lesser yellowlegs, spruce grouse, ruffed grouse, red squirrel, pine marten, beaver, coyote, wolf, black bear, wood bison, and moose. Contaminant exposures for rusty blackbird, winter wren, three-toed woodpecker, northern goshawk, gray wolf,

183

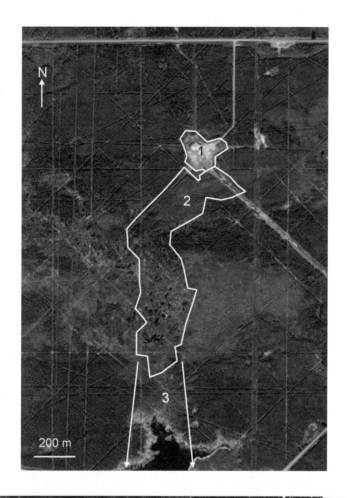

and wood bison are all the more significant due to the sensitive conservation status of these species.

Neither the company nor the regulator presented data on impacts to vegetation but mapping by the Global Forest Change program detected dead spruce, larch, and birch as a result of the spill (plate 12.3). By 2016, much of the spill footprint had been converted to open water due to both excavation and to the toxic effects of the salt. Immediately south of the spill, direct habitat loss was due to excavation of the bog-fen (figure 12.11). Although the regulator found "no affect" on habitat or wildlife, the ecological damage was severe enough to be mappable from satellite imagery.

Given the extensive damage, the slow response and failure to notify the Dene Tha for an entire month, and the persistent effects of the Apache spill, the administrative penalty of $16,500 served as an incentive to continue business as usual. In comparison, in 2016, a $2.1 million civil penalty was imposed by the US EPA on the Slawson Exploration Company for violations of the Clean Air Act at its storage tanks in North Dakota where excessive emissions of VOCs, methane, and hazardous air pollutants such as benzene were observed. Slawson agreed to take actions that will cost $4.1 million to reduce its annual emissions of VOCs, methane, and hazardous air pollutants (EPA 2016). The contrast with the situation in Alberta is sobering (see chapter 15 under "Poor Record Keeping and Enforcement"). Low rates of enforcement for noncompliance and insignificant financial penalties, which have characterized the AER's enforcement record, contribute to the frequent environmental incidents. Because environmental costs are borne by society, company profit is maximized by letting system components fail, responding to incidents, and replacing the failed component rather than maintaining and replacing corroded

Figure 12.10 *Opposite top* Undated prespill image of part of the aerial footprint of the Apache 15-09 saline spill as delimited during spill response. Numbered divisions were defined by Apache. Note the high density of linear disturbances. Extensive wetland damage in Division 2 was detected (see plate 12.3b). Unsafe levels of aluminum, chromium, copper, selenium, silver, iron, zinc, methanol, ammonia, and phenols were observed in surface water in all four divisions. Soil exceedences were reported for boron, molybdenum, selenium, methanol, benzene, toluene, ethylbenzene, xylene, and F2, F3, and F4 hydrocarbons. For a map of the spill divisions, see web 12.2.

Figure 12.11 *Opposite bottom* The excavated pond at the Apache 15-09 spill. What was formerly a healthy bog-fen has been replaced by a pond with impaired chemistry, essentially devoid of life, and posing a risk to wildlife. Note the salt-killed conifers in the distance. See plate 3.1b for an aerial view of the fen at the time of the spill.

pipelines and other components before they fail. It's more profitable to expose wildlife to contaminants.

EXPOSURE TO HIGH SALINITY AT THE BP ZAMA (APACHE ZAMA) SALINE SPILLS

Documenting the spill and disturbance history for the BP Zama spill site was challenging because the AER's records are equivocal. The locations for the spills are imprecise; it's unclear what was spilled, where it was spilled, how much was spilled, and how much was recovered; and there's always the prospect of unrecorded spills. Although soil chemistry information does exist, and was requested from the regulator and from industry, none was provided. Of twenty-two spill records, twelve refer to a crude oil group battery, seven to a water pipeline, one to "miscellaneous," one to "other pipeline," and one to a custom treating facility. After poring over the information obtained through FOIP (AER 2017c), I found eight reported spills and 96 m³ of unrecovered saline water near or in the pipeline ROW near Plot 6.

Evidence from the fieldwork, the FIS records, and the documents obtained through FOIP demonstrate that the soils in the vicinity have been contaminated for years, perhaps decades (figure 12.12; Alberta Environment 2001) despite the facts that some soil and site reclamation took place circa 2008 and the spills have been remediated to a level acceptable to the regulator. The impaired vegetation is composed of salt-tolerant and disturbance-tolerant plants and introduced species.

SUMMARY

Field evidence documents ecological damage, persistent contamination, no effective wildlife deterrents, and no monitoring at spill sites. Postspill excavations create contaminated ponds that lure wildlife into danger. Tens of thousands of sites with impaired environments are distributed across Alberta and tens of thousands more are distributed across North America wherever hydrocarbons are exploited. Let's think about that for a moment. Organisms are exposed to contaminants on a daily basis. The exposure is chronic, but no agency monitors the effects. Although it's the regulator's responsibility to protect the

Figure 12.12 Multiple saline spills at the BP Zama site have rendered the soil permanently contaminated. Part of the Apache sour gas plant is visible north of the plot. Plot 6, 21 June 2016.

environment in Alberta, it does little more than issue press releases that it's protecting the environment for its stakeholders. Its failure to acknowledge spill effects in its FIS database is negligence pure and simple. Under its auspices, the regulator oversees and approves activities that result in long-term ecological damage. If industrial sites are ever to be remediated, it's the taxpayer that will pay the price – more on this topic in later chapters. In the next chapter we compare rates of damage to habitat and wildlife reported in the regulator's data and the scientific data.

CHAPTER 13

The Regulator's Failure to Document Spill Effects on Habitat and Wildlife

Progress is a nice word. But change is its motivator. And change has its enemies.

Robert F. Kennedy, speech, 25 May 1964

INTRODUCTION

Suppose we're siblings and our mother has not been well for some months. She drags herself to the doctor who examines her and does some tests. The doctor calls a few days later to say that he can't find anything amiss and suggests it's all in our mother's head. She grows more ill. A year passes and she goes to another doctor with the same result. Two years pass and our mother's health has declined further. A third doctor does some tests and then his office calls and asks our mother to come for a consultation. There we learn that our mother has terminal stage colorectal cancer. The doctor says if they had caught the cancer earlier, they could have operated but now it's too late. In this real world situation that some of us have experienced, we never learn why the doctors failed to find the cancer. Let's suppose that, instead of doing nothing, we confronted the first two doctors. The first doctor saw evidence of the cancer but he didn't want to deliver bad news and therefore said nothing. The second doctor had no data so he made up something that we wanted to hear. We would be justifiably outraged. But that's precisely what happens when industry reports to the regulator and the regulator reports to the public. We ask and we are told nothing or happy news like perfect spill recovery, or the relevant data can't be found or were never gathered.

Whenever any of us ask an authority for information, we want good news, but most of all we want the truth. We don't expect to be answered with silence or be told there's no information or be given misinformation. Family members should not have to run biomarker analyses or interpret x-rays for their loved ones. Nor should citizens be required to gather soil, vegetation, and wildlife observations or interpret technical data about their ecosystems. That's why we have regulators.

Although the question of whether spills affect habitat and wildlife may seem rhetorical, the regulator's data reveal surprising results. Few would argue that crude oil and saline spills do not affect the environment. The regulator's data, however, indicate that spills have little or no ecological effects. In this chapter, we examine the regulator's habitat and wildlife damage data, provide a scientific estimate of damage rates, then discuss the regulator's data in the context of scientific evidence. We will observe that the regulator is unable to provide credible assessments of habitat and wildlife impacts. When we're deprived of accurate and timely information, bad surprises are in store.

DO CRUDE OIL AND SALINE SPILLS AFFECT HABITAT AND WILDLIFE?

The regulator uses four categories to classify the effect of spills on wildlife and habitat. These are (1) "No affect" [*sic*], (2) "Habitat affected," (3) "Conversion from ENV system" (meaning no data), and (4) "Animal(s) injured or killed." Only from 2002 onwards do most records contain habitat/wildlife data. In 77 per cent of crude oil spills and 69 per cent of saline spills, the regulator has no habitat affected data (web 13.1, 13.2). When we omit the spills for which there are no habitat effects data, we find that according to the regulator, habitat is affected in 1.2 per cent of crude oil spills and animals are injured or killed in 0.1 per cent of those spills. The regulator observes no effect in 98.7 per cent of crude oil spills. For saline spills, the regulator finds that habitat is affected in 0.9 per cent of spills and animals are injured or killed in 0.02 per cent of spills. Remarkably, the regulator observes no effect in 99.1 per cent of saline spills.

So, the majority of spills have no information on wildlife and habitat effects, and for those that do, only a tiny proportion of spills show effects on habitat and wildlife. It's uncertain why this is so because the criteria used by industry or the regulator to assess wildlife and habitat effects, if any criteria exist, are not known. The regulator does not apply nor does it require standard methods to assess habitat and wildlife effects. The judgment of industry that there has been no effect is simply accepted. It's another example of industry and the regulator working together to misinform the public. It's no wonder that wildlife are disappearing while the regulator claims it's protecting the environment.

Given that the industry has been active in Alberta since 1902, why have regulators and government so poorly documented wildlife and habitat effects of spills? It's a recipe for disaster. When a journalist asked the regulator how it can report such low rates of damage to habitat and wildlife, a spokesperson stated that prior to 2013 the regulator tracked only what was in its mandate and impacts on wildlife and wildlife habitat were not under its jurisdiction. He added, "If the spill caused damage to a sensitive area or wildlife/livestock outside of the regulator's jurisdiction, it may have been marked (for lack of a better option in the system) as not affected" (Nikiforuk 2017a). This bit of smoke blowing is typical of the regulator's explanations. The regulator explains away problems as bookkeeping issues and thereby tacitly acknowledges that its database is not credible, it shifts responsibility to another agency such as the ERCB (its former name!), and it misinforms by stating that it did not record environmental damage prior to 2013; it has tracked environmental damage since 2002.

There are four possible explanations for AER's reporting that no animals were killed as a result of a spill: (1) there were no animals killed; although this outcome is possible, it requires credible scientific evidence which it does not provide; (2) animals were killed, but no study was conducted; (3) study was conducted but its timing and methods failed to meet acceptable standards; or (4) animal deaths were reported, but AER did not record those deaths. Let's examine a credible estimate of damage.

In their study of spills in Oklahoma, Fisher and Sublette (2005) determined the industry-reported median volumes that resulted in environmental injury for crude oil and saline water spills. Applying the same spill volume thresholds for harm (table 13.1), how does the Oklahoma estimate compare to the AER wildlife and habitat harm rates? Oklahoma's spill harm rates are forty times greater for crude oil spills and thirty-nine times greater for saline spills than the regulator's harm rates.

Table 13.1 Harmful crude oil and saline spills in Oklahoma and Alberta: a comparison of estimates

Spill class	Harmful crude oil spills	Harmful saline spills
Oklahoma, total harmful spills	15,069	9,106
Oklahoma, harmful spills/year	357.9	216.3
Alberta, total harmful spills[a]	379	237
Alberta, harmful spills/year	9.0	5.6
Harm ratio Oklahoma:Alberta	39.8	38.6

Note: Threshold for harmful crude oil spills is set at ≥ 1.6 m³ for crude oil and at ≥ 9.5 m³ for saline spills based on Fisher and Sublette (2005).
[a] Alberta spill harm rate based on the proportion of spills reporting harm to wildlife or habitat.

EVIDENCE OF WILDLIFE AND HABITAT EFFECTS

Failure to record habitat damage or animal deaths is insidious because it's difficult to document if observations are not made and/or records and reports are not available to the public. Although the rate of failures to report wildlife and habitat effects can't be determined directly due to lack of studies, we needn't look far to realize there's a significant problem of failure to report environmental effects. Such is the culture of misinformation and denial within the regulator that it's good to remind ourselves that failure to report environmental effects is simply that – a failure to report – rather than an absence of effects. Here are some examples.

For a Plains Midstream spill of April 2011, the AER database states "Habitat affected," not that animals were injured or killed. However, an investigation found eleven beavers, four bears, ten frogs, twenty-eight ducks, fifty "small birds (shoreline and songbird)," and three mice were "affected" (ERCB 2013a). The mortality count, as reported by Plains Midstream, was eleven beavers, eleven frogs, seventy-nine birds, six mice, one vole, and one toad (ERCB 2013a). Although 109 animals were found dead, the regulator failed to record any animal deaths in its database. Moreover, the industry-reported mortality count was based on animals found dead during cleanup operations, which represents an unspecified fraction of the true mortality count. Recall that in the Pine River oil spill, fish found dead represented only about 6–11 per cent of the estimated total fish mortality.

The regulator has no record of the May 2005 spill of crude oil into the Waskahigan River. But a study (AAR 2006) documented reproductive effects in sculpins, and PAH metabolites were detected in longnose sucker and lake chub.

On 19 July 2011, 130–160 m³ of crude oil spilled from a Pembina Pipeline Corporation pipeline northeast of the town of Swan Hills. Crude oil flowed overland into a forest and a creek. About 3.6 km of the creek and creek bank were affected. A report stated, "Monthly sampling of the creek water is being conducted by a Pembina contractor; no impacts have been reported to ESRD. An affected area where excavation activities occurred due to ineffective flushing operations has been backfilled and recontoured with the exception of a few localized areas" (ERCB 2013b). The regulator accepted the lack of environmental impacts as reported by industry. In spite of extensive damage, the AER database states that there was "no affect" on wildlife or habitat.

The regulator's failure to document wildlife impacts continues today. I illustrate with a 29 May 2019 saline spill by Obsidian Energy. The spill, initially reported as 80 m³ then raised to 400 m³, took place northwest of Drayton Valley and flowed into a wetland tributary of the Pembina River (Rieger 2019). Although the regulator was unable or unwilling to confirm the well type involved in the spill (Heidenreich 2019), the spill took place at an injection well. On its online compliance dashboard, the regulator, without conducting an investigation, repeated the company's assessment that "no impacts to wildlife" were reported, but a saline spill of 400 m³ is forty-two times larger than the median volume found to harm the environment (table 13.1). Spokespersons for the regulator and Obsidian Energy both declined a request for an interview with Global News (Heidenreich 2019). For this spill, and tens of thousands of other spills, the regulator's careful choice of words is a clever evasion. The regulator can truthfully state that no wildlife impacts were reported by industry, which avoids stating whether there were impacts. Because the regulator accepts industry's statements without verification, it can maintain plausible deniability. Should any impacts be found by a third party, the regulator can profess ignorance, a position it adopts with practiced ease.

The regulator has even failed to document wildlife and habitat effects for the four largest saline spills in Alberta history. The lack of documentation of effects for these spills is stunning. The largest release, that from Peace River

Oils #1 ("Old Salty"), is missing from the FIS database and was discussed in chapter 8. I describe other large saline spills below. For context, recall that the extensive damage documented for the Apache 15-09 spill involved a release of 15,363 m³ of saline water, one-half to one-third the size of the following three releases.

The fourth largest saline spill in Alberta history reported a release of 30,000 m³ on 30 August 1985 at an abandoned well northeast of McLennan, Alberta. The volume recovered field is blank. The regulator concluded there was "no affect" on wildlife/habitat and that the area was not sensitive, even though the spill occurred in a shoreline area 600 m west of a large lake. Equally remarkable is the release cleanup date of 17 March 2015; in other words, there was a thirty-year delay between the spill and its being entered into the FIS database.

The third largest recorded saline spill, a release of 32,000 m³, occurred at a BP Canada water pipeline on 7 August 1984, east of Utikuma Lake. Despite the fact that zero volume was recovered, the wildlife/habitat affected field contains no data and the regulator did not consider the area to be sensitive. The spill occurred in a large wetland complex and wetlands are known for their sensitivity to spills.

The second largest saline spill in Alberta history took place west of Edmonton during a well blowout on 12 December 2004. The blowout released 8.1 million m³ of raw production gas, 436 m³ of crude oil, and 48,079 m³ of saline produced water; zero volumes were recovered. More than 500 people were evacuated. We are asked to believe that this shockingly large release was contained in an area smaller than 10 m x 10 m, and that there was no effect on habitat or wildlife. I searched for documentation and found one report (EUB 2005) on emergency response in regard to public safety, the evacuation, and air monitoring for hydrogen sulphide. I found no study of environmental impacts. Given the large volumes of saline water and crude oil released, and the fact that the blowout and wind dispersed toxic materials in a plume towards the northeast, it's difficult to understand how the regulator concluded that the incident caused no effects on wildlife or habitat. See web 13.4 for more information on this spill.

The final example illustrates a failure to report environmental impacts. On 18 May 2006, a release of steam resulted from cap rock failure at Total's Joslyn Creek steam-assisted gravity drainage operations (figure 13.1). According to the AER, the blowout released 5,000 m³ of process water and, miraculously, all 5,000 m³ of process water were recovered and there was "no affect" on wildlife or habitat. In contrast, studies documented significant impacts. Roche (2010) reported that Total was exceeding the approved steam injection pressure when the reservoir cap rock was breached, which blew out a "huge crater" and hurled rocks hundreds of metres into the air. An ERCB (2010) report observed that the steam release created a surface disturbance about 125 m by 75 m with a triangular-shaped crater. The main release zone contained heaved and rotated ground, subsidence zones, and tensile cracks formed in response to the ejection of soil and bedrock. A fine dust settled over an area about 1 km long by 100 m wide. Rock projectiles were thrown up to 300 m from the main crater, and probably greater than this distance vertically. About 1,400 to 1,700 m³ of soil and bedrock were blown skyward. The peatland and its habitat were obliterated. The habitat surrounding the incident was later stripped of natural vegetation and the landscape desiccated. By examining satellite imagery I also found that the location for the incident as provided by the regulator was incorrect by about 505 m (figure 13.1).

194

Figure 13.1 *Above and opposite* The blowout at Total's Joslyn Creek caprock failure and steam explosion. (a) Before the blowout and steam explosion. (b) Immediately after the blowout, showing crater; the ellipse outlines part of the displaced material deposit. Average concentrations in the deposit were 1,168 mg/kg, 15,875 mg/kg, and 7,900 mg/kg for F2, F3, and F4 hydrocarbons. Average levels of conductivity, sodium, and sulphate were 1,720 μS/cm, 461 mg/L, and 573 mg/L. Elevated hydrocarbons and salinity were also observed in a deposit of displaced material that extended over one kilometer from the blowout. Wildlife were exposed to the contaminants through contact and ingestion

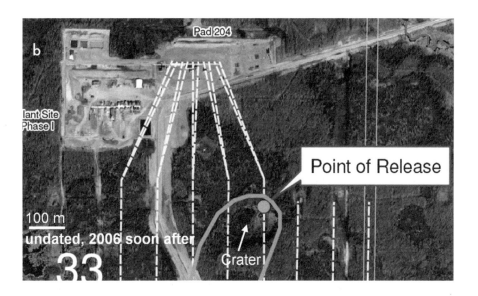

of vegetation, soil, and foods. Groundwater transported contaminants to Joslyn Creek (Millennium 2007). (c) Two years after the blowout. The top thumbtack marks the incorrect location of the incident as reported by AER, the bottom thumbtack marks the correct location, ~ 505 m to the southeast. Note the increasing industry footprint evident as habitat loss.

"Loss" of the Total blowout impact study (Millennium 2007) was equally troubling. When I contacted Alberta Environment and Parks in order to procure the report, staff informed me that the report, if it existed, would have to be requested via a FOIP application. When I persisted, AEP told me that the report could not be found and had probably been destroyed. I complained to the environment minister and, *mirabile dictu*, the report was "found" and sent to me. The report revealed significant environmental impacts. Near the blowout, about two hectares were covered with a layer of displaced material with strongly elevated hydrocarbons and salinity. That the regulator would maintain that this explosion did not harm wildlife or habitat and that process steam blown hundreds of metres into the air was fully recovered demonstrates the length to which the regulator will go to deny reality.

THE NEED FOR CREDIBLE EFFECTS MONITORING

Because public access to spills is prohibited in Alberta, independent observers can't provide real-time information. Were people free to observe animals in distress and to report those observations to an agency that provided public access to those observations, the public would be outraged at the death toll. Freedom to observe and report to a public agency can serve the public interest and help distressed wildlife (figure 13.2). In the wake of a single spill, the Enbridge Kalamazoo River, Michigan spill, the public reported more animal observations than are present in the entire AER database. Twenty-six kinds of animals and 405 oiled individuals were reported. The Michigan data illustrate the concept of "observability." The oiled animals most often reported were large, familiar, or slow moving and therefore readily observable, such as geese, ducks, and turtles. Less observable animals were reported infrequently, such as mice, frogs, toads, and crayfish. These small, difficult to observe animals, are more abundant than are geese, ducks, and turtles. The reported rate of oiling for difficult to observe animals is considerably underestimated. Transparent and public monitoring after spills can provide important insight into postspill effects.

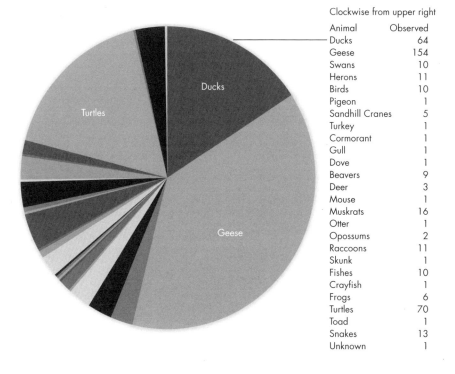

Figure 13.2 Wildlife hotline calls by species. The public effectively reported distressed wildlife although large and familiar vertebrates such as ducks and geese are easy to observe and therefore tend to be overrepresented relative to other animals. In response to the Kalamazoo River spill, Enbridge developed an "Oiled Wildlife Hotline" that allowed citizens and spill responders to report observations so that field crews could respond to distressed wildlife in a timely manner. A similar reporting system is long overdue in Alberta.

CAN THE PUBLIC USE FIS DATA TO ASSESS HABITAT AND WILDLIFE EFFECTS?

The short answer is no. The regulator does not provide credible information on habitat and wildlife effects, on the areal extent of damage, and on the contaminants remaining after a spill. Neither does it provide accurate location data and reliable volumes released and recovered nor does it monitor the environmental impacts over time.

To demonstrate the degree to which FIS misinformation can hamper the evaluation of a spill's effects, consider a major 2015 Nexen pipeline spill (figure 13.3). The AER responded to the spill as if it were solely crude oil and failed to recognize that saline water was involved that would spread into the nearby water body. Although the presence of saline water was immediately brought

Figure 13.3 Aerial view of the July 2015 Nexen pipeline spill of bitumen and saline wastewater emulsion near the Long Lake facility, looking NNE. Arrows mark the apparent linear extent of the spill. According to a confidential source, the lake adjacent to the pipeline was also affected.

to the AER's attention, a significant delay ensued before response efforts included the affected water body. The Alberta Environmental Monitoring, Evaluation and Reporting Agency offered its scientific and technical assistance, but its offer was declined by the AER (W. Donahue, pers. comm., January 2020). As reported by the regulator, the spill released 5 m³ of saline produced water (zero recovered), along with a recovery of 5 m³ of contaminated surface water and 202 m³ of waste. The area affected was given as 100–1,000 m² and there was "no affect" on habitat or wildlife. Court documents, however, stated that the release totalled about 5,000 m³, that the release was an emulsion of bitumen, "wastewater," and sand, and that the affected area was 21,900 m² (Mertz 2017). Given that the spill affected the lake adjacent to the pipeline, the court-stated spill footprint is also an underestimate. At the minimum, the regulator underestimated the spill area by at least a factor of twenty-two, underestimated the spill volume by a factor of 1,000, provided misinformation on the substances spilled, was offered and declined expert assistance, and failed to adequately respond to the spill. It's significant that the Nexen spill took place at a new, technologically advanced, double-walled pipeline; that the automatic spill detection equipment failed (Mertz 2017); and that AER's location for the spill was wildly inaccurate (see chapter 6, "Inaccurate Locations"). I leave it to you to decide if the spill had no effect on habitat.

Unreliable industry-reported data on spills are ubiquitous. In every case for which I could find comparison data, the regulator's figures underestimated spill volumes, habitat and wildlife impacts, and areas affected. To make matters worse, the AER failed to update its database when new, more accurate figures became available. Industry's underreporting of effects is by no means restricted to Alberta (see chapter 15). When Calgary-based TC Energy (formerly Trans Canada) reported its Keystone Pipeline had spilled 1,400 m³ of crude oil in eastern North Dakota, the state regulator reported that the spill covered 0.2 ha; it was later found that the spill footprint had been underestimated by a factor of nine (Associated Press 2019).

SUMMARY

In spite of clear evidence of effects, the regulator rarely admits to effects on habitat or wildlife. Its decisions about environmental effects appear to be based not on science but rather on ideology. Failure to report animal and habitat effects is yet another reason that the regulator's data are not credible. The regulator doesn't have the expertise to evaluate environmental effects in a scientifically credible manner.

Failure to document spill effects has been occurring for decades, which undermines both environmental management and faith in the regulatory system. Industry-reported data from Oklahoma indicate that crude oil and saline spills harm habitat and wildlife at a rate about forty times higher than suggested by the regulator's data. The science on spill effects is clear and consistent – spills cause detectable and persistent effects. The regulator's data portray an alternative reality disconnected from science. The AER, as the sole authority over fossil fuel industry spills, is failing to protect the environment in Alberta.

In the next chapter we examine how failing to protect the environment causes significant cumulative effects.

CHAPTER 14

Cumulative Effects

If no one asks, then no one answers, that's how every empire falls.

R.B. Morris, "That's How Every Empire Falls"

INTRODUCTION

It's long been known that the fossil fuel industry can exert lasting impacts on ecosystems. Forty-eight years ago in the early days of arctic oil and gas development in Canada, two ecologists (Bliss and Peterson 1973) pondered the future. They worried that ecological information might not be incorporated into the design, construction, and operations of hydrocarbon development. Until that was done they felt that little more than lip service would be paid to maintaining viable arctic ecosystems and the ways of life for northern native peoples. They wondered how successful we would be at blending engineering and ecological understanding to achieve in the arctic what we have failed to do elsewhere.

Forty-eight years later we find that the growth of ecological knowledge has lagged behind the rate of exploitation and that the incorporation of that knowledge into industrial operations has failed. There are several reasons for that failure, but the inherently destructive nature of hydrocarbon exploitation is probably the foremost. It's impossible for a carbon-based economy to not cause pervasive ecological harm. The harm can be lessened with best practices, but the industry determined years ago that it's less expensive to damage ecosystems when the costs of prevention are borne by industry while the costs of damage are borne by society. Investment in public relations and regulatory capture provided larger financial gains than did changing operations to protect the environment. Whatever the reasons for the failure to incorporate ecological understanding, the result has been a multidecadal expansion of cumulative effects worsened by climate change.

In chapters 4 and 5, we examined studies on the impacts of spills, well pads, pipelines, and seismic lines. Other chapters have documented the impacts of spills and the reliability of the regulator's data. Those impacts provide a basis to understand how the industry creates cumulative effects and how the regulator's data mislead about those effects. In this chapter, we broaden the focus to examine those cumulative effects. We first summarize the effects of hydrocarbon exploitation and estimate the landscape footprint for Alberta. We then examine the landscape conversion process, how cumulative effects are expressed on industry leases, the multiplier effect of climate change, and the challenges of predicting future cumulative effects. For a discussion of the impacts of industrial roads and the concerns arising from liabilities at contaminated sites, orphan wells, failed reclamation, and impacts upon First Nations please see web 14.2–14.4.

201

CUMULATIVE EFFECTS OF THE FOSSIL FUEL INDUSTRY

The importance of assessing the cumulative effects of fossil fuel industry activities grows more urgent with each year. The effects of the industry are well documented (table 14.1 provides a summary). What we don't know is how those effects interact with each other nor how extensive those effects are. The areal extent of those interacting effects is the cumulative effect. How large is the effect? We don't know because we don't know all their interactions or their underground impacts. Nor can we simply total the extent of the land conversion because the effect of a disturbance is more extensive than its footprint. Placing all industry disturbances on the same metric as areal extent can mislead. By that measure, a skin abrasion would be more serious than a stab wound. With these reservations in mind, we can begin by asking, how big is the footprint?

Table 14.1 Effects of fossil fuel industry activities

Effects at ecosystem level

landscape perforation, dissection, fragmentation, and attrition

habitat loss; decreased cover of forests, wetlands, woody vegetation, and interior habitat; increased edge habitat and grass vegetation

domain shifts (persistent changes in ecosystems)

noise pollution (effects on songbirds and quality of life)

air pollution (hydrocarbons, VOCs, sulphur dioxide, hydrogen sulphide, metals, greenhouse gases, particulates); increasing concentrations of greenhouse gases in the atmosphere have altered the Earth's climate and driven planet-altering changes to ecosystems worldwide

light pollution

water and groundwater pollution, damage to riparian zones and fish habitat, increased erosion, siltation of streams, barriers to fish movement

disruption of lateral surface water flows and nutrient regimes (desiccation, ponding)

consumption of fresh water

soil and sediment pollution

reduced soil nutrients, reduced organic matter, increased bare ground, changes to soil biota

soil compaction, erosion; loss of soil carbon, especially from peatlands

salinization

increased wildfires

increased depth of thaw layer (permafrost degradation)

Effects at population and community level

decline in fisheries

changes to animal populations

increased poaching

increased predation along linear disturbances

changes in the movements and migrations of animals, plants, and microbes

increased exotic, weedy, and pollution-tolerant species

decreased native biodiversity

decline or loss of rare or sensitive species

increased metabolic and respiratory stress and reproductive impairment

increased mortality (example: loss of migratory birds due to spills, power line and vehicle collisions, and contact with oil and brine pits and tailings ponds)

Social and political effects

separation of politically powerful areas of consumption from impoverished areas of production permits the creation of environmental sacrifice zones (winners and losers, haves and have nots)

loss of traditional use and treaty rights

loss of clean drinking water and productive agricultural land

increased costs and uncertainty to local governments and the public from undocumented contaminated sites

privatization of profits, increased financial liability to taxpayers

regulatory capture

erosion of democratic institutions and loss of trust in government

The Fossil Fuel Industry Footprint in Alberta

Hydrocarbon exploitation creates a large and growing landscape footprint (figures 5.1, 12.10, 14.1–14.2, plates 12.2, 14.1–14.4). Although its footprint in Alberta as of 2014 was estimated as 11,993 km² (Schieck et al. 2014) that estimate was based on satellite imagery that underestimates the extent of narrow linear features such as seismic lines and pipelines. Multiple disturbances can further muddy the industrial footprint when, for example, evidence of energy features is obscured when affected areas lie within areas also disturbed by logging, forest fires, road building, agriculture, or other developments. So what is a reasonable estimate of Alberta's fossil fuel industry footprint?

Summing the footprints (web 14.1) for pipelines, seismic lines, well pads, and roads yields a subtotal of 23,924 km². The area of tailings ponds and open pit bitumen mines adds 1,500 km² (Timoney 2015) for a footprint of the industry of 25,424 km². This is the minimum footprint because the footprint grows each year, especially for *in situ* bitumen exploitation, and the seismic footprint is a gross underestimate. We then need to add an unknown footprint for industry batteries, power lines, facilities, camps, processing plants, and airstrips. And that estimate does not account for the ecological impacts due to edge effects, landscape fragmentation, and effects on animal and plant movements and water quality. Conservatively, the total Alberta footprint exceeds 30,000 km². It's important to realize that the biota and soils of this industrial footprint are permanently damaged (chapters 4 and 5, web 4 and 5). Despite claims of "certified" reclamation of industrial sites, there is no scientific evidence for successful reclamation, and that includes the estimated 100,000 oil and gas well sites that have been "certified" reclaimed in Alberta since 1963.

But whatever footprint we calculate underestimates the areal ecological effect because effects extend outward from disturbances for various distances. The extent of the edge effects vary whether we are considering noise pollution (which can extend for kilometres) or effects on climate and soils, mammals, birds, lichens, mosses, or flowering plants. Sensitivity to disturbance varies even between closely related species such as winter wrens and house wrens. If, for example, we placed a 100 m buffer around all industry disturbances to account for edge effects, the footprint would increase by more than a factor of ten and cover more than one-half of Alberta. At a certain density, industrial development obliterates interior habitat and the entire landscape becomes edge habitat (figures 14.1–14.2).

The Landscape Conversion Process

The hydrocarbon industry is by no means the only source of permanent habitat loss and ecosystem degradation. In some regions, agriculture and logging cause more habitat loss than does hydrocarbon exploitation. Independent of the source of the disturbance, most landscapes experience a similar process as they're converted to human uses (plate 14.2). We can conceptualize cumulative effects by imagining an ecosystem as a human body. Spills, production and disposal wells, and fracking are puncture wounds that perforate and inject toxins into our bodies. Seismic lines, pipelines, roads, and powerlines dissect the body into a network of lacerations. Well pads, batteries and other facilities, clearcuts, towns and cities, and farms and fields fragment the body's surface into a patchwork of wounds; here the ecosystem is experiencing fragmentation and habitat loss. When the wounds grow in extent and coalesce and deepen, we lose body parts such as an arm or leg. At this stage, we lose ecosystem services, populations, and communities, a landscape process known as attrition but more familiar as the processes of extirpation and extinction. Finally, the body or the ecosystem succumbs to the cumulative effects of the injuries.

We experience the landscape omnipresence of cumulative effects as a psychological footprint. Unless we're in a national park, we know that agricultural fields, cutblocks, roads, pipelines, wells (both active and abandoned), and seismic lines are nearby, and increasingly we know that a spill or a contaminated site is nearby.

A Fishery Biologist Speaks Out
Although scientists are aware of industry's cumulative effects, many won't speak out because they fear retribution or loss of income. Some voice their concerns off the record and perhaps at night their dreams are troubled, but publicly they remain silent. Ecological interactions mean that something as simple as constructing a pipeline stream crossing can have multiple unforeseen effects. Here fisheries biologist Dave Mayhood provides a rare glimpse behind the scenes (pers. comm., April 2019):

> I assessed stream habitats and fish populations and monitored the effects of pipeline construction in Muddy and Pinto creeks and their tributaries. These streams drain to the Wapiti River, part of the Peace River drainage southwest of Grande Prairie, Alberta. I monitored pipe-

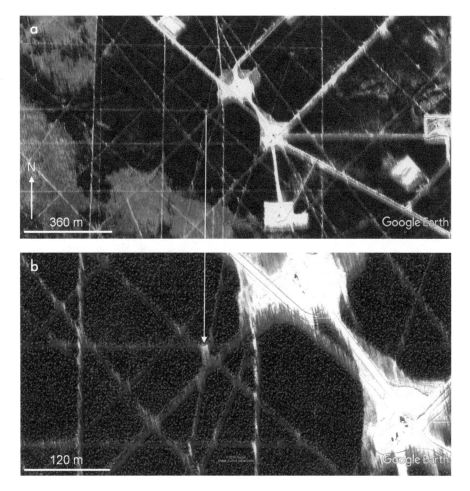

Figure 14.1 (a) Degraded landscape of boreal conifer and deciduous forests in the territory of the Dene Tha First Nation fragmented by a network of seismic lines, pipelines, wells, and roads. (b) Close-up. Because ecological effects extend beyond the physical footprint, no interior habitat remains undisturbed or unimpaired in this landscape. Location 59° 1′ 45″ N, 118° 56′ 25″ W, 20 km SW of Zama City, 27 February 2005.

line stream crossings as they were being constructed. Typically a backhoe would reach across the creek and cut a deep trench across the channel. The trench would fill up with water, cutting off flow and draining the channel dry for some distance upstream and downstream in this low-relief terrain. Dewatering the channel extended for sometimes hundreds of metres upstream and down, sending a wave of dryness downstream for many kilometres until the trench was full and flow was restored. Ice cover, now unsupported by water, collapsed at intervals for many kilometres downstream.

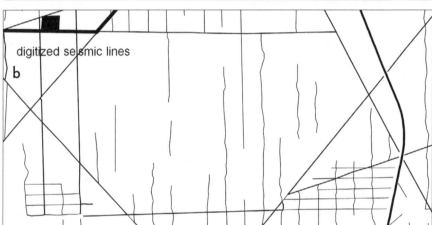

Figure 14.2 Actual compared to mapped linear disturbances such as high-density seismic lines, pipelines, and a road network in a forest wetland complex. (a) The network as annotated onto a Google Earth image. (b) The network as digitized by ABMI (2017). Less than one-half of the seismic line network was captured by the ABMI image analysis. Location 56° 48′ 53″ N, 113° 35′ 3″ W.

But that was just the beginning. After the pipe was lowered into the trench at the crossing, the trench was backfilled with sand and clay. Backfilling caused waves of muddy water to flow downstream for many kilometres. This muddy water would flow over the collapsed ice and freeze solid, creating a barrier to fish movement. Although total suspended sediments were often high, and persisted only long enough to cause sublethal effects on fishes, the impaired movement caused by the ice blockages imposed greater impacts by exposing fish to freezing. Ice collapse due to unprotected trenching extended at least 6.5 and 12 km downstream in two cases. It was a big eye-opener for me. I just hadn't expected it.

The project proponent [pipeline company] didn't provide for follow-up studies, and the responsible government agencies didn't require them. It is a great failing to ignore follow-up monitoring to determine the effects of projects. Postproject evaluations would make future environmental assessments easier, cheaper, and more reliable, and future crossings less damaging.

Looking at the region on Google Earth today, I see it has been overwhelmed by a dense network of roads, pipelines, wells, seismic lines, and clearcuts. The science tells us that the extensive landscape disturbance will have reduced stream carrying capacity for fish. Widened channels caused by bank erosion will have made streams shallower with fewer pools suitable for overwintering. Chronic siltation will have reduced the productivity of bottom-dwelling invertebrates and reduced spawning habitat quantity and quality. The stream crossings with hanging and blocked culverts will have created impassable barriers that prevent fish use of critical habitat.

Habitat damage of this kind is one of the major factors accounting for the decline of native trout, char, whitefish, and grayling populations throughout Alberta's eastern slopes and western boreal regions. Athabasca rainbow trout are now federally listed as endangered, westslope cutthroat trout and bull trout are federally listed as threatened, and Arctic grayling and mountain whitefish have declined throughout much of their Alberta range. These are the probable impacts, but where are the studies?

THE MULTIPLIER EFFECT OF CLIMATE CHANGE

Climate change exacerbates the stresses imposed by humans upon the Earth's ecosystems. Species and communities that are not extirpated directly by habitat loss must cope with background stressors and, increasingly, must cope with changes in disturbance regimes, water availability, drought, temperature, and growing season. In western Canada, a combination of habitat disturbance, wetland drainage, and increased aridity are contributing to long-term declines in wetland extent. The desiccating effects of salinization are exacerbated by increases in aridity (Timoney 2015). Application of road salts, municipal and industrial wastewater discharge, climate change, and the agriculture, hydrocarbon, and mining industries all contribute to ecosystem salinization and now threaten the health of aquatic systems worldwide (Kerr 2017; Laceby et al. 2019). In southern Alberta, rising salinity since the 1980s is threatening the sustainability of aquatic ecosystems (Kerr 2017). In central Alberta, from 1987 to 2017, concentrations of chloride, sodium, and potassium increased in aquatic systems downstream of Edmonton (Laceby et al. 2019). The rising salinity is due to a combination of road salting (54 per cent of the increase), agriculture (20 per cent), and industrial effluent (15 per cent). An ecologically unsustainable six tonnes of chloride are now added per km² every year to aquatic systems downstream of Edmonton and the ecosystem retains 56 per cent of the chloride.

Climate warming in recent decades across much of the boreal zone has resulted in declines in conifer growth and forest productivity (Lloyd and Bunn 2007; Berner et al. 2011; Tei et al. 2017). Despite predictions that the boreal forest will migrate northward in a warming climate, an increased areal extent of burned forests was the largest change we observed over the period 1960–2010 in a vast 960,000 km² subarctic region (Timoney and Mamet 2019). Fire severity and extent in western North America are predicted to increase significantly over the twenty-first century, with attendant ecological, economic, and social impacts (Flannigan et al. 2005; Balshi et al. 2009; de Groot et al. 2013). Wildfires can increase the abundance of cyanobacteria in shallow boreal lakes (Charette and Prepas 2003) and increase mercury and nutrient loading and lake productivity, and thereby restructure aquatic food webs and exacerbate the effects of contaminants (Kelly et al. 2006). Overall the prospects for forests, wetlands, forest-dependent and wetland-dependent species, and water quality are not good.

In western and central Canada, the most salient effects of increased wildfire activity are a net reduction in forest extent; declines in forest age, stature, and stored carbon; a reduction in conifers in favour of deciduous trees; melting of permafrost in ice-cored peatlands; increases in savannah, grass, and shrub vegetation; and increased weed and exotic species populations. The role that humans have played in Alberta in exacerbating the impacts of wildfires has not received adequate attention. Indeed, half of all wildfires in Alberta are started by humans. Significantly, two of the largest and most destructive wildfires in Alberta history were started by humans (plate 14.5). Although it's tempting to

Human-Caused Fires: The Beast in the Room

Although the Alberta government hesitates to acknowledge the fact, humans recently caused two of the largest, most destructive and costly wildfires in Alberta history (plate 14.5).

The Richardson River wildfire north of Fort McMurray burned 576,649 ha in 2011 (Timoney 2015). I asked the Alberta government to provide the cost of the wildfire but it declined. The Fort McMurray wildfire (nicknamed the Beast) burned 589,552 ha in 2016 and caused $9.9 billion of damage and tremendous hardship.

The Richardson River wildfire began on a seismic line. The Fort McMurray wildfire began in the Horse River trail area and is believed to have been caused by recreation vehicles, a campfire, industry, a power line, or arson. Lightning has been ruled out as a cause for both fires. Although evidence of human-caused ignition exists for both fires, no prosecutions were pursued. Why? Would the prosecutions have exposed that the fossil fuel industry is causing extensive harm and costing the public billions of dollars? Would the insurance companies on the hook for the Beast have sued the responsible parties for compensation? Is it a surprise that the Alberta government refused to tell me the cost of the Richardson River wildfire? Is it a surprise that an increasing number of insurance companies are refusing to insure fossil fuel industry companies? Northeastern Alberta lies in the crosshairs of cumulative effects.

209

blame the 2011 Richardson River and 2016 Fort McMurray wildfires on climate change, those fires were the result of fossil fuel industry activities; climate change acted as an effect multiplier.

Climate change increases the risks of spread of exotic species that are associated with industrial development (Nixon et al. 2015) and can induce range contractions and local extirpations. From his study of changes in the ranges of 976 species, Wiens (2016) concluded that extirpations are already widespread, most often at the "warm" edge of ranges, in tropical species, in animals, and in freshwater habitats; 47 per cent of the species showed evidence of local extinctions. Climate changes that have already occurred have been sufficient to extirpate local populations, suggesting that many species can't shift their ranges rapidly enough to track climate change and landscape disturbance.

Those losses include birds near and dear to many of us such as northern go-shawk, long-eared owl, least flycatcher, Lincoln's sparrow, black-backed wood-pecker, and northern waterthrush.

The combined stresses imposed by human activities and climate change are causing major changes in biodiversity (IPBES 2019). In the coming decades, local population extinctions may become more widespread as climate change intensifies. Species persistence might depend largely on their abilities to shift their ranges to higher latitudes or elevations in order to remain within their domains of ecological tolerance. These shifts may be impeded by a lack of suit-able habitat or soil, or by barriers to dispersal, or dispersal or adaptation may be too slow to keep pace with climate change (Wiens 2016). The pace of en-vironmental change may create unstable ecosystems (Hansen et al. 2001). The stresses may be too great to permit the persistence of the ecosystem mosaics prevalent in the twentieth century and familiar to most of us.

CUMULATIVE EFFECTS LARGE AND SMALL

We can arrange industrial disturbances along a gradient from least to greatest impairment: low-impact seismic lines, conventional seismic lines, and tem-porary airstrips; pipelines, roads, and utility corridors; well sites; and finally batteries, waste pits and dumps, tailings ponds, and processing plants. For all intents, industry sites have undergone a domain shift and will not return to their predisturbance condition in our lifetimes. Whether you feel that's good or bad or you're indifferent is your personal choice, but those are the facts. In-dustry leases will serve as a reminder of our collective failure to protect eco-systems from harm.

To review, we know how particular processes such as spills and construction of well pads and pipelines affect ecosystems. Similarly, we have an idea of the minimum ecological footprint. We know that disturbances from agriculture and the fossil fuel, mining, and forest industries interact to exacerbate effects and we call this interaction cumulative effects. We know that climate change is an effect multiplier. What we don't know, and will take years of study to un-ravel, is the web of interactions of those effects. When disturbances occur, the effects are more complex than a chain reaction. Instead the effects spread out-ward and interact like the strands of a web. In short order, these effects become too complex to model. Let's consider an example.

Say seismic exploration detects hydrocarbons and a network of wells is drilled that requires development of a network of pipelines, roads, powerlines, and batteries. That infrastructure makes it more economical for other companies to follow and the disturbance network increases in intensity and extent (figures 12.2, 14.1–14.2, plate 14.1). The disturbances destroy most or all of the native biota within the footprints. The seismic lines, pipelines, powerlines, and roads change how water moves and how moose, caribou, wolves, and other animals move. Those same features attract recreational hunters, poachers, and off-roaders. Increased human activities from industry and the public increase the area burned by wildfires. Spills contaminate the soil and groundwater. Mammals, birds, and fishes are exposed to contaminants in water, soils, and waste pits; some die and some become sick or have trouble reproducing. Stream crossings cause siltation, and hanging culverts block fish movements. Water quality declines and fishes decline and animals that eat fish decline. Interior and old forest species decline and other sensitive species like wolverine, lynx, or fisher decline or disappear. Noise pollution causes declines in bird breeding success and quality of life for humans. Woodland caribou decline while white-tailed deer and cowbirds increase. Biodiversity declines and exotic species spread. First Nations people have to spend more money and time to reach now distant animals. They have to buy and carry bottled water because the streams from which they used to drink have taken on a strange taste. Culturally important animal populations decline and people have to resort to store-bought food. Their nutrition and health suffer; their happiness and life satisfaction decline; they stop going out on the land and traditional knowledge is lost. While we piece together this web of interactions to understand cumulative effects, the landscape footprint grows and the climate continues to change. In short, we experience the changes first and try to understand them later. This is not how a modern, rational society is supposed to function.

Understanding cumulative effects sufficiently to predict the future is not possible. Instead, cumulative effects studies typically focus on a region or single facility and attempt to predict effects on particular species such as woodland caribou or to predict the effects of say, acid deposition on soils. These studies are most often conducted as part of environmental impact assessments of major industrial projects. The most noteworthy failure to assess cumulative impacts is perhaps the industry-funded Regional Aquatics Monitoring Program whose objective was to assess the effects of the bitumen industry on regional water quality in northeastern Alberta. Repeated assessments of the

211

program concluded that it was unable to measure and assess development-related environmental change due to a combination of poor study design, loss or degradation of reference sites, and lack of integration with other monitoring (Ayles et al. 2004; Dowdeswell et al. 2010; RAMP Review Panel 2011). Despite having no scientific credibility, RAMP monitoring continues to provide public relations cover for the industry.

The status of air monitoring is equally unacceptable. After decades of environmentally significant air emissions in the bitumen sands region, emission measurements still require improvements, and understanding of their cumulative impacts remains incomplete (Brook et al. 2019). But more funding and more and better data will not prevent the damage. Waiting for a complete understanding of the cumulative impacts isn't necessary. It doesn't require multimillion dollar research efforts to know that the cumulative impacts have been significant. The science is clear. One such study examined the effects of hydrocarbon development in a 7,000 km^2 Canadian boreal region over a sixty-year period. Development caused the ecosystem to exceed its normal range of variability, which was formerly driven by wildfire (Pickell et al. 2015). Oil and gas activities caused a net reduction in living forest cover and an increase in low quality edge habitat. In some areas, development had generated novel landscapes with no historical analogue.

Hydrocarbon development has contributed to significant declines in the abundance of breeding birds. In western Canada, 11,840 to 60,380 bird nests are destroyed each year due to seismic exploration, clearing of pipelines and well pads, and bitumen sands mining (Van Wilgenburg et al. 2013). When natural mortality is accounted for, this nest destruction results in the annual loss in the range of 10,200 to 41,150 birds. At the local scale, in the Swan River area of north-central Alberta, an area subjected to industrial disturbances, the number of breeding bird species and the overall abundance of breeding birds declined over the period 1987–2017. Over that thirty-year period, the number of breeding bird species declined about 14 per cent while the overall abundance of birds declined about 47 per cent (web 14.5). Declines from predisturbance conditions are actually larger than these numbers indicate because bird monitoring began decades after industrial development. At the regional scale, as early as 1968, development in the Swan Hills was already causing significant land degradation (Lengellé 1976). At the subbiome scale, of the ninety-three breeding bird species with medium to high data reliability in the Alberta portion of the boreal taiga plains region, 38 per cent of species declined in abundance while only 10 per cent of species increased over the period 1970–2015 (web 14.6).

The woodland caribou is sensitive to human disturbance and serves as a good indicator of cumulative effects. The species has been suffering range contraction and population decline for decades. Degraded habitat conditions in Alberta can't sustain caribou populations (Alberta Government 2017b). In the winter range of the La Peche caribou herd, 88 per cent of the landscape has been disturbed; the entire winter range has been allocated for logging and 95 per cent has been made available for hydrocarbon development. In the Bistcho caribou range north of the Hay-Zama Lakes (plate 14.5), only 6 per cent of the landscape remains undisturbed due to the extensive fossil fuel industry footprint and wildfires. Unfortunately, the Alberta government has taken the view that woodland caribou can be restored while industry continues to create extensive disturbances. Instead of restricting the encroachment of industry into caribou range, the government has resorted to killing wolves and is considering raising caribou in large penned enclosures. The view that caribou conservation must "not unduly impact industry" (Alberta Government 2017b) defines corporate profit as the bottom line and amounts to a death warrant for many caribou populations. When it comes to protecting endangered species in conflict with industry, endangered species have no chance. We know enough to know that urgent action is needed. What we lack is the will to act.

FAILURE TO ADDRESS CUMULATIVE EFFECTS

Pervasive subjectivity and lack of consistency and rigour were recently exposed in a review of impact studies of hydrocarbon projects in northeastern Alberta (Campbell et al. 2019). Validated models observed twice the level of adverse effects on wildlife for the same habitat loss as did unvalidated models and were less confident in the effectiveness of mitigation, a process that would require 50–150 years to be measured. The reviewers observed that 91 per cent of the 1,681 applications submitted to the AER were approved, and that of energy projects that predicted significant adverse effects submitted to the federal review process, 74 per cent of the projects were approved. The authors questioned whether demonstrating that a project will have significant negative effects has any bearing on project approval. Dr Adam Ford, one of the authors, observed that the tens of thousands of pages of impact assessments on file at the AER reveal little about the ecological condition of the landscape. There are people whose lives depend on the land and its wildlife and "we're telling them we're pretty much making this up … You would have to go out of your way to make it this bad" (Weber 2019). The AER declined to comment on the scientific review.

Bogus environmental review and regulatory approval continued with the July 2019 approval of the Teck Resources Frontier Mine. An AER review panel recognized that the 29,217 hectare open pit bitumen mine, the farthest north to date and only 30 km south of the globally significant Peace–Athabasca Delta and Wood Buffalo National Park, will cause significant detrimental effects on ecosystems, wildlife, and local people. The panel observed that the Frontier Mine will cause significant loss of old-growth forests, migratory birds, species at risk, 14,000 hectares of wetlands, and biodiversity. In spite of major and permanent impacts, the AER concluded that the project is in the public interest. It did so by defining the "public interest" as the "orderly and efficient development of oil sands resources." But in February 2020, Teck Resources withdrew its Frontier Mine application citing low oil prices, financial challenges, and the lack of a defensible regulatory framework that reconciles resource development with climate change (Connolly 2020). Teck's withdrawal is an admission that the AER's scorched earth policy of hydrocarbon development is resulting in loss of the industry's social licence and the confidence of investors.

The environmental and social extremism of the AER is further exemplified by its June 2018 approval of the Prosper Petroleum Ltd bitumen sands project in the sacred Moose Lake area in northeastern Alberta. In 2001, the Fort Mckay First Nation began negotiations with the government of Alberta to protect Moose Lake within a 10 km-wide buffer. In 2015 Alberta premier Jim Prentice signed a letter of intent to protect the area. But in 2018, the AER approved a 10,000-barrel-a-day mine that would have encroached to within 2 km of Moose Lake and broken the agreement to protect the area. The Fort Mckay First Nation appealed the decision to the Alberta Court of Appeal where the AER argued that its mandate forbids it from considering issues of Indigenous consultation and cumulative effects. In April 2020, the AER approval was overturned (Weber 2020a). Justice Sheila Greckoll wrote, "The honour of the Crown … does require that the Crown keep promises made during negoti-

214

ations designed to protect treaty rights ... It certainly demands more than allowing the Crown to placate (the band) while its treaty rights career into obliteration. That is not honourable. And it is not reconciliation." Greckol further observed that the AER was wrong to maintain that management of cumulative effects lies beyond its purview. Justices Barbara Veldhuis and Jo'Anne Strekaf wrote that "The public interest mandate can and should encompass considerations of the effect of a project on Aboriginal Peoples ... To preclude such considerations entirely takes an unreasonably narrow view of what comprises the public interest." Prosper CEO Brad Gardiner wrote that "This decision reflects a failure of the regulatory framework for the energy industry and a failure of the Crown to address the concerns of Fort McKay First Nation."

SUMMARY

Hydrocarbon exploitation continues to outpace the advance of knowledge of its effects and the monitoring and expertise needed to minimize harm. A significant body of knowledge has accumulated that, if incorporated into operations, could mitigate much of the ecological damage. In large part, incorporation of that knowledge has not occurred. Instead, we observe the persistence of practices that cause permanent and pervasive ecosystem damage. Critical data are not being gathered and the public is not being informed.

People who live in the midst of the "oil patch" have been disproportionately affected. The rights of Indigenous peoples, recognized in international agreements by the United Nations, have been infringed upon and violated by the fossil fuel industry, their regulators, and governments. First Nations are aware of their rights and Canada's Supreme Court has consistently upheld them in the face of government resistance or refusal to honour them. Conflicts will continue for the foreseeable future unless governments listen and act.

Bogus environmental reviews and failures to control cumulative effects and the extinguishment of treaty rights are the fruits of a regulator acting to dishonour the Crown while it undermines the social licence of the fossil fuel industry. The financial liability for cleanup of Alberta's fossil fuel industry sites was estimated at $260 billion as of 2018 (web 14.2, and chapter 17, "Risks and Liabilities"). But the situation is even worse when we consider the limited capacity to return industrial sites to a state of ecological health. Public financial liabilities and permanently damaged ecosystems may prove to be the most lasting legacy of the fossil fuel industry.

In Alberta, the energy regulator has the mandate to assess cumulative effects and use them to guide operational procedures, but it has neither the scientific capacity nor the will to do so. The industry has created a large and growing landscape footprint that exceeds 30,000 km^2 in Alberta. But this figure underestimates the true effect of the industry's disturbances which extend well beyond footprint boundaries in a web of complex interactions above and below ground that affect all of us. Species and natural community diversity and abundance are declining. Pervasive ecological effects and failed reclamation lead to an inescapable conclusion: the industry is causing wholesale, long-term damage to ecosystems. The effects of agriculture, forestry, and climate change exacerbate the damage. Cumulative effects are already serious and vary in scale from local to global. Increasing rates of ecological and climatic change may overwhelm the stability of society.

PART FIVE

OUT OF THE RABBIT HOLE AND INTO THE LIGHT

CHAPTER 15

Misinformation and the Metaorganization

To be a scientist is to be naive. We are so focused on our search for truth,
we fail to consider how few actually want us to find it … Where I once would
fear the cost of truth, now I only ask: what is the cost of lies?

Craig Mazin, *Chernobyl*

INTRODUCTION

Energy regulators have a responsibility to provide timely, complete, and accurate information about industry activities. Previous chapters have evaluated the veracity and reliability of regulatory data. This chapter begins with an evaluation of how the AER responds to questions about spills. This is followed by a discussion of the regulator's reliance on industry-reported data, and how it reports online incident information. We then compare the regulator's information to energy information provided by other agencies. We'll observe that timely, accurate, and complete information is rare while misinformation, underreporting, and poor record keeping are characteristic of the hydrocarbon metaorganization.

What is the structure of the metaorganization? Hydrocarbon production companies lie at the hub of a wheel whose spokes are money (figure 15.1). Producers interact most closely with their production partners and regulators, which together possess most of the information about the environmental effects of their activities. This information lies behind a firewall, a small fraction of which is available to the public. Governments provide legislation and policy to support the network but do little to manage the effects and possess little of the relevant environmental data. Other components surround and support the producers. These are (clockwise from the top of figure 15.1): industry-funded monitoring groups that provide the appearance of monitoring; educational and research institutions that act as enablers; enforcement, security, and surveillance; lobby groups and industry organizations; goods and services providers; the financiers and insurers; legitimators and promoters such as think tanks; legitimators in the media; and political parties and governments captured by the industry. The sole weakness of this vast and powerful meta-organization is that it runs on the money and security provided by banks, asset managers, and insurance companies. Remove those inputs and the network disintegrates. This is why the industry and its allies are terrified of divestment.

THE REGULATOR AS AN INFORMATION SOURCE

The Regulator's Self-Concept

At this juncture it's instructive to contrast the self-concept of the AER with the evidence gathered. The regulator (AER 2016a) states that it "Ensures the safe, efficient, orderly, and environmentally responsible development of energy resources … We make sure energy development doesn't damage any aspect of our province's environment." It sees itself as a credible and transparent organization that demonstrates "empathic engagement," "stellar competence," and "regulatory excellence … that moves us closer to being truly protective, effective, efficient, and credible … to deliver results for the AER and our many stakeholders – the people who live here … Albertans have told us they want an energy regulator that protects the public and the environment and that enforces the rules."

As for stellar competence and regulatory excellence, the regulator fails to provide credible, empirical data on spill frequency, spill locations, spilled and recovered volumes, recovery efficiencies, environmental effects, wildlife effects, and sensitive areas. When it does supply information, that information tends to be incomplete, inaccurate, subjective, and subject to significant delay. Although the regulator states that it practices empathic engagement, demonstrates stellar competence, protects the environment, and enforces the rules, the evidence does not support those views. Given the organizational structure of the regulator, industry, consultants, government, co-opted universities, pro-

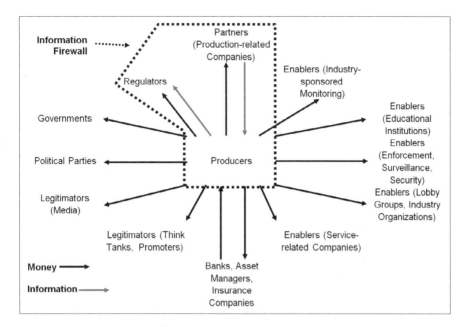

Figure 15.1 Components of the hydrocarbon metaorganization. The black and gray arrows identify the main flows of money and information. For details, see web 15.

moters, and enablers, information made available to the public has little chance of being accurate, credible, unbiased, or timely.

Failure to provide timely, accurate, credible information and failure to notify affected parties is an oft-recurring criticism of the AER. Although obligated to inform affected parties, the AER functions quasi-independently as an agency rather than a government department. When the regulator fails to supply information, there's little recourse. Although in theory the regulator is accountable to the government, in practice, government doesn't exercise oversight.

Response of the Regulator to Questions

Questions posed to the regulator do not receive timely answers and the answers received are not supported by evidence. For example, in June 2013, Timoney and Lee (2013) posed written questions to the regulator. Six months later, the regulator responded (web 15.1). We learned that the regulator accepts, without empirical data, industry statements for volumes spilled and recovered. The regulator provides no independent and quantitative verification of spill volumes and recovered volumes. It depends upon industry to determine environmental impacts. It has no electronic data available on spills in Alberta prior to 1975 and did not admit that post-1974 spills are missing from its database. The regulator stated that it inspects about 10–15 per cent of spills but provided no evidence in support. I checked that assertion. As of 15 May 2019 for the period dating back to June 2013, the regulator had investigated 6.7 per cent of 1,835 incidents on its Compliance Dashboard, some of which included nonspills such as operating without a licence. Reports were available for 0.1 per cent of incidents. Of the regulator's reports, what proportion is a credible environmental assessment? Certainly its report on the Pace-Spyglass spill is not.

During the course of this study, I occasionally asked technical and scientific staff at AER for clarification. Then, in February 2017, soon after I gave a public presentation at the University of Alberta about the AER and industry spills, I received an anonymous email from the regulator (see web 11.2.2) that stated, "The AER is asking that all future engagement from yourself or the organizations you are representing, be submitted to the stakeholder engagement branch by e-mail at stakeholder.engagement@aer.ca." In place of direct, timely communication with knowledgeable staff, the regulator instituted a policy of slow and uninformative communication with public relations staff (for correspondence, see web 15.1.1). The regulator's prohibition of direct communication between the public and scientific and technical staff is all about information control. It's like having questions about your heart. You need to consult your cardiologist but the hospital has instituted a new policy. You're told you can't speak with your cardiologist but someone at the information desk will answer your questions.

How the Regulator Responded to the Freedom of Information Request

In summer 2015, I first requested information about four spills. A year later, I submitted a FOIP request for reports and data pertaining to nine locations over the period 1 January 1970 to 6 September 2016 (web 2.1). AER compiled 3,890 pages related to the information request (Mori 2016), which comprised a subset of the requested information – I know this only because the Dene Tha supplied me with reports that were not disclosed by the AER.

The difficulty and delay I experienced in attempting to access AER information exacerbated the problems posed by the unreliable data. Part of the delay was due to the third party consultation process, which allows a company to block public access to information for months simply by filing an objection. Although the experience produced little information in relation to the effort, time, and expense, it provided evidence of the difficulties the public faces when requesting information from the regulator. I obtained most of the useful environmental information about the spills from the Dene Tha, not from the regulator. The regulator supplied thousands of pages of often irrelevant or redundant information. The FOIP experience demonstrated what one Alberta journalist has referred to as the alternate meaning of FOIP: "F**k Off, It's Private."

Despite related requests, industry supplied no information. Given that all evidence indicates that spills result in persistent environmental impacts, it's not surprising that requests made to industry for documentation on cleanup and environmental effects were met with silence. Although industry is under no obligation to supply spill information to the public, its failure to provide information raises concerns. If spills are not causing harm and industry possesses data that support that view, why not release the evidence? The most revealing response from industry was to ignore my information request and instead contact the Dene Tha with an offer of short-term tree planting jobs at a spill site – in essence, an offer of a job in exchange for silence.

In summary, I made repeated requests for information about the spills to the regulator. Eight months later, information was supplied for four spills. That request was followed by my submission of a FOIP request, and eight months later, by AER closing the file. The regulator provided information for three spills over a six-month period; information for two spills entailed an eight-month wait and no information was received for four spills. The two information requests spanned twenty-one months. The requests delivered a mixture of relevant, irrelevant, incomplete, and erroneous information or failed to supply any information. If your head is spinning at this point, mine was too. Sometimes what isn't divulged reveals more than what is (see web 11.2 for a record of the correspondence).

AER's Online Incident Reporting

You'd be justified in asking if recent changes at the regulator have resulted in improved spill reporting. One such change is online reporting, which, at first impression, would seem an improvement over past practices. How does the online reporting compare to the old system? When I compared online reporting with the FIS database for the years 2014–16, I found that online releases represented only 16 per cent of those reported in the FIS releases (table 15.1). Specific to crude oil and saline water, 59 per cent of spills were missing from online reporting. Furthermore, location information had been changed from the township and range system, which was approximate at best, to a vague statement such as "Cold Lake 45 km NW" that makes it impossible to locate a spill (see web 2.8 and web 15.2). On the positive side, in 2019, the AER placed its FIS data online. That's progress (see chapter 17).

RELIANCE ON INDUSTRY-REPORTED SPILL AND RECOVERY VOLUMES

Reporting to a regulator can provide an incentive to present "optimistic" assessments of a company's efforts to control or reduce pollution (deMarchi and Hamilton 2006). Industry has a strong incentive to underreport volumes released, exaggerate volumes recovered, and minimize impacts to the environment. Furthermore, industrial data are difficult to verify. The regulator requires no standard assessment techniques and accepts whatever volumes are reported by industry. Reliance on industry-reported data is a major source of unreliability.

In a letter to me, the AER (web 15.1) danced around but didn't admit that its spill volumes are not measured: "The AER requires that the volume of a released substance be reported when a pipeline release has occurred. The accuracy of the reported release volumes varies, as not all pipelines are equipped with metering and sometimes the starting time of an event is unknown. Best estimates are based on production rates, pipeline capacities, metering, and measurement of contaminated area." The AER makes no attempt to quantify the accuracy of spill and recovery volumes – which would require scientific data it doesn't have. Instead, after all these years and thousands of spills, the AER accepts unverified, self-reported information and distributes this information without warnings that the data may be misleading. Once we blow away the smoke we can also see that the regulator failed to address measuring spill volumes at the majority of crude oil spills – which don't take place at pipelines (see chapter 3 and web 3.2). Uncritical acceptance of industry's self-reported data combined with minimal field inspections and the failure to pro-

Plate 14.1 Damaged wetland near the Amber oil spill site. This wetland illustrates some of the impacts of industrial roads. Industrial roads act as vectors for undesirable species such as foxtail barley (the blond grass) and scentless chamomile (the white-flowered forb), a restricted weed. Foxtail barley reduces native biodiversity and thrives on salinized or otherwise disturbed, fine-textured soil. The compacted road surface impedes horizontal flow of water. Surface flows accumulate to the right (north) of the road, resulting in ponding, dieback of trees, and conversion of bog to marsh adjacent to the road. To the left (south) of the road, the peatland is desiccating due to deprivation of water. 20 July 2016.

Plate 14.2 Ecological effects accumulate as natural landscapes are converted by human activities. Effects are set in motion when seismic lines are cut and industrial roads open an area to development (figures 14.1–14.2, plate 14.1). (a) When hydrocarbons are found, wells are drilled. On well pads, the native vegetation and topsoil are removed and the site is prepared to receive heavy machinery such as drill rigs. Note the liquid waste pits (circled); 53° 51′ 7″ N, 112° 5′ 40″ W, 29 September 2015. The dominant plants here in 2019 were sweet-clover, foxtail barley, and summer-cypress. (b) Pipelines are then built to carry well production to regional batteries or waste facilities. Although the Chinchaga Wilderness is "protected," its protection has not stopped natural gas resource development; 57° 3′ 53″ N, 119° 45′ 40″ W, 21 July 2006.

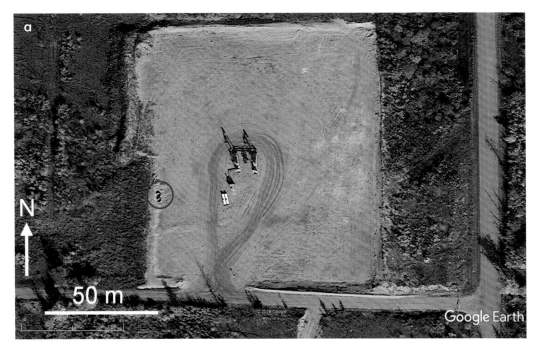

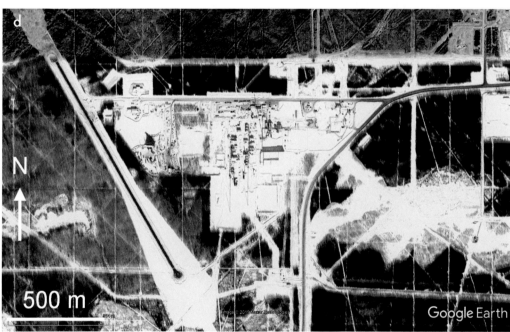

Plate 14.2 *continued* (c) Facilities such as this crude oil group battery are constructed to gather, store, and separate the hydrocarbons and waste. The barren soil is typical. All plant species in the vicinity are exotics; 53° 49' 57" N, 112° 57' 48" W, 5 August 2018. (d) Larger facilities process hydrocarbons in the upstream production chain. Here we see the multiple disturbances typical of the industrialized landscape such as the Apache Sour Gas plant, roads, an airport, seismic lines, and pipelines. There were thirty-three spills recorded in the area of this image; 59° 3' 53" N, 118° 52' 41" W, 27 February 2005.

Plate 14.2 *continued* (e) In the Swan Hills, spills (red dots), roads, pipelines, well sites, and forest clear-cutting combine to degrade the boreal forest; 54° 50' 1" N, 115° 26' 4" W, 20 August 2019. (f) We're told that the hydrocarbon industry reclaims their leases with the assumption that nature has been restored. This isn't the case. Here we see the Harbor-Liege airstrip built to service a remote oil field. Although the airstrip was reclaimed twenty-six years before this photo, it's covered with an exotic meadow community of alsike clover, timothy, smooth brome, slender wheat grass, and red fescue; 56° 59' 1" N, 113° 30' 3" W, 21 September 2009.

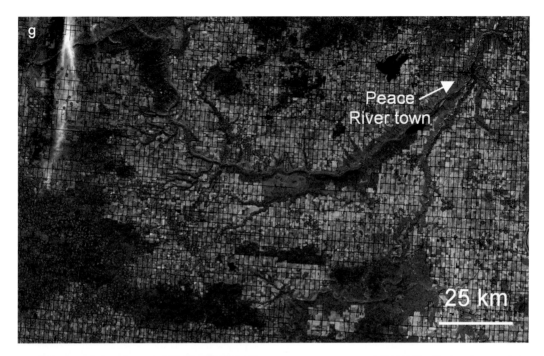

Plate 14.2 *continued* (g) Agriculture is a major cause of habitat loss. Here near the town of Peace River, most of the region has been converted to agricultural fields serviced by a dense network of roads that result in an advanced degree of habitat loss and fragmentation. The red dots plot 1,069 spills; many sites experienced multiple spills. (h) Agricultural expansion into the boreal forest exacerbates the stresses posed by the hydrocarbon and forest industries. Here, 20 km southeast of La Crete, large-scale loss of habitat continues today as boreal wetlands are drained and converted to fields with permanent loss of biodiversity and stored carbon; 58° 6' 26" N, 116° 6' 14" W, 28 April 2016.

Plate 14.3 Use of herbicides by the fossil fuel industry is widespread. A broad-spectrum herbicide was applied to the wet meadow at this pipeline riser in Strathcona County, Alberta. 5 August 2018.

Plate 14.4 The industrial footprint disproportionately impacts First Nations such as here on the lands of the Lubicon Cree. Cleanup of the Plains-Midstream 2011 crude oil spill of 4,500 m³ of crude oil near Little Buffalo, Alberta. (a) Portion of impacted beaver pond community. (b) Part of the cleanup operations. Note the oil slick on the water surface. Yellow arrows point to beaver lodges; white arrows point to active beaver channels; turquoise arrows point to humans in white hazmat protective coveralls; orange arrows point to active beaver dams. See web 14.3.

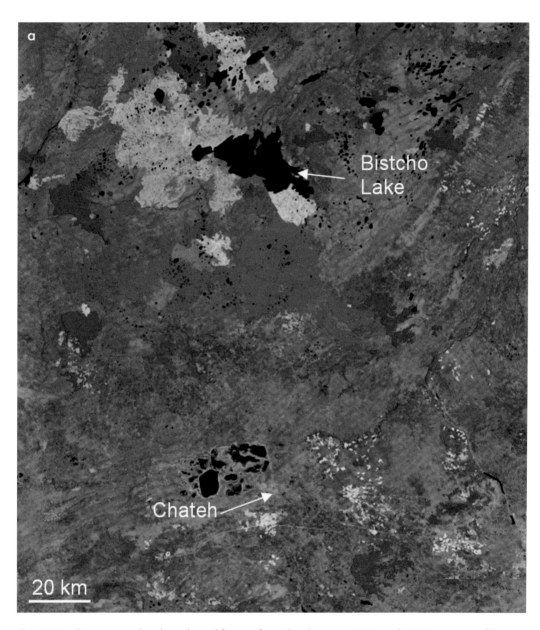

Plate 14.5 The recent onslaught on boreal forests: forest loss between 2000 and 2016 as mapped by Global Forest Change. (a) northwestern Alberta and (b) northeastern Alberta and adjacent Saskatchewan. Large nongreen polygons are wildfires; small polygons are wildfires, logging, and fossil fuel industry disturbances. Linear disturbances are not visible at this scale. This is a large proportion of the landscape to experience forest loss over a seventeen-year period.

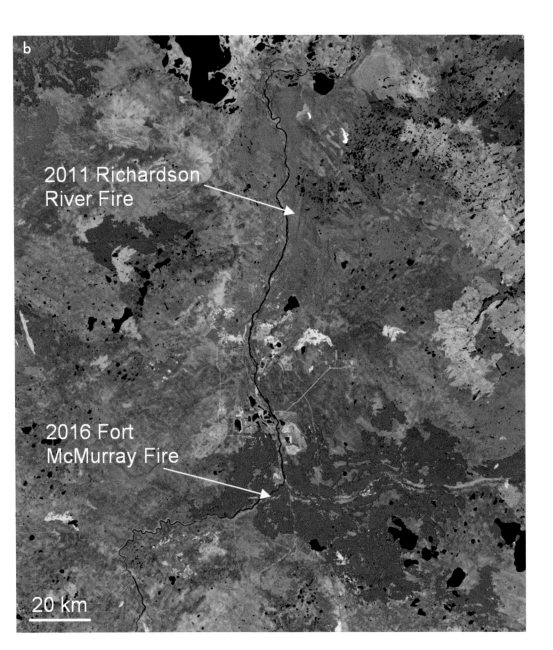

b

2011 Richardson
River Fire

2016 Fort
McMurray Fire

20 km

Plate 17.1 The industry disturbance signature can help us identify damaged ecosystems and toxic sites that hide in plain sight. (a) The salt-contaminated soil along this pipeline corridor in northwestern Alberta is recognizable by its dominance of foxtail barley and other halophytes. (b) This harmless-looking verdant landscape, part of a 200-hectare EPA Superfund site near Liberty, Texas, belies the contaminants hidden at the former Petro-Chemical Systems Inc. facility. Dumping of waste oils in unlined pits along the road continued until the mid-1970s, which resulted in contamination of soil and groundwater with naphthalene, chrysene, fluorene, benzene, styrene, and lead. Despite this danger, the land was later developed and subdivided into residences. Following legal actions, in 1988 local residents were relocated, the site was excavated, and the area fenced to protect humans from contaminated soil and dust. As of 2014, site remediation was ongoing. Image centre at 29° 55' 13" N, 94° 41' 15" W.

Plate 17.1 *continued* (c) Establishment of pollution-tolerant common cattail in the crude-oil-contaminated soil at the Pace-Spyglass spill misled the Alberta Energy Regulator to conclude that remediation was successful. Invasion by pollution-tolerant marsh plants into a contaminated fen is a typical disturbance signature. Marsh plants and open water draw wildlife into contaminated areas and can result in mortality sinks. (d) Seventy years after the Atlantic No. 3 blowout near Devon, Alberta, plants struggle to survive in the water-repellent soil. Pollution-tolerant grasses and exotics such as brome, Canada thistle, common dandelion, and blue-green algal mats provide a disturbance signature.

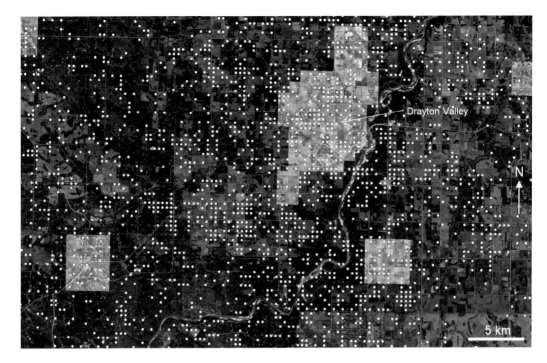

Plate 17.2 The hidden scourge of spills imposes environmental uncertainty on society. Here, near Drayton Valley, Alberta, we see a network of 3,924 spills. The density of spills is greater than it appears because multiple spills at single sites are mapped as single points.

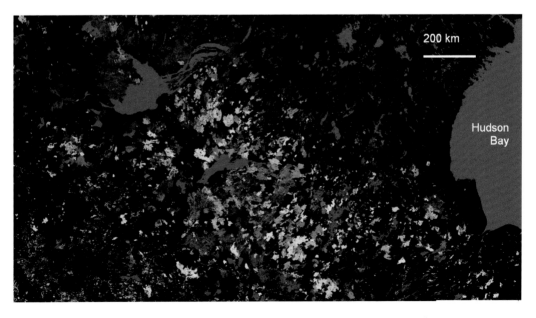

Plate 18.1 Rapid loss of forest cover (coloured polygons) over the nineteen-year period 2000–18 in boreal and low subarctic north-central Canada driven by an increase in wildfire activity.

Plate 18.2 Contaminated landscapes as our gift to the future. (a) This soil at a well site near Bruderheim, Alberta is permanently impaired (conductivity 18,860 μS/cm). The only recorded spill took place thirty years ago, a release of 1 m³ of crude oil and 15 m³ of saline water. The regulator reported perfect spill recovery. Apparently the recovery was not perfect or there were other unrecorded spills. 5 May 2019.

Plate 18.2 *continued* (b) Damage from saline produced water released during oil production at Skiatook Lake, Oklahoma, persists as a treeless disturbance signature documented by the US EPA. Although production ceased about eighty years before this 2020 image, soil and vegetation damage remain evident in the photo centre. EPA "Site A," 36° 23' 10" N, 96° 10' 57" W, 10 November 2020. Image modified from Google Earth.

c

Plate 18.2 *continued* (c) The vegetation at this abandoned compressor station and pipeline in the boreal forest of northeastern Alberta reveals the familiar disturbance signature of weedy exotic vegetation, here indicated by white sweet-clover, common dandelion, and weedy grasses. Elevated levels of hydrocarbons, phenols, chromium, zinc, and nitrogen were detected in the water and sediments of a lake 400 m to the NE of here. The source of the contaminants is not known in this intensively disturbed landscape (Timoney 2011). SW of Chipewyan Lake, 56° 50′ 46″ N, 113° 34′ 29″ W, 19 September 2009.

Plate 18.2 *continued* (d) In the fragmented and disturbed boreal peatlands in the Dene Tha territory in northwestern Alberta, an excavated salt-contaminated pond surrounded by weedy exotic saline vegetation is the legacy of the Apache2 11-26 2013 spill. Pond at 59° 16′ 40″ N, 119° 14′ 30″ W. Image modified from US Geological Survey, undated, postspill.

e

Plate 18.2 *continued* (e) Chronic pollution, failed reclamation, unmonitored wildlife mortalities, damaged ecosystems, and environmental liabilities are the legacy of a corrupt regulator. Here an oil- and salt-contaminated soil is covered in pollution-tolerant exotics such as alsike clover, reed canary grass, sow-thistle, and foxtail barley. Chronic leaks from storage tanks often go unrecorded or noted under the euphemism "oil or salt water staining." Amber site, 58° 55' 4" N, 118° 56' 3" W, 20 July 2016.

Plate PS.1 *this page and opposite* An unhealthy salinized ecosystem five years after spill and reclamation: the Apache 15-09 spill. (a) A salt crust on the shore of the excavated pond reveals that saline conditions persist after "completion" of contaminant removal. (b) Semibarren saline mud on the shore of the pond and an exotic-dominated weedy meadow demonstrates persistent damage to the soil and vegetation. (c) Pollution-tolerant plant species in the impaired weedy meadow and marsh include sow-thistle, foxtail barley, stunted common cattail, and planted wheatgrasses (*Elymus*). (d) Even pollution-tolerant common cattail is reduced in stature in the saline soil. Note the lack of aquatic plants.

Plate PS.1 *continued* (f) Planted wheatgrasses and white spruce struggle to survive on the saline soil. (e) One of many dying planted white spruce seedlings indicates that residual salinity will result in failed tree establishment.

Table 15.1 Number of primary releases, 2014–16, for all substances and for crude oil + saline water

Year	All releases, FIS	All releases, Online	Ratio of Online to FIS (%)	Crude oil + saline, FIS	Crude oil + saline, Online	Ratio of Online to FIS (%)
2014	2,400	420	17.5	646	240	37.2
2015	2,303	339	14.7	442	192	43.4
2016	1,966	302	15.4	397	171	43.1
Total	6,669	1061	15.9	1485	603	40.6

Note: As reported in the AER FIS database and online at http://www1.aer.ca/compliancedashboard/incidents.html. Due to inconsistencies in the way substances are named in the FIS and online data, I combined crude oil and saline spills for comparison purposes.

vide scientific evidence raise governance and ecological concerns. Unreliable environmental data and reports are the responsibility of both the companies hired to conduct the work and the regulator that accepts the work. Industry provides what the regulator accepts, no less, no more. If the regulator accepts superficial and subjective assessments, that's what industry will provide.

The next section illustrates how the regulator manipulates information to present a favourable version of its performance.

PIPELINE SPILL RATES IN ALBERTA: LESSONS IN REPORTING

This section presents two examples of the regulator's reporting of spill rates in Alberta. The first example focuses on the year 2012 and compares National Energy Board and AER data. The second example assesses the accuracy of a report of pipeline performance.

Pipeline Spill Rates in Alberta

The objective of this section was to compare provincial pipeline spill rates in Alberta (AER 2013) with federal pipeline spill rates reported by the National Energy Board (NEB 2015, 2016). The comparison was difficult because the two regulators did not report spill rates in ways that allowed for direct comparisons because different years were reported by the regulators and because both reports contained errors. The most direct comparison possible was for the period 2008–12. The spill rate for liquid hydrocarbons was 0.45 spills/1,000 km operating pipeline/year for NEB pipelines. In comparison, the 2012 crude oil spill rate for provincial pipelines was 2.04 spills/1,000 km of operating pipeline, about 453 per cent of the spill rate from interprovincial pipelines.

Although the Alberta provincial crude oil pipeline spill rate is far higher than the crude oil spill rate on NEB pipelines, which is bad enough, the comparison blatantly understates the actual crude oil spill rate in Alberta. The regulator's reporting of crude oil spills from only crude oil pipelines, which account for only 4 per cent of crude oil spills and 24 per cent of crude oil volume spilled in Alberta, distracts attention from the larger problem of crude oil spills. It serves as an example of how the regulator selectively reports information that places its activities in a positive light (for more, see web 3.2 and 15.3).

Pipeline Performance in Alberta: Assessing the Accuracy of AER Reporting

In early 2017, the AER published an assessment of pipeline performance (AER 2017d) for the year 2016 and provided some comparisons of incident rates for the period 2007–17. In order to assess the accuracy of the online data presented by the regulator, I determined pipeline releases for four comparison years from the FIS data (web 15.4). The comparison reveals underreporting of pipeline releases in Alberta. For the years 2013–16, the online report excluded 27 per cent of pipeline spills.

I asked AER why their online report did not include all pipeline releases. Two months later, the regulator explained (web 11.2) that its reporting excluded "all pressure tests, integrity tests, HDD frac-outs … [and] pipeline incidents associated with AUC [Alberta Utilities Commission] licensees." That explanation doesn't provide the rationale for not reporting all spills. For example, HDD frac-outs occur when pressurized drilling lubricant inadvertently enters a water body or a location where it may enter water (Alberta Government 2013). HDD frac-outs can pose a threat when they occur beneath sensitive habitats, waterways, and in areas of cultural importance. To exclude hundreds of spills from consideration when those spills are ecologically or culturally relevant is not acceptable.

MISINFORMATION ISN'T RESTRICTED TO THE AER

We've seen how the regulator struggles to provide accurate and credible information about spills. The following sections document how other agencies and groups similarly struggle to provide accurate and credible information.

Poor Record Keeping and Enforcement: Alberta Government

Poor record keeping is an important cause of environmental misinformation. Study of Alberta's Environmental Management System data on 9,262 bitumen industry incidents in northeastern Alberta (1996–2012) found that reported incidents represented a fraction of the true number of incidents. Underestimation resulted from a combination of missing or redacted records, multiple contraventions subsumed under a single record, and the fact that other kinds of incidents, such as pipeline spills, were typically not reported (Timoney and Lee 2013). The volume, duration, and chemical composition of the releases to air, land, and water were typically unspecified or unknown. There was a twenty-nine-year data gap extending from the beginning of bitumen operations in 1967 to the beginning of electronic records in 1996 for which the Alberta government holds no retrievable information. Enforcement actions were taken in only 0.9 per cent of alleged contraventions, an enforcement rate seventeen times lower than pursued under the Clean Water Act in the United States. Minimal oversight and enforcement contributed to the poor record keeping, which limited the ability to understand industrial impacts and allowed industry to underreport releases and emissions.

227

Alberta Environment and Parks (AEP) shares responsibility with AER for monitoring contaminated sites, but AEP does not have a proactive program to identify contaminated sites. Instead, it depends on landowners or leaseholders to notify the government. AEP doesn't have credible data on the frequency, location, and toxicity of contaminated sites in Alberta. In 2017, the City of Calgary learned that more than 1,000 contaminated sites existed in the city but was unable to access sufficient documentation held by the Alberta government (Anderson 2017).

When an investigative reporter for CBC News contacted AEP to determine how many contaminated sites were located in Calgary, AEP "was either unwilling or unable to provide clarity on how many sites it's aware of in the city of Calgary. After several months and repeated requests for information, the ministry said there were 1,766 sites. But CBC News had to inform a spokesperson [for AEP] that figure only applied to locations that had undergone an environmental site assessment. Information regarding how many of those areas are actually contaminated was either not known or not shared ... Several requests to speak with someone at the ministry with knowledge of contaminated sites went unanswered." Calgary's mayor, Naheed Nenshi, added that although AEP holds the authority, it lacks the ability to remediate contaminated sites, which does not serve citizens well (Anderson 2017). If the City of Calgary can't access contaminated site records or enjoin the responsible authority to clean up contaminated sites, how can a private citizen, a farmer, or a county planner have any hope? Failure to keep accurate environmental records imposes inexcusable uncertainty and risk on all of us.

Other Alberta government branches also behave as a captured regulator. Looking back on his experiences with Alberta Fish and Wildlife, Carl Hunt, a retired fisheries biologist, told me that chronic understaffing meant that government was unable to adequately monitor the more than 400 streams in the northeastern slopes region (pers. comm., March 2019). Understaffing, along with senior-level government reluctance to prosecute fossil fuel industry violators, led to low levels of monitoring and enforcement. He revealed,

> In the early days [1970s] we investigated and successfully prosecuted a spill into Prairie Creek southwest of Rocky Mountain House and a pipeline overflow into Deep Valley Creek near Fox Creek. But by the 1980s, we'd investigate and the prosecution would often get cancelled in Edmonton ... We investigated many pipeline spills, but after numerous investigations but no charges, we just quit investigating ... One of my last investigations (~1995) was a series of pipeline breaks reported in Swan Hills that spilt brine into headwater beaver dams, often during winter. We discovered this brine was full of sulphates and other toxic materials. I learned from Edmonton [head office] that the twelve to fourteen spills reported from Whitecourt and Swan Hills were just those noted by our Fish and Wildlife Officers, and that in the Judy Creek field alone [south slope of Swan Hills], there were around 100 spills each year.

The Fish and Wildlife branch was not being informed by industry or the regulator; it was aware only of the spills that their officers detected. Here again we see that the reported rate of spills represents a fraction of the actual rate of spills.

Unreliable Assessments and Self-reporting by Industry

The unreliability of environmental data held by the regulator stems from an untenable situation. The company responsible for the spill is also responsible for producing reliable environmental data, and an environmental impact report if one is required. Those reports are usually produced by contractors hired by the energy company. In a competitive field, the incentive for the contractor to produce information that portrays the company in a favourable light is overwhelming; the conflict of interest is patent. This is not to say that all impact reports are *de facto* suspect, but analysis of the reports examined in this study points consistently to unreliable results (for another example, see web 4.3). In a commentary on how the regulator responded to the Apache 15-09 spill, Jones (2013) concluded that the regulator was more concerned with controlling the information about the spill than it was with informing the public.

Consultants willing to escape that information control and divulge what is actually happening on the landscape are rare. One such consultant is the fisheries biologist Dave Mayhood. He writes of his experience attempting to ensure environmental protection during construction of pipeline stream crossings (pers. comm., March 2019):

> I was saddened by the lack of support and authority from government regulatory staff and corporate leadership. Although I was expected by both groups to ensure environmental protection, I was given no authority to shut down operations when the construction crews refused to comply. Government regulators saw me as a company agent yet refused to attend during crossing construction to enforce my (and their) directions. Conversely, company supervisors simply ignored my demands for environmental protection measures. On one occasion I was told that a flume would be installed at a stream crossing to divert clean water around the work area during installation, and that I should be there at 8 AM to monitor the construction. When I arrived on time, an open-cut crossing had been made, the creek was a wreck, and the foreman just laughed, knowing that there was nothing I could do about it.

229

The tendency to underestimate impacts is consistent across the industry. Despite the fact that the fossil fuel sector is responsible for a large proportion of greenhouse gas emissions, industry-reported data consistently underestimate actual emissions. Measurements of atmospheric concentrations of carbon dioxide near four bitumen-processing facilities in northeastern Alberta observed that mean emissions were 13, 36, 38, and 123 per cent higher than reported emissions at Suncor, CNRL, Shell Albian Jackpine, and Syncrude Mildred Lake, respectively (Liggio et al. 2019). As a result, total carbon dioxide emissions from the four facilities were roughly 64 per cent higher, and for the entire bitumen sector 30 per cent higher, than industry reported.

Industrial Reporting of Volatile Organic Compound Emissions

Underreporting of volatile organic compound emissions further illustrates the unreliability of industry-reported data (Li et al. 2017). The authors measured VOC emissions and compared them to industry-reported emissions from four bitumen operations in northeastern Alberta. Industry underestimated total emissions by factors of 200, 310, 450, and 410 per cent at the four facilities and underestimated emissions for eighty-two of the ninety-three VOC compounds. Depending on the facility, industry failed to report any emissions for nine to fifty-three of the VOCs for which emissions reporting is mandatory. For individual VOC species, measured emission rates were 4.5 to 375 times higher than reported emission rates. In a landscape in which emissions of VOCs range from fifty to seventy tonnes per day at each of the four facilities, missing information and underreporting of air emissions have implications for ecosystem and human health. That such wholesale discrepancies between measured and reported emissions would be discovered fifty years after emissions began in the bitumen sands region demonstrates a systemic failure by the Alberta government, the province's energy and environmental regulators, and industry to gather credible scientific information. It's a betrayal of the public trust.

To ascertain if unreliable reporting of VOC emissions extends outside Alberta's bitumen sands region, I conducted Benford analyses of annual emissions data for total VOCs from various jurisdictions (web 15.5–15.6). Annual total VOC emissions reported by industry in Alberta, British Columbia, Saskatchewan, Ontario, and Quebec do not conform to the Benford distribution while Manitoba VOC data do conform. Of the six Canadian provinces analyzed, the largest deviations, suggesting the largest influence of human bias in the choice of numbers, were observed in Alberta. To place the Canadian emissions data in perspective, I examined voc emissions from four American states (web 15.5–15.6). Deviations from the expected Benford distribution were lower in the American data than in the Canadian data. Reported voc emissions in Oklahoma, Ohio, and North Dakota conformed to the Benford distribution, and those from Texas nearly conformed. In Canada, and in particular in Alberta, unreliable data for industrial emissions of vocs present risks to the environment and the public. That Alberta produces the least reliable reporting of vocs may stem from the dysfunctional relationship that exists between government and industry. But fossil fuel industry misinformation is, of course, not restricted to Alberta.

231

Misinformation: British Columbia and the Canadian Federal Government

On 27 May 2018, the government of British Columbia reported a spill of one hundred litres of crude oil at a Kinder Morgan pipeline pump station north of Kamloops (cbc 2018b). Two weeks later, Kinder Morgan announced that 4,800 litres of crude oil had been spilled, forty-eight times larger than the volume reported by government. In response, the Ministry of Environment communicated to Kinder Morgan the "importance of accurate spill volume reporting." Who is responsible for the misinformation: the company or the government for accepting, without verification, industry's account of the incident?

Environment Canada–Health Canada (2016, using aer's data) reported 531 natural gas condensate spills with a total volume released of 2,204 m^3 for the period 2002–11. In contrast, I observed 573 condensate spills with a total volume of 2,466 m^3 using the same data. It's unclear why there is a discrepancy in the values. More importantly, the regulator's condensate releases underestimate actual releases because condensates are found in raw production gas and are therefore hidden in the bookkeeping. So, what is a more defensible estimate of condensate releases? There were 4,852 unplanned releases of raw production gas over the comparison period that reported a total release of 314.5 million m^3. The estimated total volume of condensate contained in those raw production gas releases is about thirty-six times higher than the Environment Canada–Health Canada estimate of condensate released (see web 15.7 for details). The devil is always in the bookkeeping.

Peer-Reviewed Misinformation

One of the dangers of misinformation is its tendency to spread via uncritical repetition. Myriad examples of widespread false information exist, such as "evidence" for the belief that vaccines cause autism. The following example, a review of crude oil impacts, illustrates that even scientific reports are not immune to the contagion of misinformation.

In 2015, the Royal Society of Canada (RSC) published a review of the effects of crude oil spills in water (Lee et al. 2015). The review, although useful in many respects, contained misleading information. It stated that "spills of crude oil into marine or freshwater systems in Canada from oil production facilities, tankers, pipelines, rail and truck transport are infrequent" but noted that statistics for inland spills into fresh water were not readily available. Why then would the report conclude that inland spills were infrequent? The report presented a table (their table 1.5) that indicated an average of 7.4 pipeline spills of unspecified hydrocarbons per year for all of Canada and cited the National Energy Board (NEB) as the source. As an astute reader you know that the NEB has jurisdiction over interprovincial pipelines only, spills from which comprise a small fraction of pipeline spills in Canada, and an even smaller fraction of total crude oil spills.

To understand the effect of relying on NEB data to estimate crude oil spill rates we can compare spills from provincial pipelines in Alberta with spills from NEB pipelines in Alberta over the same period (web 15.8). In Alberta provincial pipelines, the crude oil spill rate was 128 times higher and the total volume spilled was thirty-nine times higher than in Alberta interprovincial pipelines. By reporting spills from only NEB pipelines, the Royal Society underestimated the crude oil spill rate and therefore underestimated the effects of crude oil spills in Canada. For further perspective, consider that over the period 2008 to July 2019, there were forty-four crude oil spills in interprovincial pipelines with a total spill volume of 1,682 m³ according to the NEB for all of Canada. In comparison, over that same period, in Alberta alone, there were 5,693 intraprovincial crude oil spills from all sources with a total volume of 33,644 m³. In short, crude oil spills in Alberta were 128 times more frequent than the national pipeline spill rate and the Alberta volume spilled was twenty times higher than the national total. That the Royal Society, in attempting to quantify the rate of crude oil spills, would not consult provincial spill data is difficult to understand.

Particular to the Pace-Spyglass spill, the Royal Society report stated, "no wildlife or aquatic life mortalities noted; remediation efforts reported as being effective with vegetative regrowth noted." The statement is essentially a quote from the AER 2014 report on the Pace-Spyglass spill (see chapter 11). The AER's assessment of the spill was not credible. For the Royal Society to reiterate the regulator's assessment of the spill without appraisal of its veracity doesn't serve the public interest.

Mistakes are understandable when industry information is accepted without evaluation of the underlying data. But what is most significant is that the Royal Society report was authored by a team of scientists. It's unclear how a report on crude oil spills could, for Alberta alone, underestimate the number of pipeline spills by a factor of 128 and the volume of pipeline spills by a factor of twenty. Suppose you go to a carnival stand where a man guesses your weight. Say you weigh eighty kilograms but the man guesses four kilograms, one-twentieth your actual weight. You might wonder if the man were joking. Incidentally, funding for the RSC review was provided by the Canadian Energy Pipeline Association and the Canadian Association of Petroleum Producers.

Misinformation: Gulf of Mexico, United States

The ongoing Taylor Energy oil spill in the Gulf of Mexico illustrates that industry misinformation is international in scope. Here we review the main facts (Fears 2018; Macdonald 2018; CBC 2018c; Mason et al. 2019). On 15 September 2004, Hurricane Ivan, a Category 4 storm, unleashed 230 km/hour winds and waves that reached 21 m in height. The storm and a sub-marine mudslide toppled the Taylor Energy platform located about 20 km off the Louisiana coast. The platform and its well infrastructure were subsequently buried under 50 m of marine mud. Over the past seventeen years, the site has been the source of one of the largest oil spills in United States history.

For six years, no one outside of Taylor Energy and the regulator were aware of the ongoing oil release because Taylor Energy, with the cooperation of the US Coast Guard National Response Center, had kept the spill a secret. In 2008, the Coast Guard informed Taylor Energy that the ongoing release posed a significant threat to the environment. Then in 2010, an environmental watchdog group monitoring the BP Deepwater Horizon spill from an aircraft, observed oil slicks unrelated to the BP site and the public finally learned of the Taylor spill.

The response followed the familiar pattern of denial of effects followed by ever-increasing estimates of spill rates. Taylor initially argued that there was no evidence that their wells were leaking. Then the company reported that one of the wells was leaking 0.05 barrels of crude oil per day. Nearly a decade later, the government determined that the oil release was between one and fifty-five barrels per day. Various methods have since been applied to estimate the daily release of crude oil from the site. The estimates range from an extreme low of 0.125 barrels/day reported by Taylor Energy, to four estimates ranging from about 20–150 barrels/day, to a maximum of 1,652 barrels/day (Mason et al. 2019).

Under the Oil Pollution Act, industry must report spills to government, but there is no penalty for underreporting. Like the Alberta Energy Regulator, the US Coast Guard National Response Center accepts the industry-reported data without attempting to verify release volumes. Analysis of the National Response Center spill data has determined that their reports are not reliable. No laws in the United States require industry or government to report spills to the public. The Clean Water Act, however, requires that public participation in the enforcement of any regulation shall be provided for, encouraged, and assisted.

Taylor Energy maintained in 2016 that the storm was an act of God as the company sought to recover $450 million in trust funds put aside to stop the leaks. The company argued that the release issuing from a mass of mud and buried infrastructure could not be contained. Although Taylor Energy has plugged nine of the thirty-five wells, the release of crude oil continues today. The federal government has yet to determine the impact of the spills on the marine ecosystem. In July 2018, Earthjustice sued the National Oceanic and Atmospheric Administration for failing to produce a timely study required by policy. The suit stated that "Taylor has failed to provide the public with information regarding the pace and extent of the oil leaks and Taylor's efforts to control the leaks."

Discovery of the spill by an environmental group and twelve years of continuous release from the Taylor wells were required for the federal government to begin investigating the environmental damage. In November 2018, after fourteen years of continuous oil release, the US Coast Guard ordered Taylor Energy to eliminate the surface oil sheen and avoid deficiencies associated with prior containment attempts; the company will be fined $40,000 per day for failing to comply (Baurick 2018). If the oil release is not staunched, it may continue for another one hundred years. The environment, the tourism and fishing industries, and the public kept in the dark for years, continue to suffer the liability with no means of redress and no solution in sight. Meanwhile, the offshore oil industry plans to expand up the east coast of the United States while climate change intensifies the storms that wreak havoc on human communities, ecosystems, and offshore oil platforms.

SUMMARY

In an ideal world, the public would be provided with accurate, reliable, and timely information about the impacts of the fossil fuel industry. In reality, misinformation and disinformation are ubiquitous. At the national and global scale, the industry and its partners engage in a disinformation campaign that has been successful in sowing confusion and preventing substantive action to curb the impacts of hydrocarbon exploitation and use. Private profit predicated on public liability is a recipe for disaster.

A deep dive into industry-reported data is a plunge into murky waters. Estimating the rate of industry incidents from publicly available information is fraught with difficulty. Industry, regulators, and their partners provide information that minimizes ecological effects and places their activities in a favourable light. Missing and withheld information is a chronic deficiency. Formal information requests take months, after which the information may be incomplete or fail to address the questions. Covert spills can go undetected for years. Detection of a spill can depend upon a serendipitous observation by the public.

If justice requires that the truth be known, then failure to provide the truth constitutes obstruction of justice. If the hydrocarbon industry did not damage ecosystems, industry and the regulator would be eager to share the good news in order to maintain the social licence. The reluctance of the regulator and industry to provide accurate and timely information speaks volumes about the true impacts. In the absence of evidence proving that no ecosystem damage has occurred, the approach followed by industry and the regulator has been to simply not report impacts. If no impacts are reported, the regulator can maintain that it's doing a good job. Provision of misinformation is characteristic of a captured regulator, a topic to which we now turn.

CHAPTER 16

A Captured Regulator

It may well be that the greatest tragedy of this period of social transition
is not the glaring noisiness of the bad people, but the appalling silence
of the good people.

Martin Luther King, speech, "The Christian Way of Life in Human Relations"

INTRODUCTION

The regulator in its various incarnations has been a captured organization
for decades. The consistent failure of the agency and its government partners
to monitor activities, gather credible data, manage the industry, and enforce
regulations has undermined the public interest and done irreparable harm
to ecosystems. Its disregard for credible information imposes uncertainty,
hampers decision making, undermines democracy, and presents dangers to
our environment and our society. How did we end up with such a broken
system? The answer is regulatory capture. Social scientists, policy analysts,
and legal scholars have discussed various aspects of regulatory capture and
I'll not try to duplicate their efforts. In this chapter, we examine regulatory
capture as a font of misinformation and disinformation.

THE REGULATORY ENVIRONMENT

Although the Alberta government establishes policy and implements this
policy and associated regulations for all sectors, it does not regulate the
hydrocarbon industry. The Alberta government established its first energy

regulator in 1938 after facing bitter resistance from petroleum producers that included inflammatory advertising, political campaigns, and a challenge taken to the Supreme Court of Canada (Taft 2017). Since 1938, the energy sector has been regulated by a semi-independent agency, first by the Petroleum and Natural Gas Conservation Board, then by the Energy Utilities Board (EUB), then by the Energy Resources Conservation Board (ERCB), and most recently by the AER. The regulator's mandate has focused on facilitating the efficient exploitation of hydrocarbons while minimizing waste of resources. Its mandate has also included maintenance of environmental quality with a focus on controlling pollution. George Govier, chairman of the ERCB from 1962 to 1978, described the agency's approach to regulation: "If government's standards, regulations, and enforcement are sound, they will be realistically based upon the facts. They will be sensitive to the wishes of the community – those are facts too – but they will also recognize the hard facts of technology and economics. Our environment must be preserved but realism must prevail – we cannot frustrate the development and use of our energy resources" (Jaremko 2013).

The ERCB settled disputes between energy companies and the public by converting conflicts over land use, access, and environmental harm into financial decisions. It calculated measurable losses in terms of dollars and its decisions could not be appealed (Penfold 2016). Its actions ensured that hydrocarbon exploitation would not be frustrated by the public. In 2013, the AER, formed under the Responsible Energy Development Act, replaced the ERCB. The act placed all regulatory authority for energy development under the AER. In 2014, environmental acts were also transferred to the AER including the Environmental Protection and Enhancement Act, parts of the Mines and Minerals Act, and the Public Lands Act. In principle, but not in practice, the AER evaluates energy projects based on their predicted social and economic effects, environmental effects, and impacts to landowners. The AER is responsible for gathering all environmental information related to energy industry activities.

Although the regulator maintains that it protects the environment and that credibility and transparency are cornerstones of its activities, previous chapters have demonstrated that these beliefs are either hyperbole or self-deception. Rhetoric aside, the essential attribute of the AER is that it is not a government regulator; it is an industry-funded agency. For years, the question has been

237

whether the same agency can be entrusted to manage development of the resource, protect the public interest, and provide truthful information. The answer to that question is now painfully clear.

SYSTEMATIC DISTORTION OF INFORMATION

Organizations distort information whenever filters are applied to emphasize information that is favourable to the organization (Bella 1987). Distortion does not require unethical behaviour nor need it be the outcome of conscious intent or wilful deceit. Information distortion increases in proportion to the strength of previously held beliefs (Russo 2018). Distortion simply requires that an individual accept the role of a functionary whose responsibilities are limited to completion of assignments. People who are competent and honest can sustain systematic distortions by merely fulfilling their organizational roles. Indeed this is the most troubling aspect of organizational distortion of information. Were it solely the result of wilful deceit, malefactors could be rooted out and the problem solved. But such is not the case. Few scientists or engineers involved in environmental impact studies are aware of how the information that they prepare is used, vetted, or modified. Most are content to serve the role of a functionary, oblivious to their larger societal obligations. They're only taking orders – that's how every empire falls.

Within the core of the hydrocarbon industry metaorganization, there's a code of silence analogous to the mafia's code of omertà. If you work in the industry and want to keep your job, you remain silent. If scientists want funding or journalists want to be published, they need to speak the code words used by the metaorganization, such as "oil sands" instead of the scientifically correct "bitumen sands." If a consulting company, scientist, or organization want funding, they study what the industry and government want them to study and say what their funders want to hear. They become enablers willing to practice self-censorship. With the industry's takeover of university funding, some academics have retired in disgust, some have lost their jobs, and some have gone quiet, afraid to speak out. Then there are those who have chosen the role of useful idiots who take the industry's money and sing its praises. They've become compromised quislings who have traded their independence for income.

238

Organizations can develop complex technological systems of immense power and simultaneously sustain self-deception concerning the risks of those systems. As a result, an organization can be incapable of addressing the catastrophic possibilities that it creates (Bella 1987). Unless countered vigilantly, organizations selectively produce, sustain, and distribute information that contributes to the perception that their behaviours, actions, and decisions are responsible, reasonable, and justified. Favourable information that underestimates risks, uncertainties, or impacts is rarely scrutinized; favourable speculation based on no evidence can be accepted and communicated to superiors and the public. Conversely, information that does not support organizational objectives is challenged or dismissed. Yet it's precisely this "bad news" that allows an organization to correct its deficiencies. The organization rejects unfavourable information and hampers, intimidates, or removes troublemakers. It selects and shares favourable information, a process reinforced by conformity and social trust within the organization, with the effect that a distorted view of reality becomes dogma. The organization promotes staff who act as enablers to produce and distribute that good news. Without accurate, unbiased information, an organization is unable to learn from its mistakes (figure 16.1).

An organization can address information distortion in two ways. It can do nothing and wait for catastrophes. Or it can recruit the active participation of those who ask hard questions and pursue unfavourable enquiries. Without such participation, checks and balances are undermined and the risks of catastrophic failures increase as the scope and power of technology and organizations increase. If no checks and balances exist to detect and correct errors, then disinformation persists. Change personnel and still the problem persists. The only solution is to change the organizational behaviour.

How and Why Misinformation Arises

As we scale up from data pertaining to individual incidents to the impacts of the fossil fuel industry at national and global scales, the proportion of intentional disinformation increases. At the local scale, misleading information can arise out of poor training, subjectivity, poor oversight, or failure to gather relevant data. But at larger scales, misinformation is planned; it's disinformation intended to deny the public its right to know. No better example exists than

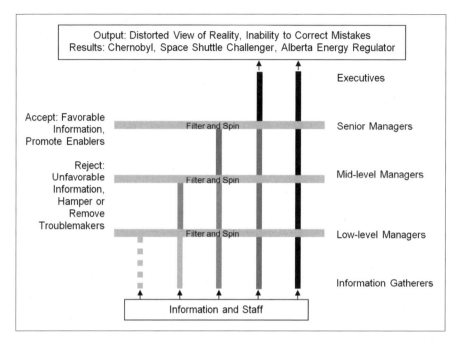

Figure 16.1 Information and personnel within an organization are subject to filtering at successive organizational levels. Only favourable information is released to the public and only enablers rise to the top (black). Troubling information and troublemakers (light gray) are rejected or filtered and spun to be favourable (increasingly darker grays). Information distortion increases the probability of disastrous consequences.

industry's successful campaign to confuse the public about the climatic and ecological impacts of fossil fuel use. The hydrocarbon industry has known for decades that burning fossil fuels affects global climate, but has pursued a disinformation campaign modelled after that of the tobacco industry. Its disinformation reduces understanding of climate change and support for climate action, nullifies accurate information, polarizes the public along political lines, and suppresses dialogue (Cook et al. 2019). Disinformation maintains the industry's grip on power.

Misinformation and disinformation can arise from intrinsic and extrinsic sources. Intrinsic distortion stems from cognitive biases that are common in organizations. Confirmation bias (the tendency to believe whatever confirms a belief), anchor bias (the tendency to lend greater weight to early information than to later information), bandwagon bias (the tendency to believe what others around you believe, also known as groupthink), and the ostrich bias (the tendency to reject unfavourable information) can all play a role in information distortion within an organization. Of extrinsic sources of information distortion, government censorship (hiding data and forbidding scientists to communicate) is the most prevalent (Fischetti 2019). Bias and misrepresentation (the mischaracterization of science and the discounting of science in policy making) is also a potent way to undermine science. Interference with education through control of curricula in schools and the funding of research programs at universities are widely used tools of the antiscience movement. Budget cuts and manipulating personnel provide further tools to weaken the influence of science. Research hindrance (destruction of data, pressuring scientists to alter their findings, and prevention of publication) and self-censorship (the voluntary suppression of information) also distort information and are notoriously difficult to document in that they require whistleblowers. I illustrate with an example of censorship in Alberta.

Recently, a scientist colleague observed difficulties in finding information about seismic lines and wrote to me about the experience. However, when approval was sought to publish the experience in this book, the scientist's director prohibited release because "it does not reflect well on the Government." Let's consider the significance of that decision. The information was censored not because it was false but because a manager thought it was unfavourable. The experience demonstrates how censorship can prevent us from learning from our mistakes and how when environmental information is lost, history is effaced. To protect the scientist, I've removed identifying details and revised the experience in my own words.

A Seismic Event
Some years ago, I studied plant succession on seismic lines in black spruce-dominated peatlands and aspen-dominated uplands. I thought that knowing a bit about the history of these lines would be useful. Who constructed them? When? Over what period? Who has been using them over the years, and are they still in use? If not for what they were originally intended, then for what reasons? I thought that it should not be difficult to find this information. I was wrong.

After a visit to the provincial government office, the local energy industry office, the forestry company office, and the local college, I was none the wiser. No one knew anything about these lines. Finally, I was told that if I collect the information on the metal plaques nailed to trees along the seismic lines, someone in the provincial government should be able to help me decode the information. I photographed every plaque and entered the information into a spreadsheet, and sent it off to the person I was told to contact.

After several weeks I inquired if anything had been learned. I was informed that no – the codes on the plaques meant nothing to anyone. I was also informed that the archival system had been changed in the year 2000, so the seismic lines "do not exist in the system anymore." There was no way of tracing them based on location and the information from the metal plaques. At that point at least I knew that the lines were cut before 2000 and had not been used since then. I then studied aerial photos taken between 1950 and 1990, and found that some of the seismic lines were constructed before 1950 and the others were cut over time until 1986. Who made them and who has been using them remain a mystery. Decades have passed and the seismic lines, especially the ones in peatlands, are not showing much regeneration. Active restoration will be necessary for their recovery. But who should do it? After all, no one knows who is responsible for the seismic lines in the first place.

The information was lost not out of malice but by people being unaware of the importance of historical data. It's like a janitorial crew going through a museum and chucking out all the old junk. To a scientist, the older the information the better because old data help us reach farther back in time to reconstruct environmental change. In previous chapters, we saw how loss of information about spills undermines our ability to document environmental impacts. The same is true of seismic lines.

CASE STUDIES OF INFORMATION DISTORTION

The Chernobyl nuclear reactor and Space Shuttle Challenger disasters illustrate how information distortion can result in tragedy. In the case of Chernobyl, a failed regulatory regime, poor communication about risks and design flaws, and the general lack of a safety culture set the stage for the disaster. In the case of Challenger, the problem began with a faulty design of the solid rocket joint. Both NASA and its contractors failed to recognize the problem, then once recognized, failed to fix the problem, and later treated it as an acceptable risk. As late as the night before the launch, engineers familiar with the booster joint and the effects of low temperature had argued against the launch. Their concerns were not communicated to those in charge of the launch decision. Filtering of information had been occurring for years with the result that self-deception had shaped the perceptions of flight managers who, protected from unfavourable information, believed the risks of failure were remote. Managers perceived the risk of solid-fuelled booster failures as 1:100,000 whereas engineers estimated the failure risk as 1:100, a thousandfold difference. The actual failure rate of solid-fuelled boosters at that time was about 1:25.

The reemergence of malaria mosquitoes in Sri Lanka illustrates how the perceived necessity of a successful result can lead to corruption of information and public harm. After an apparently successful eradication effort in the 1960s, the continued pressure to report success led to a change in data gathering that resulted in disaster (Spielman and D'Antonio 2001). By the government's data, the malaria mosquito eradication should have been complete. Why malaria later resurfaced would have remained a mystery but for the efforts of a public health entomologist who studied Ministry of Health files held in Colombo. Documents buried in manila folders reported the plan of attack, the supplies used, and the fieldwork and surveillance results. Hidden in the minutiae of data the entomologist found a memo from a government official that decreed a change in methods for reporting mosquito resistance to DDT. In the beginning of the eradication campaign, DDT effectiveness was confirmed if all mosquitoes died in a one-hour-long test. If so, insecticide resistance was absent and the spraying program could continue. Halfway through the malaria testing program, the time limit for the test was doubled to two hours. Why the method of data gathering was changed wasn't revealed in the memo, but investigation found that mosquitoes were developing DDT resistance. In order to achieve the required 100 per cent mosquito mortality, the test duration was doubled so that the mortality target could be met and the spraying program justified. The change allowed officials to reassure the public and political leaders that their efforts were successful. The reverse was true: the change in data gathering obscured the fact that malaria mosquitoes were developing insecticide resistance. The need to believe what they hoped was true prevented health officials from seeing the truth. The public paid the price in a resurgence of malaria.

Other examples of information distortion that led to catastrophic failures include Big Tobacco's campaign to suppress the health effects of smoking, the Bay of Pigs invasion, and the Vietnam War (Larson and King 1996). Although it would be reasonable to hope that societies learn to recognize and thwart disinformation, that doesn't seem to be the case. The most recent tragedy is the eighteen-year-long war in Afghanistan, the longest war in United States history, documented in "The Afghanistan Papers" in an exposé by the *Washington Post* in December 2019. Interview transcripts with participants involved in the disinformation campaign revealed that US officials repeatedly misled with statements they knew to be false. It was common to distort statistics to make it appear that the United States was winning; "every data point was altered to present the best picture possible" (Whitlock 2019). Truth was rarely welcome at headquarters in Kabul and Washington. Bad news was suppressed or spun to appear positive, such as portraying suicide bombings as a sign of the Taliban's desperation. The result was a trillion-dollar expenditure, 157,000 people killed, rampant corruption, a crippled country that has become the world's largest opium producer, and a resurgent Taliban.

Alberta's Home-Grown War on Truth

Despite all the evidence, the AER and the Alberta government contend that they and their industry partners are world leaders in the "science of solutions." They see their organization as setting global standards for reducing environmental impacts and supporting the development of greener communities (AER 2016a; Alberta Energy 2017). The acceptance of such beliefs in contradiction of the facts is an example of organizational groupthink. Beliefs that support and sustain a chosen social group, legitimize its power, and cast its activities in a positive light are fervently held and defended. Organizational self-deceptions, like religious beliefs, are propagated over time in spite of evidence that those beliefs are unfounded.

The Alberta Energy Regulator distorts information to meet its needs and the needs of its funders (see web 6.1, 12.1, 15.1, and 16 for examples). Although the regulator defines its stakeholders as "the people who live here," the regulator's record demonstrates that its controlling stakeholder is industry. The temptation might be to conclude that the regulator is corrupt. Is the regulator abusing its power by suppressing information? It's possible that many involved, especially low-ranking staff, have no conscious intent to mislead. But the result is the same: the organization is unable to address deficiencies and therefore continues to distort information and fails to protect the public interest.

The AER is resistant to change because it's working exactly as designed. Regulatory capture has placed important scientific decisions in the hands of engineers, managers, and others lacking the competence to make those decisions. Combine that deficiency with a lack of legal training of those implementing our environmental laws and we end up with an incompetent regulator controlled by a culture aligned with industry priorities rather than with protection of the public interest. The AER serves the interests of its clients and funders, the industry, by facilitating hydrocarbon exploitation while providing the appearance of oversight. The costs of irreparable harm to ecosystems, damage to the global climate, and stunning levels of unsecured liabilities never appear on the company balance sheets. Those externalized costs are deferred to the public and to future generations. An organization such as the AER, blinded to or unconcerned about its deficiencies, is dangerous to society. Because accurate and timely information form the basis for rational decisions and actions, distorted information poses societal risks. Normally, a regulator would take a dim view of any entity producing misinformation in the industry that it regulates. Ironically, in the case of the AER, it's the regulator itself that distributes the misinformation.

245

INDUSTRY'S CAPTURE OF THE ALBERTA ENERGY REGULATOR

Regulatory capture occurs when the decisions, actions, or resources of a regulator are directed away from the public interest in favour of a private interest through the actions of that interest (Taft 2017). The industry has played a long game to ensure that policies, regulations, and their application have been redirected away from the public interest to instead support the interests of the industry. It has done so by hitting the grand slam of regulatory capture. First base: corrosive capture or deregulation; second base: coercive capture by threats of political and/or legal retaliation or of catastrophic economic consequences; third base: cultural capture through ensuring that the regulator and the industry share the same ideology, personnel, and allegiances; and home run: acquisitive capture by acquiring legislation that ensures industry's minions control all aspects of hydrocarbon exploitation (MacLean 2016).

The ability of the energy regulator to protect the public interest has ebbed and flowed over the decades. In its incarnation as the Energy Resources Conservation Board (ERCB), the agency built a reputation for competence and quasi-judicial independence, although its intimate relationship with industry and its mandate to promote development hampered its effectiveness.

Its capture by the fossil fuel industry took major strides with the election of Ralph Klein, who served as Alberta's premier from 1993 to 2006, and later, in 2013, with establishment of the AER.

During the "Klein revolution," government opened the doors to industry's rise to power by effecting severe cutbacks in budgets, capacities, and autonomy of the civil service, municipal governments, universities, school boards, health authorities, and the regulator; meanwhile, it lowered energy royalties and taxes (Taft 2017). Government sold its interests in the Alberta Energy Company, the Husky upgrader, and Syncrude under the slogan "get government out of the business of business." An unprecedented transfer of public wealth to private interests occurred as publicly owned resources were sold at bargain prices. Politicians and industry executives shifted back and forth between positions of government power and industrial power. Ministers previously in the industry sat on and chaired committees with responsibilities for setting royalties, environmental policies, and regulating the industry. The revolving door between government and the industry pervaded all levels of government such that professional and personal relationships blurred the lines between public interest and private interest. In perhaps the most blatant abuse of privilege, three Alberta cabinet ministers joined with four other Progressive Conservative members of the legislature to form an anonymous numbered company that invested in oil and gas drilling that they owned and operated while in public office with the knowledge of both Premier Klein and the cabinet (Taft 2017).

In 2013, in the wake of a revelation that the regulator was spying on the public during an environmental hearing, the ERCB was replaced by the AER. The new regulator was given an expanded set of responsibilities that removed previous references to protection of the public interest. Responsibility for funding the agency was shifted entirely to the fossil fuel industry. Professional staff were transferred en masse from various branches of government into the AER. The responsibility, and the ability, to lay charges for contravention of the laws related to all aspects of the industry shifted from government to the industry-controlled regulator.

Much has been written about the "revolving door" between the regulator and the fossil fuel industry. The professional and personal relationships that unite government, regulators, universities, industry-funded agencies, companies, and lobby groups constitute a resilient, self-reinforcing network of mutual interests. The best example is perhaps Gerry Protti who in 2013 was appointed the chair of the AER (Taft 2017). Protti is a founding member of the lobby group Energy Policy Institute of Canada, the founding president of the lobby group Canadian Association of Petroleum Producers, former assistant deputy minister of Alberta Energy, and a former executive with Encana Corporation.

At Alberta's universities, drying up of government research funding was followed by major increases in industrial funding of research with the effect that universities increasingly came to serve industrial interests rather than the public interest. Money always comes with strings attached. Recipients of funds who are willing to break those strings and tell the hard truths are rare. Industry's funding of virtually all studies pertaining to their activities is a fundamental reason for misinformation about the effects of the fossil fuel industry. Cutbacks in government environmental monitoring resulted in the rise of industry-funded monitoring agencies whose scientific credibility and independence have been questioned. Into this vacuum of funding, capacity, and autonomy, industry expanded its power by "getting into the governing of government" (Taft 2017).

247

The AER and the Alberta and federal governments, as the key institutions within the network with responsibilities to protect the public interest, have structured their policies, regulations, and practices to suppress any challenges to the fossil fuel industry (Urquhart 2018). In 2013, the AER assumed all regulatory, monitoring, public land management, and environmental responsibilities pertaining to the fossil fuel industry in Alberta. In so doing, critical functions of environmental monitoring, ecosystem management, and enforcement were transferred *in toto* to an agency with neither the expertise nor the inclination to carry out those functions. Changes instituted under the Responsible Energy Development Act represented not so much a coup as it did completion of the industry's long-term goal of regulatory capture. Public concerns over regulatory capture aren't restricted to Alberta.

THE BEHAVIOUR OF A CAPTURED REGULATOR

In order to advance their mutual interests, the regulator and its partners produce information that places their activities in a positive light; other information is lost, ignored, or resides safely behind a firewall (figure 16.1). Lines of inquiry that might lead to inconvenient truths receive no funding from the

Regulatory Capture in Newfoundland

Questions about the ability of the Canada–Newfoundland and Labrador Offshore Petroleum Board to regulate the offshore oil industry surfaced in November 2018 after Husky Energy announced it was responsible for an offshore oil spill (CBC 2018d). The crude oil spill, whose volume was estimated by Husky at 250 m³ (without independent verification or evidence), was caused by a broken line connector beneath the SeaRose drilling platform. The spill occurred while Husky was restarting production in stormy conditions at a time when all other companies in the region had, for safety reasons, suspended operations. Concerns have been raised for years that the board defers to the wishes of the oil companies and operates under outdated, inadequate legislation. Its unhealthy relationship with industry was highlighted when it was revealed that the board privately advised Husky on how to communicate with the public about Husky's decision to continue operations when an iceberg came dangerously close to the platform. Bob Cadigan, former CEO of the Newfoundland & Labrador Oil & Gas Industries Association, notes that the provincial government needs to rethink its relationship with the board. Cadigan and others observe that it is dishonest of the provincial government to distance itself from responsibility when incidents occur. The government can't fault the board for its ineffectiveness because the government is responsible for providing all powers that the regulatory board may require.

network. The result is misinformation on a large scale. I asked a senior official within the AER how environmental misinformation arises. The source, speaking on condition of anonymity, explained (pers. comm., May 2017),

I do not believe for the most part this is intentional distortion. Based on my experience at AER – it is complete disorder, the databases are in disarray and basic knowledge of scientific method does not exist. Public Affairs does not understand the value of provision of scientific data and reports or of the value of open and transparent scientific debate. In fact, the only group associated with AER that does publish and has a critical

mass of competent scientists is the Alberta Geological Survey. That reflects the ERCB's [now AER's] mandate of knowing the resource for
extraction. That same capacity for [knowing the] environment does
not exist. As a result – nonscientists are providing data they do not
understand and Public Affairs is providing the interpretation ... Pipeline engineers understand pipeline integrity – not how to quantify an
environmental impact associated with a spill of specific toxicological
properties ...

... When a manager starts playing engineer – that is when the trouble
begins. We have seen this as well with the regulator ... as their core com-
petencies are engineering ... the same risks are unfolding. You do not
know what you do not know and if a structure is not created for that
voice to be heard and have authority – then it will be overruled simply
based on organizational and background biases.

The lack of credible scientific information on spills is due in part to inadequate capacity within the AER. A source within AER explained that those
evaluating spill impacts are usually enforcement officers; they are not toxicol-
ogists or ecologists. The same source revealed that many spill reports exist only
in paper copy and many reports can't be found. Spills in the FIS database are
edited manually by AER staff without proper documentation or quality assu-
rance/quality control procedures.

Whistleblowers

So effective are the regulator's and the industry's information control that we
seldom learn of unfavourable information. But a recent investigation by the
Alberta ethics commissioner, Marguerite Trussler, provides a glimpse behind
the AER's information firewall (Seskus and Bakx 2019). When a whistleblower
came forward to express concerns about serious wrongdoing in the operation
of the AER's International Centre of Regulatory Excellence (ICORE), a confi-
dant of the AER CEO Jim Ellis texted to Ellis, "If it is Corey I will crucify him
on the private side with everything in my possession." Trussler concluded that
Ellis had displayed "reckless and wilful disregard" in the management of public
funds. In a related report, public interest commissioner Marianne Ryan wrote,
"What struck me was almost like an atmosphere of arrogance and, on the other

hand, a culture of fear." Even the name of ICORE, touting its excellence, speaks of the culture of arrogance. The person suspected by Ellis as the whistleblower, Corey Froese, observed that "these [concerns about wrongdoing] were things that people whispered about but nobody wanted to come out and say … I got to know how those people worked and how they treated people that didn't move along with their direction." Ten days after Froese brought his concerns to Ellis and human resources, his employment was terminated. Commissioner Ryan concluded that AER staff felt that recommending a change of course or being critical of ICORE could result in adverse consequences, including termination of employment.

Industry whistleblowers from Alberta and Saskatchewan note that lying on official paperwork is rarely caught and part of a "systemic problem of oilpatch rule breaking in which good people are incentivized to lie" (McSheffrey 2019). Former oil and gas workers admit to lying or omitting facts in order to avoid being fired. Industry observers find that a failed regulatory regime allows companies to endanger workers as part of a "culture of silence that favours profit over employees." Lying is a "systemic cancer in the oilfield work culture … in which pressure to falsify often comes 'from above' and is almost always verbal." Those brave enough to step forward rarely feel free to provide their names to journalists in order to protect family members or for fear of losing their jobs or being shunned. They know too well that whistleblowers are viewed as troublemakers and so they lie whenever necessary knowing that their livelihood is at risk if they don't do what is expected by management.

Information received, produced, maintained, and distributed by the regulator and its partners flows from a complex metaorganization. Energy companies report to the regulator. Consulting companies, remediation contractors, industry organizations, lobby groups, think tanks, banks, industry-funded universities and academics, and favoured media outlets act as enablers and legitimators. The Alberta government provides the legislative authority to the regulator and acts as its political arm. Distortion of information can occur within any of these organizations and be propagated through the social network. For those hired by industry, their livelihoods depend upon providing favourable information to their clients. For industry, its reputation and social licence depend upon providing favourable information to the regulator. For government, favourable information from the regulator justifies its surrender of responsibilities and provides political cover when industrial incidents occur.

For the captured regulator, favourable information facilitates its objective of hydrocarbon production. The public, outside the firewall protecting the meta-organization, receives distorted information. For documentation of the fossil fuel industry metaorganization, see CMP (2019.)

The Portrayal of Ecoterrorism

In the late 1990s, government and media attention was directed towards a few isolated acts of energy infrastructure vandalism in northwestern Alberta. These acts were portrayed as "ecoterrorism" committed by "fringe lunatics" while the sincere concerns, fears, and frustrations widely held by people impacted by the industry received little attention (Marr-Laing and Severson-Baker 1999). The most publicized of these acts of "ecoterrorism" was in fact perpetrated jointly by the RCMP and the Alberta Energy Company in an effort to entrap suspects. In reality, vandalism is an insignificant source of spills, responsible for 0.4 per cent of the volume of crude oil spills and 0.1 per cent of the volume of saline water spills (web 7.10). There is zero evidence that ecoterrorists in Alberta have caused any spills. Yet government and the regulator have presented a different view to the public.

251

The RCMP dirty tricks operation, code-named Operation Kabriole, involved the blowing up of a shed at a well site on 14 October 1999. One week later, Alberta Energy Company hosted two tense town hall meetings at which local people were told that they were the victims of "ecoterrorists" (CBC 1999). I leave it to the reader to decide upon the advisability of the RCMP and industry instilling terror in a community by spreading fake news. In contrast to fake news, Alberta Energy Company was responsible for 1,205 reported spills in Alberta over the period 1978–2002. The Alberta government was a major shareholder in the Alberta Energy Company.

A 2014 report authored by the RCMP stated, "There is a growing, highly organized and well-financed anti-Canada petroleum movement that consists of peaceful activists, militants and violent extremists who are opposed to society's reliance on fossil fuels … If violent environmental extremists engage in unlawful activity, it jeopardizes the health and safety of its participants, the general public and the natural environment" (McCarthy 2015). In a related development, in June 2015, the federal government enacted the Anti-Terrorism Act (Bill C-51). This law defines activity that undermines the security of

Canada as anything that interferes with economic or financial stability or critical infrastructure and permits the Canadian Security and Intelligence Service (CSIS) to take measures to reduce those perceived threats. Although Bill C-51 was presented as a means to deal with Islamic extremism, the bill expanded the powers of government to infiltrate, surveil, and undermine any groups that the government believes may promote civil disobedience, such as groups opposed to the Northern Gateway Pipeline in British Columbia (McCarthy 2015). Has it done so?

That question is difficult to answer because covert operations are, by definition, secret. However, the BC Civil Liberties Union alleged in September 2018 that CSIS had broken the law by spying on peaceful pipeline protestors and had shared its information with the RCMP, the National Energy Board, and oil and pipeline companies (CBC 2018e). The executive director of the BC Civil Liberties Union stated that it is "not the job of Canada's spy and police agencies to be reporting to corporations on the democratic activities of citizens." A hearing into the complaint was to take place but its results will not be made public. In November 2019 it came to light that Trans Mountain was surveilling people it considers "persons of interest" who oppose completion of the Trans Mountain pipeline (Barrera 2019) and was sharing that information with police and Natural Resources Canada. Human rights activists are concerned that Trans Mountain's activities infringe upon citizens' rights of free expression.

Those Who Express Concern Are the Enemy

Those who voice concerns about the impacts of the industry find themselves at odds with a network of immense power. Opponents may be deprived of funding, have their legal rights denied, may be fired or have their careers curtailed, or be subjected to public *ad hominem* and libellous attacks. I've been attacked and abused several times but I hold no animus; I use the experiences as data points. The career curtailments and attacks are not limited to those outside the regulator. The case of Dr Monique Dubé has already been alluded to. I could name others who have been similarly attacked, but other than to reopen wounds, to what would it avail?

In Alberta, two recent examples of the regulator's treatment of concerned citizens demonstrate the behaviour of a captured regulator. A 2013 court case brought forward by the Pembina Institute and the Wood Buffalo Environmental Association exposed Alberta government bias in favour of the fossil fuel industry. The plaintiffs were denied their right to appeal a decision to approve expansion of a Southern Pacific bitumen project in northeastern Alberta that required significant water removals from the Mackay River (Taft 2017). The trial uncovered a briefing note prepared for the deputy minister of Alberta Environment Jim Ellis, who later became the CEO of the AER, the same Ellis at the centre of recent AER scandals.

The briefing note recommended that the complainants be denied their right to appeal because those groups were "less inclined to work cooperatively" with industry and government and because one of the complainants had published "negative media on the oil sands." In short, the complainants were denied their legal rights because they disagreed with government. Justice Marceau found that the briefing note had been used repeatedly to prevent uncooperative groups from mounting appeals. The judge found that the briefing note "clearly violated the principle that one has the right to be heard, and in this case, to answer allegations made against it in secret." The judge noted that the process followed by Alberta Environment was fatally flawed and tainted by the briefing note, which he interpreted as a formula for rejecting future submissions. He concluded "a well-informed member of the public ... would perceive that the valid object of the Environmental Protection and Enhancement Act to give the citizens of Alberta as much input as reasonable into environmental concerns that arise from industrial development is hijacked by the Briefing Note ... It is difficult to envision a more direct apprehension of bias ... the Director's decision breaches all four of the principles of natural justice and must be quashed" (Taft 2017).

Another relevant case is that of Jessica Ernst who struggled to have concerns about the effects of hydraulic fracturing on her water supply taken seriously. Ms Ernst was repeatedly denied access to the regulator's investigation and complaints process because the regulator believed that she constituted a "criminal threat of violence." The regulator even referred to Ms Ernst as a "terrorist" in a 2012 court document filed by the AER (Stenson 2015). The AER concluded that it "owed no duty of care" to protect groundwater and that an ecoterrorist's Charter rights could be violated by a regulator. A 2013 court ruling concluded that the AER is immune from legal claims, essentially placing it above the law. In spite of being branded an ecoterrorist, Ms Ernst conducted no activities that resulted in damage to energy infrastructure. Why did the regulator label a citizen as an ecoterrorist? It uses inflammatory rhetoric as a dog whistle to rally support and justify denying citizens their rights.

A recent attack was directed at a member of the AER's board of directors, Ed Whittingham, who resigned from his post in April 2019 (Bennett and Weber 2019). Mr Whittingham was "subjected to a smear campaign without precedent in Alberta for a public appointment held by a private citizen." Jason Kenney, the new Alberta premier, had accused Mr Whittingham of economic sabotage and stated that one of his first tasks upon assuming office would be to fire Mr Whittingham and replace the entire AER board of directors on the grounds that, in his view, approval of energy projects takes far longer in Alberta than in competing jurisdictions (Bennett and Weber 2019). In his resignation letter, Whittingham stated that he fears Kenney's new AER team will approve projects at the expense of the environment.

Mr Whittingham may prove to be only one of many casualties in a war promised by Kenney against those who, he says, are conspiring to hamstring Alberta's fossil fuel industry. In December 2019, Mr Kenney announced the opening of his $30 million "war room" to respond to those he says spread falsehoods about the industry. To put things into perspective, the annual budget for the "war room" is approximately 50 per cent greater than the approved budget for all provincial environmental monitoring of air, water, and biodiversity for Alberta. The enemies of Mr Kenney include banks such as HSBC that have chosen to stop investing in Alberta's bitumen industry. Mr Kenney says Alberta will boycott them in retaliation (Flavelle 2020) – this from a government whose ideology demands that government not interfere with private business. It's unlikely that the belligerence and bluster will intimidate major financial institutions. More likely, the war room is a ploy to appeal to Kenney's political base and his funders in the industry.

Another of Mr Kenney's initiatives is his $2.5 million "Public Inquiry into Funding of Anti-Alberta Energy Campaigns." Conflicts of interest have been alleged from the outset of Mr Kenney's inquiry. Principal actors in the inquiry and beneficiaries of sole source contracts and campaign contributions comprise a select group that includes the Alberta Justice Minister Doug Schweitzer (Rusnell 2020). Kenney's foreign funding conspiracy theory has already been disproven in an investigation of funding data (Garossino 2019). Conversely, foreign ownership of Alberta bitumen sands profits increased to 58 per cent from 2012 to 2016 while Canadian ownership of profits declined to 42 per cent

(Environmental Defence et al. 2020). But reality hasn't deterred the inquiry, which may in time prove to be nothing more than a ruse to attack Ecojustice, the Pembina Institute, the David Suzuki Foundation, and other environmental groups Kenney considers hostile to the fossil fuel industry. The inquiry has, without justification, repeatedly denied requests by CBC News and Ecojustice for disclosure of individual submissions, summaries of meetings, and an interim report of the findings (Rusnell 2020). Ecojustice argued that the inquiry fails to follow the basic rules of disclosure for a public inquiry and submitted a legal challenge stating that the inquiry was established for an improper purpose outside the Alberta Public Inquiries Act. In July 2020, an industry consortium was granted intervener status to oppose the Ecojustice challenge of the legality of Mr Kenney's inquiry (Martin 2020). In November 2020, an Alberta court rejected the Ecojustice challenge.

255

Other promises by Kenney include boycotting of companies that boycott bitumen companies and challenging the charitable status of groups that oppose the bitumen industry. Kenney's roll back of environmental initiatives such as the provincial carbon tax, which funds the solar rebate program, are misguided and damaging to the public interest. Both Whittingham and former environment minister Shannon Phillips are concerned that the Kenney government will undermine Alberta's environmental credibility and cost jobs and investment. Alberta's 2020 budget signalled its intention to tie Alberta's future to a commodity that the world is turning away from by tying its hopes on a resurgence of the fossil fuel industry while paying lip service to climate change (Boyd and Leavitt 2020). It's budgeting underlain by scorched earth ideology. Gill McGowan, president of the Alberta Federation of Labour, has observed, "If they take money from the public sector, from the public purse and use it to prop up oil and gas projects that have been rejected by global investors, that's money that's being taken away from education, health care, infrastructure, all those things that are already being underfunded. This is a recipe, from our perspective in the labour movement, for economic disaster" (De Souza and Yourex-West 2020).

Fear of losing investment dollars may be the driving force behind the "war room." In 2018, HSBC, Europe's largest bank, announced it would no longer finance new bitumen sands projects or pipelines. In 2019, Moody's downgraded Alberta's credit rating to its lowest level in twenty years and the insurance giant The Hartford decided to stop insuring and investing in Alberta oil production, just weeks after Sweden's central bank chose to stop holding

Alberta bonds. In February 2020, BlackRock, the world's largest asset manager, announced its green-oriented fund would stop investing in Alberta bitumen operations (Flavelle 2020). In July 2020, Deutsche Bank joined other banks and insurance companies when it announced it would prohibit investing in Arctic oil and gas projects, in projects that use fracking in countries with scarce water supplies, and in new bitumen sands projects (Healing 2020). Also in July 2020, Total, the multinational energy corporation, wrote off $9.3 billion in its northern Alberta bitumen assets, stating that these assets were now stranded due to the company's carbon reduction targets. Total also withdrew from the Canadian Association of Petroleum Producers because the lobby group's promotion of carbon-intensive activities are misaligned with Total's policy to reduce carbon emissions. These divestments are part of a growing global movement in which more than $6 trillion have been diverted away from fossil fuels on behalf of more than 1,000 institutional lenders.

The power of divestment was made clear in late February 2020 when Teck Resources withdrew its application for the Frontier Mine. In explaining the company's decision, Teck CEO Don Lindsay wrote that "global capital markets are changing rapidly and investors and customers are increasingly looking for jurisdictions to have a framework in place that reconciles resource development and climate change, in order to produce the cleanest possible products" (Connolly 2020). He added that the project would not be economical unless the price of oil was at $75/barrel or higher. Mr Kenney was quick to blame Teck's decision on Indigenous rights protesters and Prime Minister Trudeau. Kenney tweeted that "Teck's decision to pull its application, in part because of 'public safety concerns,' is deeply troubling." Alberta's finance minister Travis Toews blamed rail blockade protesters for Teck's cancellation and added "we have a federal government who [*sic*] didn't categorically confirm its support" for Teck (Boyd and Leavitt 2020). These attempts to link Teck's financial decision to the recent wave of protests and blockades in support of Indigenous rights lack substance. In truth, Teck made no statement about public safety concerns.

Science Denial

Science denial is used extensively by the metaorganization and is facilitated through the use of five techniques summarized by the acronym FLICC: Fake experts, Logical fallacies, Impossible expectations, Cherry picking, and Conspiracy theories (Cook et al. 2019). Fake experts are portrayed as highly qualified sources despite their lack of relevant education or publications. Logically flawed arguments such as non sequiturs are used to lead people to erroneous conclusions. Unrealistic standards of certainty are required before action is taken. Data are cherry picked that support a favoured conclusion while ignoring all data that support a different conclusion. And finally, conspiracy theories of secret plans by shadowy forces aimed at undermining society are used to confuse people and manipulate public opinion.

Jason Kenney's taxpayer-funded "war room" (the Canadian Energy Centre) provides a good example of FLICC at work. In the words of Mr Kenney, his war room is a "response to a campaign of lies, of defamation and disinformation based on torqued, dated and incomplete and out of context attacks on our energy sector" (Anderson 2019). The war room uses fake experts, including staff portrayed as journalists, to lead people to logical fallacies to polarize and paralyze the public to therefore undermine the transition to a carbon-neutral economy. The war room itself is rooted in a debunked Orwellian conspiracy theory: that foreign-funded outsiders are undermining Canadian society by spreading misinformation.

Twenty million dollars in the war room's annual funding come from the carbon tax (intended to support the transition to carbon neutrality) and ten million dollars come from the government's advertising budget. The war room's spin doctors have written that Canada needs more pipelines, that it's time for the Canadian hydrocarbon industry to play a larger role on the world stage, that there's a swell of support from Indigenous groups for the Trans Mountain pipeline, and that oil and gas pipelines will fuel Canada's economic recovery from COVID-19. Because war room products are not journalism, the Canadian Association of Journalists has requested that war room employees cease referring to themselves as reporters when in truth they act as "PR professionals, content writers, and spin doctors." Other accomplishments of the war room include its questioning the credibility of the *New York Times*, its misrepresentation of data and statistics, the war room's logo, copied from an American software company, and its March 2021 attacks on *Bigfoot Family*, a cartoon movie on Netflix. Attacks by Mr Kenney's war room may have unintended effects – they may further erode the social licence of the fossil fuel industry.

257

The Dysfunction Is Not Accidental

Misinformation is not due to budget constraints. Industry contributed $270 million to the regulator's budget for both 2016 and 2017 from administrative and orphan well levies alone (AER 2017e). The regulator has the financial capability to deliver credible environmental information but instead has delivered misinformation along with poor monitoring and enforcement for decades. Why? Because the dysfunction serves the interests of the industry and its regulator, neither of which want publicly available accurate environmental information when it only agitates people to ask questions.

The dysfunction extends through the entire industry metaorganization. Metaorganizations form whenever the prospects of large profits align with political power and the costs of exploitation can be shifted to the public. It's a familiar story with predictable results. We need look no further than the example that began the book, that of chemical companies dumping toxic wastes in Ocean County, New Jersey. Back in 1964, twelve years after the Toms River Chemical Company began contaminating the drinking water of thousands of people, with full knowledge of the Toms River Water Company that supplied the drinking water, and twenty years before the public began to learn that their water had been poisoned, the New Jersey government not only failed to enforce the terms of the company's discharge permits, it advised the chemical company on how to hamper citizens' efforts to uncover the truth. The government encouraged Toms River Chemical to adopt a policy of "complete silence" because its news releases were "only agitating people and supplying them with information."

The industry's most profound offence may be the way it uses misinformation to undermine public dialogue, education, and decision making (Taft 2017). Regulatory capture is a symptom of a broader malignancy in which vested interests have undermined our democratic institutions, our governments, our education systems, the media, monitoring agencies, and our schools and universities, not only in Canada but worldwide. In Saskatchewan, the fossil fuel industry has captured the province's school curriculum in order to block a transition to a postcarbon economy (Eaton and Gray 2019). The curriculum presents a favourable picture of the industry, one in which a life without fossil fuels poses a threat to freedom, in which fossil fuel production is compatible with environmental sustainability, and in which there is no climate emergency. The curriculum is designed to produce young adults with skills useful to industry who view themselves as members of a benign social-economic order that mustn't be challenged. A similar undermining of critical thinking in Alberta's school curriculum is underway. In January 2020, the Alberta government announced plans to place teaching children about climate science on equal footing with indoctrination of students about the importance of the fossil fuel industry. Education Minister Adriana LaGrange has advanced the conspiracy theory of bogeymen teaching "extremist views" about the impacts of the fossil fuel industry. This is, of course, nonsense and is a good illustration of how FLICC techniques are used to undermine science.

SUMMARY   259

In Canada, the path to regulatory capture has followed an incremental process as the industry, under the guise of streamlining regulations and oversight, has exerted increasing control over a host of agencies and institutions. Alberta lies at the epicentre of the regulatory capture. A metaorganization composed of the fossil fuel industry, the regulator, government, lobby groups and other enablers, consultants, academics, and monitoring agencies exchanging information, money, and staff represents pervasive regulatory capture that damages our democracy and our ecosystems and cripples our society. If adopting a policy of silence, depriving the public of credible information, and intimidating people to remain silent sound extreme, they are. Demanding silence is a form of violence.

CHAPTER 17

Conclusions: Better Sad Truths Than Happy Lies

Only when ruling elites become worried about survival do they react. Appealing to the better nature of the powerful is useless. They don't have one.

Chris Hedges, *America, the Farewell Tour*

INTRODUCTION

This book grew out of successive observations best understood by an analogy. A police officer pulls over a vehicle for a broken taillight. He asks the driver for his licence only to learn that the driver has no licence. This raises a red flag. The officer looks more closely at the driver and sees that his shirt and pants are spattered with blood and feathers. He asks the driver to step out of his vehicle, calls in backup, and finds, hidden under a tarp in the trunk, the bloody carcass of an endangered whooping crane. A broken taillight can sometimes uncover a federal crime.

I began this investigation with an analysis of reported rates of spill recovery and found that recovery rates were too good to be true. That result planted a nagging doubt about the truth of the regulator's data that set me on a path of inductive logic. If recovery rates are not credible, are other industry-reported data not credible? If so, what are the actual environmental impacts of the fossil fuel industry and how did it come about that the regulator accepts unreliable information and distributes it to the public? What forces created a dysfunctional regulator? Are the same forces undermining our democratic institutions?

Reasoning from the specific to the general led me to a wider analysis and the realization that perfect spill recovery was but one symptom of a disease corrupting the entire body of the regulator's evidence. I found thousands of undocumented spills, missing data, inaccurate spill locations, underestimated spill volumes, failure to assess environmental impacts and failure to record animal deaths and habitat damage, wildly inaccurate information on sensitive areas, and other biased, unempirical, or dubious data. Those findings led me to compare the regulator's data with the science. I found that residual contamination was rampant and that ecological effects were pervasive and persistent. That finding led to the realization that the data corruption was the result of regulatory capture, a form of legal corruption. Regulatory capture proved to be nested within a pervasive undermining of our democratic institutions by vested interests.

In the preface I posed several questions. The answers to those questions are now clear. Does the regulator provide scientifically credible and timely data on spill composition, location, spill and recovery volumes, environmental impacts, and sensitive areas? It does not. Is there evidence of residual contamination after cleanup? Yes, there is. Are the regulator's data complete? No, they are exceedingly incomplete. Are spills resulting in significant impacts? Most certainly. Is the regulator protecting the environment? It is not. Let's review how those conclusions were reached.

AN OVERVIEW OF THE FINDINGS

Crude oil and saline water spills are the two most common spills that occur during the production and transport of hydrocarbons. In Alberta, spills continue to occur daily and are more frequent than in Saskatchewan, North Dakota, or Montana. Over the period 1975 through 2018 in Alberta, there were 30,329 crude oil spills reporting a cumulative volume spilled of 1.8 million barrels at a rate of 1.9 spills/day. Over the same forty-four-year period, there were 26,669 saline water spills reporting a cumulative volume spilled of 6.2 million barrels at a rate of 1.7 spills/day. The total reported volume of saline water released was 3.4 times greater than the total reported crude oil spilled volume. These are minimum estimates because reported spill volumes underestimate actual spill volumes and because untold thousands of spills have not been reported or are outside the monitoring of the regulator. With rare exception, no one knows where the undocumented spills occurred.

Where do spills originate? Most crude oil spills occur at multiphase pipelines, crude oil group batteries, and oil wells. By spill volume, crude oil group batteries, crude oil pipelines, and multiphase pipelines are responsible for the largest releases. Most saline spills occur at water pipelines, crude oil group batteries, and multiphase pipelines. By volume, water pipelines are the single largest source of saline water spilled, followed by crude oil group batteries and oil wells. Pipelines of all types account for 32 per cent of crude oil spills and 52 per cent of saline spills in Alberta. Crude oil pipelines account for only 4 per cent of crude oil spills. Pipeline spill rates for crude oil and saline water are similar in Saskatchewan and Alberta.

There is a strong tendency of industry to underestimate spill volumes. Wherever I found data, initial spill volumes underestimated later volumes, such as by eight to ten times for the Lodgepole sour gas blowout, by forty-eight times for a crude oil release in British Columbia, by 160 times for the crude oil released at the Pace-Spyglass spill, by 500 times for the Apache 15-09 saline spill, and by 1,000 times for the Nexen saline spill near Long Lake. To make matters worse, the regulator does not routinely update its database with revised spill volumes and in many spills fails to report any volumes.

The regulator underreports the occurrence of sensitive areas at spills by a factor of 171 times for saline spills and 220 times for crude oil spills. Similarly, the regulator underreports habitat and wildlife damage and fails to record animal deaths or injuries in its database. Relying upon industry to investigate its environmental effects is ludicrous. We should not be surprised when we hear there are no effects. The surprise is that industry and the regulator have gotten away with this scam for decades.

One of the certainties arising from the research is not a comforting one: the total volume of crude oil and saline water released into the environment in Alberta since operations began in 1902 greatly exceeds the volumes reported. How large an underestimate? It's impossible to know. What little is known of early incidents reveals that some were appallingly large (figure 17.1). The effects of the Atlantic No. 3 blowout, the largest crude oil spill in Canadian history and six times larger than the *Exxon Valdez* spill, still persist seventy years after the spill. Atlantic No. 3 released 82 per cent of the total crude oil volume reported by the regulator for *all* crude oil spills in Alberta. "Old Salty's" eighty-seven years of saline discharge dwarfs the regulator's entire reported saline spill total release; it released 112 times the total saline volume reported by the regulator for *all* saline spills. The release by "Old Salty" is almost too large to contemplate; it released 136 times the volume of crude oil released by the BP Deepwater Horizon spill.

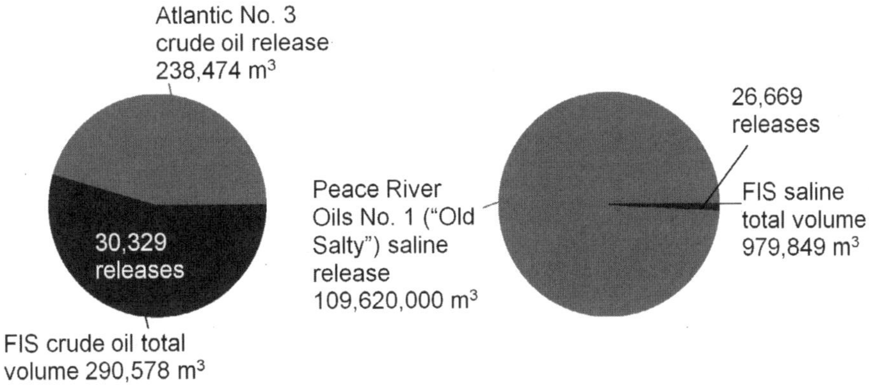

Atlantic No. 3
crude oil release
238,474 m³

30,329
releases

FIS crude oil total
volume 290,578 m³

Peace River
Oils No. 1 ("Old
Salty") saline
release
109,620,000 m³

26,669
releases

FIS saline
total volume
979,849 m³

263

Figure 17.1 Total reported spill volumes in the Alberta regulator's database comprise a small fraction of actual spill volumes from upstream activities. Here we compare total reported volumes for 30,329 crude oil and 26,669 saline water releases in the regulator's FIS database (1975–2018) with two unrecorded catastrophic releases. The dark area within each pie chart represents the total recorded spill volumes in the FIS database for all crude oil (left) and saline water spills (right) relative to the spill volumes from the catastrophic unrecorded spills of Atlantic No. 3 (left) and Old Salty (right).

The Industrial Signature and Domain Shifts

Once a native community has been removed and its living soil degraded, there is no going back. This is so because profound disturbances undermine the ecological relationships that support biodiversity, productivity, and resilience. Landscape "conversion" in the oil patch is a one-way street. A large and growing industry footprint, landscape-level effects on ecosystem function, and the failure of reclamation to achieve healthy soils and vegetation demonstrate that the industry causes wholesale, long-term damage to ecosystems. Responsibility for widespread ecosystem impacts doesn't rest solely with captured regulators. Provincial and federal governments and industry share that responsibility, as do the scientific community and the public for our collective silence and complacency. We pay for these changes through loss of ecological goods and services.

Industry disturbances create winners and losers whose abundance increases or decreases as a result of disturbance. Species that increase in abundance with fossil fuel industry disturbances are predominantly common weedy species.

Vegetation communities favoured by industrial disturbances are typically exotic weedy meadows, salinized barrens, and various exotic nonwoody plant assemblages. The vast majority of native species and communities are losers. Once we learn to recognize the disturbance signature, we can see the hand of the industry all around us, hiding in plain sight (plate 17.1).

SIGNIFICANCE OF THE FINDINGS

A hydrocarbon-fuelled economy is inherently destructive. Whether it's during the exploration and production phases, during processing and refining, during transportation via pipeline, railway car, transport truck, or container ship, or burning the hydrocarbons, the fossil fuel economy damages our land, water, and atmosphere.

Spills pose a greater threat to society and ecosystem health than industry and government would have us believe. But spills comprise only one form of damage. The cumulative effects of the industry can be likened to a full-body injury. Spills are like puncture wounds: they're not really extensive but they are intensive in their effects. In Alberta alone, there are tens of thousands of spills with unknown spill volumes remaining in the environment after cleanup and untold thousands of undocumented spills. The lack of scientifically credible postspill monitoring presents major environmental unknowns. What we don't know can hurt us.

Despite their toxicity, fresh saline spills are essentially invisible because they resemble water-soaked ground. Because saline spill volume was more than three times that of crude oil spill volume and because contamination from saline spills may persist longer than that from crude oil spills, the impacts from saline spills exceed those from crude oil spills.

Failure to acknowledge and act to control the impacts of the fossil fuel industry places an ever-increasing burden on future generations. The network of spills represents a legacy of damaged and contaminated sites that future generations will have to manage (plate 17.2). The industry has bequeathed future generations with inherited danger, uncertainty, and costs.

Companies responsible for spills want to be seen as conscientious, reasonable, and justified in their actions. They therefore tend to underestimate spill volumes and ecological damage, and overestimate recovered volumes and prospects for reclamation or remediation. The motivation to report preferred outcomes results in a cognitive bias reinforced by knowledge that the data are unlikely to be scrutinized. The outcome of this distortion of information is to report best-case scenarios that minimize spill volumes, maximize recovery volumes, and minimize environmental impacts. Crude oil and saline spills are never "good news" stories. They occur daily, they damage ecosystems, and their effects linger. If spills did not damage ecosystems, industry and the regulator would be eager to share the good news. I observed the opposite. All requests made to industry for postspill results and reports were ignored. Information requests made to the regulator met with inordinate delays and mixed results. There is no credible evidence to support statements that spill sites have been successfully reclaimed to healthy conditions.

Gathering high quality environmental data and protecting its integrity are not priorities of the regulator nor does it appreciate the importance of environmental data. Reliance on industry's unverified, self-reported data is the hallmark of a captured regulator. The data are of poor quality and incomplete, spill reports fail to address environmental impacts or are unavailable, transparency is inadequate, and third party review and scientific scrutiny are not used. Of the thousands of environmental reports submitted by industry, many are never reviewed by staff nor are the findings of such reports readily accessible. Furthermore, most industry environmental reports are not credible in the first place. Adding to the lack of credible information, about 93 per cent of incidents are not investigated by the regulator and only about 0.11 per cent of incidents result in available investigation reports. The regulator lacks the scientific competence, capacity, and inclination required to understand and manage environmental impacts and risks.

Regulatory capture has emasculated regulations and resulted in poor enforcement and poor gathering and dissemination of information. The industry is free to damage ecosystems under cover of a complicit regulator. The public is kept uninformed while the abuses continue and the ecological and financial liabilities accumulate. The regulator does not practice "empathic engagement," demonstrate "stellar competence," or enforce the rules and protect the environment. Were the regulator to admit that its information is misleading, that it has little environmental expertise and competence, has no empathy for the public, and has no intention of protecting the environment it would be less offensive than its continued patent dishonesty.

265

Replacement of the regulator's executives might provide temporary improvement in the regulator's performance, but the dysfunction of the regulator runs deeper. It's the structure of the captured organization itself – its mission to maximize hydrocarbon production, its conflicted mandate of production and protection, its immunity from judicial remedy, its independence from the electorate, its funding by the industry, its staffing by the industry, its culture of intolerance of dissent and debate, its culture of treating the public as adversaries and requests for information as hostile, and its lack of ecological and environmental expertise – that render the regulator dysfunctional. Pruning a tree of its upper branches is ineffective if the roots are corrupted with rot.

The Alberta Energy Regulator needs to be replaced, not made more dysfunctional, which was the apparent objective of the 2020 round of restructuring and layoffs precipitated by a reduction in the AER's budget. The budget cutbacks, the result of the Kenney government's reduction in the levy paid by industry to the regulator, meant an AER budget loss of $147 million over a four-year period. A spokesperson explained the cutbacks: "The energy sector requires a well-designed, single regulator for our energy resources, which is why we committed to a review of the organization in our platform" (Da Silva 2020). Changes to the AER are designed to better serve the fossil fuel industry, not the public interest.

Risks and Liabilities

Due to the unfunded reclamation financial liability, it's likely that Alberta's vast network of spills, wells, pipelines, seismic lines, facilities, and other intensively disturbed sites will receive either no reclamation or the reclamation will be funded by the taxpayer. What of the underground releases that we never see and the spreading effects of hydraulic fracturing? What will be the costs to municipalities and landowners who find they have built on contaminated land? These uncertainties have more than academic implications. Not only can we not document sites we can't find or don't know exist – we can't determine whether those sites are close to our homes or water sources.

As of 2018, the financial liability for cleanup of Alberta's fossil fuel industry sites had reached $260 billion. Only 0.6 per cent of this liability has been funded, the result of a corrupt regulatory regime captured by the industry responsible for the damage. Do these costs include incidents that are "off the books" such as the catastrophic Atlantic No. 3 blowout and underground releases? We don't know because we don't have access to the cost accounting.

In late 2019, the Alberta government asked the federal government for financial aid to address the growing liability of abandoned wells. This is a rich irony given that the management of hydrocarbon development lies solely within provincial jurisdiction and any federal involvement is bitterly opposed by the Alberta government. It's a cynical political move. Premier Kenney knows that well abandonment is a provincial liability that is supposed to be funded through levies paid by the hydrocarbon companies.

Due to gross mismanagement over the decades, we now face hundreds of billions of dollars of unsecured financial and environmental liability. So why not contrive to get the Canadian taxpayer to foot the bill? Even better, why not procure the funds under the guise of COVID-19 relief? That ruse came to fruition in April 2020 when Prime Minister Trudeau announced $1.7 billion to remediate orphan wells in Alberta, Saskatchewan, and British Columbia bundled with aid for rural businesses and people working in arts and culture (Harris 2020). The federal bailout of the provinces' failure to manage impacts may sound significant but it's chump change relative to the unsecured financial liabilities. More importantly, we the public are being forced to pay for the damage caused by private corporations.

Given the urgent need to decarbonize the world economy, it's pertinent to ask what proportion of federal COVID-19 taxpayer-funded financial support in Canada has gone to the fossil fuel industry compared to support for clean energy companies. Between January and June 2020, 98.2 per cent of financial support ($16 billion) was paid to the fossil fuel industry compared to 1.8 per cent ($0.3 billion) to support clean energy companies (Rabson 2020). In Alberta, the COVID-19 crisis has been used even more cynically to undermine the public interest. In May 2020, the Alberta government announced it would step in to pay industry levies to the AER for the first half of 2020, effectively stealing $114 million in taxpayers' money. Then, in a podcast hosted by the Canadian Association of Oilwell Drilling Contractors, Alberta's energy minister Sonya Savage stated in reference to the Trans Mountain pipeline, "Now is a great time to be building a pipeline because you can't have protests of more than 15 people. Let's get it built" (Weber 2020b). Environment Minister Jason Nixon defended Savage, "Because of COVID, there is probably less people [*sic*] taking the opportunity to go out and protest pipelines." The government has introduced new legislation that imposes large fines and possible jail terms for anyone interfering with the operation of energy infrastructure (although such acts are already illegal). An even greater ruse perpetrated under the guise of COVID-19 relief came in May 2020 when the AER suspended environmental monitoring requirements for the entire fossil fuel industry in Alberta (De Souza and Vernon 2020). Tellingly, companies continue to have production staff in the field, but 95 per cent of all environmental monitoring has ceased. Former Alberta premier and current NDP leader Rachel Notley summed up the situation: "This is an utterly idiotic decision and an idiotic rationale … a cynical and exploitative use of this pandemic in order to bring about the extreme agenda of Jason Kenney, which is to stop any work to protect the land, air, and water that Albertans care about."

According to the AER, the decision to cease environmental monitoring was made at the behest of companies unable or unwilling to meet the COVID social distancing requirements (Omstead and Fida 2020). But most monitoring is conducted remotely with instrumentation – with no human involvement – or by one or two people, which can be done safely. When asked for evidence, the AER replied that the requests were made by phone and email and that it did not keep a record of the requests. In essence, the AER was stating that, without public consultation, it made the momentous decision to cease monitoring based on requests from unnamed corporate entities but was unable to produce evidence of such requests. In July 2020, in response to a freedom of information request by Global News, redacted evidence was released indicating that the AER had provided misinformation: it had kept records. The evidence revealed that the regulator had collaborated with industry (principally Suncor and Syncrude) to suspend monitoring without consulting the public or First Nations (De Souza 2020).

And if we thought things could not get worse, in June 2020 the Alberta government removed restrictions on the strip mining of coal in Alberta's foothills. Then in August 2020, after secret negotiations, the federal and Alberta government agreed to major reductions in environmental monitoring in the bitumen sands region in northeastern Alberta (Weber 2020c). No affected parties were consulted. Under the new agreement, there will be no environmental fieldwork on the Athabasca River downstream of the bitumen operations, no water quality assessments in Wood Buffalo National Park, no studies of wetlands, fishes, or insects, and a study of the risks posed by tailings ponds has been dropped. Removal of restrictions on strip mining of coal and suspension of monitoring are the actions of a profoundly corrupt meta-organization. Given the degraded landscapes that are the legacy of the fossil fuel industry, the AER and the Kenney government truly are carrying out a scorched earth policy.

The costs of ecological degradation are borne by society, not by the companies responsible. The unsecured reclamation liabilities alone are enormous, growing each day, and sufficient to threaten the solvency of government and the funding of our health care, education, social, and environmental programs. But these costs are optional in that political will is necessary to enjoin the companies to clean up their leases. History tells us how that play will end: companies will temporize or declare bankruptcy and taxpayers will foot the bill. Or not. The most likely outcome is that most sites will never be reclaimed to a state of ecological health. Where is the moral outrage for the pervasive environmental degradation? People can't be outraged if they are uninformed or misinformed.

269

The Personal Costs

Spills are more than just uncontrolled releases of liquids that damage eco-systems. For those of us with direct experience, spills inflict wounds that refuse to heal. An animal care first responder recalls her experience after the Wabamun Lake oil spill:

The western grebes were in the midst of their breeding cycle with young about one to two weeks old. It was tragic. It took us close to three weeks before we could even begin to start washing birds due to the lack of resources. Inside the holding area at the Spruce Grove Recovery Centre, there was row after row of quickly made wooden net-bottom boxes to hold and support over 200 birds, 3–4 birds per box. I and another responder were shutting down after another long day of feeding, washing, and drying birds. The lights were low and all was quiet. As we were about to leave for the night, the grebes started calling out to each other. Were they trying to locate their mates or their young? Were they trying to ask each other – what happened here? It was so poignant, the tears filled my eyes as I tried to comprehend this from their perspective. We tried hard not to break down and, to this day, that image and odours are burned in my mind – the low light, the boxes, the smell of oil and the birds calling

… The saddest part is that this could happen again here in Alberta and we would be almost as badly off in terms of response. (K. Blomme, pers. comm., 8 May 2019)

Another Wabamun spill first responder writes,

What impacted me most was the large number of animals that required euthanasia. The initial triage site for animal intake was set up at the local arena. I can still remember feeling overwhelmed. I worked for hours triaging injured and oil-coated wildlife in the poorly lit change rooms overfilled with animals in cardboard boxes and plastic dog crates. Before Wabamun, I never imagined that part of an oil spill, the part where animals are rescued from the spill site but still do not survive. We had to euthanize animals that were too heavily oil covered and those who sustained additional injuries such as broken beaks, legs, and wings from attempting to move through the heavy oil. I left Wabamun not celebrating the animals who were in holding pens waiting to be washed. Instead, I left grieving the many animals whose lives had ended for merely being in the wrong place at the wrong time. (name withheld, pers. comm., 26 April 2019) (figure 17.2)

Images from spills are burned into our conscience – of a family of oiled beavers dying in their lodge, wood bison hock deep in crude oil, killdeer feeding on an oily shore, frogs floating belly up in toxic brine, and a ghastly morgue of great blue herons on the shore of a waste pond. Spills are not silent events. Our memories are haunted by the voices of dazed and dying Canada geese, of western grebes calling out to each other from crates in a rescue facility, of First Nations people warning and those in power responding by asking how much it will cost for silence. The smell of the spills can't be erased; recalling them brings on nausea. Spills make us sick in our hearts; they're the collateral damage of our reckless exploitation and voracious consumption. Whispering to us beneath all the noise, the voice of moral reckoning asks if hydrocarbons come at too high a price.

Beyond the moral costs, we face the social and public health unknowns. Are we facing covert contamination similar to that faced by the people of Toms River and Ocean County, New Jersey? With the tools of science, wherever we look we find persistent effects, whether that's at Turner Valley,

Figure 17.2 Oil-coated Canada goose being held at the Wabamun arena after the spill. 4 August 2005.

in Calgary, the Swan Hills, the bitumen sands region in northeastern Alberta, the Atlantic No. 3 site, at the Peace River Oils No. 1 site, or in the homeland of the Dene Tha in northwestern Alberta. In our favour, the chemicals in New Jersey were more toxic than most chemicals released in crude oil and saline spills, and few of us drink directly from contaminated sources. Working against us is the sheer scale and volume of the spills and the tens of thousands of undocumented contaminated sites. The concerns stem not only from spills but also from abandoned wells, flare pits, waste ponds, dumps, and places where drilling wastes were ploughed under and covered with topsoil. We don't know how dangerous these sites are and no agency is gathering the needed data. Nor do we have the legislation in place to require agencies to investigate suspected contaminated sites.

Scientists tend, by training, to think that more studies will help. We have become doctors afraid to tell our patient she has cancer until we're certain that the cancer is terminal. When we temporize and understate the dangers for fear of being labelled alarmists, we err on the side of recklessness. As scientists, we need to have the gumption to state the facts that our data tell us. Waiting for more data defers action that should be taken immediately and makes enablers and tools of injustice out of well-meaning people. "We need more data" is too often used to support the *status quo* and to avoid addressing even more pressing problems such as lack of trust, poor oversight, and exclusion of public participation (Moore et al. 2018). "We need to study the problem" is coded language meaning that those in power are going to stick the problem where the sun never shines. In many respects we don't need more data. We have sufficient information to know what's wrong and why. Science can't fix this mess.

SUMMARY

Crude oil and saline spills are the most common releases that occur during production of hydrocarbons. They occur daily. Industry disturbances result in permanent degradative changes in ecosystems. The ecological and financial liabilities of this ecological degradation threaten our future.

For decades, the regulator has failed to provide complete, truthful, reliable, and timely information and has failed in its responsibility to provide effective monitoring, enforcement, and protection of the environment. The regulator's industry-reported values for spill frequency and volume, the extent of affected areas and sensitive areas, rates of habitat and wildlife damage, the locations for spills, and values for spill recovery are not credible. Tens of thousands of spills report perfect recovery, an unsupported finding so unlikely it can be dismissed as fiction. Spill and recovery volumes are based on unempirical decisions influenced by human biases. The falcon or faked data effect, a signature of the spill data, results from recovery volumes that are chosen by humans who prefer particular fractions of the spill volume. The reported impacts of the industry represent a fraction of the true impacts. Corrupted data are like contaminated soils – everything that grows out of them must be tested to determine if it's safe to consume.

If the results of this study are surprising, it's a testament to the effectiveness of regulatory capture. Distorted information has crippled our society and blinded us to the dangers of hydrocarbons. We have become confused sheep drinking from a contaminated water trough. Without accurate information, we are kept in the dark while governments waste time, money, and resources on fruitless or harmful initiatives. The hidden scourge of fossil fuel exploitation extends beyond the degradation of ecosystems to the corruption of our democracy.

CHAPTER 18

The Way Home

The heavy heart at the waking hour is expecting heavy weather.
David Francey, "The Waking Hour"

INTRODUCTION

The fossil fuel industry derived its social licence through practices that served the public interest. When a regulator, industry, or government provides untruthful information they undermine their social licence, sow mistrust, and fuel discord. The industry and its regulators have provided misinformation about the effects of their activities since hydrocarbon exploitation began in the early twentieth century. How could it be otherwise? It's naive to expect an industry that is inherently destructive to tell the truth. A culture of fear, silence, intimidation, and distorted information has poisoned the regulator, the industry, and our government. Like it or not, we live behind the Oil Curtain.

In Canada, and in Alberta especially, the fossil fuel network has infiltrated all branches of civil society from the government, regulators, monitoring agencies, political parties, financial institutions, universities, and the media on down to primary schools. The infiltration has a simple goal: to maintain the economic and political power of the fossil fuel industry. In so doing, it provides disinformation to obstruct environmental and climate justice and the green energy transition, the obscenity of which deepens when we realize that the perpetrators will be dead before the monstrous reality they've wrought reaches it full savagery.

It would be idle to debate the facts about spills, ecological impacts, and regulatory capture. What we can debate and discuss is what to do about those facts. First, let's recognize that the findings of this investigation will not effect positive changes within the regulator. The regulator will ignore the recommendations. In its view, the regulator serves its client well. Unfortunately, that client is the fossil fuel industry. Anything short of replacing the regulator is to acquiesce in further ecological degradation and financial risk, the burden of which is borne by all of us and, increasingly, by future generations. But replacing the Alberta Energy Regulator, and indeed all captured regulators worldwide, will amount to putting lipstick on a pig if we can't overcome our carbon addiction. I propose an action plan to fix the mess made by regulatory capture in web 18. In brief, we need people of many backgrounds to work together: policy experts, politicians, engineers, universities, and most of all we need an informed, concerned public. We need to replace the policies, subsidies, and tax incentives that favour the fossil fuel *status quo* that is undermining planet Earth and the pillars of civilization with those that facilitate the transition to a life-affirming economy. Society must recognize that captured regulators are corrupt enterprises whose goal is to defraud the public of its financial and environmental security. We need new federal legislation that will tax industries to fund an agency empowered to document and remediate hazardous sites. We need a political movement with the power to redirect captured governments and regulators toward protecting the public interest. Fines for spills and other contraventions should be commensurate with the offenses, large enough to serve as a deterrent rather than so small that they encourage business-as-usual. All monitoring, environmental protection, and enforcement mandates should be taken over by government and therefore placed under the control of voters. In our schools, we need to reclaim the primacy of free discussion rather than indoctrination; we need to teach ecology, not ideology. Studies of the environment, regulators, and industry are needed to help establish a new regulatory regime. These initiatives could be funded by taxing a small fraction of the profits of hydrocarbon companies.

In these final pages it's fitting to focus on the global perspective and our prospects for the future.

275

THE BIG PICTURE

Pervasive daily spills, covert contamination, a growing footprint of ecological degradation, disinformation, and corrupt data are symptoms of a life-threatening disease caused by our addiction to carbon. But even if we could wave a magic wand and alleviate these symptoms, we would still be in deep trouble because our carbon addiction has destabilized the planet. In this concluding section, we examine the global crisis created by a voracious over-abundant species.

We find ourselves living in the Anthropocene, a period of overexploitation of Earth's life support systems driven by human overpopulation and overconsumption (Steffen et al. 2011). We have altered the climate and the chemistry of the atmosphere primarily through the emission of greenhouse gases, 77 per cent of which stem from the use of fossil fuels. Atmospheric concentrations of the major greenhouse gases continue to increase. Over the past three decades, global temperatures have increased faster than at any time over the past 2,000 years; sea levels are rising, Arctic sea ice and permafrost are declining, the rate of loss of glacial ice from Greenland is increasing, and extreme rainfall and heat events are becoming more frequent (Hayhoe and Stoner 2019).

The continued rise of planet-threatening carbon emissions can be attributed largely to regulatory capture writ large in that the fossil fuel industry has continued to successfully extort subsidies from world governments. In its 2019 assessment, the International Monetary Fund (IMF) determined fossil fuel industry subsidies for 191 countries (Coady et al. 2019). Globally, subsidies totalled $4.7 trillion (6.3 per cent of global GDP) in 2015 and were projected to reach $5.2 trillion (6.5 per cent of global GDP) in 2017. The IMF determined that if prices accurately reflected the true costs of fossil fuels, including the environmental damage, consumption would have decreased such that 2015 global carbon emissions would have fallen by 28 per cent, fossil fuel-related air pollution deaths would have fallen by 46 per cent, and government revenue would have increased by 3.8 per cent of GDP. Our collective failure to make the changes needed to ensure a liveable planet is due in large measure to fossil fuel subsidies, disinformation, and policy obstacles put in place by the hydrocarbon metaorganization. Continuing fossil fuel subsidies is a death sentence for our atmosphere, climate, ecosystems, and global security. By subsidizing futile technologies such as carbon capture that lock us into a climate-destroying carbon dependency death spiral, precious time is lost and resources are diverted from genuine solutions. When all carbon emissions are accounted for, even the best carbon capture technologies may sequester only about 10 per cent of total emissions from burning fossil fuels to generate electricity (Jacobson 2019). When pollution, health, economic, and climate change impacts are factored in, carbon capture worsens the damage by promoting the falsehood that a carbon-intensive economy can be made ecologically sustainable. It cannot.

The use of fossil fuels creates significant climate-disrupting externalities that markets are not yet capable of addressing. The winner of the 2018 Nobel Prize for Economics for integrating climate change into long-run macroeconomic analysis, William Nordhaus, has shown that the economics of climate change are straightforward: the fairest and most effective way to address climate externalities is to price carbon pollution. Pricing carbon achieves four objectives: it tells consumers which goods and services are more carbon-intensive; it tells producers which activities are most carbon-intensive; it propels and funds innovation; and is the best means to convey these signals within well-functioning markets. Carbon pricing is not radical. It's supported by conservative monetary agencies such as the OECD, the World Bank, and the IMF. The World Trade Organization has shown that market-based instruments led by pricing have the least distortionary effects on markets, competitiveness, and trade.

The economic, social, and environmental benefits of carbon pricing are clear justification for the federal Greenhouse Gas Pollution Act of 2018. So who would oppose the principle of making polluters pay for the damage they create? The fossil fuel industry and its allies. The February 2020 decision by the Alberta Court of Appeal that the federal carbon tax infringes on provincial jurisdiction is little more than a demonstration of a captured judicial system. Protecting the atmosphere lies clearly within federal jurisdiction and is a matter of national concern. The fight against carbon pricing has been led by industry-captured governments in Alberta, Saskatchewan, and Ontario. In September 2020, the Supreme Court of Canada heard provincial appeals of the carbon tax. Finally, in March 2021 the court concluded that human-caused climate change causes harm beyond provincial boundaries and constitutes a national concern under the peace, order, and good government clause of the Constitution. Every day we delay in curtailing carbon emissions only deepens the ultimate costs.

Climate change is altering everything we know, decreasing the length of winter and the depth of snowpacks, driving greater extremes in droughts,

277

floods, and storms, increasing wildfires, and causing shifts in the ranges of species (US EPA 2016). Rates of biodiversity loss and climate change and changes in the global nitrogen cycle have already exceeded safe planetary thresholds (Rockström et al. 2009). Meanwhile, by mid-2021, Earth's human population had reached 7.9 billion and our population increases by about 223,000 people each day. The new normal is change, a constantly shifting baseline of destabilizing and planet-altering effects known as the Great Acceleration.

The most important driver of change in the past fifty years has been habitat loss resulting from conversion of natural landscapes to agricultural and industrial uses (Steffen et al. 2011). The global extent of ecologically intact landscapes, which provide life-supporting ecological goods and services, declined 3.3 million km² over the past two decades (Watson et al. 2016). Three-fourths of the land surface of the planet have been significantly altered by humans; two-thirds of the ocean's area shows evidence of cumulative impacts; and 85 per cent of the world's wetlands have been lost (IPBES 2019). Land degradation has reduced productivity in 23 per cent of terrestrial areas and pollinator loss threatens to reduce agricultural output by $235 to $577 billion per year.

About one-fourth of all assessed animal and plant groups are threatened; about one million species face extinction. The global extinction rate is tens to hundreds of times higher than it has averaged over the past ten million years; extinction rates are increasing. Among terrestrial vertebrates, 322 species have become extinct since 1500 (Dirzo et al. 2014). But defaunation, the decline in the abundance of animal species, poses an even greater threat than extinction. Populations of terrestrial vertebrate species have declined an average of 25 per cent while the abundance of two-thirds of monitored invertebrate species has declined an average of 45 per cent. Over the period 1970 to 2016, the average abundance of 20,811 monitored populations of 4,392 vertebrate species decreased by 68 per cent (WWF 2020). The chief causes of this shocking loss of biodiversity are habitat loss and degradation, overexploitation, invasive species and diseases, pollution, and climate change. Pervasive changes in animal abundance are creating cascading ecosystem effects such as dieback of coral reef communities. Algal blooms and coastal dead zones grow in extent while sea levels rise and coastal areas are inundated both by rising water and stronger storms. Climate change is driving changes in the seasonal timing of flowering and fruiting, and the abundance of pollinators, insects, and diseases.

We are dangerously close to triggering as many as nine global tipping points such as irreversible losses of summer Arctic sea ice, the Greenland Ice Sheet, and portions of the Antarctic Ice Sheet, and loss of the boreal ecosystem as we know it (plate 18.1; Lenton et al. 2019). The time we have left to prevent irreversible changes may have already shrunk to zero whereas the reaction time to achieve carbon neutrality is thirty years at best. The only bright spot is that we may have the ability to control the rate at which damage accumulates. The stability and resilience of our planet and our global civilization are in peril and international action must reflect this state of emergency. Our Earth system is so complex and so full of feedbacks and nonlinear responses that by the time we identify the multitude of changes occurring, the opportunity to minimize harm will have passed. We need to act now on the scientific warnings.

Closer to home, in Alberta, our climate has already changed significantly over the past several decades (Hayhoe and Stoner 2019). From 1950 to 2013, average temperatures increased for all seasons, with average increases of 0.5 to 1° C/decade for winter and 0.1 to 0.3° C/decade for summer. The frequency of cold days (below -30° C) is decreasing while the frequency of warm days (above 25° C) is increasing and the frost-free season length is increasing by about two weeks per degree of warming. The proportion of precipitation that falls as snow is decreasing at 2 to 4 per cent/decade. The rate of these and other changes is expected to increase, and, because northern latitudes are more sensitive to climate change, future Alberta temperatures are expected to increase by 2° C for every 1° C increase in global temperatures. The observed and future climate changes will affect every facet of our society, our economy, and our ecosystems.

In Alberta's future, we can expect a net decline in natural ecosystem biomass and primary productivity driven by the combined effects of climate change, drought stress, habitat loss, and habitat degradation. White spruce, black spruce, jack pine, and mixed-wood forests on boreal uplands will decrease as will their dependent life forms such as arboreal lichens and old-growth dependent warblers and caribou. Boreal conifer forests may be largely replaced by a mixture of deciduous forest, savannah, shrub, and meadow vegetation. Fire-mediated change in Alberta boreal forests could convert about one-half of Alberta's upland mixed-wood and conifer forest to deciduous woodland and grass-dominated areas by 2100 (Stralberg et al. 2018). The future of Alberta's boreal wetlands, which cover 30–40 per cent of the boreal landscape, is in doubt. Many wetlands will desiccate and burn and release their stored carbon to the atmosphere. Many of our boreal wetlands are being sold to farmers who then destroy them to make agricultural fields. Deforestation, in particular, loss of old-growth forest, will be exacerbated by logging and the fossil fuel industry. The future of the southern boreal – northern prairie eco-tone, called the aspen parkland in western Canada, is difficult to predict be-cause the native ecosystems have been largely replaced by agriculture. Therefore, as the southern boreal climate desiccates and warms, and forests retreat northward, what communities will replace them when the natural eco-systems have already been lost from the aspen parkland? What species will constitute the predicted savannahs and grass-dominated areas when the native grasses have been extirpated and the boreal soils differ from the aspen parkland soils? Most likely we'll see the emergence of novel communities dominated by disturbance-adapted generalists and exotics. Beyond these general observa-tions and predictions, the only certainty is that there will be surprises.

As the COVID-19 pandemic demonstrated, warnings seldom engender pre-ventative action. Action required people dying in increasing numbers, then panic spread faster than the virus. Within a matter of days, financial markets, global trade, and economies faltered, while disease surveillance and response struggled to contain the outbreak, streets and schools emptied, and worried people stripped grocery store shelves. COVID-19 is a warning of the exponential speed and power of a global emergency. If we fail to address the global climate and ecological emergency, if we wait for crop failures and drowning coastal cities, it will be too late. The foundations of modern advanced civilization may be unable to withstand the chaos.

By ones and twos, inexorably our native species and ecosystems are declin-ing. It's like the night sky. Each year, the light pollution grows and by ones and twos the stars are blotted out. Over time, we forget the starry brilliance of a winter night and gaze up at a pale semblance of what once was and ask our-selves what's missing. If we're not paying attention, gathering data, it's easy to dismiss all the change. The problem with shifting baselines is that we lose our moorings. Without still points in our lives, without ecological baselines, we drift, unable to recognize approaching perils. Every year brings more change, everything is in motion. Instead of change being a departure from the norm, the norm has become change. Climate refugees are on the move. Our own home places are beginning to feel strange. Summer in western Canada now feels like a bad version of *Let's Make a Deal*. Door number one is weeks of lurid orange skies and choking smoke from wildfires, door number two is drought, and door number three is torrential rain and storms. This is not normal.

Even if we had the capacity to establish native species and communities after disturbance, we can't restore damaged ecosystems to the conditions that existed in the mid- and late-twentieth century. Those conditions no longer exist. We are not approaching ecological thresholds. We have passed them. By driving extinctions, defaunation, declines in biodiversity, changes in species ranges, and the spread of exotic species, we are changing the course of evolution. We are breaking the circle of life.

It doesn't help that denial has become a prevalent way to assuage our growing unease with a deteriorating world. Instead of facing the fact that our actions are leading to planetary catastrophe, many have chosen to attack the science. Science denial is a last-ditch attempt to defend a privileged minority composed of the hydrocarbon and finance industries, their captured regulators, and their quisling politicians (Taylor 2019). That minority will fight to the death to defend the *status quo*. The short-term profit motive requires that the liquid money underground must be extracted and sold even if doing so requires the undermining of democracy and the endangerment of life.

In the past, one sure way to undermine a civilization was to salinize the agricultural fields, a fatal mistake that contributed to the collapse of the Sumerians and other civilizations. We are repeating that mistake in many parts of the world including North America's oil-producing regions (plate 18.2). Today, the surest way to undermine global civilization is to contaminate the one thing we all share, our atmosphere, such that destructive climate change destabilizes planetary life support systems. The presently dangerous and increasing greenhouse gas concentrations in our atmosphere pose an existential threat to advanced civilization and the ecosphere. We can't immediately turn off the hydrocarbon taps – we need them to grow food and produce a myriad of useful products, but most of all we need them to power our transition to sustainable energy systems. If it's not obvious that we must rapidly wean ourselves off burning hydrocarbons, then nothing is obvious. The wise, short-term use of hydrocarbons can power the ship that carries us through the energy transition.

We are past the point where incremental change can save us. We need transformational change. Because previous efforts to rein in greenhouse gas emissions have failed, by 2030, emissions will need to be 55 per cent lower than 2018 emissions if we are to limit global warming to the least destructive 1.5° C (UN 2019). If current trends continue, we will reach the 1.5° C threshold by 2040 and are headed for warming in excess of 3° C, which will be catastrophic for global society (UNDP 2019). But let's say that we don't care about

281

worldwide ecological devastation, declining biodiversity, more destructive storms, flooding of cities, and disproportionate impacts to the world's poorest and most vulnerable peoples. Let's say that we can tolerate bad air quality, drowning cities, a billion climate refugees, increasing wildfires, food shortages, and scarcity of clean water and can live without caribou, polar bears, tigers, and elephants. Let's say that business-as-usual is what we want. We can't have that because, as the world becomes more ecologically and climatically unstable, with inexorable declines of return on energy invested and ever greater expenditures needed to maintain a liveable environment, there is no business-as-usual. There can be no return to the good old days of clean coal and ethical oil. They don't exist and they never have. In place of business-as-usual, if we fail to adapt, we face the prospect of mass migrations of desperate people and a breakdown of international trade and alliances. The signs are all around us. For each year that our destructive activities continue unabated, we increase the likelihood that the Earth's systems will become inimical to advanced civilization.

I reach these conclusions as a Canadian and an Albertan. Some of my family, friends, and neighbours are involved in the fossil fuel industry. All of them care and many of them are troubled with what's happening. Some are frightened. But suppose I were an "outsider" (as extremists like to refer to those who oppose their views), the conclusions would be the same. The facts are the facts and the facts are ominous. With our eyes on a clock ticking down to midnight, we look to our leaders, many of whom are working to discredit science and sow mistrust and confusion. Time, and our luck, are running out.

Afterword

I hate bullies, especially adults who bully young people, and, as a rule, I don't attend rallies. But when I learned that Greta Thunberg was to speak at a rally to combat the climate crisis and that supporters of the fossil fuel industry planned to disrupt the event, I knew that I had to go. So on 18 October 2019, I attended a noon rally on the Alberta legislature grounds in Edmonton. Throngs of climate action supporters poured onto the site for more than an hour. At its peak, around six to eight thousand people of all ages were there, from toddlers and school children to senior citizens.

The so-called "counter rally" consisted of scattered small groups, some of which heckled the speakers with boos and shouts of "Greta go home." They were assisted by big trucks cruising the perimeter while their drivers stood on their air horns in an attempt to drown out the speakers. Based on the signs they held and those cheering vs booing, those in favour of addressing the climate crisis outnumbered those opposed by about seventy-five to one.

Those in support of addressing the climate crisis carried a diverse array of homemade signs with messages such as "Grow up, so I can" carried by a child; "Greta > Gretzky"; "Joan of Arc 2.0" with an image of Greta Thunberg; and "Save the planet, change your diet." In contrast, most supporters of the fossil fuel industry carried the same mass-produced "I love oil and gas" sign manufactured for canadaaction.ca, a lobby group that refuses to divulge its sources of funding.

After impassioned speeches by young Albertans working for climate justice, Greta was the last to speak. She focused on the science and of our need to work together to address the climate crisis. She noted that school children are striking not because it's fun but because they have to act in hopes of averting global catastrophe. The hecklers, coordinating by phone with the truckers and their air horns, attempted to prevent the rally from hearing Greta's message. No one demonstrates being on the wrong side of history as well as adults trying to bully young people into silence.

I thought supporters of the hydrocarbon industry couldn't sink any lower but I was mistaken. In late February 2020 it was revealed that someone associated with X-Site Energy Services of Red Deer, Alberta, had published an image depicting a naked female seen from behind with long braided hair being pulled by a pair of hands; the name "Greta" was written on the young woman's back and the logo of the company appeared below the young woman (CBC 2020). X-Site denied involvement and declined requests for media interviews.

The fossil fuel industry would do well to repudiate the support it receives from antidemocratic elements, misogynists, bullies of young people, and other extremists speeding loss of the industry's social licence. It's a hopeful sign that many in the industry have realized that the climate crisis presents an opportunity to transform to a sustainable global society. The industry can choose to be part of the energy transition or be left behind. It can persist in its obscene undermining of life in pursuit of profits or it can play a major role in a global transformation and thereby find redemption. The fate of everyone and everything are at stake. In his poem "Questionnaire," Wendell Berry wrote, "State briefly the ideas, ideals, or hopes, the energy sources, the kinds of security, for which you would kill a child. Name, please, the children whom you would be willing to kill." History is littered with the remains of industries that failed to adapt to changing conditions and of civilizations that failed to address clear and present dangers. We must adapt and improvise or be overcome. If we can't address this existential crisis, we should get out of the way and let the young people lead.

Postscript

In late 2018, I received updated information from the Dene Tha First Nation on four of the spills in northwestern Alberta.

The Amber oil spill and battery site: The Boneyard was reportedly remediated. I have no additional information.

The Pace-Spyglass oil spill: As of June 2018, the site remained much the same as it was in 2016. Although the contaminated material stockpile was removed and taken to a landfill, the wetland still smells of oil. The AER recommended to SanLing (the company now responsible for the site) that it should begin water sampling. Yes, you read correctly – SanLing should *begin* water sampling. Wildlife continues to be exposed to contaminants on a daily basis.

As to the fate of the ecosystem at the Pace-Spyglass site, more bad news came in early March 2021 when the AER was forced to suspend SanLing's operating licence for its 2,266 wells, 227 facilities, and 2,170 pipelines. The reason? The company has repeatedly failed to comply with orders relating to improper storage of oilfield waste, improper abandonment of pipelines and wells, failing to follow rules in its operation and maintenance of pipelines, failing to remediate damaged sites, and failing to pay a security deposit. SanLing currently owes the AER $67 million in unpaid security deposits. Then on 21 April 2021 it was announced that SanLing would cease operations on 30 April. The Orphan Well Association (OWA) has applied for a court order to require a receiver to liquidate SanLing's assets. Any remaining assets will be assigned to the OWA.

How could these abuses have been tolerated for so long? Companies can damage ecosystems and kill wildlife as long as they don't embarrass the regulator with publicized flagrant violations. As an enabler of serial abuse, the AER has sown the wind and now we all reap the whirlwind.

The Nuvista oil and saline water spill: Three years after the spill, the Dene Tha remained concerned about failed remediation and elevated levels of heavy metals. A visit with AER and Dene Tha was conducted on 18 June 2018. In a follow-up letter, the AER wrote, "It is also important that this discussion include [*sic*] how to address determining the source of the increase in heavy metals." Three years after the spill and the regulator, whose responsibility it is to protect the environment, still has not done the basic environmental chemistry; it is placing the onus on the Dene Tha to gather the needed data. The regulator added, "The AER is unable to provide input into what the data collection and remediation process should be as this would affect our neutrality; rather it is our responsibility to assess a proposed plan and actions for adequacy." The regulator's position would be laughable were it not tragic. The AER is not a competent evaluator of environmental impacts or of the adequacy of remediation plans.

Upon reading the regulator's Nuvista report, an environmental consultant working for the Dene Tha wrote, "It seems to me to be the classic government attitude of total unhelpfulness. The comment 'The AER is unable to provide input into what the data collection and remediation process should be' ... is particularly infuriating. As their mandate is to ensure oil and gas development is done responsibly, I don't see how neutrality comes into any of their decision making. At some point they are going to have to take a side ... as a former regulator myself, I'm very critical of AERs attitude that they are some kind of neutral observer ... [This is] compounded by the fact that the AER risk assessor told me she was 'too tired' after the site visit to look at the metals data."

The Apache 15-09 saline spill: As of July 2018, the area was showing signs of long-term impairment. Dene Tha observers informed me that healthy vegetation is not reestablishing around the excavated areas. The reason is not clear but in addition to soil salts, they observe that soil compaction by heavy machinery may be inhibiting plant growth. These observations contrast with the opinion of Paramount Resources Ltd (now responsible for the site). A company representative wrote that the affected area "displays a healthy vegetation community, with observations of ducks and amphibians using the area." A Paramount document (June 2018) stated, "25 local species are present, most of them planted: 6 trees, 5 shrubs, 6 forbs and 8 grasses provides [*sic*] a diverse foundational vegetation structure for the recovery of the site." This is, of course, nonsense. Twenty-five species would comprise a depauperate flora. Nor do we know what species are present, how many are halophytes or weedy exotics, and why most of the species have had to be planted rather than reestablish naturally. It's likely that no mosses and lichens are noted because the soil is too toxic. How many of the planted species observed in one year are dead the next year? In other words, what is the turnover rate? The two-page report by the company is not a credible assessment.

Photographs from a site visit on 23 September 2018 attest to the persistent damage at the Apache saline spill (plate PS.1). A salt crust on the shore of the excavated pond reveals that contaminant removal, although deemed complete, has left behind residual salt. The semibarren saline mud on the shore of the pond, a virtual absence of aquatic plants, and an impoverished exotic-dominated weedy meadow and marsh demonstrates an impaired plant community. Species present are well known pollution tolerators such as sow-thistle, foxtail barley, and common cattail. Planted white spruce seedlings are succumbing due to the excess soil salts. Planted wheatgrasses struggle to survive. These results would be expected by anyone with even a basic knowledge of ecology. How is this still happening?

One final observation sounds an ominous note. In spring 2017, while Dene Tha members Baptiste and Lorny Metchooyeah were hunting, they discovered a saline water spill on their traditional lands. They contacted the regulator; it was not aware of the spill. The company responsible for the spill produced an August 2018 report that assured the reader that the "surrounding area is green and flourishing" without "dying plants or browning of trees." The blurry photographs provided in the report tell a different story. Stressed and impacted vegetation surrounds the four saline water pits.

The regulator and the energy companies remain negligent. How many other spills continue to go undetected? It's not acceptable that First Nations people are required to act as spill detection personnel for the industry and the regulator. The regulator remains not only steadfastly incapable of protecting the environment, it does not understand that environmental protection is its responsibility. It is not its role, as it maintains, to act as a neutral arbiter between companies damaging the environment and people trying to protect the environment. Its role is to protect the environment on behalf of the people.

Acknowledgments

I thank Keepers of the Water Council for their support and encouragement; Baptiste Metchooyeah (deceased), Warren Danais, Gabriel Didzena, Matt Munson, Joe Chonkolay, and Norm Chonkolay of the Dene Tha First Nation for their traditional knowledge, support during the fieldwork, and provision of reports and data; Dorothy Fabijan (University of Alberta Herbarium); Brett Feland and Allan Harms (University of Alberta Natural Resources Analytical Laboratory) for chemical analyses of soil and water; Maxxam Analytics for hydrocarbon analyses of soil; Dr Pete Kershaw, Dr Brett Purdy, and Mae Elsinger for vegetation and soils data; Alberta Environment and Parks for ecologically sensitive area information; Anne Robinson for her work on bryophytes and lichens and for field, office, and editorial assistance; Ed Zwolinski for local knowledge on chemical dumping in the New Jersey Pine Barrens; investigative journalist Leslie Young (Global News) for the 1975–2013 FIS spills database, and the Alberta Wilderness Association for the 1975–2017 FIS database.

Funding in support of publication was provided through the generosity of The Gavia Group Inc., Laura Jackson and Patrick Lamb, Robert A. Cameron, Cecile Fausak and Bruce Jackson, Evelyn and Harvey Scott, Keepers of the Water, and the Federation for the Humanities and Social Sciences.

I thank all those, named and anonymous, who provided eyewitness observations and testimony in personal communications.

ACKNOWLEDGMENTS

I am indebted to Alan Dunn P.Eng., Dr William Donahue, Mae Elsinger, Dr Geoff Holroyd, Dr John Honsaker, Dr Tristan Lee-Jones, Dr Pete Kershaw, Geoff Kershaw, Peter Lee, Joseph Maslen, Anne Robinson, Cliff Wallis, and several anonymous reviewers for their critical reviews.

Most of all, I thank my wife Anne who supported me on a years-long journey down a dark rabbit hole. Without her unflagging help and encouragement, this book would have never seen the light of day.

290

Glossary of Concepts, Abbreviations, and Terms

ACIMS: Alberta Conservation Information Management System is a publicly available database that provides reliable biodiversity information; the public can access data at: https://www.albertaparks.ca/albertaparksca/management-land-use/alberta-conservation-information-management-system-acims/

accurate: A description that corresponds closely to credible evidence; in statistics, a number whose value corresponds closely to the true value

active layer: In a permafrost soil, the layer that thaws during summer; due to climate change, active layers are becoming thicker and more persistent

adverse effect: Defined by the AER (in 2016b) as "'impairment of or damage to the environment, human health, or safety or property.' Adverse effect may be determined by any number of factors, including the following: the chemical and physical characteristics of substance released, the receiving media, the location of the release, and the risk to the environment. The onus is on the person who causes, permits, or has control of the release to determine whether there is a potential adverse effect." The definition absolves the regulator of the responsibility of determining the adverse effect.

AER: Alberta Energy Regulator, the agency responsible for regulating the energy industry in Alberta; formerly the ERCB (see below)

AESRD: Alberta Environment and Sustainable Resource Development (ESRD), formerly known as Alberta Environment and recently renamed Alberta Environment and Parks (AEP)

Agreed Statement of Facts: In a court proceeding, a document that describes the facts on which the opposing parties agree

agronomic species: Plants used in agriculture, typically nonnative species selected and bred for desirable traits such as rapid growth; synonym: cultivar

alkyl: Any alkane (noncyclic saturated hydrocarbon such as $-CH_3$) group missing one hydrogen atom; compare alkylphenols

alkylphenols: A family of hydrocarbons with an alkyl group attached to a phenol ring; they are used in detergents, paints, herbicides, pesticides, plastic polymers, and oil field chemicals and can be found in fossil fuel industry spills; they are xenoestrogens, synthetic compounds that mimic the hormone estrogen and are known to be weak endocrine disruptors that are chemically stable and can bioaccumulate; examples include bisphenol A (BPA) and nonylphenol

battery: As used in the fossil fuel industry, a collection of infrastructure such as compressor stations, production machinery, buildings, tanks, equipment, pipes, and wells used together to accomplish a set of tasks; crude oil group batteries are a major source of spills

bellhole: A bell-shaped hole or widening of a trench that creates work space for people and equipment involved in maintenance or repair of energy infrastructure

Benford analysis: A statistical procedure used to detect datasets that are influenced by human bias; in this study, the procedure is used to detect datasets composed of numbers that have been chosen rather than randomly assigned through measurement; the analysis uses the frequency distribution of first significant digits; it has been used to detect inaccurate industry-reported concentrations of environmental toxins; in accounting it is routinely applied to detect fraud

bimodal: In statistics, the mode is the most frequently occurring value in a set of values; a bimodal distribution is therefore a dataset with two frequently occurring values; for example, a bimodal dataset of 500 observations with values ranging from zero to one hundred might include one hundred zero values (the first mode), one hundred observations for the numbers one through ninety-nine, and 300 values of one hundred (the second mode); bimodal distributions in AER spill recovery data might arise from three populations of observations: (1) spills in which recovery was judged to be perfect (100 per cent recovery); (2) spills in which no attempt was made to recover the spill (0 per cent); and (3) spills in which an attempt was made to quantify the recovery (intermediate values)

blowout: An uncontrolled pressurized release from a well; blowouts are typically liquid or gas, but under extreme pressure, solids can be expelled such as in the Joslyn blowout

BTEX: Acronym for a group of short-chain (F1) hydrocarbons; B = benzene, T = toluene, E = ethylbenzene, and X = xylene

CCME: Canadian Council of Ministers of the Environment

certified reclaimed: Although a consensus definition of "certified reclaimed" should exist, there isn't one. Prior to 1993, there were no criteria for certifying well sites as reclaimed; an inspector would use personal judgment. In Alberta, "reclaimed" means that the land is able to support land uses, but those land uses need not be those that existed prior to disturbance. Reclaimed can also mean that equipment or buildings have been removed or that attempts have been made to decontaminate the site or that the land has been recontoured or resurfaced. Various attempts have been made to define reclamation for various ecosystems. One example: currently, in forest ecosystems, the Alberta government (ESRD 2013) specifies for certified sites reclaimed after June 2007, with natural recovery, a minimum of 25 per cent cover of herbs and a minimum of 25 per cent cover of woody species, or, a minimum one stem for every 2 m². In practice a certified reclaimed site could be covered in exotic species growing on contaminated soil. "Certified reclaimed" is not a high standard. By adopting such a low bar for certified reclamation, the Alberta government and industry have assumed a false equivalency between biodiverse natural communities and depauperate human-created communities – the equivalent of equating a tall grass prairie with a cornfield. See reclamation

chromatogram: A graph of the concentration (y-axis) of a mixture of hydrocarbons identified along the x-axis by the number of carbon atoms

cluster analysis: A method of identifying groups of related items (such as study sites or species) whose group memberships are based upon shared responses to the environment; vegetation cluster types are communities composed of repeating species groups

condensate: A family of liquid hydrocarbons containing two to thirty carbon atoms, but mostly having five to fifteen carbons; most have a specific gravity of 0.5–0.8; in an underground hydrocarbon reservoir, high temperatures maintain the mixture as a gas; when pumped to the surface, the decrease in temperature causes some gases to condense to liquids; condensates are also found in natural gas processing plants and gas pipelines; synonyms include pentanes plus, natural gasoline, drip gas, and natural gas liquids; common examples include pentane and hexane; the toxicity of condensates depends on their composition

contaminant: A substance that is introduced into a system by human agency; also, a substance normally present in a system but whose concentration has been increased by human agency

contamination: The presence or super-abundance of a substance or organism in an ecosystem; specific to spills, there are two kinds of environmental contamination: addition of substances, such as petroleum hydrocarbons, that are absent under natural conditions, and, for substances that are normally present, such as sodium and chloride, increase in their concentrations to levels outside the range of natural variation of those substances within that ecosystem corrupt: A corrupt action occurs when a person acts dishonestly in return for personal gain; alternatively, a dataset, program, or system is corrupt when it has been made unreliable by errors, misinformation, or alteration, or by loss of information; a dataset or an agency can be corrupted intentionally or unintentionally, but the result is the same

credible: Offering reasonable grounds for belief and based on demonstrable evidence

crude oil: A complex mixture of volatile and nonvolatile hydrocarbons in combination with varying amounts of natural gas, carbon dioxide, saline water, sulphur compounds, nitrogen, metals, and minerals; the oil component comprises four classes of chemicals: saturates, aromatics, resins, and asphaltenes; the toxicity of crude oil is determined by its composition and the nature of the receiving environment. See Lee et al. (2015) for a description of the composition of crude oil

crude oil group battery: A site with one or more wells, accompanied by storage tanks, sump pits, pipes, machinery, and buildings involved in the production of crude oil

crude oil wastewater disposal facility: A site where produced water is stored in ponds; evaporation of the water concentrates the chemicals present; sodium levels in some evaporation ponds are toxic to waterfowl

cryptogamic crust: A fragile soil crust composed of bound inorganic and organic soil particles created by a network of lichens, mosses, fungal mycelia, algae, and cyanobacteria; these crusts cover and stabilize soils in arid, semi-arid, arctic, alpine, and other environments; they are also called biological soil crusts; "cryptogam" means hidden gamete, i.e., plants without flowers; loss of cryptogamic crusts can result in long-term site degradation

cultivar: A plant species bred to have particular qualities such as fast growth, disease resistance, or salt tolerance; synonym: agronomic species

custom treating facility: A facility composed of tanks and other equipment that receives trucked in oil/water emulsion that it separates into components for further transport or disposal dehydrator tank: An open-topped tank used to store and evaporate water separated from natural gas at a production facility; these open-topped tanks are a major cause of bird mortality at western United States production facilities; most birds killed at dehydrator tanks are songbirds

disinformation: False or misleading information intended to deceive

DTFN: Dene Tha First Nation

electrical conductivity: A measure of the ability of soil or water to conduct an electrical current; it is an indirect measure of the concentration of dissolved materials such as salts; 1,000 µS/cm = 1 dS/m

296

empirical: Originating in or based on observation; capable of being disproved by observation, data, or experiment

ERCB: Energy Resources Conservation Board, the predecessor of the Alberta Energy Regulator, and the successor to the Energy Utilities Board; in 1938, the first energy regulator was formed (Petroleum and Natural Gas Conservation Board)

error of commission: When a fact, event, or datum is recorded incorrectly

error of omission: When a fact, event, or datum is omitted or missing from a dataset

evidence: A body of valid data or knowledge

exotic: A species that is not native to a region; because an exotic species did not evolve in the region, it may lack the predators, competitors, or diseases that typically control a species' abundance; exotic species can cause major disruptions, such as the population crashes of American chestnut and American elm caused by introduced diseases, the introduction of rabbits, red foxes, and domestic cats to Australia, zebra mussels to the Great Lakes, and brome grass to North America; exotic species introduction has become a major global cause of species endangerment

F1F4: A shorthand for classes of hydrocarbons based on the number of carbon atoms; F1 refers to hydrocarbon chains with 6 to 10 carbons (C6 to C10); F2 refers to C11 to C16; F3 refers to C17 to C34; F4 refers to C35 and above

fact: Information that is demonstrably true, supported by evidence

falcon effect: A falcon-shaped pattern in a graph of data points that results from values that are subjective judgments constrained by choosing pre-ferred fractions of spill volume; this constraint imposes smooth, arcuate structures to scatter plots that produce falcon-like shapes; the subjective nature of the data can be confirmed by Benford analysis; the falcon effect is a signature of subjectively chosen numbers, i.e., faked data

297

fiction: An erroneous account of a phenomenon; a supposition known to differ from fact but conventionally accepted; synonym: alternative facts

fiduciary: Held or founded in trust; public responsibilities entrusted to an agency

first significant digit: The first nonzero digit in a number; examples are underlined: 10.2, 0.5, 0.03; the frequency of the first significant digits 1–9 follows the Benford distribution in a large number of numeric datasets derived from measurement

FIS: Acronym for Field Inspection System, the AER's database of spills; also referred to as Field Information System

flare pit (pond): A flare pit or flare pond is an excavated depression near a flare stack that stores oil or other liquids released from the flare stack; they present a chronic hazard to wildlife

flaring: The process of disposing waste gas through burning at a flare stack

flowline: A term used in Saskatchewan for the pipeline connected to a well; it conveys produced crude oil, water, and gases from the wellhead to process equipment

FOIP: A formal information request submitted to an agency of the Alberta provincial government under its Freedom of Information and Protection of Privacy (FOIP) Act; documents requested under the Act are said to be FOIPed

forb: A broad-leaved herb

forensic: Pertaining to or suitable for public discussion and debate; pertaining to the application of scientific facts to legal problems; the use of specialized methods of evidence detection

fracking: The process of injecting acids such as hydrochloric acid, biocides such as glutaraldehyde, gel breakers such as ammonium persulfate, clay stabilizers such as tetramethyl ammonium chloride, corrosion inhibitors such as methanol, crosslinkers, friction reducers, and gelling agents such as petroleum distillates, citric acid for iron control, sodium hydroxide for pH adjustment, scale inhibitors such as sodium polycarboxylate, surfactants such as lauryl sulfate, and sand under high pressure in order to fracture rock and open existing fissures to allow trapped oil and gas to escape; for a list of chemicals commonly used in fracking, see https://fracfocus.org/chemical-use/what-chemicals-are-used; serious unknowns exist about the environmental and social risks of fracking

fraud: False representation of a matter of fact, or concealment of what should have been disclosed, intended to deceive another so that the individual will act upon it to his or her injury; legally, fraud involves a false statement of a material fact, knowledge on the part of the defendant that the statement is untrue, intent to deceive, justifiable reliance by the victim on the statement, and injury to the victim as a result

frequency: How often something happens per unit of time, such as spills per year

fresh water: As used in fossil fuel industry spills, "fresh water" means water that is not predominantly saline produced water or process water; "fresh water" spills in the AER database contained thirty-five different nonfresh water substances, the most common of which were saline produced water, waste, raw production gas, and crude oil; "fresh water" spills come from a variety of sources including water, crude oil, sour gas, multiphase, "other," and natural gas pipelines, crude oil group batteries, and gas, drilling, oil, service, and suspended wells; according to AER's media relations (August 2019), "Fresh water is shown as nonsaline water within the FIS incident data. Nonsaline water has a total dissolved solids content of 4000 mg/L or less and may require treatment before it can be used for domestic or agricultural purposes. Nonsaline water can include lake or river water, surface runoff water, and groundwater"; this statement is important because it illustrates misinformation; there is no such term as "nonsaline water" in the FIS data; furthermore, water of 4000 mg/L total dissolved solids can indicate degraded water quality; species richness in Canadian fresh water ecosystems decreases as salinity increases with most of the decrease occurring at salinities ranging from 1,000 to 3,000 mg/L (Environment Canada 2001)

GIS: Geographic information system; a computer-based system used to store, manipulate, analyze, and present geographic or spatial information; GIS are widely used in ecological, planning, and engineering decision-making to minimize environmental impacts and to maximize efficiency of operations

graminoid: A grass-like plant; the group includes grasses, sedges, rushes, cattails, bulrushes, and other plants with grass-like stems and leaves

hydraulic fracturing. See fracking

hydrotest fluids: Fluids used to test the integrity of pressure vessels such as tanks and pipelines; hydrotest fluids are a mixture of water with substances such as propylene glycol, potassium acetate, and methanol

inaccuracy: Deviation from the true value of a parameter

indicator value: A numeric value that measures the strength of affinity of a species to a defined group such as spill sites and natural control sites; a species with an indicator value of 100 per cent would be found exclusively at sites belonging to a single site type; formally, it refers to the value generated by indicator species analysis (ISA) as developed by Dufrêne and Legendre

injection: The process of disposing waste products underground via an injection well

ISA: Indicator species analysis (ISA) is a method of identifying species whose abundance is influenced by defined environmental conditions, for example species that increase in abundance when a site is disturbed

legal location: A method of specifying a geographic location based on the township and range system and widely used by the fossil fuel industry; a "legal" of 15-9-116-06-W6 means legal subdivision 15 in Section 9 of Township 116 in Range 6, west of the 6th meridian; spills located by a legal subdivision are accurate to 16 ha (forty acres); finding spills based on "legals" can be impossible without local knowledge

m^3: Volume used for crude oil and saline water release and recovery; one m^3 is equivalent to 6.29 petroleum barrels, 264 US gallons, or 1,000 litres

median: In numeric datasets, the middle value; example: say you have nine observations and you arrange them from smallest to largest (0,0,0,1,3,3,7,8,9), counting from smallest to largest, the fifth (middle) value is the median, 3; the mode (the most common value) is 0, and the mean (average) is 3.44

mg/L: A measure of the concentration of a substance in milligrams per litre of liquid (usually water), equivalent to parts per million; whether the concentration is cause for concern depends upon the substance, the organism exposed, the length of exposure, and other factors; mg/kg is a similar measure but is used to express concentrations of substances in solids (such as soil)

misinformation: Incorrect information that misleads by errors of omission and commission; as used here, misinformation does not imply intent; compare disinformation multiphase pipeline: A pipeline that conveys a mixture of crude oil, gas, saline production water, "fresh water," and other materials from an oil well; the mixture is also known as "oil effluent"

natural gas: "Dry natural gas" is a mixture of about 90 to 95 per cent methane with small amounts of ethane, propane, butane, and impurities; synonyms: raw production gas, production gas, raw gas; "wet natural gas" contains varying amounts of water, condensates, and other fluids that must be separated from the natural gas at treater or dehydration units

nonnormal: In statistics, data that do not meet the requirements of a normal distribution; to describe such data and test for differences, a different set of techniques is used than for parametric data; nonparametric statistics are robust in that they make few or no assumptions about the underlying data

normal distribution: In statistics, data whose frequency distribution assumes a bell-shaped curve centred on the mean; such a distribution has only one peak, the mean equals the median, and two-thirds of the observations lie within one standard deviation; compare bimodal, skewed

ordination: A set of statistical methods that objectively arranges entities (such as plots or species) along axes based on the relationships amongst those entities; more specifically, ordination arranges entities along axes based on their responses to variables such as soil chemistry; nonmetric multidimensional scaling (NMS) is a powerful and flexible ordination method that uses the pair-wise ranked differences among entities in order to arrange those entities along axes with minimal stress; the computations, rather than the user, determine the optimal number of axes

p-value: The probability that the result could be observed by chance; a p-value of 0.001 indicates that the result, on average, could be observed by random chance once in 1,000 trials

PAH: Polycyclic aromatic hydrocarbon; a large family of hydrocarbons containing more than one aromatic carbon ring; PAHs are major constituents in fossil fuels and can also be formed during combustion of organic matter; PAHs are widely distributed in air, water, sediments, and soil; their chemical structure determines their environmental mobility and toxicity; PAHs have a high affinity for organic carbon and can therefore accumulate in peatlands and organic sediments

PHC: Petroleum hydrocarbon; see F1F4; total hydrocarbons (THC) is a similar designation but THC can include biogenic hydrocarbons (those made by organisms)

phenol: An aromatic organic ring compound composed of a phenyl group ($-C_6H_5$) bonded to a hydroxyl group (-OH); a common petroleum derivative; compare alkylphenol

302

primary spill: Refers to spills in which the named substance is the first component listed, often with the largest volume of the spilled substances; a primary crude oil spill may contain other components such as saline produced water; similarly, primary saline water spills often contain hydrocarbons and other substances

process water: Water supplied or required for industrial processes and whose quality is changed as a result of its use in industrial processes; compare produced water

produced water: Water released from its geological formation during hydrocarbon production; produced water flows up the well bore in a mixture with the oil or gas being produced; the chemical properties of produced water arise from its geological setting; compare saline produced water, process water

quaternary spill: Refers to spills in which the named material is the fourth substance listed

reclamation: As defined by the regulator, the process of returning land to a "productive state"; this may entail addressing contamination, land contouring to ensure drainage and establish topography similar to pre-disturbance, and revegetation; the AER's revegetation criteria are abstruse, but for all intents there are no requirements to return the land to its previous natural vegetation; "certified reclaimed" means that the condition of the land has been accepted by the regulator, it is not an indicator of ecological health; see certified reclaimed

regulatory capture: A state in which the decisions, actions, or resources of a regulator are consistently directed away from the public interest in favour of a private interest through the actions of that interest

release: An unplanned emission of liquids or gases; there are three types of unplanned releases: (1) spills are unplanned releases of liquids, with or without gases, from pipelines, wells, tanks, etc. onto land or water or into air; (2) underground releases occur when pipelines, well bores, and fractured reservoirs allow liquids or gases to escape and migrate underground; these releases are hidden from view, difficult to detect, and constitute a poorly understood risk; (3) blowouts occur when pressurized liquids or gases are expelled into the atmosphere as a result of loss of vessel or bedrock containment; a catastrophic blowout can be sufficiently powerful to expel soil and bedrock

release cleanup date: Defined by the AER as the "'date the release was determined to be cleaned up' … the date the area was cleared of any released substance including any contaminated soil/water. This date is not an indicator of any ongoing remediation that may be required at the site including (but not limited to) contamination testing, bioremediation and soil replacement"

reportable release: Defined by the AER (2016b) as "any substance release that may cause, is causing, or has caused an adverse effect; any unrefined product release of more than 2 m³ on lease; unrefined product release off lease; any substance release into a waterbody; any pipeline release or pipeline break (including during pressure testing); pipeline hits; any uncontrolled gas release of more than 30,000 m³; any well flowing uncontrolled; any fire caused by a flare or incinerator; any fire causing a loss of more than 2 m³ of oil or 30,000 m³ of gas, or causing damage to a wellhead; any fire that occurs on an oilsands site that results in the deployment of major firefighting equipment"; these criteria for a reportable spill are more inclusive than those used in the online compliance dashboard; as defined online, "reportable releases" under FIS exclude many releases, such as spills of ≤ 2 m³ that remain on leases and do not enter a water body or come from a pipeline; to what extent the criteria are followed is unknown, however, because the FIS database reports spills that do not meet the reporting criteria; the AER's online "compliance dashboard" reports a subset of spills reported in the FIS database; please refer to web 6.21 for data

reserve pit: An earthen pit on a drilling pad used to store either drilling mud or drilling waste; these waste ponds are open to the air and thus pose a danger to wildlife due to contaminant exposures; at the end of drilling, the pit contents may be removed to a certified landfill or plowed into the ground on site, a reclamation technique known by the euphemism "land farming"

rhizosphere: The living upper layer of a soil that includes plant roots, bacteria, fungi, protists, and animals; where the important biological, chemical, and physical processes that control the function and health of terrestrial ecosystems occur

row-column summary: Within PC-Ord, a means of summarizing species richness, diversity, and other attributes from a species by plot data file (McCune and Mefford 2011)

saline produced water: A by-product of oil and gas production; its composition varies in concert with its geological source, but it is usually saline and may contain volatile organic compounds (VOCs), polycyclic aromatic hydrocarbons (PAHs), alkylphenols, heavy metals, and naturally occurring radioactive material; synonyms: brine, salt/produced water, saline water

saline spill: An unplanned release of saline produced water by the fossil fuel industry; the composition and concentration of the saline spills vary, but typically the brine is predominantly sodium chloride and the electrical conductivity exceeds that of seawater; compare release

salinity: The amount of salt in a system indicated by measures such as total dissolved solids, electrical conductivity, and the concentrations of ions such as sodium and chloride salinization: The human-caused accumulation of salts within soils, subsoils, or waters of an ecosystem with attendant ecological impacts; the three major causes of salinization are irrigation agriculture, fossil fuel industry spills, and road salting

satellite: A structure, such as a well, that is spatially isolated from similar structures

secondary spill: Refers to spills in which the named material is the second component listed, often with the second largest volume

seismic line: A linear removal of vegetation and disturbance of the soil sur-face to allow passage of a seismic survey crew; seismic waves, produced on the land surface, flow through the subsurface and reflect back to receptors on the land surface; the pattern of reflections is used to infer the underlying geologic structure, location, and volume of hydrocarbon deposits; millions of kilometres of seismic lines exist in Alberta and the length increases every year; seismic line width varies from ~2–10 m; seismic lines cause significant ecological impacts

signature: A set of attributes that, like a written signature, identifies an entity; a saline water spill, for example, can leave a signature in the form of salinized and impaired soil dominated by exotic halophytic grasses and forbs; the falcon effect is a signature left in data that identifies the numbers as chosen by humans rather than produced by measurement

skewed: In statistics, nonnormal data with a frequency distribution that extends as a long tail to one side of the mean; most of the spill data are positively skewed, meaning that a small number of spills have volumes far greater than the mean volume

skim pit: A pit on a well pad in which waste emulsions of crude oil and water are stored; the oil is later skimmed off the top; these pits present a chronic hazard to wildlife

sodicity: A measure of the amount of exchangeable sodium in soil or water; the soils, vegetation, and growth potential of sites high in sodium are impaired sodium absorption ratio (SAR): The ratio of the amount of soil sodium relative to the amount of soil calcium and magnesium; adding sodium to soils can collapse soil structure and inhibit water and gas movements; soils with a high SAR limit the growth of most plants

soil structure: The organization of clay, silt, sand, and organic soil particles into compound particles called aggregates that take the form of granules, blocks, prisms, or plates; soils without structure can be either massive or single grain; soil structure results from the expression of biological, chemical, and physical processes over time; soil structure influences the movements of air and water and the density and distribution of roots and soil organisms; structure can be degraded by crude oil and saline spills, by excavation, topsoil stripping, and plowing, and by compaction with heavy equipment; loss of soil structure is, on human time scales, permanent

standard deviation: A measure of the amount of variation in data observations around the mean; a small standard deviation indicates that most of the data cluster around the mean; in normal distributions, about two-thirds of the observations lie within one standard deviation of the mean

statistics: The practice of organizing, processing, analyzing, summarizing, and drawing conclusions from data; numerical description of the state or behaviour of a system; a means to test generalizations, assumptions, and hypotheses

Superfund Site (Act): Contaminated land identified by the United States Environmental Protection Agency as a candidate for cleanup because it poses a risk to human health and/or the environment; they include manufacturing facilities, processing plants, landfills, mining sites, and illegal dump sites; remediation of these sites is authorized under the Superfund Act, formally known as The Comprehensive Environmental Response, Compensation, and Liability Act adopted in 1980

suspended well: A well on which operations have been discontinued but which has not been plugged and abandoned permanently tertiary spill: Refers to spills in which the named material is the third substance listed

timely: Arriving promptly, at the appropriate time, in time to be useful

tonne: 1,000 kg, a metric ton, or 2,200 pounds

volatile organic compounds (vocs): A large group of human-made and natural organic chemicals with a low boiling point that causes them to sublimate or evaporate and enter the atmosphere as a gas; common natural vocs include isoprene and dimethyl sulphide; human-made vocs come from a wide array of products such as fossil fuels (e.g., gasoline, propane, benzene), paints and protective coatings, cleaning products, perfumes, refrigerants, solvents, adhesives, car exhaust, cigarette smoke, and carpets; exposure to vocs such as benzene, perchloroethylene, methylene chloride, and formaldehyde can pose serious health risks

waste: A generic term for a mixture of materials associated with a spill which can include hydrocarbons, saline water, and mineral and organic materials

Tables, Figures, and Plates

TABLES

FIGURES

PLATES

References

AAR (Applied Aquatic Research Ltd). 2006. "Crude Oil Exposure and Its Effects on Resident Fishes and Benthic Invertebrates in the Waskahigan River, Alberta." *Waskahigan River Oil Leak Biomonitoring Program*. Grande Prairie: Canadian Natural Resources Ltd.

ABMI (Alberta Biodiversity Monitoring Institute). 2017. *Human Footprint Inventory 2014. Geospatial Centre, Version 1*. March. Document: HFI2014_V2_Metadata.pdf.

ACIMS (Alberta Conservation Information Management System). 2013. "List of all Species and Ecological Communities within the ACIMS Database 2013." Excel file containing species names, common names, tracked community names, and conservation ranks. Edmonton: Alberta Government. This file is no longer available from government. It has been replaced by separate files for vascular plants, mosses, lichens, etc., available from: https://open.alberta.ca/dataset?q=list+of+all+elements&sort=score+desc.

AER. 2013. Report 2013-B: Pipeline Performance in Alberta, 1990–2012. Calgary: Alberta Energy Regulator.

– 2014a. *Alberta's Energy Reserves 2013 and Supply/Demand Outlook 2014–2023*. Calgary: Alberta Energy Regulator. Document: ST98-2014.pdf.

– 2014b. "Pace Oil and Gas Ltd. Wellhead Piping Failure License No. W0057420 May 19, 2012." *AER Investigation Report*, 3 March. Calgary: Alberta Energy Regulator.

– 2015a. "Order under Section 113 of the Environmental Protection and Enhancement Act." *Nexen Energy ULC*, 17 July. Calgary: Alberta Energy Regulator. http://www.aer.ca/documents/orders/NexenEPOJuly2015.pdf.

– 2015b. *Investigation Summary Report 2013-004: Apache Canada Ltd. License No. P36753-33.* October. Calgary: Alberta Energy Regulator.

– 2016a. *15/16 Annual Report Executive Summary.* Document: AER2015–16Annual ReportExecutiveSummary.pdf. Calgary: Alberta Energy Regulator.

– 2016b. *Release Reporting Requirements.* Document: AER-ReleaseReporting Brochure.PDF. Calgary: Alberta Energy Regulator.

– 2017a. *FOIPed Materials Relating to the Pace-Spyglass 2012 Spill.* Calgary: Alberta Energy Regulator. Documents: Redacted Records-Location 3-Applicant Copy_ Part8.pdf, Redacted Records-Location 3-ApplicantCopy_Part1.pdf, and Redacted Records-Location 3-Applicant Copy_Part2.pdf.

– 2017b. "Syncrude Charged with Blue Heron Deaths." Accessed 15 August. www.aer.ca/about-aer/media-centre/news-releases/news-release-2017-08-03.

– 2017c. *Pipeline Performance.* Accessed 24 February. www.aer.ca/data-and-publications/pipeline-performance.

– 2017d. *FOIPed Materials Relating to the Apache 15-09 and BP Zama (Apache Zama) Saline Spills.* Calgary: Alberta Energy Regulator. Document: Remaining Redacted Records – Applicant Copy.pdf.

– 2017e. *Management's Discussion and Analysis.* http://www1.aer.ca/AnnualReport/ media/AER2016–17AnnualReportFinancials.pdf. Calgary: Alberta Energy Regulator.

– 2018. *Crude Oil Production.* https://www.aer.ca/providing-information/data-and-reports/statistical-reports/crude-oil-production. Calgary: Alberta Energy Regulator.

Alberta Culture and Tourism. 2018. "Conventional Oil. Blowouts and Fires." http://www.history.alberta.ca/energyheritage/oil/energy-crises-political-debates-and-environmental-concerns-1970s-1980s/blowouts-fires-and-waste-prevention/ blowouts-and-fires/default.aspx.

Alberta Energy. 2017. *Our Business.* http://www.energy.alberta.ca/OurBusiness.asp.

– 2018. *Alberta Energy History Prior to 1970.* http://www.energy.gov.ab.ca/About_Us/ 3997.asp.

Alberta Environment. 1989. *Peace River Oils # 1 Study Environmental Assessment.* Edmonton, Alberta: Alberta Environment. No. Oll6z W8910. Document: 8957.pdf.

– 2001. *Salt Contamination Assessment and Remediation Guidelines.* Edmonton: Alberta Environment. Publ. No. T/606.

– 2003. *Siting an Upstream Oil and Gas Site in an Environmentally Sensitive Area on Private Land.* http://aep.alberta.ca/forms-maps-services/publications/ documents/SitingUpstreamOilGasSiteSensitive-2003.pdf.

Alberta Government. 2013. *Code of Practice for Pipelines and Telecommunication Lines Crossing a Water Body, Made under the Water Act and the Water (Ministerial) Regulation Consolidated to Include Amendments in Force as of June 24, 2013.* Edmonton: Alberta Government. http://www.qp.alberta.ca/documents/codes/PIPE LINE.PDF.

– 2017a. *Alberta Wild Species General Status Listing 2015.* Edmonton: Alberta Government. Document: SAR-2015wildspeciesgeneralstatuslist-mar2017.pdf.

– 2017b. *Draft Provincial Woodland Caribou Range Plan.* Edmonton: Alberta Government. Document: DRAFT-CaribouRangePlanAndAppendices-Dec2017.pdf.

Alberta Oil. 2010. "Anatomy of Alberta's Worst Oil-well Blowout. Atlantic No. 3 Woke Up a Sleeping Giant for Regulators and Policymakers Alike." https://www.albertaoilmagazine.com/2010/09/anatomy-of-albertas-worst-oil-well-blowout/.

Alberta Provincial Court. 1983. *R. v. SUNCOR (Fisheries Act), decision of Judge Horrocks, Provincial Court 3, Fort McMurray, 3 June 1983.* Accessed 23 April 2020. https://archive.org/stream/fisheriespolluti03cana/fisheriespolluti03cana_djvu.txt.

Allen, B. 2019. "Oil and Gas Leaks among 15,000 Spills on New Map of Saskatchewan." CBC News, 15 November. https://www.cbc.ca/news/canada/saskatchewan/oil-gas-leaks-spills-map-saskatchewan-1.5360963.

Allison, E. and B. Mandler. 2018a. "Spills in Oil and Natural Gas Fields." *American Geosciences Institute.* https://www.americangeosciences.org/critical-issues/factsheet/pe/spills-oil-natural-gas-fields.

– 2018b. "Abandoned Wells." *American Geosciences Institute.* https://www.american geosciences.org/criticalissues/factsheet/pe/abandoned-wells.

Anderson, D. 2017. "Lead, Oil, Salt: Calgary's Push for Control over Potentially Hundreds of Contaminated Sites." CBC News, 19 June. http://www.cbc.ca/news/canada/calgary/calgary-contaminated-toxic-sites-cleanup-city-charters-1.4150058.

– 2019. "Alberta's Energy 'War Room' Launches in Calgary." CBC News, 26 December. https://www.cbc.ca/news/canada/calgary/alberta-war-room-launch-calgary-1.5392371.

Ash, M. and I. Ash (compilers). 2004. *Handbook of Preservatives. Second edition.* Endicott, NY: Synapse Information Resources.

Associated Press. 2019. "10 Times More Land Affected by Leak from Keystone Pipeline Than First Thought." CBC News, 18 November. https://www.cbc.ca/news/canada/calgary/alberta-north-dakota-keystone-spill-oil-tc-energy-1.5363633.

Ayles, G.B., M. Dubé, and D. Rosenberg. 2004. *Oil Sands Regional Aquatic Monitoring Program (RAMP), Scientific Peer Review of the Five Year Report (1997–2001).* Ft McMurray: Regional Aquatics Monitoring Program.

Bachu, S. and T. Watson. n.d. *Factors Affecting or Indicating Potential Wellbore Leakage.* Edmonton: Alberta Energy and Utilities Board.

Baker, K.A. 1990. *Forests as an Ecological Monitoring Tool for Catastrophic Events. A manuscript report prepared for the Canadian Environmental Assessment Research Council.* http://publications.gc.ca/collections/collection_2018/acee-ceaa/En107-3-31-1991-eng.pdf.

Bakx, K. 2019. "Old, Unproductive Oil and Gas Wells Could Cost up to $70B to Clean Up, Says New Report." CBC News, 8 April. https://www.cbc.ca/news/business/orphan-wells-alberta-aldp-aer-1.5089254.

Balshi, M.S., A.D. McGuire, P. Duffy, M. Flannigan, J. Walsh, and J. Melillo. 2009. "Assessing the Response of Area Burned to Changing Climate in Western Boreal North America Using a Multivariate Adaptive Regression Splines (MARS) Approach." *Global Change Biology* 15(3): 578–600.

Barrera, J. 2019. "Trans Mountain Monitoring Anti-Pipeline Activists, Labelling Some as 'Persons of Interest.'" CBC News, 25 November. https://www.cbc.ca/news/indigenous/tmx-docs-reports-1.5370221.

Baurick, T. 2018. "Coast Guard Orders Taylor Energy to Stop 14-Year Oil Leak." *The Times-Picayune*, 20 November. https://www.nola.com/environment/2018/11/coast-guard-orders-taylor-energy-to-stop-14-year-oil-leak.html.

Bella, D.A. 1987. "Organizations and Systematic Distortion of Information." *Journal of Professional Issues in Engineering* 113(4): 360–70.

Belvederesi, C., M. Thompson, and P.E. Komers. 2017. "Canada's Federal Database is Inadequate for the Assessment of Environmental Consequences of Oil and Gas Pipeline Failures." *Environmental Reviews* 25(4): 415–22. dx.DOI.org/10.1139/er-2017-0003.

Benford, F. 1938. "The Law of Anomalous Numbers." *Proceedings American Philosophical Society* 78: 551–72.

Bennett, D. and B. Weber. 2019. "Alberta Energy Regulator Official Quits before He Can Be Fired by Incoming Jason Kenney." *National Post*, 29 April. https://nationalpost.com/news/politics/alberta-energy-regulator-official-quits-ahead-of-being-fired-by-incoming-premier.

Berg, S.A. and L.L. Williams. 2015. *Wildlife Response Activities for the July 25–26, 2010 Enbridge Line 6B Oil Discharges near Marshall, MI.* US Fish and Wildlife Service. [Appendix C of US Fish and Wildlife Service, Nottawaseppi Huron Band of the Potawatomi Tribe, and Match-E-Be-Nash-She-Wish Band of the Potawatomi Indians (2015), cited below.]

Berner, L.T., P.S.A. Beck, A.G. Bunn, A.L. Lloyd, and S.J. Goetz. 2011. "High-latitude

Tree Growth and Satellite Vegetation Indices: Correlations and Trends in Russia and Canada (1982–2008)." *Journal of Geophysical Research* 116, Issue G1. DOI: 10.1029/2010JG001475.

Birtwell, I. 2008. *Comments on the Effects of Oil Spillage on Fish and their Habitat – Lake Wabamun, Alberta. Hearing Order OH-001-2014, Upper Nicola IR #2, Document B.* Document: C363-10-3_-_OH-001-2014_Upper_Nicola_IR_2_Doc_B_Birtwell._2008._Comments_on_the_effects_of_oil_spillage_on_fish_and_their_habitat_(00228022xC6E53)_-_A4G6Q2.pdf.

Bishop, F.G. 1976. *Observations on the Biological Effects of an Oil Spill in the Moosehorn and Swan Rivers, Alberta.* Peace River: Alberta Environment.

Bliss, L.C. and E.B. Peterson. 1973. "The Ecological Impact of Northern Petroleum Development." 2–5 May. In: *Fifth International Congress on Arctic Oil and Gas: Problems and Possibilities,* 1–26. Le Havre, France.

Boufadel, M., B. Chen, J. Foght, P. Hodson, K. Lee, and S. Swanson. 2015. *The Behaviour and Environmental Impacts of Crude Oil Released into Aqueous Environments.* Ottawa: The Royal Society of Canada.

Boyd, A. and K. Leavitt. 2020. "If Teck Offered Lessons, It's Not Clear Alberta Is Learning Them." *The Star,* 27 February. https://www.thestar.com/news/canada/2020/02/27/experts-say-alberta-hasnt-learned-the-lesson-about-climate-change-and-oilsands-development.html.

Bredl, S., P. Winker, and K. Kotschau. 2012. "A Statistical Approach to Detect Interviewer Falsification of Survey Data." *Survey Methodology* 38(1): 1–10. Statistics Canada, Catalogue No. 12-001-X.

Brook, J.R., S.G. Cober, M. Freemark, T. Harner, S.M. Li, J. Liggio, P. Makar, and B. Pauli. 2019. "Advances in Science and Applications of Air Pollution Monitoring: A Case Study on Oil Sands Monitoring Targeting Ecosystem Protection." *Journal of the Air & Waste Management Association* 69(6): 661–709.

Brooks, M.L., C.M. D'Antonio, D.M. Richardson, J.B. Grace, J.E. Keeley, J.M. Di Tomaso, R.J. Hobbs, M. Pellant, and D. Pyke. 2004. "Effects of Invasive Alien Plants on Fire Regimes." *BioScience* 54(7): 677–88.

Burt, M. and T. Crawford. 2014. *Seeking Tidewater: Understanding the Economic Impacts of the Trans Mountain Expansion Project.* Ottawa: The Conference Board of Canada.

Calgary Herald. 1973. "Oil Pipeline Breaks." Page 25, 7 August. https://news.google.com/newspapers?id=BW1kAAAAIBAJ&sjid=L30NAAAAIBAJ&dq=alberta%20oil-spill&pg=6446%2C2329553.

Calvert, A.M., C.A. Bishop, R.D. Elliot, E.A. Krebs, T.M. Kydd, C.S. Machtans, and

G.J. Robertson. 2013. "A Synthesis of Human-related Avian Mortality in Canada." *Avian Conservation and Ecology* 8 (2): 11. http://www.ace-eco.org/vol8/iss2/art11/.

Campbell, Mac A., B. Kopach, P.E. Komers, and A. Ford. 2019. "Quantifying the Impacts of Oil Sands Development on Wildlife: Perspectives from Impact Assessments." *Environmental Reviews*, 31 January. https://DOI.org/10.1139/er-2018-0118.

Campion-Smith, B. and T. MacCharles. 2018. "Trans Mountain Pipeline 'Will be Built,' Trudeau says." *The Star*, 15 April. https://www.thestar.com/news/canada/2018/04/15/prime-minister-premiers-meet-over-controversial-trans-mountain-pipeline.html.

Canadian Press. 1970. "Oil Spill Nearly Cleaned Up." *The Regina Leader-Post*, page 15, 12 September. https://news.google.com/newspapers?id=U95UAAAAIBAJ&sjid=ajwNAAAAIBAJ&dq=alberta%20oil-spill&pg=2965%2C2044749.

– 1972. "Oil Spill Burn Off Allowed." *Calgary Herald*, page 17, 24 February. https://news.google.com/newspapers?id=TG9kAAAAIBAJ&sjid=e30NAAAAIBAJ&dq=alberta%20oil-spill&pg=1886%2C1422501.

– 2012. "Alberta Oil Spill: Up to 3,000 Barrels Spill Near Red Deer River Reports Plains Midstream Canada." *Huffington Post*, 8 June. http://www.huffingtonpost.ca/2012/06/08/alberta-oil-spill-red-deer-river_n_1581008.html.

– 2018. "QuickQuotes: Ottawa's $4.5B Trans Mountain Play Welcomed, Condemned." *The Star Phoenix*, 16 May. https://thestarphoenix.com/pmn/news-pmn/canada-news-pmn/morneaus-pledge-to-backstop-pipeline-expansion-draws-criticism/wcm/92b3005c-f1b6-4364-aee4-881ead6f87ee.

– 2019a. "Crash and Fuel Spill from Tanker Carrying Crude Prompts BC Ministry Monitoring." *North Shore News*, 18 November. https://www.nsnews.com/crash-and-fuel-spill-from-tanker-carrying-crude-prompts-b-c-ministry-monitoring-1.24011597.

– 2019b. "Syncrude to Pay $2.75M after Blue Heron Deaths at Alberta Oilsands Mine." Global News, 2 February. https://globalnews.ca/news/4809118/syncrude-fined-dead-great-blue-herons/.

CBC. 1999. "More Details of RCMP 'Dirty Tricks' Revealed." 30 January. http://www.cbc.ca/news/canada/more-details-of-rcmp-dirty-tricks-revealed-1.168362.

– 2009. "Soil Contamination Saga Ends for Calgary Neighbourhood." 29 June. https://www.cbc.ca/news/canada/calgary/soil-contamination-saga-ends-for-calgary-neighbourhood-1.810559.

– 2018a. "As Trans Mountain Changes Hands, Coldwater Couple Not Sure Who Will Clean Up Lingering Oil Spill." 10 June. http://www.cbc.ca/news/indigenous/trans-mountain-spill-coldwater-reserve-janice-antoine-1.4686604.

– 2018b. "Spill at Kinder Morgan Station near Kamloops, BC Was Larger Than First Stated by Province." 9 June. http://www.cbc.ca/news/canada/british-columbia/kinder-morgan-oil-spill-darfield-1.4699763.

– 2018c. "How One of the Worst Active Oil Spills in US History Has been Kept 'Under the Radar.'" CBC Radio, *As It Happens*, 26 October. https://www.cbc.ca/listen/shows/as-it-happens/segment/15620920.

– 2018d. "After Massive Oil Spill, Spotlight Shifts to Agency Regulating NL Offshore Industry." 21 November. https://www.cbc.ca/news/canada/newfoundland-labrador/cnlopb-in-question-after-spill-1.4914163.

– 2018e. "CSIS Surveillance of Pipeline Protesters Faces Federal Review." 27 September. https://www.cbc.ca/news/canada/british-columbia/csis-surveillance-of-pipeline-protesters-faces-federal-review-1.3188231.

– 2019. "Pipeline Rupture Sends 40,000 Litres of Oil into Alberta Creek." 19 August. https://www.cbc.ca/news/canada/calgary/bonterra-energy-pipeline-spill-1.5251723.

– 2020. "Alberta Oilfield Company Draws Fire for Sexually Graphic 'Greta' Image." 27 February. https://www.cbc.ca/news/canada/edmonton/greta-thunberg-xsite-energy-sexual-image-1.5478561.

CCME (Canadian Council of Ministers of the Environment). 2008a. *Canada-Wide Standards for Petroleum Hydrocarbons (PHC) in Soil*. Ottawa, Ontario.

– 2008b. *Canada-Wide Standards for Petroleum Hydrocarbons (PHC) in Soil: Scientific Rationale, Supporting Technical Document*. Ottawa, Ontario.

CFIA (Canadian Food Inspection Agency). 2008. *Invasive Alien Plants in Canada – Technical Report*. http://www.inspection.gc.ca/english/plaveg/invenv/techrpt/techrese.shtml.

Charette, T. and E.E. Prepas. 2003. "Wildfire Impacts on Phytoplankton Communities of Three Small Lakes on the Boreal Plain, Alberta, Canada: A Paleolimnological Study." *Canadian Journal of Fisheries and Aquatic Sciences* 60: 584–93.

CMP (Corporate Mapping Project). 2019. "Fossil-Power Top 50." https://www.corporatemapping.ca/database/fossil-power-top-50/. Detailed information on the fossil fuel industry metaorganization is available at: https://www.corporatemapping.ca/database/ and https://littlesis.org/partners/corporate-mapping-project#cmp-full-network.

CNRL (Canadian Natural Resources Limited). 2013. *Current Status of Primrose Operations*. http://www.cnrl.com/upload/media_element/648/03/0731_primrose-operations.pdf.

Coady, D., I. Parry, N.-P. Le, and B. Shang. 2019. "Global Fossil Fuel Subsidies Remain

Large: An Update Based on Country-Level Estimates." *International Monetary Fund, Working Paper* WP/19/89. Document: WPIEA2019089.pdf.

Cody, W.J., K.L. MacInnes, J. Cayouette, and S. Darbyshire. 2000. "Alien and Invasive Native Vascular Plants along the Norman Wells Pipeline, District of Mackenzie, Northwest Territories." *Canadian Field-Naturalist* 114(1): 126–37.

Colgan, W. III., M.C. Vavrek, and J. Bolton. 2002. "Re-Vegetation of an Oil/Brine Spill: Interaction between Plants and Mycorrhizal Fungi." In: *Proceedings of the Annual International Petroleum Environmental Conference*. Albuquerque, NM.

Connolly, A. 2020. "Teck Resources Has Abandoned Its Frontier Mine Plan." Global News, 25 February. https://globalnews.ca/news/6588026/teck-frontier-oilsands-mine-cancelled/.

Cook, J., G. Supran, S. Lewandowsky, N. Oreskes, and E. Maibach. 2019. "America Misled: How the Fossil Fuel Industry Deliberately Misled Americans about Climate Change." *George Mason University Center for Climate Change Communication*. Fairfax, VA. https://www.climatechangecommunication.org/america-misled/.

Cozzarelli, I.M., K.J. Skalak, D.B. Kent, M.A. Engle, A. Benthem, A.C. Mumford, K. Haase, A. Farag, D. Harper, S.C. Nagel, L.R. Iwanowicz, W.H. Orem, D.M. Akob, J.B. Jaeschke, J. Galloway, M. Kohler, D.L. Stoliker, and G.D. Jolly. 2017. "Environmental Signatures and Effects of an Oil and Gas Wastewater Spill in the Williston Basin, North Dakota." *Science of the Total Environment* 579: 1781–93.

CTV Edmonton. 2010. "Abandoned Gas Well in Calmar Leads to More Questions." 3 June. https://edmonton.ctvnews.ca/abandoned-gas-well-in-calmar-leads-to-more-questions-1.518785.

Cunningham, N. 2020. "Canada's TransMountain Pipeline Faces Another Major Setback." *Oil Price*, 23 July. https://oilprice.com/Energy/Energy-General/Canadas-TransMountain-Pipeline-Faces-Another-Major-Setback.html.

Cushing, L.J., K. Vavra-Musser, K. Chau, M. Franklin, and J.E. Johnston. 2020. "Flaring from Unconventional Oil and Gas Development and Birth Outcomes in the Eagle Ford Shale in South Texas." *Environmental Health Perspectives* 128(7). https://doi.org/10.1289/EHP6394.

Cwiak, C.L., N. Avon, C. Kellen, P.C. Mott, O.M. Niday, K.M. Schulz, J.G. Sink, and T.B. Webb, Jr. 2015. *The New Normal: The Direct and Indirect Impacts of Oil Drilling and Production on the Emergency Management Function in North Dakota*. https://www.ndsu.edu/fileadmin/emgt/FINALThe_New_Normal_January_2015_a.pdf.

Dabros, A., M. Pyper, and G. Castilla. 2018. "Seismic Lines in the Boreal and Arctic Ecosystems of North America: Environmental Impacts, Challenges and Opportunities." *Environmental Reviews* e-First Article. https://DOI.org/10.1139/er-2017-0080.

Dance, J.T., R.D. Huddleston, L.G. Garrett, and T. Robbie. 2015. *Risk Assessment and Abandonment Strategy Petroleum Production Field.* http://www.esaa.org/wp-content/uploads/2015/06/02-07DancePaper.pdf.

Da Silva, T. 2020. "Alberta Energy Regulator Continues Restructuring, Laying off Staff." Global News, 12 February. https://globalnews.ca/news/6543455/alberta-energy-regulator-more-layoffs-february/.

de Groot, W.J., M.D. Flannigan, and A.S. Cantin. 2013. "Climate Change Impacts on Future Boreal Fire Regimes." *Forest Ecology and Management* 294: 35–44.

de Marchi, S. and J.T. Hamilton. 2006. "Assessing the Accuracy of Self-Reported Data: An Evaluation of the Toxics Release Inventory." *Journal of Risk and Uncertainty* 32: 57–76.

De Souza, M. 2020. "Emails Show How Oilpatch Lobbied Alberta Energy Regulator for Coronavirus Relief." Global News, 17 July. https://globalnews.ca/news/7185882/coronavirus-capp-aer-suncor-emails-monitoring/.

De Souza, M. and T. Vernon. 2020. "Alberta Energy Regulator Suspends Monitoring Requirements Across Oil and Gas Industry." Global News, 21 May. https://global news.ca/news/6968696/aer-suspends-monitoring-nhl/.

De Souza, M. and H. Yourex-West. 2020. "Alberta Government Took Six Months to Release Alarming Climate Report." Global News, 27 February. https://global news.ca/news/6600989/alberta-buried-climate-report/.

Di, Q., L. Dai, and Y. Wang. 2017. "Association of Short-term Exposure to Air Pollution with Mortality in Older Adults." *Journal of the American Medical Association* 318(24): 2446–56. DOI: 10.1001/jama.2017.17923.

Diekmann, A. 2007. "Not the First Digit! Using Benford's Law to Detect Fraudulent Scientific Data." *Journal of Applied Statistics* 34(3): 321–9.

Dirzo, R., H.S. Young, M. Galetti, G. Ceballos, N.J.B. Isaac, and B. Collen. 2014. "Defaunation in the Anthropocene." *Science* 345(6195): 401–6.

Dowdeswell, L., P. Dillon, S. Ghoshal, A. Miall, J. Rasmussen, and J. Smol. 2010. *A Foundation for the Future: Building an Environmental Monitoring System for the Oil Sands.* Ottawa: Environment Canada. http://www.ec.gc.ca/pollution/E9 ABC93B-A2F4-4D4B-A06D-BF5E0315C7A8/1359_Oilsands_Advisory_Panel_report_09.pdf.

Drollette, B.D., K. Hoelzer, N.R. Warner, T.H. Darrah, O. Karatum, M.P. O'Connor,

325

R.K. Nelson, L.A. Fernandez, C.M. Reddy, A. Vengosh, R.B. Jackson, M. Elsner, and D.L. Plata. 2015. "Elevated Levels of Diesel Range Organic Compounds in Groundwater near Marcellus Gas Operations Are Derived from Surface Activities." *Proceedings National Academy of Sciences* 112(43). www.pnas.org/cgi/DOI/10.1073/pnas.1511474112.

Eaton, E.M. and N.A. Day. 2019. "Petro-Pedagogy: Fossil Fuel Interests and the Obstruction of Climate Justice in Public Education." *Environmental Education Research.* DOI: 10.1080/13504622.2019.1650164.

Edwardson, L. 2018. "Notley's Bill 12 'Shows Bold Leadership,' Say Alberta Oil and Gas Producers." CBC News, 17 April. http://www.cbc.ca/news/canada/calgary/alberta-oil-gas-producers-support-notley-government-bill-12-1.4622717.

Elsinger, M.E. 2009. "Reclamation Status of Plains Rough Fescue Grasslands at Rumsey Block in Central Alberta, Canada after Oil and Gas Well Site and Pipeline Disturbances." M.Sc. thesis. University of Alberta, Edmonton, Alberta.

Environment Canada. 2001. *Priority Substances List Assessment Report. Road Salts.* Ottawa, Ontario.

Environment Canada – Health Canada. 2016. *Screening Assessment Petroleum Sector Stream Approach Natural Gas Condensates.* http://www.ec.gc.ca/ese-ees/7933A3C7-9ACC-4F80-9339-85451B59FFD0/FSAR%20PSSA4%20NGCs%202016-12-12.pdf.

Environmental Defence, Équiterre, and Stand.Earth. 2020. "Who Benefits? An Investigation of Foreign Ownership in the Oil Sands." *Stand.Earth*, 12 May. https://www.stand.earth/sites/stand/files/report-foreign-ownership-oilsands.pdf.

EPA (Environmental Protection Agency). 1994. EPA *Superfund Record of Decision: Jackson Township Landfill.* EPA ID: NJD980505283 OU 01. ROD/R02-94/233. 09/26/1994. US Environmental Protection Agency, document: R0200549.pdf.

– 2010. *Dixie Oil Processors Superfund Site, Harris County, Texas.* EPA ID# TXD089793046. EPA *Region 6.* Washington, DC: US Environmental Protection Agency.

– 2016. *Slawson Exploration Company, Inc. Clean Air Act Settlement.* https://www.epa.gov/enforcement/slawson-exploration-company-inc-clean-air-act-settlement.

– 2018. "Wilson Farm, Plumstead Township, NJ, Operable Units." https://cumulis.epa.gov/supercpad/SiteProfiles/index.cfm?fuseaction=second.ous&id=0200740.

ERCB (Energy Resources Conservation Board). 2010. ERCB *Total E&P Canada Ltd. Surface Steam Release of May 18, 2006 Joslyn Creek* SAGD *Thermal Operation* ERCB *Staff Review and Analysis. February 11, 2010.* Calgary: Energy Resources Conservation Board.

– 2013a. *Plains Midstream Canada* ULC NPS *20 Rainbow Pipeline Failure, License 5592, Line No. 1, April 28, 2011.* Calgary: Energy Resources Conservation Board.

– 2013b. *Pembina Pipeline Corporation, Pipeline Failures, License No. 2349, Line No. 10, July 20 and August 15, 2011.* Calgary: Energy Resources Conservation Board.

– 2014. *Plains Midstream Canada* ULC NPS *20 Rangeland South, Pipeline Failure and Release into the Red Deer River, License No. 5844, Line 1, June 7, 2012.* Calgary: Energy Resources Conservation Board.

ESRD (Environment and Sustainable Resource Development). 2013. *2010 Reclamation Criteria for Wellsites and Associated Facilities for Forested Lands (updated July 2013).* Document: 2013-2010-reclamation-criteria-wellsites-forested-lands-2013-07.pdf.

Etkin, D.S. 2009. "Figure 32." In *Analysis of U.S. Oil Spillage.* Publication 356. Washington, DC: American Petroleum Institute, Regulatory and Scientific Affairs Department.

EUB (Energy and Utilities Board). 2005. ACC *Acheson 2-26-52-26, Acheson Field, December 2004 Blowout,* EUB *Investigation Team Post-Incident Analysis and Recommendations.* https://archive.org/stream/accacheson22652200albe/accacheson22652200albe_djvu.txt.

European Commission. 2011. *Toxicity and Assessment of Chemical Mixtures.* Scientific Committee on Health and Environmental Risks (SCHER), Scientific Committee on Emerging and Newly Identified Health Risks (SCENIHR), and Scientific Committee on Consumer Safety (SCCS). Brussels, Belgium: European Commission.

Fairbarns, M. 1990. *The Salt Meadows of Northwestern Alberta: A Reconnaissance Biophysical Inventory.* Edmonton: Alberta Forestry, Lands and Wildlife, Natural Areas Program.

Fagin, D. 2013. *Toms River, A Story of Science and Salvation.* New York: Bantam.

Fears, D. 2018. "A 14-Year Gulf Oil Spill Verges on Becoming One of Worst in US History." *Washington Post,* 25 October. https://www.washingtonpost.com/national/health-science/a-14-year-long-oil-spill-in-the-gulf-of-mexico-verges-on-becoming-one-of-the-worst-in-us-history/2018/10/20/f9a66fd0-9045-11e8-bcd5-9d911c784c38_story.html?noredirect=on&utm_term=.97b268e89608.

Financial Post. 2015. "Oilsands Pipeline Projects Look Doomed after Nexen Oil Spill Leaves 'Two Big Football Fields of Black Goo.'" 28 July. https://business.financialpost.com/commodities/energy/oilsands-pipeline-projects-look-doomed-after-nexen-oil-spill-leaves-two-big-football-field-of-black-goo.

Fischetti, M. 2019. "Silencing Science." *Scientific American* 320(5): 88.

Fisher, J.B. and K.L. Sublette. 2005. "Environmental Releases from Exploration and Production Operations in Oklahoma: Type, Volume, Causes, and Prevention." *Environmental Geosciences* 12(2): 89–99.

Flannigan, M.D., K.A. Logan, B.D. Amiro, W.R. Skinner, and B.J. Stocks. 2005. "Future Area Burned in Canada." *Climatic Change* 72: 1–16.

Flather, C.H., M.S. Knowles, and I.A. Kendall. 1998. "Threatened and Endangered Species Geography." *Bioscience* 48: 365–76.

Flavelle, C. 2020. "Global Financial Giants Swear Off Funding an Especially Dirty Fuel." *New York Times*, 12 February. https://www.nytimes.com/2020/02/12/climate/blackrock-oil-sands-alberta-financing.html.

Freedom House. 2020. *Freedom in the World 2020: A Leaderless Struggle for Democracy*. https://freedomhouse.org/sites/default/files/2020-02/FIW_2020_REPORT _BOOKLET_Final.pdf.

Garossino, S. 2019. "A Data-Based Dismantling of Jason Kenney's Foreign-Funding Conspiracy Theory." *National Observer*, 3 October. https://www.nationalob server.com/2019/10/03/analysis/data-based-dismantling-jason-kenneys-foreign-funding-conspiracy-theory.

Geodiscover. 2018. "Map of Abandoned Wells in the Devon, Alberta Area." https://geodiscover.alberta.ca/GDAHTML/Viewer/?viewer=GDAHTML&layer Theme=&scale=144447.638572&layers=2XXxVP2h8B%2fy&center=-12655332. 453140557%2c7046774.507596623.

GISD (Global Invasive Species Database). 2018. "*Bromus inermis.*" http://issg.org/ database/species/impact_info.asp?si=1223&fr=1&sts=&lang=EN.

Gleason, R.A. and B.A. Tangen, eds. 2014. *Brine Contamination to Aquatic Resources from Oil and Gas Development in the Williston Basin, United States Scientific Investigations Report 2014-5017.* US Dept of the Interior and US Geological Survey.

Gordon, G., I. Stavi, U. Shavit, and R. Rosenzweig. 2018. "Oil Spill Effects on Soil Hydrophobicity and Related Properties in a Hyper-Arid Region." *Geoderma* 312: 114–20.

Gorman, H.S. 2001. *Redefining Efficiency.* Akron, OH: University of Akron Press.

Goss, G., D. Alessi, D. Allen, J. Gehman, J. Brisbois, S. Kletke, A. Z. Sharak, et al. 2015. *Unconventional Wastewater Management: A Comparative Review and Analysis of Hydraulic Fracturing Wastewater Management Practices across Four North American Basins.* Edmonton: Canadian Water Network, University of Alberta. http://www.cwn-rce.ca/assets/resources/pdf/Hydraulic-Fracturing-Research-Reports/Goss-et-al.-2015-CWN-Report-Unconventional-Wastewater-Manage ment.pdf.

Hansen, A.J., R.P. Nielson, V.H. Dale, C.H. Flather, L.R. Iverson, D.J. Currie, S. Shafer, R. Cook, and P.J. Bartlein. 2001. "Global Change in Forests: Responses of Species, Communities, and Biomes." *Bioscience* 51(9): 765–79.

Harris, K. 2020. "Trudeau Announces Aid for Struggling Energy Sector, Including $1.7B to Clean Up Orphan Wells." CBC News, 17 April. https://www.cbc.ca/news/politics/financial-aid-covid19-trudeau-1.5535629.

Harrison, S.S. 1983. "Evaluating System for Ground-Water Contamination Hazards Due to Gas-Well Drilling on the Glaciated Appalachian Plateau." *Ground Water* 21(6): 689–700.

Hayhoe, K. and A. Stoner. 2019. *Alberta's Climate Future, Final Report 2019*. Report for Alberta Environmental Protection by ATMOS Research and Consulting.

Healing, D. 2020. "Total writes off $9.3B in oilsands assets, cancels CAPP membership." Global News, 29 July. https://globalnews.ca/news/7233046/total-writes-off-oilsands-assets-alberta-capp/.

Heidenreich, P. 2019. "Cleanup Underway after 400,000-Litre Produced Water Leak at Obsidian Energy Well near Drayton Valley." Global News, 31 May. https://globalnews.ca/news/5341494/well-produced-water-spill-obsidian-drayton-valley-alberta/.

Hellebust, A., B. Hanna, R.G. Sheath, M. Gergis, and T.C. Hutchinson. 1975. "Experimental Crude Oil Spills on a Small Subarctic Lake in the Mackenzie Valley, N.W.T.: Effects on Phytoplankton, Periphyton, and Attached Aquatic Vegetation." In *Proceedings of the 1975 International Oil Spill Conference, March 1975*, 509–15. Washington, DC: American Petroleum Institute.

HERMIS (Heritage Resources Information Management System). n.d. "Alberta Register of Historic Places. Atlantic No. 3 Wild Well Site." https://hermis.alberta.ca/ARHP/Details.aspx?DeptID=1&ObjectID=4665-1073.

Hogge, H.L., R.J. Allman, M.J. Paetz, R.E. Bailey, and E.E. Kupchanko. 1970. *Alberta Government Committee Report on Great Canadian Oil Sands Oil Spill to Athabasca River, June 6, 1970*. Edmonton: Alberta Environment.

Hollebone, B.P., B. Fieldhouse, G. Sergey, P. Lambert, Z. Wang, C. Yang, and M. Landirault. 2011. *The Behaviour of Heavy Oil in Fresh Water Lakes*. Paper submitted to the 34th Arctic and Marine Oilspill Program (AMOP) Technical Seminar on Environmental Contamination and Response, 4–6 October. Calgary.

Howat, D.R. 2000. *Acceptable Salinity, Sodicity and pH Values for Boreal Forest Reclamation, Report ESD/LM/00-2*. Edmonton: Alberta Environment, Environmental Sciences Division.

Hutchinson, T.C. and W. Freedman. 1978. "Effects of Experimental Crude Oil Spills

on Subarctic Boreal Forest Vegetation near Norman Wells, N.W.T., Canada."
Canadian Journal of Botany 56: 2424–33.

IAHS (International Association of Hydrological Sciences). 1990. "Groundwater
Contamination Risk Assessment: A Guide to Understanding and Managing
Uncertainties." In *Working Group on Groundwater Contamination Risk Assessment
of the IAHS International Commission on Groundwater*, edited by E. Reichard,
C. Cranor, R. Raucher, and G. Zapponi, Publ. 196. Washington, DC: International
Association of Hydrological Sciences.

IPBES (Intergovernmental Science-Policy Platform on Biodiversity and Ecosystem
Services). 2019. *Summary for Policymakers of the Global Assessment Report on
Biodiversity and Ecosystem Services*. Unedited advance version. https://assets.
documentcloud.org/documents/5989433/IPBES-Global-Assessment-Summary-
for-Policymakers.pdf.

Jacobson, M.Z. 2019. "The Health and Climate Impacts of Carbon Capture and
Direct Air Capture." *Energy and Environmental Science* 12, 12, 21 October. DOI:
10.1039/C9EE02709B.

Jaremko, G. 2013. *Steward 75 Years of Alberta Energy Regulation*. Calgary: Energy
Resources Conservation Board. Document: Steward_Ebook.pdf.

Jones, C.F. 2014. *Routes of Power: Energy and Modern America*. Cambridge, MA:
Harvard University Press.

Jones, J. 2013. "Alberta Regulator Falls Short on Disclosure." *The Globe and Mail*,
17 June. https://www.theglobeandmail.com/report-on-business/rob-commentary/
executive-insight/alberta-regulator-falls-short-on-disclosure/article12618777/.

Kallal, C.A. 2016. *In the Provincial Court of Alberta Criminal Division Between: Her
Majesty the Queen and Apache Canada Ltd., October 2013 Incident. Docket No.
151257771P1*. Edmonton: Alberta Crown Prosecution Service.

Kandalepas, D., M.J. Blum, and S.A. Van Bael. 2015. "Shifts in Symbiotic Endophyte
Communities of a Foundational Salt Marsh Grass following Oil Exposure from
the Deepwater Horizon Oil Spill." *PLOS One*. DOI: 10.1371/journal.pone.0122378.

Keiffer, C.H. and I.A. Ungar. 2002. "Germination and Establishment of Halophytes
on Brine-Affected Soils." *Journal of Applied Ecology* 39(3): 402–15.

Keller, J. 2020. "Trans Mountain Pipeline Expansion Cost Balloons to $12.6-Billion."
The Globe and Mail, 10 February. https://www.theglobeandmail.com/canada/
alberta/article-trans-mountain-expansion-cost-balloons-to-126-billion/.

Kelly, E.N., D.W. Schindler, V.L. St Louis, D.B. Donald, and K.E. Vladicka. 2006.
"Forest Fire Increases Mercury Accumulation by Fishes via Food Web Restructuring and Increased Mercury Inputs." *Proceedings National Academy of Sciences*,
online: www.pnas.org_cgi_DOI_10.1073_pnas.0609798104.

Kerr, A. 1986. *Atlantic No. 3.* Self-published. ISBN 0889257183 / 9780889257184.

Kerr, J.G. 2017. "Multiple Land Use Activities Drive Riverine Salinization in a Large, Semi-Arid River Basin in Western Canada." *Limnology and Oceanography,* online. DOI: 10.1002/lno.10498.

Kershaw, G.P., L.J. Kershaw, E.S. Kershaw, J.M. Kershaw, and G.G.L. Kershaw. 2013. *70 Years of Natural Recovery of Vegetation on Canol Crude-Oil Spills.* Report for the Contaminated Sites Programme. Yellowknife, NT: NT Region, Aboriginal and Northern Affairs Canada.

Kershaw, G.P., L.J. Kershaw, E.S. Kershaw, J.M. Kershaw, and G. Kershaw. n.d. "Canol Crude – 70 Years of Natural Revegetation." Presentation for Earthwatch Canada. Provided by G.P. Kershaw to the author.

Kharaka, Y.K. and N.S. Dorsey. 2005. "Environmental Issues of Petroleum Exploration and Production: Introduction." *Environmental Geosciences* 12(2): 61–3.

Kheraj, S. 2011. "Alberta's Oil Spill History." http://activehistory.ca/2011/05/albertas-oil-spill-history/.

– 2019. "A History of Oil Spills on Long-Distance Pipelines in Canada." *Canadian Historical Review.* DOI: 10.338/chr.2019-0005.

Laceby, J.P., J.G. Kerr, D. Zhu, C. Chung, Q. Situ, S. Abbasi, and J.F. Orwin. 2019. "Chloride Inputs to the North Saskatchewan River Watershed: The Role of Road Salts as a Potential Driver of Salinization Downstream of North America's Northern Most Major City (Edmonton, Canada)." *Science of the Total Environment* 688: 1056–68.

Larson, E.W. and J.B. King. 1996. "The Systematic Distortion of Information: An Ongoing Challenge to Management." *Organizational Dynamics* 24(3): 49–61.

Lauer, N.E., J.S. Harkness, and A. Vengosh. 2016. "Brine Spills Associated with Unconventional Oil Development in North Dakota." *Environmental Science and Technology* 50: 5389–97.

Lee, E.-H., K.-S. Cho, and J. Kim. 2010. "Comparative Study of Rhizobacterial Community Structure of Plant Species in Oil-Contaminated Soil." *Journal of Microbiology and Biotechnology* 20(9): 1339–47. DOI: 10.4014/jmb.1003.03022.

Lee, K., M. Boufadel, B. Chen, J. Foght, P. Hodson, S. Swanson, and A. Venosa. 2015. *The Behaviour and Environmental Impacts of Crude Oil Released into Aqueous Environments.* Ottawa: Royal Society of Canada.

Lengellé, J.G. 1976. *Anthropogenic Erosion Swan Hills, Alberta.* Edmonton: Environment Conservation Authority of Alberta, Government of Alberta.

Lenton, T.M., J. Rockström, O. Gaffney, S. Rahmstorf, K. Richardson, W. Steffen, and H.J. Schellnhuber. 2019. "Climate Tipping Points – Too Risky to Bet Against." *Nature,* 27 November. https://www.nature.com/articles/d41586-019-03595-0.

331

Li, Shao-Meng, A. Leithead, S.G. Moussa, J. Liggio, M.D. Moran, D. Wang, K. Hayden, A. Darlington, M. Gordon, R. Staebler, P.A. Makar, C.A. Stroud, R. McLaren, P.S.K. Liu, J. O'Brien, R.L. Mittermeier, J. Zhang, G. Marson, S.G. Cober, M. Wolde, and J.B. Wentzell. 2017. "Differences Between Measured and Reported Volatile Organic Compound Emissions from Oil Sands Facilities in Alberta, Canada." *Proceedings National Academy of Sciences,* E3756-E3765, 24 April. DOI: 10.1073/pnas.1617862114.

Liggio, J., S.-M. Li, R.M. Staebler, K. Hayden, A. Darlington, R.L. Mittermeier, J. O'Brien, R. McLaren, M. Wolde, D. Worthy, and F. Vogel. 2019. "Measured Canadian Oil Sands CO_2 Emissions Are Higher than Estimates Made Using Internationally Recommended Methods." *Nature Communications* 10: 1863. https://DOI.org/10.1038/s41467-019-09714-9.

Linnitt, C. 2018. "Pipeline Spills 290,000 Litres of Crude Oil Emulsion in Northern Alberta." *The Narwhal,* 17 April. https://thenarwhal.ca/pipeline-spills-290-000-litres-crude-oil-emulsion-northern-alberta/.

Lloyd, A.H. and A.G. Bunn. 2007. "Responses of the Circumpolar Boreal Forest to 20th Century Climate Variability." *Environmental Research Letters* 2:045013. DOI: 10.1088/1748-9326/2/4/045013.

Macdonald, I. 2018. "Remote Sensing of Persistent Oil Slicks in Mississippi Canyon 20." Gulf of Mexico Oil Spill and Ecosystem Science Conference, Hyatt Regency Hotel, New Orleans, LA, 5–8 February. Remote Sensing of Persistent Oil Slicks in MC20.pptx.

MacInnes, K. 2017. *Blast from the Past: Atlantic No. 3.* https://resource.aer.ca/blast-from-the-past-atlantic-no-3/.

MacLean, J. 2016. "Striking at the Root Problem of Canadian Environmental Law: Identifying and Escaping Regulatory Capture." *Journal of Environmental Law and Practice* 29: 111–28.

Marr-Laing, T. and C. Severson-Baker. 1999. *Beyond Eco-Terrorism: The Deeper Issues Affecting Alberta's Oilpatch.* Drayton Valley: The Pembina Institute.

Martin, K. 2020. "Industry Group Can Help Fight Ecojustice's Bid to Derail Oilpatch Foreign Interference Inquiry: Court." *The Province,* 17 June. https://theprovince.com/news/local-news/industry-group-can-help-fight-ecojustices-bid-to-derail-oilpatch-foreign-interference-inquiry-court/wcm/6f95ff22-3c89-4dd8-9373-71f475ea9405.

Mason, A.L., J.C. Taylor, and I.R. MacDonald, eds. 2019. *An Integrated Assessment of Oil and Gas Release into the Marine Environment at the Former Taylor Energy*

MC20 Site. NOAA National Ocean Service, National Centers for Coastal Ocean Science. NOAA Technical Memorandum 260. DOI: 10.25923/kykm-sn39.

McCarthy, S. 2015. "'Anti-Petroleum' Movement a Growing Security Threat to Canada, RCMP Say." *The Globe and Mail*, 17 February. https://www.theglobeand mail.com/news/politics/anti-petroleum-movement-a-growing-security-threat-to-canada-rcmp-say/article23019252/.

McCune, B. and M.J. Mefford. 2011. PC-ORD. *Multivariate Analysis of Ecological Data. Version 6.09*. Gleneden Beach, OR: MjM Software.

McCune, B., and H.T. Root. 2015. "Origin of the Dust Bunny Distribution in Ecological Community Data." *Plant Ecology* 216(5): 645–56. DOI: 10.1007/s11258-014-0404-1.

McSheffrey, E. 2019. "Cover-Ups, Lies 'A Systemic Cancer' in World of Oilpatch Health and Safety Breaches: Whistleblowers." Global News, 20 August. https://globalnews.ca/news/5774195/coverup-canada-oilpatch-health-safety-breaches-whistleblowers/.

Meehan, M, K. Sedivec, T. DeSutter, C. Augustin, and A. Daigh. 2017. *Environmental Impacts of Brine (Produced Water)*. https://www.ag.ndsu.edu/publications/en vironment-natural-resources/environmental-impacts-of-brine-produced-water. Document: r1850.pdf.

Mertz, E. 2017. "5 Charges Laid Against Nexen for Massive July 2015 Long Lake Pipeline Spill." Global News, 6 July. https://globalnews.ca/news/3580278/5-charges-laid-against-nexen-for-massive-july-2015-long-lake-pipeline-spill/.

Millennium. 2007. DCEL *Steam Release Incident, LSD 09-33-095-12-W4M, Volume I Executive Summary, and Volume II Soil Delineation Program: Summary Report*. Millennium EMS Solutions Ltd, report prepared for Deer Creek Energy, December 2006, File 04-101. Edmonton: Alberta Environment and Parks.

Monenco Consultants. 1983. *Environmental Assessment Lodgepole Sour Gas Well Blowout*. Public Advisory Committee, Environment Council of Alberta, Edmonton, Alberta.

Moore, B.J., P.E. Hardisty, and J.V. Headley. 1997. *Hydrocarbon Attenuation in Natural Wetlands*. http://info.ngwa.org/gwol/pdf/972963344.PDF.

Moore, M.-L., K. Shaw, and H. Castleden. 2018. "'We Need More Data!': The Politics of Scientific Information for Water Governance in the Context of Hydraulic Fracturing." *Water Alternatives* 11(1): 142–62.

Mori, A. 2016. "Re: Freedom of Information and Protection of Privacy Act ('Act') Request for Access to Records. Alberta Energy Regulator Reference No. 2016-

G-0040." Calgary: Alberta Energy Regulator. Document: Letter to Applicant re access decision-Nov.29'16.pdf.

Mosimann, J.E., C.V. Wiseman, and R.E. Edelman. 2008. "Data Fabrication: Can People Generate Random Digits?" *Accountability in Research* 4(1): 31–55. https://DOI.org/10.1080/08989629508573866.

Munn, D.A. and R. Stewart. 1989. "Effect of Oil Well Brine on Germination and Seedling Growth of Several Crops." *Ohio Journal of Science* 4: 92–4.

Naugle, D.E., ed. 2011. *Energy Development and Wildlife Conservation in Western North America.* Washington, DC: Island Press.

NEB (National Energy Board). 2015. *Archived – Reportable Liquid Releases by Year, January 2008 to April 2013.* https://www.neb-one.gc.ca. Accessed 17 December 2016.

– 2016. *Archived – Pipeline Incidents: Spills of Hydrocarbon Liquids.* https://www.neb-one.gc.ca. Accessed 17 December.

Newcomb, S. 1881. "Note on the Frequency of Use of the Different Digits in Natural Numbers." *American Journal of Mathematics* 4(1): 39–40. https://www.jstor.org/stable/2369148.

NFB (National Film Board). 1946. *The Story of Oil.* https://www.nfb.ca/film/story_of_oil/.

Nikiforuk, A. 2017a. "On Oil Spills, Alberta Regulator Can't Be Believed: New Report." *The Tyee.* https://thetyee.ca/News/2017/02/09/Oil-Spills-Alberta-Regulator/.

– 2017b. "Alberta Failing on Risk From Leaking Oil and Gas Wells, Says Expert." *The Tyee.* https://thetyee.ca/News/2017/07/04/Alberta-Failing-Leaking-Oil-Gas-Wells-Risk/.

– 2017c. "Energy Industry Legacy: Hundreds of Abandoned Wells Leaking Methane in Alberta Communities." *The Tyee.* https://thetyee.ca/News/2017/06/28/Energy-Industry-Legacy/.

Nixon, A., C. Shank, and D. Farr. 2015. *Understanding and Responding to the Effects of Climate Change on Alberta's Biodiversity.* Edmonton: Alberta Biodiversity Monitoring Institute.

North Dakota Oil Spill Data. 2011. "Oil Spill Data 2010–2011." http://www.saltedlands.org/documents/research/OilSpills2010-2011.pdf.

NWWG. 1988. *Wetlands of Canada.* Ecological Land Classification Series No. 24. Ottawa: National Wetlands Working Group, Canadian Wildlife Service.

Ohio EPA. 2010. *Guidance for Assessing Petroleum Hydrocarbons in Soil.* Number: DERR-00-DI-033 ISSUED: 4/14/04 (4/2/10 update), STATUS: Final.

Omstead, J. and K. Fida. 2020. "First Nations appeal Alberta Energy Regulator decision to suspend monitoring requirements." CBC News. https://www.cbc.ca/news/canada/edmonton/first-nations-appeal-aer-monitoring-requirements-oil-companies-1.5602501.

Pace. 2012a. "Attachments to 12 July 2012 Letter from Pace Oil & Gas Ltd. to ERCB Field Surveillance and Operations Group." Document: PACE ERCB Covering Letter.pdf, digital attachment with photographs. Materials provided by Dene Tha First Nation.

– 2012b. "Letter to Chief Ahnassay, re: Remediation Plan, In Situ Controlled Burn, Pace Spill 14-21-108-7W6." Documents: Remediation letter to Chief Ahnassay Final 2.docx, Burn excavation and bio remediation plan.pdf. Materials provided by Dene Tha First Nation.

Paraskova, T. 2020. "Third Major Blow For Pipelines: Keystone XL Project Stays Blocked." *Oil Price*, 7 July. https://oilprice.com/Energy/Crude-Oil/Third-Major-Blow-For-Pipelines-Keystone-XL-Project-Stays-Blocked.html.

Penfold, S. 2016. "Petroleum Liquids." In *Powering Up Canada: A History of Power, Fuel, and Energy from 1600*, edited by R.W. Sandwell, 274–99. Montreal, QC: McGill-Queen's University Press.

Pezeshki, S.R., M.W. Hester, Q. Lin, and J.A. Nyman. 2000. "The Effects of Oil Spill and Clean-Up on Dominant US Gulf Coast Marsh Macrophytes: A Review." *Environmental Pollution* 108: 129–39.

Pickell, P., D. Andison, N. Coops, S. Gergel, and P. Marshall. 2015. "The Spatial Patterns of Anthropogenic Disturbance in the Western Canadian Boreal Forest Following Oil and Gas Development." *Canadian Journal of Forest Research*. DOI: 10.1139/cjfr-2014-0546.

Pimblett, B., and J. Mitton. 2015. "The Wabamun Story." Presentation downloaded from the website of the Environmental Services Association of Alberta. https://www.esaa.org/wp-content/uploads/2015/06/06-Pimblett-Mitton.pdf.

Purdy, B.G., S.E. Macdonald, and V.J. Lieffers. 2005. "Naturally Saline Boreal Communities as Models for Reclamation of Saline Oil Sand Tailings." *Restoration Ecology* 13: 667–77.

Rabson, M. 2020. "Aid For Energy Industry Heavily Leaned Towards Fossil Fuels Over Clean Tech." *Huffington Post*, 15 July. https://www.huffingtonpost.ca/entry/clean-energy-industry-coronavirus_ca_5f0fae36c5b6d14c3362b213?ncid=other_huffpostre_pqylmel2bk8&utm_campaign=related_articles.

Ramirez, P. Jr. 2010. "Bird Mortality in Oil Field Wastewater Disposal Facilities." *Environmental Management* 46: 820–6.

– 2013. "Migratory Bird Mortality in Oil and Gas Facilities in Colorado, Kansas,

Montana, Nebraska, North Dakota, South Dakota, Utah, and Wyoming." *US Fish and Wildlife Service, Region 6. Environmental Contaminants Program Report Number R6/726C/13.*

Ramirez, P. and K. Johnson. 2011. "Bird mortality in oil and gas production facilities can be prevented." *US Fish and Wildlife Service*, 19 August 2011. https://www.fws.gov/mountain-prairie/pressrel/11-64.html.

RAMP Review Panel. 2011. *2010 Regional Aquatics Monitoring Program (RAMP) Scientific Review.* [Review Panel composed of Drs D. Burn, D.G. Dixon, M. Dubé, J. Flotemersch, W.G. Franzin, J. Gibson, K. Munkittrick, J. Post, and S. Watmough.] Report on Behalf of Alberta Innovates – Technology Futures, Calgary.

Rieger, S. 2019. "AER Orders Obsidian Energy to Suspend Well After Produced Water Spills into Wetland." CBC News. https://www.cbc.ca/news/canada/calgary/obsidian-energy-produced-water-spill-1.5162309.

Robson, D.B., J.D. Knight, R.E. Farrell, and J.J. Germida. 2004. "Natural Revegetation of Hydrocarbon-Contaminated Soil in Semi-Arid Grasslands." *Canadian Journal of Botany* 82: 22–30.

Roche, P. 2010. "Total Abandoning Joslyn SAGD After Steam Injection Blew Hole in Ground." *Daily Oil Bulletin*, 25 February. http://www.airwaterland.ca/issues/article.asp?article=dob%5C100225%5Cdob2010_fp0004.html.

Rockström, J., W. Steffen, K. Noone, Å. Persson, F.S. Chapin III, E.F. Lambin, T.M. Lenton, M. Scheffer, et al. 2009. "A Safe Operating Space for Humanity." *Nature* 461: 472–5.

Rooney, R.C. and S.E. Bayley. 2011a. "Setting Reclamation Targets and Evaluating Progress: Submersed Aquatic Vegetation in Natural and Post-Oil Sands Mining Wetlands in Alberta, Canada." *Ecological Engineering* 37: 569–79.

– 2011b. "Development and Testing of an Index of Biotic Integrity Based on Submersed and Floating Vegetation and Its Application to Assess Reclamation Wetlands in Alberta's Oil Sands Area, Canada." *Environmental Monitoring and Assessment*, DOI: 10.1007/s10661-011-1999-5.

Rooney, R.C., S.E. Bayley, and D.W. Schindler. 2012. "Oil Sands Mining and Reclamation Cause Massive Loss of Peatland and Stored Carbon." *Proceedings National Academy Sciences*, 109(13): 4933–7. DOI: 10.1073/pnas.1117693108.

Roy, J.L. and W.B. McGill. 1998. "Characterization of Disaggregated Nonwettable Surface Soils Found at Old Crude Oil Spill Sites." *Canadian Journal of Soil Science* 78(2): 331–44.

Rusnell, C. 2020. "Ecojustice Alleges Unfairness in 'Secret' Public Inquiry into Anti-Alberta Energy Campaign." CBC News, 11 March. https://www.cbc.ca/news/

canada/edmonton/ecojustice-alleges-unfairness-in-secret-public-inquiry-into-anti-alberta-energy-campaign-1.5492804.

Russo, J.E. 2018. "Bayesian Revision vs. Information Distortion." *Frontiers in Psychology* 9: 1550. DOI: 10.3389/fpsyg.2018.01550.

Schieck, J., P. Sólymos, and D. Huggard. 2014. "Human Footprint in Alberta." *ABMI Science Letters*. Edmonton: Alberta Biodiversity Monitoring Institute.

Seburn, D.C. and G.P. Kershaw. 1997. "Changes in the Active Layer of a Subarctic Right-of-Way as a Result of a Crude-Oil Spill." *Canadian Journal of Earth Sciences* 34(12): 1539–44.

Seburn, D.C., G.P. Kershaw, and L.J. Kershaw. 1996. "Vegetation Response to a Subsurface Crude Oil Spill on a Subarctic Right-of-Way, Tulita (Fort Norman), Northwest Territories, Canada." *Arctic* 49(4): 321–7.

Sensitive Ecosystems Inventories. 2017. "A spatial database of rare and fragile terrestrial ecosystems in British Columbia, used to encourage land-use decisions that will ensure the continued integrity of these ecosystems." Accessed 12 April. Victoria: British Columbia Government. https://catalogue.data.gov.bc.ca/data set/sensitive-ecosystems-inventory-sei-detailed-polygons-with-short-attribute-table-spatial-view.

Seskus, T. and K. Bakx. 2019. "'I will crucify him': Inside the Workplace Culture at Alberta's Energy Regulator." CBC News. https://www.cbc.ca/news/business/alberta-regulator-whistleblower-1.5312463.

Shannon, D. 2015. "Letter to Syncrude Canada Regulatory Affairs, Re: File No. 2015-019 from Alberta Energy Regulator, 11 August 2015." Calgary: Alberta Energy Regulator.

Shield, D. 2019. "'All I could see was flames': Sask. Crude Oil Train Derailment Fills Sky with Smoke, Fire." CBC News, 9 December. https://www.cbc.ca/news/canada/saskatoon/cp-rail-derailment-sask-plunkett-guernsey-1.5389011.

– 2020. "Sask. Village Evacuated after Train Derailment Sparks Massive Fire." CBC News, 6 February. https://www.cbc.ca/news/canada/saskatoon/sask-train-derail ment-1.5453942.

Smith, M. 2020. "1.2M Litres of Oil Spilled in Saskatchewan Train Derailment." *The Star Phoenix*. https://thestarphoenix.com/news/local-news/1-2m-litres-of-oil-spilled-in-saskatchewan-train-derailment.

Spielman, A. and M. D'Antonio. 2001. *Mosquito: A Natural History of Our Most Persistent and Deadly Foe*. New York: Hyperion.

St Clair, C.C. 2016. "Bird protection from tailings ponds in the minable oilsands: Review of current approaches, knowledge gaps, and recommendations for better practice." https://www.scribd.com/document/489963319/Bird-protection-from-tailings-ponds-in-the-minable-oilsands-Review-of-current-approaches-knowledge-gaps-and-recommendations-for-better-practice.

Steffen, W., Å. Persson, L. Deutsch, J. Zalasiewicz, M. Williams, K. Richardson, C. Crumley, P. Crutzen, C. Folke, L. Gordon, M. Molina, V. Ramanathan, J. Rockström, M. Scheffer, H.J. Schellnhuber, and U. Svedin. 2011. "The Anthropocene: From Global Change to Planetary Stewardship." *AMBIO*. DOI: 10.1007/s13280-011-0185-x.

Stenson, F. 2015. "Landowner Rights. How Big Oil Trumps Private and Public Good." *Albertaviews – The Magazine for Engaged Citizens,* 1 June. https://albertaviews.ca/landowner-rights/.

Stewart, J. 1988. *Blowout at Atlantic No. 3.* Published by the Glenbow Museum, 2 November 2016. https://www.youtube.com/watch?v=ciWbci3KuKA. Film based on the book by Aubrey Kerr.

Stralberg, D., X. Wang, M.-A. Parisien, F.-N. Robinne, P. Sólymos, C.L. Mahon, S.E. Nielsen, and E.M. Bayne. 2018. "Wildfire-Mediated Vegetation Change in Boreal Forests of Alberta, Canada." *Ecosphere* 9(3): e02156. DOI: 10.1002/ecs2.2156.

Struzik, E. 1982a. "Suncor Lawyer Challenges his Client's Records." *The Edmonton Journal,* 19 October. Clipping on file at the Alberta Environmental Law Centre, Edmonton.

– 1982b. "Possible Impact of Suncor Spills Cited." *The Edmonton Journal,* 23 October. Clipping on file at the Alberta Environmental Law Centre, Edmonton.

Sublette, K.L., G. Thoma, and K. Duncan. 2006. *Risk Reduction and Soil Ecosystem Restoration in an Active Oil Producing Area in an Ecologically Sensitive Setting. Final Report.* Report DE-FC26-01BC15332. https://www.etde.org/etdeweb/servlets/purl/881050/.

Taft, K. 2017. *Oil's Deep State: How the Petroleum Industry Undermines Democracy and Stops Action On Global Warming in Alberta, and in Ottawa.* Toronto: James Lorimer & Company.

– 2018. "Kevin Taft on What Turned Rachel Notley from Crusading Critic to Big Oil Crusader." *National Observer,* 19 April. https://www.nationalobserver.com/2018/04/19/opinion/kevin-taft-what-turned-rachel-notley-crusading-critic-big-oil-crusader.

Tasker, J.P. and K. Harris. 2018. "After Federal Court Quashes Trans Mountain, Rachel Notley Pulls out of National Climate Plan." CBC News, 30 August. https://www.cbc.ca/news/politics/trans-mountain-federal-court-appeals-1.4804495.

Taylor, A. 2019. *Democracy May Not Exist, But We'll Miss It When It's Gone.* New York: Henry Holt and Company.

Taylor, S.W., B.S. Lollar, and L.I. Wassenaar. 2000. "Bacteriogenic Ethane in Near-Surface Aquifers: Implications for Leaking Hydrocarbon Well Bores." *Environmental Science and Technology* 34(22): 4727–32.

Tei, S., A. Sugimoto, H. Yonenobu, Y. Matsuura, A. Osawa, H. Sato, J. Fujinuma, and T. Maximov. 2017. "Tree-Ring Analysis and Modeling Approaches Yield Contrary Response of Circumboreal Forest Productivity to Climate Change." *Global Change Biology.* DOI: 10.1111/gcb.13780.

Testa, S.M. and J.A. Jacobs. 2014. *Oil Spills and Gas Leaks: Environmental Response, Prevention, and Cost Recovery.* New York: McGraw-Hill Education.

Thormann, M. and S. Bayley. 2008. *Impacts of the CN Rail Oil Spill on Softstem Bulrush-Dominated Lacustrine Marshes in Wabamun Lake.* Edmonton: Report for Alberta Environment.

Timoney, K.P. 2001. "String and Net-Patterned Salt Marshes: Rare Landscape Elements of Boreal Canada." *Canadian Field-Naturalist* 115(3): 406–12.

– 2011. *Aboriginal Community Sustainability and Resource Extraction in Northern Alberta. A Study on Behalf of the Community of Chipewyan Lake, Alberta, Ecological and Landscape Component: A Study of the Environment of the Chipewyan Lake Area, Alberta.* Edmonton: University of Alberta.

– 2013. *The Peace-Athabasca Delta: Portrait of a Dynamic Ecosystem.* Edmonton: The University of Alberta Press.

– 2015. *Impaired Wetlands in a Damaged Landscape: The Legacy of Bitumen Exploitation in Canada.* Cham, Switzerland: Springer International Publishing.

Timoney, K.P., and P. Lee. 2013. *Environmental Incidents in Northeastern Alberta's Bitumen Sands Region, 1996-2012.* Edmonton: Global Forest Watch Canada. https://databasin.org/galleries/0267510a7beb4142a55857290b8f922a#expand=15225 6%2C152270. Document: 20130723A_Envir_Incidents_July-22-2013.pdf.

– 2014. *CNRL's Persistent 2013–2014 Bitumen Releases near Cold Lake: Facts, Unanswered Questions, and Implications, Final Report, 6 February 2014.* Edmonton: Global Forest Watch Canada. Report: 20140206A_CNRL_Release_Bulletin.pdf. https://databasin.org/galleries/0267510a7beb4142a55857290b8f922a#expand=15225 6%2C152270.

Timoney, K.P. and S. Mamet. 2019. "No Treeline Advance over the Last 50 Years in Subarctic Western and Central Canada and the Problem of Vegetation Misclassification in Remotely Sensed Data." *Écoscience.* https://DOI.org/10.1080/11956 860.2019.1698258.

Timoney, K.P. and R.A. Ronconi. 2010. "Annual Bird Mortality in the Bitumen Tailings Ponds of Northeastern Alberta, Canada." *The Wilson Journal of Ornithology* 122(3): 569–76.

Tolppanen, B.P. 2014. *Churchill in North America, 1929.* Jefferson, NC: McFarland and Company.

Trail, P.W. 2006. "Avian Mortality at Oil Pits in the United States: A Review of the Problem and Efforts for Its Solution." *Environmental Management* 38: 532–44.

Turcza, A. 2004. *The Effectiveness of Alberta's Solutions to the Orphan Well Problem.* University of Alberta, Business Economics 463 term paper. Edmonton, Alberta. Document: orphanpapercorrected.pdf.

UN (United Nations). 2019. *Emissions Gap Report 2019.* Document: EGR2019.pdf. Nairobi, Kenya: UN Environment Programme.

UNDP (United Nations Development Programme). 2019. *The Heat Is On. Taking Stock of Global Climate Ambition.* NDC Global Outlook, Report 2019. Document: NDC_Outlook_Report_2019.pdf. United Nations, New York: United Nations Development Programme.

Urquhart, I.T. 2018. *Costly Fix: Power, Politics, and Nature in the Tar Sands.* Toronto: University of Toronto Press.

US EPA (Environmental Protection Agency). 2016. *Climate Change Indicators in the United States. Fourth Edition.* EPA 430-R-16-004. www.epa.gov/climate-indicators.

USFWS (US Fish and Wildlife Service). 2011. *The Ineffectiveness of Flagging to Deter Migratory Birds from Oilfield Production Skim Pits and Reserve Pits.* https://www.fws.gov/mountain-prairie/contaminants/documents/Flagging_oil_pits.pdf.

Vanderklippe, N. 2013. "Toxic Waste Spill in Northern Alberta Biggest of Recent Disasters in North America." *The Globe and Mail*, 12 June. http://www.theglobeandmail.com/report-on-business/industry-news/energy-and-resources/apache-pipeline-leaks-60000-barrels-of-salty-water-in-northwest-alberta/article12494371/.

Vanderklippe, N. and D. Walton. 2012. "Cleanup of Latest Alberta Oil Spill Could Take All Summer." *The Globe and Mail*, 8 June. http://www.theglobeandmail.com/news/national/cleanup-of-latest-alberta-oil-spill-could-take-all-summer/article4241238/.

Van Wilgenburg, S.L., K.A. Hobson, E.M. Bayne, and N. Koper. 2013. "Estimated Avian Nest Loss Associated with Oil and Gas Exploration and Extraction in the Western Canadian Sedimentary Basin." *Avian Conservation and Ecology* 8(2): 9. http://dx.DOI.org/10.5751/ACE-00585-080209.

Vavrek, M.C., H. Hunt, W. Colgan III, and D.L. Vavrek. 2004. "Status of Oil Brine

REFERENCES

Spill Site Remediation." *Proceedings of International Petroleum Environment Conference, October 12–15, Albuquerque, NM*. https://www.researchgate.net/publication/251554598.

Wang, Z., M. Fingas, S. Blenkinsopp, G. Sergy, M. Landriault, L. Sigouin, and P. Lambert. 1998. "Study of the 25-Year-Old Nipisi Oil Spill: Persistence of Oil Residues and Comparisons between Surface and Subsurface Sediments." *Environmental Science and Technology* 32: 2222–32.

Watson, J.E.M., D.F. Shanahan, M. Di Marco, J. Allan, W.F. Laurance, E.W. Sanderson, B. Mackey, and O. Venter. 2016. "Catastrophic Declines in Wilderness Areas Undermine Global Environment Targets." *Current Biology* 26: 2929–34. http://dx.DOI.org/10.1016/j.cub.2016.08.049.

Weber, B. 2003. "Alta Oil Well Finally Capped after 87 Years of Spewing Pollutants into River." *Canadian Press Newswire*, 2 October. http://ezproxy.ae.talonline.ca/login?qurl=https%3A%2F%2Fwww.proquest.com%2Fwire-feeds%2Falta-oil-well-finally-capped-after-87-years%2Fdocview%2F359560541%2Fse-2%3Faccountid%3D46585.

– 2019. "'Making this up': Study Says Oilsands Assessments Marred by Weak Science." Global News. https://globalnews.ca/news/4972075/oilsands-assessments-weak-science-study/.

– 2020a. "Alberta's Top Court Overturns Approval of Oilsands Mine Following Land Concerns." Global News, 24 April. https://globalnews.ca/news/6864561/alberta-moose-lake-fort-mckay-first-nation-oilsands-mine/.

– 2020b. "'Pointing Out the Obvious': Alberta Government Stands by Energy Minister's Comments." CTV News, 27 May. https://edmonton.ctvnews.ca/pointing-out-the-obvious-alberta-government-stands-by-energy-minister-s-comments-1.4956822.

– 2020c. "Alberta, Ottawa Reduce Oilsands Environmental Monitoring Budget Due to Pandemic." CBC News, 4 August. https://www.cbc.ca/news/canada/edmonton/alta-oilsands-monitoring-1.5673433.

Wein, R.W. and L.C. Bliss. 1973. "Experimental Crude Oil Spills on Arctic Plant Communities." *Journal of Applied Ecology* 10: 671–82.

Whitlock, C. 2019. "At War with the Truth." *The Washington Post*, 9 December. https://www.washingtonpost.com/graphics/2019/investigations/afghanistan-papers/afghanistan-war-confidential-documents/.

Wiens, J.J. 2016. "Climate-Related Local Extinctions are Already Widespread Among Plant and Animal Species." *PLoS Biol* 14(12): e2001104. DOI: 10.1371/journal.pbio.2001104.

Williams, J.P., A. Regehr, and M. Kang. 2021. "Methane Emissions from Abandoned Oil and Gas Wells in Canada and the United States." *Environmental Science and Technology* 55(1): 563–70. DOI: 10.1021/acs.est.0c04265.

Wollis, H., and C. Stratmoen. 2010. *Population Study of Western Grebes in Alberta 2001–2009: Implications for Management and Status Designation. Alberta Species at Risk Report No. 138.* Edmonton: Alberta Sustainable Resource Development, Fish and Wildlife Division.

WWF (World Wildlife Fund). 2020. "Living Planet Report – Bending the curve of biodiversity loss." Almond, R.E.A., M. Grooten, and T. Peterson, eds. World Wildlife Fund, Gland, Switzerland. https://www.worldwildlife.org/publications/living-planet-report-2020.

Zaporozec, A. 1981. "Ground-Water Pollution and Its Sources." *GeoJournal* 5(5): 457–71.

Index

344